PUBLIC EMPLOYEES
AND POLICYMAKING

PUBLIC EMPLOYEES AND POLICYMAKING

Alan Saltzstein

California State University, Fullerton

Palisades Publishers   Pacific Palisades, California 90272

Library of Congress Catalog Card Number: 79-87843
International Standard Book Number: 0-913530-15-8

Palisades Publishers
P.O. Box 744
Pacific Palisades, California 90272

Printed in the United States of America

CONTENTS

Preface ix

CHAPTER ONE
FROM PERSONNEL ADMINISTRATION
TO PERSONNEL POLICYMAKING

Introduction 1

CHAPTER TWO
PERSONNEL ADMINISTRATION AND
THE DYNAMICS OF PUBLIC ORGANIZATIONS

Introduction 7

1 The Bureaucracy Problem 9
   James Q. Wilson

2 Public Personnel Administration and Politics: Toward a New Public
   Personnel Administration 15
   David H. Rosenbloom

3 The Politics of Manpower: The Manager Triumphant 26
   Frank J. Thompson

4 Employee Power in the Federal Service 45
   Hugh Heclo

CHAPTER THREE
THE PERSONNEL OFFICER
AND THE FEDERAL SYSTEM

Introduction 63

5 Title VII, The Civil Rights Act, 1964 72
   U.S. Congress

6 National League of Cities et al. v. Usery 78
   U. S. Supreme Court

7 CETA: Successful Job Program or Subsidy for Local Government? 86
   Harrison H. Donnelly

CHAPTER FOUR
MANAGEMENT AND PUBLIC POLICY

Introduction 97

8   The Limits of Collective Bargaining in Public Employment 102
    Harry H. Wellington and Ralph K. Winter

9   Some Impacts of Collective Bargaining in Local Government: A Diversity
    Thesis 117
    Raymond D. Horton, David Lewin, and James W. Kuhn

10 Public Sector Bargaining Legislation and Strikes: A Case Study 130
    Charles R. Greer

11 Making Personnel Decisions by Public Referenda: Campaigns for Police and
    Firefighter Collective Bargaining in Texas 137
    I. B. Helburn and Darold T. Barnum

CHAPTER FIVE
EMPLOYMENT DISCRIMINATION AND
THE PERSONNEL ADMINISTRATOR

Introduction 147

12 Women in Top Jobs: An Opportunity for Federal Leadership 150
    Debra W. Stewart

13 Employing the Black Administrator 162
    Cortez H. Williams

14 The Reality of Equal Employment Compliance in Municipalities . . 171
    Alan Saltzstein and Grace Hall Saltzstein

15 Griggs et al. v. Duke Power Company 179
    U. S. Supreme Court

16 Washington, Mayor of Washington, D.C. et al. v. Davis 184
    U. S. Supreme Court

17 Bakke and Beyond: The Future of Affirmative Action 191
    Burt C. Buzan

18 Regents of the University of California v. Alan Bakke 203
    U. S. Supreme Court

CHAPTER SIX
PRODUCTIVITY, EFFICIENCIY,
AND PUBLIC MANAGEMENT

Introduction 221

19 The Civil Service: A Meritless System 223
    E. S. Savas and Sigmund Ginsburg

20   Public Personnel Administration: Legalistic Reforms vs. Effectiveness, Efficiency, and Economy .... 236 X
     Chester S. Newland

21   Revitalizing the Civil Service .... 247 X
     Alan K. Campbell

22   Technological Trends in Productivity Measurement 253
     Walter L. Balk

CHAPTER SEVEN
THE FUTURE AND
PUBLIC PERSONNEL POLICY

Introduction 261

23   The Public Service in a Temporary Society 263
     Frederick C. Mosher

24   The Economic Status of Minorities and Women 276
     Lester Thurow

Index 287

PREFACE

Public personnel officials make policy. They advise presidents, governors, mayors, and legislators on matters that affect the size of the budget, the role of government in the economy, and ways of reducing racial and sexual discrimination. Legislative acts are written by personnel specialists; judges hear their testimony, and they must interpret and act upon vague and often contradictory guidelines. They are, in the words of Max Weber, "politicians for hire."

The readings and essays in this book were written and selected to give the background needed to cope with today's personnel problems. Too often, public administration instructors have confused applied education with learning the minutae of administrative life in particular agencies. While knowledge of specific practices and ordinances is important, such data are of little value unless placed within a broader background which emphasizes the role of the administrator within the American federal system and the importance of personnel decisions to the problems of the larger society.

I also take issue with some over the meaning of the poorly used term "nuts and bolts." The words usually connote the practical tools of the job as opposed to the philosophy or history of the subject. "Nuts and bolts", however, are valuable only as means to accomplish a set of goals. If the personnel official is a policymaker, "nuts and bolts" must be the skills required to design a piece of legislation, understand the meaning of court decisions, and deal with the administrative rulings of other agencies that may affect one's jurisdiction. This book provides "hands on" experience in these concerns. It also contains examples of legislation, court decisions, and narratives of the administrative process as they influence personnel. The selections were further chosen to raise the practical and moral problems of today's administrator.

A book is never written in isolation; and I am particularly indebted to the many contributors who together supply us with much of what we know about personnel policy. My colleagues at California State University Fullerton's Department of Political Science provided a setting for sound practical education and good scholarship. Without the many excellent students at CSUF, I would know much less about this topic. My friend John C. Bollens of UCLA gave hours of encouragement, assistance, and able counsel. Bert Buzan performed valuable detective work in tracking down the text of the Bakke case, and cleverly and accurately condensed the words of the court. If his skills were used by that august body, administrators might come to understand the law more clearly.

Ideas occur when one relates to others with concern, understanding and love. I dedicate this book to my wife Grace.

A.L.S.

CHAPTER ONE

From Personnel Administration to Personnel Policymaking

Striking Teachers Want Smaller Classes
Court to Rule on Affirmative Action
Los Angeles Hires First Woman Firefighter

Public personnel policies are the decisions concerning who is hired, fired and retained and the conditions under which government employees work. These headlines reveal the prominence of personnel policy in the news. Numerous kinds of personnel decisions affect all branches and levels of government as well as all public employees.

Interest groups regularly count the number of women and minorities appointed to positions and make decisions of support based in part on such calculations. Public employee organizations are a significant element of the voting public and politicians court them assiduously for support. An employee strike can stifle a city's economy and alter the well-being of the citizens.

The importance of personnel for the government administrator is apparent from the pressures revealed by the issues cited above. Additionally, new personnel policies have altered many basic working procedures of the administrator. Policies emanating from the courts, the federal government and state institutions have radically affected how personnel decisions must be made. Public officials cannot allocate funds in isolation of the budget office; they must await the outcome of negotiations with organized employees. Department heads may be unable to hire the assistants with which they feel most comfortable; they must concern themselves with equal employment guidelines or face long and costly legal battles. Promotional opportunities and dismissals cannot be determined solely by the desires of supervisors; court-approved procedures must be followed. Minority and women's groups can legitimately make demands upon the once isolated purview of the civil service or personnel commission. Today, personnel officers cannot assume that fairness has governed their actions; they must prove that they have been unbiased, or otherwise they risk the imposition of procedures by the courts or the federal government.

Consequently, the modern public personnel administrator cannot separate herself or himself from the important social and political concerns of the environment, and the chief administrator, department head, and aides to these officials must be very much involved in personnel matters. Personnel policy has become the terrain of a wide range of public officials and interest groups. Court rulings, new legislation, and the acts of regulatory bodies in the personnel area influence matters such as budgets and working standards. A detailed understanding of the personnel field as it affects public policy should therefore be an important component of the education of public officials and informed citizens.

The Academic Study of Public Personnel Administration

The academic study of the public personnel process rarely emphasizes this point of view. In fact, most authors assume little connection between personnel matters and public policy. We usually label courses in this area as "Public Personnel *Administration*," implying that policymaking is a minor concern.

A closer look at course curricula and the texts assigned suggests that personnel administration has been defined as the application of rules and techniques to agreed upon goals. The study often emphasizes matters such as position classification, grievance mechanisms, employee training, the institutions of collective bargaining and benefit systems. Scant attention is usually given to the effect of personnel decisions on broader social questions or the influence of other concerns on personnel policy.

Many writers in this field have not been oblivious to the role of personnel matters in policy. They have felt, however, that a set of mutually accepted principles guided good personnel practice. To uphold these principles meant, in effect, that personnel matters could be decided by a common set of norms which were unaffected by other values and acceptable to the major interests in society. With such agreement present, conflicts over policy goals could be effectively divorced from personnel administration.

The keystone of these mutually agreed upon values is the notion of the "merit system". O. Glenn Stahl, author of what has been the leading public personnel administration text for the past forty years, defines the merit system as ". . . a personnel system in which comparative merit or achievement governs each individual's selection, and progress in the service and in which the conditions and rewards of performance contribute to the competency of the service".[1] A good personnel system, then, develops the means to insure that merit or achievement is the basis for all decisions. Stahl assumes that personnel officials have the ability to make merit determinations; that merit, in fact, will be the only criteria applied, and that the applications of the principles of merit will result in public policy that is efficient and value free. He has much confidence in the techniques of civil service and acceptance of the general public's acceptance of merit principles. He states, "The merit method has no substitutes in providing the continuous competence and continuity that are essential to the operation of the complex ma hinery of modern government. Undoubtedly the principles and practices of good management could never have been extended to the sphere of public administration had not civil service reform created a stable body of qualified public employees."[2]

To Stahl, then, the purpose of public personnel administration is the application of merit to all phases of personnel work. The purpose of research and teaching in the personnel field is to develop techniques that promote the use of merit criteria in all decisions. Policies affecting public personnel that impinge on the merit concept, such as certain affirmative action rulings and some forms of organized activities of public employees, are criticized. The use of personnel policies to pursue goals such as representation and the desire of employees to influence organization policy through political activity are questioned (Stahl, pp. 22, 132, 382).

Problems With the Principles of Merit

The goal of those who adhere to the merit position is one that most public administration practitioners and writers support—the creation of a society where all individuals advance according to their own skills and desires, and governmental policy is created democratically by elected policymakers and implemented efficiently and effectively. But the creation of such a system rests on the acceptance of three assumptions:

1. The social and economic system provides equality of access to those with similar skills and desires. A merit civil service assumes that merit principles govern access to those institutions that help citizens develop skills and desires to gain employment. Educational institutions and training opportunities therefore must provide equal opportunity for all if the concept of merit in the civil service is to be realized. If educational institutions fail to do this, a "merit" civil service will perpetuate biases within the larger society rather than selecting the most fit.

2. The governmental system provides a mechanism for the electorate or their representatives to make policy that truly represents the public's desires. Elected decisionmakers understand the wishes of their constituents, have the means to convert these wishes to policies, and can enforce their policy directives. If merit is the guide for personnel decisions, administrators are concerned strictly with the implementing of policy. Appointed officials should have no role in policymaking and must assume that their elected superiors make all important policy decisions. The job of the administrator is not to represent any particular position or point of view; it is to carry out policy in the most efficient and effective manner possible under the guidance of the policymaker.

3. Personnel officers using civil service procedures have the ability to implement a merit system. It is assumed that procedures have been developed that can clearly select, retain, and promote those who can most competently perform the required tasks. The merit philosophy assumes that the techniques of the merit system are not simply ways of making personnel decisions; it assumes that personnel processes select, develop, and promote the most fit.

Analyses of contemporary American society and governmental practices question the validity of these just stated postulates:

1. Equality of access to educational and training institutions has been

questioned by social theorists and the Supreme Court. Many researchers have argued that the American educational system systematically favors the middle and upper classes and hinders the educational progress of members of minority groups and the lower class.[3] Others have contended that the social and educational system discourages women from acquiring the skills to enter certain occupations.[4] If systematic biases in the education and social system prevent some individuals from acquiring the education and skills needed to pass civil service entrance examinations, the merit system may be simply perpetuating these biases rather than selecting the most able people.

2. Analysts of the American political system have concluded that, in fact, elected decisionmakers do not clearly articulate and enforce public policy. Some have pointed out that policy is made by an attentive public which does not necessarily represent the interests of the general public.[5] More importantly, studies of the policymaking process at all levels of government have frequently shown that important policy decisions are often made by appointed officials. Policy proposals that lead directly to actions are often prepared by bureaucrats. It is common for many appointed officials to be given wide discretionary powers with little or no policy guidance from their elected superiors.[6]

   If, in fact, appointed officials make policy, criteria other than technical skills and commitment to the public service may be important standards for selection. Policy decisions are often judgments that must be assessed on one's support of a given set of values. What an individual believes therefore determines the kind of policy he or she will make. To make decisions, more than the traditional neutral nonpartisan competence is expected.

3. Studies of the procedures used by many civil service systems have demonstrated that the skills tested for an entry or promotion and those required on the job may be two separate matters.[7] Tests, in fact, have often been devised to screen out applicants rather than determine who is most able to do the tasks required of the job. Developing tests that accurately measure the traits required to perform a job well is often beyond our understanding of human and organization behavior. Until recently, the personnel field in general has given little thought to the relationship between tests and the job to be performed. Accordingly, the merit principle may not be actually practiced in many personnel decisions.

From Personnel Administrator to Personnel Policymaker

If one accepts the validity of the challenges to the merit principle, a different perspective on the public personnel field must follow. The public personnel administrator becomes a public personnel policymaker. He or she must become aware of the kinds of conflicts that surround the decisions that must be made. Agreement on the role and the principles of good practice are lacking. Merit remains a relevant and important value, but certainly not the only one. The problems of the larger society and the importance of past discriminations become matters that must influence actions.

The personnel official's most important task is to try to understand the strains and problems in his or her environment and *make* policy that tries to satisfy the divergent surrounding interests. Nobody is likely to tell him or her whether the possible walk-out of employees is more important to the legislative body than a proposal to increase these workers' salaries until after the recommendation has been made. The personnel official in this situation must develop an understanding of the ramifications of different courses of action. His or her superiors are likely to assume that he or she can handle the situation unless past actions indicate otherwise. Thus, the personnel administrator's job is not necessarily to apply previously defined rules, but rather to satisfy creatively these diverse and often conflicting pressures.

The Public Personnel Policymaker

With challenges to the merit principle now much a part of American politics, the new personnel administrators are called on to defend practices that used to be accepted, or they are asked to devise new policies with little guidance or histories of experience. Often one finds different agencies expecting distinctly different kinds of decisions on the same matter. When organized employees demand that layoffs be based on seniority while minority groups object because their members will be released first, different court rulings and administrative orders may support both positions. The job of the personnel administrator in that situation is to try to resolve conflicting demands with little guidance from either merit principles or political superiors. Only knowledge of the political and social setting of the organization, the actions and influences of other governments and the courts, and the experience of other people in a similar predicament can assist this person. No longer is there a clear set of principles to form a course of action.

This book is designed to illuminate the kinds of problems that face the modern personnel policymaker. It is assumed initially that personnel officials are policymakers, not only administrators. The goal is to provide knowledge and understanding of the complex tasks that must be accomplished. The personnel administrator exists in a volatile environment where different people and groups expect divergent actions from him or her. He or she is also surrounded by federal rules, regulatory commissions, and court actions which ask him/her to do conflicting things. The personnel administrator is also responsible to a chief executive to assist in accomplishing organization goals in the most efficient manner.

These are not easy tasks. They require a knowledge of the techniques of good administration, a sensitivity to divergent perspectives, and an ability to make decisions without clearly defined guiding principles. The personnel officer is not a technician. The job is an exciting one that is deeply involved in many of the society's important problems.

This book is written to present to the reader this broader perspective on the public personnel policy process. Understanding requires knowledge of the conflicts faced by contemporary administrators, a view of the political environment of American government, and a detailed analysis of the three most important present issues: labor relations, equal employment opportunity, and economy and efficiency.

Chapters One and Two examine the environment of public personnel policy. The selections and essays discuss both organizational and inter-governmental influences.

Chapter Three considers the three important contemporary problems in detail. Differing views are presented on the influence of public employee organizations, equal employment pressures and conflicts surrounding attempts to improve productivity in government. Policy guidelines as presented in court cases and legislation are included.

Finally, in Chapter Four, the reader becomes familiar with possible changes in the personnel process. Personnel policy is an important component of many policy changes. Government intervention in the economy may require an expanded role in the training of the unemployed. Can personnel systems respond to this task? Scientific advances require new technical personnel in government. Will this demand alter the personnel system? To make policy, as all personnel employees do, one must anticipate the kinds of changes required by a dynamic society.

Notes

1. O. Glenn Stahl, *Public Personnel Administration,* 7th ed., (New York, Harper and Row, 1976), p. 42.

2. *Ibid,* p. 53.

3. See James S. Coleman et al. *Equality of Educational Opportunity,* (Washington, D. C., United States Government Printing Office, 1966). Fredrick Mosher and Daniel Patrick Moynihan, eds., *On Equality of Educational Opportunity* (New York: Random House, 1972) and Christopher Jenks et al., *Inequality: A Reassessment of the Effect of Family and Schooling in America* (New York: Harper and Row, 1972).

4. Carolyn Bird, *Born Female* (New York: David McKay, 1968).

5. This point is brought out in most American and urban government textbooks. See particularly Kenneth Dolbeare and Murray J. Edelman, *American Politics: Policies, Power and Change,* 2nd ed. (Lexington, Mass: D. C. Heath, 1974.), pp. 316-346, or for a discussion of constraints on the President in the making of foreign policy. See Robert Lineberry and Ira Sharkansky, *Urban Politics and Public Policy,* 3rd ed., (New York: Harper and Row, 1978), for an analysis of decisionmaking processes in local government.

6. This point is made in most public administration textbooks. See, for example, Ivan L. Richardson and Sidney Baldwin, *Public Administration: Governments in Action* (Columbus, Ohio: Merrill, 1976).

7. *See Griggs et al.,* v. *Duke Power Company* and *Washington* v. *Davis,* both of which are selections in this volume.

CHAPTER TWO

Personnel Administration and the Dynamics of Public Organizations

Introduction

If you spent a day with a public personnel officer, you might see that some of his or her time goes to consultation with major department heads and the chief administrator in discussions of general organizational policy as well as specific personnel matters. The official would probably confer with personnel officers in other jurisdictions or levels of government. Reading material and discussions would brief him or her on current court cases, pieces of legislation at the state or federal level and happenings in the private sector. On his or her desk you will find copies of the *Wall Street Journal,* AFL-CIO publications, briefs of court cases, and *Public Personnel Management.* During the day he or she will deal with union representatives, insurance specialists, and safety inspectors from the Federal Occupational Safety and Health Administration. Other department heads may telephone him or her to discuss potential employee grievances, proposed training programs, or disputes they are experiencing over the meaning of terms in an employee contract.

Life Within the Organization

The daily routine of the personnel officer is varied and hectic. He or she is a part of the management team in the organization. As a member of this team this individual influences policy in areas other than those of his or her immediate area of responsibility. However, the officer is also influenced by the concerns of others. His or her desire for improving the working conditions of the employees may be tempered by the demands of others to cut costs.

The personnel officer is not a narrow specialist who is expected to deal only with such matters as employee grievances, position classifications, and collective bargaining. These matters are important, but they coexist with a need to deal with the problems of central management.

How to Make Policy

How do personnel administrators make policy? Writings in the field of public administration point out that administrators are policymakers but rarely suggest the conditions present when policy must be made or how it should be made. The first two selections in this chapter grapple with this problem and suggest where the administrator might look in his or her search for policy direction. The final two selections deal directly with the way in which personnel officers and other employees cope with personnel policy.

James Q. Wilson (Selection 1) notes that different people and groups expect varying policies from a public agency. Some want lower taxes, some others, efficiency, still others, services. Most probably want incompatible combinations of these and other goals. Any public official therefore makes decisions amid much uncertainty and considerable conflict in goal perspective among the clientele. If that is the case, ask yourself how the administrator should accomplish a given task. How could this person best organize his work to minimize these problems?

Rosenbloom (Selection 2) acquaints the reader with many important changes that have occurred in public personnel administration recently and advocates a recasting of the field to account more fully for the inherently political nature of the personnel process. If, in fact, a public administrator must deal with conflicting goals and historical changes in what is expected, and these value problems are an inherent part of personnel administration, a new perspective on public personnel administration follows.

While it is common to assume that public and private management are similar, Chapter One and these selections in Chapter Two argue that the differences between public and private management may be greater than the similarities. Wilson implies that conflict over goals is inherent in public administration. It is this condition that most clearly distinguishes public from private management. Hence, all experience from the private sector may not be transferable to public personnel management.

The final two selections in this chapter (Selections 3 and 4) discuss organization influences on personnel policy in a practical context. Both present discussions of how public personnel managers cope with the daily problems of organization survival.

The selection by Thompson (3) describes the politics of personnel decisions in Oakland, a large California city. He presents the different perspectives on personnel policy held by city managers, department heads, and personnel officers. Policy is the consequence of a bargaining process among these people. It is aided by assumed norms of operation and certain accepted routines of organization life. In the process, many goals of sound personnel practice such as up-to-date position classification, equal pay, and policies to improve employee satisfaction are altered. The personnel administrator in this setting must become involved in conflicts between the needs of the central administration, his or her professional values, and the interests of the employees.

Personal and group advancement and job enhancement and preservation are goals of most employees. Each public servant, as a member of an organization, is collectively a part of a very powerful body that can promote or impede action. His or her actions serve individuals as well as collective ends. An astute personnel administrator must be aware of the limits of his or her ability to alter established policy and procedures radically. Policy, as Chester Barnard pointed out forty years ago, flows upward, not downward. The chief administrator can influence activities in a large organization but seldom can he direct them.

In personnel matters important policies are often made or strongly influenced by employees. Heclo (Selection 4) points this out vividly in his analysis of promotional decisions in the federal government. Informal contacts, norms of self protection, and alliances with outside organizations are sources of power for employees to preserve their positions and advance their careers. While the conditions Heclo describes are those of the federal civil service, the characteristics he discovers are general organizational qualities and personal motivations that are endemic to any large organization.

1

The Bureaucracy Problem
James Q. Wilson

The federal bureaucracy, whose growth and problems were once only the concern of the Right, has now become a major concern of the Left, the Center, and almost all points in between. Conservatives once feared that a powerful bureaucracy would work a social revolution. The Left now fears that this same bureaucracy is working a conservative reaction. And the Center fears that the bureaucracy isn't working at all.

Increasing federal power has always been seen by conservatives in terms of increasing *bureaucratic* power. If greater federal power merely meant, say, greater uniformity in government regulations—standardized trucking regulations, for example, or uniform professional licensing practices—a substantial segment of American businessmen would probably be pleased. But growing federal power means increased discretion vested in appointive officials whose

---

Reprinted with permission of the author from *The Public Interest* Vol. 6, Winter, 1976, pp. 3-9, (c) by National Affairs Inc.

James Q. Wilson is Professor of Government, Harvard University. He is author of numerous books and articles on American politics including *Political Organizations, Varieties of Police Behavior: The Management of Law and Order in Eight Communities,* and *Thinking About Crime.*

behavior can neither be anticipated nor controlled. The behavior of state and local bureaucrats, by contrast, can often be anticipated *because* it can be controlled by businessmen and others.

Knowing this, liberals have always resolved most questions in favor of enhancing federal power. The "hacks" running local administrative agencies were too often, in liberal eyes, the agents of local political and economic forces—businessmen, party bosses, organized professions, and the like. A federal bureaucrat, because he was responsible to a national power center and to a single President elected by a nationwide constituency, could not so easily be bought off by local vested interests; in addition, he would take his policy guidance from a President elected by a process that gave heavy weight to the votes of urban, labor, and minority groups. The New Deal bureaucrats, especially those appointed to the new, "emergency" agencies, were expected by liberals to be free to chart a radically new program and to be competent to direct its implementation.

It was an understandable illusion. It frequently appears in history in the hopes of otherwise intelligent and far-sighted men. Henry II thought his clerks and scribes would help him subdue England's feudal barons; how was he to know that in time they would become the agents of Parliamentary authority directed at stripping the king of his prerogatives? And how were Parliament and its Cabinet ministers, in turn, to know that eventually these permanent undersecretaries would become an almost self-governing class whose day-to-day behavior would become virtually immune to scrutiny or control? Marxists thought that Soviet bureaucrats would work for the people, despite the fact that Max Weber had pointed out why one could be almost certain they would work mostly for themselves. It is ironic that among today's members of the "New Left," the "Leninist problem"—i.e., the problem of over-organization and of self-perpetuating administrative power—should become a major preoccupation.

This apparent agreement among polemicists of the Right and Left that there is a bureaucracy problem accounts, one suspects, for the fact that non-bureaucratic solutions to contemporary problems seem to command support from both groups. The negative income tax as a strategy for dealing with poverty is endorsed by economists of such different persuasions as Milton Friedman and James Tobin, and has received favorable consideration among members of both the Goldwater brain trust and the Students for Democratic Society. Though the interests of the two groups are somewhat divergent, one common element is a desire to scuttle the social workers and the public welfare bureaucracy, who are usually portrayed as prying busybodies with pursed lips and steel-rimmed glasses ordering midnight bedchecks in public housing projects. (Police officers who complain that television makes them look like fools in the eyes of their children will know just what the social workers are going through.)

Several Bureaucracy Problems

Now that everybody seems to agree that we ought to do something about the problem of bureaucracy, one might suppose that something would get done.

Perhaps a grand reorganization, accompanied by lots of "systems analysis," "citizen participation," "creative federalism," and "interdepartmental co-ordination." Merely to state this prospect is to deny it.

There is not one bureaucracy problem, there are several, and the solution to each is in some degree incompatible with the solution to every other. First, there is the problem of accountability or control—getting the bureaucracy to serve agreed-on national goals. Second is the problem of equity—getting bureaucrats to treat like cases alike and on the basis of clear rules, known in advance. Third is the problem of efficiency—maximizing output for a given expenditure, or minimizing expenditures for a given output. Fourth is the problem of responsiveness—inducing bureaucrats to meet, with alacrity and compassion, those cases which can never be brought under a single national rule and which, by common human standards of justice or benevolence, seem to require that an exception be made or a rule stretched. Fifth is the problem of fiscal integrity—properly spending and accounting for public money.

Each of these problems mobilizes a somewhat different segment of the public. The problem of power is the unending preoccupation of the President and his staff, especially during the first years of an administration. Equity concerns the lawyers and the courts, though increasingly the Supreme Court seems to act as if it thinks its job is to help set national goals as a kind of auxiliary White House. Efficiency has traditionally been the concern of businessmen who thought, mistakenly, that an efficient government was one that didn't spend very much money. (Of late, efficiency has come to have a broader and more accurate meaning as an optimal relationship between objectives and resources. Robert McNamara has shown that an "efficient" Department of Defense costs a lot more money than an "inefficient" one; his disciples are now carrying the message to all parts of a skeptical federal establishment.) Responsiveness has been the concern of individual citizens and of their political representatives, usually out of wholly proper motives, but sometimes out of corrupt ones. Congress, especially, has tried to retain some power over the bureaucracy by intervening on behalf of tens of thousands of immigrants, widows, businessmen, and mothers-of-soldiers, hoping that the collective effect of many individual interventions would be a bureaucracy that, on large matters as well as small, would do Congress's will. (Since Congress only occasionally has a clear will, this strategy only works occasionally.) Finally, fiscal integrity—especially its absence—is the concern of the political "outs" who want to get in and thus it becomes the concern of "ins" who want to keep them out.

Obviously the more a bureaucracy is responsive to its clients—whether those clients are organized by radicals into Mothers for Adequate Welfare or represented by Congressmen anxious to please constituents—the less it can be accountable to presidential directives. Similarly, the more equity, the less responsiveness. And a preoccupation with fiscal integrity can make the kind of program budgeting required by enthusiasts of efficiency difficult, if not impossible.

Indeed, of all the groups interested in bureaucracy, those concerned with fiscal integrity usually play the winning hand. To be efficient, one must have clearly stated goals, but goals are often hard to state at all, much less clearly. To be responsive, one must be willing to run risks, and the career civil service is not ordinarily attractive to people with a taste for risk. Equity is an abstraction, of concern for the most part only to people who haven't been given any. Accountability is "politics," and the bureaucracy itself is the first to resist that (unless, of course, it is the kind of politics that produces pay raises and greater job security.) But an absence of fiscal integrity is welfare chiseling, sweetheart deals, windfall profits, conflict of interest, malfeasance in high places—in short, corruption. Everybody recognizes *that* when he sees it, and none but a few misguided academics have anything good to say about it. As a result, fiscal scandal typically becomes the standard by which a bureaucracy is judged (the FBI is good because it hasn't had any, the Internal Revenue Service is bad because it has) and thus the all-consuming fear of responsible executives.

The Limits of Reform

If it is this hard to make up one's mind about how one wants the bureaucracy to behave, one might be forgiven if one threw up one's hands and let nature take its course. Though it may come to that in the end, it is possible—and important—to begin with a resolution to face the issue squarely and try to think through the choices. Facing the issue means admitting what, in our zeal for new programs, we usually ignore: *There are inherent limits to what can be accomplished by large hierarchical organizations.*

The opposite view is more often in vogue. If enough people don't like something, it becomes a problem; if the intellectuals agree with them, it becomes a crisis; any crisis must be solved; if it must be solved, then it can be solved—and creating a new organization is the way to do it. If the organization fails to solve the problem (and when the problem is a fundamental one, it will almost surely fail), then the reason is "politics," or "mismangement," or "incompetent people," or "meddling," or "socialism," or "inertia."

Some problems cannot be solved and some government functions cannot, in principle, be done well. Notwithstanding, the effort must often be made. The rule of reason should be to try to do as few undoable things as possible. It is regrettable, for example, that any country must have a foreign office, since none can have a good one. The reason is simple: it is literally impossible to have a "policy" with respect to *all* relevant matters concerning *all* foreign countries, much less a consistent and reasonable policy. And the difficulty increases with the square of the number of countries, and probably with the cube of the speed of communications. The problem long ago became insoluble and any sensible Secretary of State will cease trying to solve it. He will divide his time instead between *ad hoc* responses to the crisis of the moment and appearances on Meet the Press.

The answer is not, it must be emphasized, one of simply finding good people, though it is at least that. Most professors don't think much of the State Department, but it is by no means clear that a department made up only of professors would be any better, and some reason to believe that it would be worse. One reason is that bringing in "good outsiders," especially good outsiders from universities, means bringing in men with little experience in dealing with the substantive problem but many large ideas about how to approach problems "in general." General ideas, no matter how soundly based in history or social science, rarely tell one what to do tomorrow about the visit from the foreign trade mission from Ruritania or the questions from the Congressional appropriations subcommittee.

Another reason is that good people are in very short supply, even assuming we knew how to recognize them. Some things literally cannot be done—or cannot be done well—because there is no one available to do them who knows how. *The supply of able, experienced executives is not increasing nearly as fast as the number of problems being addressed by public policy.* All the fellowships, internships, and "mid-career training programs" in the world aren't likely to increase that supply very much, simply because the essential qualities for an executive—judgment about men and events, a facility for making good guesses, a sensitivity to political realities, and an ability to motivate others—are things which, if they can be taught at all, cannot be taught systematically or to more than a handful of apprentices at one time.

This constraint deserves emphasis, for it is rarely recognized as a constraint at all. Anyone who opposed a bold new program on the grounds that there was nobody around able to run it would be accused of being a pettifogger at best and a reactionary do-nothing at worst. Everywhere except in government, it seems, the scarcity of talent is accepted as a fact of life. Nobody (or almost nobody) thinks seriously of setting up a great new university overnight, because anybody familiar with the university business knows that, for almost any professorship one would want to fill, there are rarely more than five (if that) really top-flight people in the country, and they are all quite happy—and certainly well-paid— right where they are. Lots of new business ideas don't become profit-making realities because good business executives are both hard to find and expensive to hire. The government—at least publicly—seems to act as if the supply of able political executives were infinitely elastic, though people setting up new agencies will often admit privately that they are so frustrated and appalled by the shortage of talent that the only wonder is why disaster is so long in coming. Much would be gained if this constraint were mentioned to Congress *before* the bill is passed and the hopes aroused, instead of being mentioned afterward as an excuse for failure or as a reason why higher pay scales for public servants are an urgent necessity. "Talent is Scarcer Than Money" should be the motto of the [Office of Management and Budget].

Defining our Objectives

If administrative feasibility is such a critical issue, what can be done about it? Not a great deal. If the bureaucracy problem is a major reason why so many programs are in trouble, it is also a reason why the problem itself cannot be "solved." But it can be mitigated—though not usually through the kinds of expedients we are fond of trying: Hoover Commissions, management studies, expensive consultants, co-ordinating committees, "czars," and the like. The only point at which very much leverage can be gained on the problem *is when we decide what it is we are trying to accomplish.* When we define our goals, we are implicitly deciding how much, or how little, of a bureaucracy problem we are going to have. A program with clear objectives, clearly stated, is a program with a fighting chance of coping with each of the many aspects of the bureaucracy problem. Controlling an agency is easier when you know what you want. Equity is more likely to be assured when over-all objectives can be stated, at least in part, in general rules to which people in and out of the agency are asked to conform. Efficiency is made possible when you know what you are buying with your money. Responsiveness is never easy or wholly desirable; if every person were treated in accordance with his special needs, there would be no program at all. (The only system that meets the responsiveness problem squarely is the free market.) But at least with clear objectives we would know what we are giving up in those cases when responsiveness seems necessary, and thus we would be able to decide how much we are willing to tolerate. And fiscal integrity is just as easy to insure in a system with clear objectives as in one with fuzzy ones; in the former case, moreover, we are less likely to judge success simply in terms of avoiding scandal. We might even be willing to accept a little looseness if we knew what we were getting for it.

The rejoinder to this argument is that there are many government functions which, by their nature, can never have clear objectives. I hope I have made it obvious by now that I am aware of that. We can't stop dealing with foreign nations just because we don't know what we want; after all, they may know what *they* want, and we had better find out. My argument is advanced, not as a panacea—there is no way to avoid the problem of administration—but as a guide to choice in those cases where choice is open to us, and as a criterion by which to evaluate proposals for coping with the bureaucracy problem.

Dealing with poverty—at least in part—by giving people money seems like an obvious strategy. Governments are very good at taking money from one person and giving it to another; the goals are not particularly difficult to state; measures are available to evaluate how well we are doing in achieving a predetermined income distribution. There may be many things wrong with this approach, but administrative difficulty is not one of them. And yet, paradoxically, it is the last approach we will probably try. We will try everything else first—case work, counseling, remedial education, community action, federally-financed mass protests to end "alienation," etc. And whatever else might be said in favor, the likelihood of smooth administration and ample talent can hardly be included.

Both the White House and the Congress seem eager to do something about the bureaucracy problem. All too often, however, the problem is described in terms of "digesting" the "glut" of new federal programs—as if solving administrative difficulties had something in common with treating heartburn. Perhaps those seriously concerned with this issue will put themselves on notice that they ought not to begin with the pain and reach for some administrative bicarbonate of soda; they ought instead to begin with what was swallowed and ask whether an emetic is necessary. *Coping with the bureaucracy problem is inseparable from rethinking the objectives of the programs in question.* Administrative reshuffling, budgetary cuts (or budgetary increases), and congressional investigation of lower-level boondoggling will not suffice and are likely, unless there are some happy accidents, to make matters worse. Thinking clearly about goals is a tough assignment for a political system that has been held together in great part by compromise, ambiguity, and contradiction. And if a choice must be made, any reasonable person would, I think, prefer the system to the clarity. But now that we have decided to intervene in such a wide range of human affairs, perhaps we ought to reassess that particular trade-off.

2
Public Personnel Administration and Politics: Toward a New Public Personnel Administration
David H. Rosenbloom

Public personnel administration, as an academic field, is currently lacking in appeal for the vast majority of political scientists and even for many public policy oriented public administrationists. It has, as a recent introductory political science text noted, become little more than a "specialty 'tool,'" which is "... generally taught as a technical specialty, revolving around such topics as position classification ... and methods of recruitment and selection for the civil service."[1] This is true despite the fact that many have recognized that within the field there are several topics having widespread political ramifications.[2] The purpose of this article is to explicate the reasons for the current status of public personnel administration and to suggest a path which could be followed in order to develop a new and more useful public personnel administration.

Political Science, Public Administration, and Personnel

The current status of public personnel administration is related to intellectual developments which have taken place in the related areas of political science and public administration. Public personnel administration is a profession as well as a discipline, and as such, it has always had a practical and

---

Reprinted with permission from *Midwest Review of Public Administration,* Vol. 7 No. 2, April, 1973, pp. 98-110.

David Rosenbloom is Professor of Political Science at the University of Vermont and author of *Federal Service and the Constitution* and *Federal Equal Employment Opportunity.*

prescriptive bias. Its literature is formalistic and highly value-laden, with the standard goals being greater efficiency, economy, and procedural regularity. In the years since World War II, however, the major intellectual developments in political science and public administration have been in an opposite direction. Both have become less prescriptive, less formalistic, more value-free, and more behaviorally oriented. In addition, public administration, in particular, has undergone changes which have placed public personnel administration on tenuous intellectual grounds. Public administration, as a field, has come to recognize that to a large extent its focus must be on "public" rather than on "administration," if it is to make a *special* contribution. It is partly in this connection that public administration rejected a portion of the core of its former body of theory (or framework of "proverbs," if the reader prefers) and became far more concerned with decision making and public policymaking. As a result, some areas which were more central to public administration in the past have largely now become the preserves of other fields, including sociology and business administration. Thus, Waldo observed: "There is over-all a wide gap between the interests and activities of the scholars identified with Theory of Organization and the interests and activities of scholars trained in and identified with political science and the related or subdiscipline of public administration."[3] In terms of public personnel administration, it is especially important that there are now few, if any, who argue that the general behavioral patterns of individuals in organizations are significantly related per se to whether the organizations are public or private by definition. If behavorial patterns in public and private organizations are similar, however, *public* personnel administration, as it is now constituted, is largely without a viable rationale.[4]

The current status of public personnel administration is also related to its self-imposed narrowness of scope. Although public personnel administrationists are sometimes sweeping in their generalizations pertaining to the importance of the field, they nevertheless fail to address themselves fully to its public or political aspects, despite the fact that these might be the only legitimate basis for a *public* personnel administration. For example, O. Glenn Stahl, one of the most influential American public personnel administrationists, has concluded that "There is no single activity which will net such economy or promote such performance as may be realized through continued improvements in the quality and the motivation of public personnel."[5] His concepts of economy and performance, however, are almost totally apolitical. Public personnel administration, as a whole, has also failed to address itself to the fact that all public personnel systems are primarily political products and therefore, that terms such as "economy," "efficiency," "performance," and "best qualified" cannot be, and have not been, defined without reference to political values.

Perhaps the most important factor in public personnel administration's rejection of an approach more oriented toward politics has been its simultaneous commitment to the "merit system" and its failure to understand correctly the nature of that system. In the minds of most public personnel administrationists, the merit system is associated with efficiency, economy, procedural justice, quality, and political neutrality. It has been treated as something upon which, as a whole, there can be no legitimate disagreement, and therefore as something which is inherently apolitical. Thus, the slogan "only the best shall serve the state" became the rallying cry of public personnel administrationists, as though it were akin to a natural law, rather than a legitimizing proposition for a particular set of political arrangements.[6] Merit systems, however, were often introduced at least as much in connection with demands for a redistribution of political power, authority, and influence among members of political communities, as to secure better economy and efficiency. Civil service reform in the United States, Great Britain, and sixth [to] tenth century China present just three such examples.

In the United States, the civil service reformers thought that, in the words of Carl Schurz, "The question whether the Departments at Washington are managed well or badly is, in proportion to the whole problem, an insignificant question."[7] What they wanted, as they clearly stated, was to make it possible for a new class of politicians to emerge, or, "To restore ability, high character, and true public spirit once more to their legitimate spheres in our public life, and to make active politics once more attractive to men of self-respect and high patriotic aspirations."[8] In short, nothing less than a fundamental change in political leadership. In Great Britain, as J. D. Kingsley observed, ". . . the debate occasioned by the Northcote-Trevelyan recommendations ran clearly along class lines"[9] and the overall issue was the distribution of political power, authority, and influence, rather than more efficient administration. In China, "After several centuries of division, the Sui (589-618) and the T'ang (618-906) dynasties saw in the training and recruitment of a centralized civil service the best means of overcoming the powers of regionalism and of the hereditary aristocracy."[10] Although there is some doubt as to whether "the rise of this aristocracy of merit . . . definitely freed the dynasty from its dependence on an older, hereditary aristocracy,"[11] there is little doubt that personnel administrative reforms were introduced with this prospect in mind.

The historical relationship between merit systems and the distribution of political power, authority, and influence suggests that merit values such as selection of the best qualified, efficiency, and economy, which historically have been predominantly political values cannot be defined fully and legitimately without reference to other political values. It should be noted, in this context, that some now consider all major public administrative values to be political values as well. It is here, perhaps, that public personnel administration currently leaves the most to be desired from the point of view of political science. The field has devoted itself almost entirely to attempting to discover the principles and practices through which public personnel systems can assure the highest degree of economy and efficiency in an apolitical sense, and it has almost completely ignored the impact of these principles and practices on such politically relevant factors as bureaucratic representativeness and individual, group, and organizational political behavior. It should be noted in passing that this shortcoming of public personnel administration has itself become politically relevant in the U.S. today as members of some minority groups and women have been increasingly arguing that procedures designed to obtain the "best" civil servants tend to be racially, ethnically, and /or sexually discriminatory and, therefore, that they are inherently not the best procedures.

A final reason for the current lack of interest in public personnel administration among political scientists and many public administrationists is a more technical one: the field as a whole has failed to develop satisfactorily as either a science or an art, even within its excessively narrow confines. For example, "The cornerstone of the public personnel program is the process of selection by means of competitive examinations . . ."[12] but, ". . . hundreds of public jurisdictions have probably never done a validity study"[13] and there are many major barriers to such studies. First, there is the difficulty of determining what constitutes "job success." "A 'success rating' usually amounts to a kind of 'report card' which is made out by the employees' supervisor," and, ". . . such ratings are inevitably limited in reliability—particularly when different *supervisors are rating different people,*"[14] as is the case in the vast majority of large jurisdictions. A second limitation is that ". . . generally only a limited portion of the test-taking group ever get the chance to perform on the job."[15] Third, those appointed often have very similar scores, thereby limiting the amount of variation likely to be explained by those scores. Finally, public jurisdictions tend to be forced to give examinations having "face validity," but face validity does not necessarily coincide with content validity. As a result of these barriers, civil service examination validity coefficients are typically at about the .25 level and seldomly greater than .50.[16] In other words, performance on civil service examinations usually explains only about 6 per cent of the variance in job performance and rarely more than 25 per cent. What then of the cornerstone, not to mention the rest of the structure? The problem would not be so acute if public personnel administration were less value-laden and less ideological, and had sought to explain the remainder of the variance in some other ways. By and large, however, it has not. It is this defect in particular which has led some to conclude that the merit system and public personnel administration in general contribute little more than a means of keeping "undesirables" out of the civil service in an inexpensive and relatively neutral fashion,[17] and that therefore public personnel administration, as an intellectual endeavor, has made little contribution apart from rationalizing the political status quo.

What Must Be Done

If public personnel administration is to progress and develop more toward its full potential, at least two of its current limitations must be overcome. First, the field must develop a greater degree of self-awareness and methodological sophistication. It must seek to define its sphere of interest with a greater degree of consciousness and do more to assert an existence independent of governmental practices and practitioners, just as political science has an existence apart from law and politicians. In this connection, public personnel administration must seek to understand more fully its own development and explore further the extent to which public personnel practices and theories have been related to political variables. At the same time that the field must become less value-laden and less ideological, it must make greater efforts to become more methodologically sophisticated. It must, for example, seek to explain a far greater share of the variance in on-the-job performance, and in other personnel factors. In this regard, the field might find it useful to adopt a more experimental approach, where possible. In short, public personnel administration must seek to discover true relationships rather than presumed ones. In addition to developing greater methodological sophistication to deal with its traditional concerns, public personnel administration should also do the same with regard to what should become its new concerns. This, then, relates to the second limitation to be overcome.

In order to overcome its currently excessively narrow scope, public personnel administration must adopt a perspective which is more analytic of political relationships and political behavior. It must go beyond the value constraints of its understanding of the merit system and attempt to develop an understanding of the impact of public personnel administration on political variables, and vice-versa, rather than simply on efficiency and economy in a technical sense. At least for the time being, however, this political perspective should probably be a limited one. The field, by the very nature of its concerns, must retain some of its applied and prescriptive bias. If it is to remain, or more accurately, to become *public* personnel administration, it must also avoid following the path of modern organization theory, or of duplicating it, in rejecting a meaningful distinction between public and private organizations. Thus, in addition to normal limitations based on the relevance of public personnel administrative theory, hypotheses, principles, and practices to political variables, public personnel administration should not concern itself with political behavior which is not oriented toward or highly relevant to macro-politics. That is to say, that, at least for the present, public personnel administration should not seek to develop further understanding of individual political behavior which is essentially intra-organizationally oriented, unless such behavior is believed to be relevant to macro-politics.

The justification for the above approach, and indeed for *public* personnel administration itself is related ultimately to Weber's conception of the state as being distinguished from other organizations on the basis of its ". . . monopoly of the legitimate use of physical force within a given territory."[18] Despite the problems sometimes incurred in attempting to distinguish public from private organizations, it is always the case that central national administrative apparatuses and the people who are responsible for their functioning have a degree of direct or primary political power which is not available to the vast majority of private organizations[19] and administrators. Therefore, it is not necessary to consider whether the intra-organizationally oriented behavior of public employees differs from that of private employees, or whether the overall organizationally oriented behavior of structurally similar public and private organizations differs, as to recognize that, in general, the political outputs of each are fundamentally different in terms of their "authoritative" or binding qualities. In addition, it is probably true that civil servants employed by central administrative organizations tend to possess more political authority and influence in their extra-organizationally oriented political behavior, directly and indirectly by virtue of their association with these organizations, than do people doing similar types of tasks in private organizations.[20] On the basis of this distinction between the general political characteristics of public and private organizations, many areas into which public personnel administration could and should legitimately expand can be identified. Perhaps it will eventually prove possible to develop a general theory of public personnel administration on this basis. For the time being, however, rather than attempting to build a framework from the top down, public personnel administration would probably be better off by developing a sounder foundation. In this regard, there are at least four areas of political importance which appear to be significantly related to public personnel administrative practices, and which also appear to be fundamental to the development of a more useful public personnel administration.

A Broadened Focus

The first of these areas, and perhaps the most important, is that of bureaucratic representation. In an age in which much of the policy of all governments is formulated in public bureaucracies, the potential importance of their representativeness is hard to overestimate. It can hardly be much less important, and might even be more, for example, than the representativeness of legislatures. For the most part, however, public personnel administration, which, at least in theory, has always been concerned with the relationship between the input of manpower and the quality of bureaucratic outputs, has in practice avoided any serious consideration of whether either these "inputs" or outputs do have a representative quality, whether they have any relationship to one another in this regard, or whether the outputs are related to anything other than technical efficiency. In fact, public personnel administration has been largely oblivious to the major questions posed by the concept of representative bureaucracy, which, incidentally, has been developed almost entirely by political scientists rather than by public personnel administrationists. To understand more fully exactly what is involved here, it is necessary to briefly identify the major aspects of that concept.

The concept of representative bureaucracy has now been in the literature of political science for some time, and has received considerable attention. It was perhaps most comprehensively defined by Krislov, who concluded that it had "four intertwined meanings:"

> *The most obvious is the simple representational notion that all social groups have a right to political participation and to influence. The second can be labeled the functional aspect; the wider the range of talents, types, and regional and family contacts found in a bureaucracy, the more likely it is to be able to fulfill its functions, with respect to both internal efficiency and social setting. Bureaucracies also symbolize values and power realities*

and are thus representational in both a political and an analytic sense. Therefore, finally, social conduct and future behavior in a society may be channelized and encouraged through the mere constitution of the bureaucracy.[21]

In addition, Mosher has provided a note of clarity by distinguishing between passive (or sociological) and active (or responsible) representation. The former "... concerns the source of origin of individuals and the degree to which, collectively, they mirror the total society." In active representation, on the other hand, "... an individual (or administrator) is expected to press for the interests and desires of those whom he is presumed to represent, whether they be the whole people or some segment of the people."[22]

It is logically a task of public personnel administration to attempt to answer many of the questions posed by the concept of representative bureaucracy. Public personnel administration's sole concern with efficiency and economy might have been appropriate at an earlier time when public bureaucracies did not have important policy functions, but it is certainly inappropriate today. Broad questions, such as the following, for instance, must be approached in a far more adequate fashion: What is the relationship between active and passive representation? What is the political and administrative importance of each? And with what does it vary? What factors serve to encourage or discourage a strong relationship between the two? What personnel practices, such as examinations and protections against discriminatory treatment, serve to foster or to limit passive and active representation? What are the political and administrative effects of using personnel procedures, such as quotas for minority group hiring and promotion, which either limit or increase passive representation? Until public personnel administration deals reasonably effectively with such questions, it will remain highly underdeveloped and continue to be concerned with much that is less important.

Agency Cultures

A second and related area into which public personnel administration could profitably expand concerns the relationship between public personnel administrative practices and the development of agency cultures and patterns of behavior. The latter, of course, are inherently political and of political interest because they are directly related to public policy outputs. Although there is a considerable overlap between this area and that of representative bureaucracy, there is also a significant difference of focus. Here the concern is with the agency as a whole, its general outlook and the development of institutionalized behavioral patterns, rather than with the individual and his contribution to passive or active representation. As Seidman has observed. "Each agency has its own culture and internal set of loyalties and values which are likely to guide its actions and influence its policies."[23] He has also noted that,

... Because people believe what they are doing is important and the way they have been taught to do is right, they are slow to accept change.

Institutional responses are highly predictable, particularly to new ideas which conflict with institutional values and may pose a potential threat to organizational power and survival. Knowledgeable Budget Bureau officials estimate that agency positions on any major policy issue can be forecast with nearly 100 per cent accuracy, regardless of the administration in power.[24]

Although Seidman argues that culture and behavior are largely products of structural and organizational arrangements, personnel practices, as Downs has argued, probably also play an important role. Firstly, the development of agency cultures must depend heavily on internal socialization processes and methods of treating deviant behavior (disciplinary procedures). Both of these, of course, are largely questions for personnelists. Secondly, Downs has hypothesized that such personnel concerns as agency rates of growth and methods of promotion are important in determining agency behavior: "Fast-growing bureaus experience a rising proportion of climbers and a declining proportion of conservers," and, "if most of the officials occupying key positions in a bureau are of one type, then the bureau and its behavior will be dominated by the traits typical of that type."[25] In addition, if Downs is correct, such personnel procedures as promotion by seniority would tend to increase the proportion of "conservers" in an agency, give the total agency a conserver culture and increase the importance of bureau pathologies peculiar to that group. Other personnel practices, including recruitment and selection, position classification, status gradations, the nature and use of authority, and so forth, would also seem to be relevant here as they make agencies more or less attractive to different types of "organizational men" and therefore, presumably are also related to different kinds of organizational behavior and public policy outputs. The task of public personnel administration is, of course, to analyze the relationships between such practices, their development, and the development of organizational cultures and behavioral patterns. Again, focusing only on individual ability and proper placement of individuals in a technical sense does not seem to explain adequately agency performance and behavior, and again variables of political importance, rather than simply economy and efficiency are involved.

Another area in which public personnel administration could make an important contribution concerns the relationship between public personnel administrative practices and the general political participation and orientation of civil servants. Public personnel administration has, of course, addressed itself to a part of this subject area in its traditional concern with regulations concerning political neutrality, conflicts of interest, and adverse actions. In general, however, the treatment of these subjects has been technical, legal, and largely from a narrow administrative perspective. Little systematic effort has been made to understand the impact of these features on politics and political variables.[26] Political neutrality regulations, for example, range from almost no restrictions on the part of Scandinavian civil servants, through substantial limitations on the partisan political activities of U.S. civil servants, to an almost complete denial of political rights to some civil servants in Japan. But the consequences of these regulations for political systems is largely unknown, as is the relative commonness and importance of the political activities of civil servants where such activity is permitted. Yet without a better understanding of these activities, the consequences, and necessity, desirability, or sensibility of regulations in this area cannot be known, despite the wealth of opinion expressed upon them. The same applies with respect to conflicts of interest. In some countries civil servants cannot join a private firm for two years after they have retired from the service, if they have had official dealings with that firm. In other countries no such regulation exists. Although it could be assumed that policy formulation and the development of relationships or complexes involving public agencies and private firms or groups could be influenced by these differences, in fact very little is known about their consequences. The protections afforded civil servants against adverse actions present another case in point. These usually have been developed for administrative reasons or as a result of collective bargaining, rather than for political reasons, and they vary widely among political systems. It is reasonable to assume that they have political consequences because they largely remove sanctions against civil servants for engaging in legitimate, but disfavored political activity. Public personnel administration, however, has failed to approach this subject from this point of view and consequently very little is known about it.

Each of the above categories of public personnel regulations, and perhaps others as well, appear, on their face, to be related to the potential political behavior of civil servants and therefore, of course, to the political importance and consequences of that behavior. Developments concerning the legal-constitutional position and political participation of civil servants in the U.S. in the last decade provide a good illustration that such a relationship can exist and have significant consequences. Beginning in the 1960s and continuing to the present time, the legal-constitutional position of U.S. civil servants has undergone major changes in the direction of providing them with greater constitutional protections, including those of free speech and association, and greater due process in removals and adverse actions.[27] At the same time, a significant number of them, with at least a general awareness of their greater security, began to engage in permissible, but decidedly disfavored political activities including the signing of rather strongly worded anti-war petitions, the petitioning of departmental secretaries for changes in national policies, the organization of political pressure groups within the Federal service, and related activities.[28] These forms of political participation raise numerous questions which are legitimately the concern of public personnel administrationists and should at least be addressed, if not fully answered. For example, how direct is the relationship between a strengthening of civil servants' legal-constitutional position and their proclivity to take part in political activities? To what extent is this proclivity also related to their positions in agencies? How does the public at large react to such activities and with what does this reaction vary? How do administrative officials and politicians react to the activities and to the civil servants taking part in them? What effect does greater political participation have on internal administrative arrangements, behavior, and policy outputs? And, more normatively, how desirable is it from the point of view of various aspects of the political system?

Labor Relations

A final area in which public personnel administration should adopt a new approach involves labor relations. Regulations and practices pertaining to employee organization and collective bargaining have long been considered an important aspect of public personnel administration, but, in general, public personnel administrationists have failed in this area, as in the others, to develop an adequate political focus. The overall political relevance of public employee unionization has, perhaps, best been conveyed by Chapman in his study of public personnel practices in Western Europe: "The truth is that people employed in government service are tending to become not only self-governing but also self employed. All the evidence . . . points in this direction. The drift towards the syndical state machine is one of the unnoticed oddities of the last fifty years."[29] With regard to the power position of civil service unions, he concluded:

> *Their power now lies in their numerical strength and its potential electoral importance to politicians. This is reinforced by the fact that they are the accepted spokesmen for those employed by the state. Their aim is to protect the interests of the state in so far as those interests coincide with the interests of their members. Indeed, some extremists have held that the body of civil servants is the state.*[30]

The fact that Chapman perceived this development as having been a "drift" is significant because it speaks directly to public personnel administration's apolitical approach in an area in which politics is of fundamental importance. Although it is probably too late to drastically affect the power positions of public service unions, if that should be desirable, there are many questions which are still worth analyzing. For example, What are the public personnel administrative and political causes and effects of administrative systems in which civil service *unions* are engaged in the administration of public services? What are the public personnel administrative, general administrative, and political roots of different styles of union leadership, growth, and relative power? What happens, and under what conditions, when employee organizations seek to recast public personnel practices in a way more suitable to themselves? How do all of these affect popular control, representative bureaucracy, and other general aspects of public service?

In conclusion, public personnel administration has more or less fallen by the intellectual wayside in recent years as a result of its failure to keep up with developments in related areas in political science and public administration, its overly narrow scope, and its inability to develop satisfactorily as an art or a science within its limited realm. The field has the potential to make significant contributions in both political science and public administration and it may be able to revive itself by becoming more self-conscious and methodologically sophisticated, and by adopting a more political focus. Hopefully, this article will serve as a meaningful step toward the development of a new, and far more useful, public personnel administration.

Notes

1. Stephen Wasby, *Political Science—The Discipline and Its Dimensions* (New York: Charles Scribner's Sons, 1970), pp. 425-426.

2. *Ibid,* p. 427.

3. Dwight Waldo, "Theory of Organization: Status and Problems," in Amitai Etzioni, ed., *Readings on Modern Organizations* (Englewood Cliffs: Prentice-Hall, 1969), pp. 22.

4. Thus, there are really two principal courses open to public personnel administration. It must either develop a distinctive focus by more adequately addressing the public (especially the political and public policy-making) aspects of governmental personnel administration, or essentially merge with personnel administration in general. Remaining in its current state, as I will argue below, amounts to little more than serving to place a veneer of professional legitimacy in a peculiar set of political arrangements.

5. O. Glenn Stahl, *Public Personnel Administration* (New York: Harper and Row, 1962), p. 480.

6. See Norman Sharpless, Jr., "Public Personnel Selection—An Overview," in J. Donovan, ed., *Recruitment and Selection in the Public Service* (Chicago: Public Personnel Association, 1968), pp. 8-9.

7. Carl Schurz, *Speeches, Correspondence, and Political Papers of Carl Schurz,* ed. by F. Bancroft (New York: G. P. Putnam's Sons, 1913), II, p. 123.

8. Editorial in *Harper's Weekly,* XXXVII (July 1, 1893), p. 614.

9. J. Donald Kingsley, *Representative Bureaucracy* (Yellow Springs: Antioch Press, 1944), p. 63.

10. See *The Chinese Civil Service,* ed. by Johanna Menzel (Boston: D. C. Heath and Co., 1963), p. vii.

11. *Ibid,* p. viii.

12. Stahl, *Public Personnel Administration,* p. 67.

13. Kenneth Wentworth, "The Use of Commercial Tests," in Donovan, ed., *Recruitment and Selection,* p. 155.

14. Glenn McClung, "Statistical Techniques in Testing," *ibid.,* pp. 339-340.

15. *Ibid.,* p. 340.

16. *Ibid.,* Table 2.

17. See, for example, Samuel Krislov, *The Negro in Federal Employment* (Minneapolis: University of Minnesota Press, 1967), p. 55.

18. *From Max Weber: Essays in Sociology,* ed. by H. H. Garth and C. W. Mills (New York: Oxford University Press, 1958), p. 78.

19. Note that one could make the same argument with regard to what might be called "non-central" public organizations, such as public corporations and state farms, which are more analogous to private firms in many ways than to public administrative and public policymaking organizations in the usual sense.

20. The term "task" is intended to distinguish the nature of the work activity from its specific substance.

21. Krislov, *The Negro,* p. 64.

22. Frederick C. Mosher, *Democracy and the Public Service* (New York: Oxford University Press, 1968), p. 12. On representative bureaucracy see also V. Subramanian, "Representative Bureaucracy: A Reassessment," *61 American Political Science Review* (December 1967), pp. 1010-19.

23. Harold Seidman,*Politics, Position, and Power* (New York: Oxford University Press, 1970), p. 18.

24. *Ibid.* See also Louis Gawthorp, *Bureaucratic Behavior in the Executive Branch* (New York: The Free Press, 1969), esp. chaps. vii-ix. Gawthorp argues that agencies fall into one of two main categories, innovative or consolidative.

25. Anthony Downs,*Inside Bureaucracy* (Boston: Little, Brown and Co., 1967), p. 263, numbers 7, 6.

26. My own *Federal Service and the Constitution* (Ithaca: Cornell University Press, 1971) is an attempt to deal with this area as a whole from a political perspective.

27. See *ibid.,* chaps. vii-viii.

28. See D. Rosenbloom, "Some Political Implications of the Drift Toward a Liberation of Federal Employees," *31 Public Administration Review* (July/August 1971), pp. 420-426.

29. Brian Chapman, *The Profession of Government* (London: Unwin University Books, 1959), p. 297.

30. *Ibid.,* p. 296.

3
The Politics of Manpower:
The Manager Triumphant

Frank J. Thompson

Organizational arrangements are not neutral. We do not organize in a vacuum. Organization is one way of expressing . . . commitment, influencing program direction, and ordering priorities. Organizational arrangements tend to give some interests, some perspectives, more access to those with decisionmaking authority. . . .

Harold Seidman[1]

Officials in cities sporadically make choices that shape the formal role structures of local governments. They at least implicitly decide how to group certain sets of duties into positions (that is, promulgate a division of labor); they

Reprinted with permission from *Personnel Policy in the City: The Politics of Jobs in Oakland,* pp. 20-44. University of California Press (c) 1975 The Regents of the University of California.

Frank J. Thompson is Associate Professor, Department of Political Science, University of Georgia.

choose how many of the different kinds of positions the organization needs; and they determine where to situate work roles in the hierarchy of authority and among various departments. By so doing, officials influence the level of service the bureaucracy provides in different functional areas, the financial cost of local government, the level of work alienation among employees, the recruitment problems city officials confront, and so forth.

In appraising manpower decision making in Oakland, this chapter will focus first on the politics of numbers (for example, choices concerning how many firefighter slots to fund). Budgetary and job classification processes will consequently receive considerable attention. Then I will analyze the factors that facilitate or impede position transfers among departments. As will become apparent, the manpower arena is the city manager's main personnel success story.

The Politics of Manpower Numbers

To an outsider, decisions on whether to add or delete certain types of jobs may seem complex. Who can be sure of the political, economic, and social costs and benefits of adding more patrolmen instead of recreation or museum personnel? Who can specify precisely the relationship between the number of people in different occupational roles and organizational effectiveness? While queries like these might trouble some, Oakland officials are generally little disturbed by them.

Consider the city manager, who, more than any other actor shapes personnel outlays. For Oakland's city manager, success in the manpower arena is comprehensible in terms of its implications for revenue policies. Reinforced by the attitudes of the mayor (a Republican in a formally nonpartisan role) and council, the manager considers the tax rate to be the crucial overall indicator of his performance. Since taking office in 1966, he has struggled to minimize the need for additional revenue, while whittling down the politically hot property tax. The manager has had some success in accomplishing the latter objective. During the period from 1966 to 1971, the property tax rate declined from $3.17 per $100 assessed valuation to $2.80, a 13 percent decline.[2] The search for money is, however, unending and the sense of fiscal crisis persists.

Given his revenue aspirations the manager naturally casts a jaundiced eye on any request which will further drain the city treasury. For him the basic concern is not whether a proposal will enhance organizational efficiency. Expanded output at a lesser increment of increased cost is not the object. Rather, the point is to promote cost reduction efficiency, or on occasion simply to economize regardless of the impact on efficiency. The fact that fiscal inputs are relatively easy to measure compared to service outputs encourages this orientation. For as Anthony Downs has noted in another context, high certainty concerning costs and substantial ignorance concerning benefits often leads officials to undervalue the latter.[3] A city manager like Oakland's is all the more unlikely to seek efficiency through greater spending if there are no good productivity scorecards which tell him precisely what he is getting for spending more.

In his unrelenting war against greater costs, the manager believes that it is particularly important to resist work-force expansion. Personnel expenditures comprise more than 70 percent of Oakland's budget, in fiscal 1969/70, the city budgeted more than $45 million for employees. Furthermore, such expenses constantly threaten to mushroom. Once hired, a subordinate costs more each year. In part this is because the subordinate receives an annual step increase until he has been in the same position for five years. But it also stems from the pay and fringe benefit boosts employee leaders are constantly able to win.

Adding to the manager's problem is the "once hired, never fired" norm which pervades the organization. Civil service rules protect the tenure rights of employees after a probationary period; building the case necessary for firing consumes much time and energy. While the council and city manager have the authority to lay off employees (unlike firing, this means removing personnel for reasons other than poor performance) they are reluctant to use this resource. Concerned with showing fidelity to city bureaucrats and wishing to avoid conflict with employee organizations, council members and the manager prefer to eliminate slots only through attrition.

Even this kind of position surgery is difficult, as the experience of the Manpower Control Committee testifies. Created by the manager, this committee (consisting of the personnel director, finance director, and assistant to the city manager) meets every Friday to decide whether to eliminate or refill vacant slots. While this body may raise questions and suggest careful review during the next budgetary cycle, it seldom weeds out a position. Committee members believe that they lack the data needed for sound judgment, and that they do not have the time or staff necessary to find out whether excessive manpower slack exists.[4] Another inhibiting factor is their awareness that constant challenges to department heads, particularly where the committee has flimsy evidence, might raise antagonisms. The city manager, then, faces difficulties in reducing the size of city hall's work force.

By contrast, the manager finds it much easier to prevent increases in man-years. In this regard the main threat to his cost-cutting goals arises during the budgetary process. By and large, Oakland's departments lend credence to the claims of Parkinson[5] and Downs that "all organizations have an inherent tendency to expand."[6] Attuned to professional norms and committed to better service, agency heads request more manpower year after year. In 1970, for example, 71 percent of Oakland's fourteen major departments sought additional personnel, 14 percent held the line asking for neither more nor less, and 14 percent requested fewer slots than the previous year. For most of these agency heads, the more slots attained out of those sought the greater the sense of having achieved success in this arena. (As will become clearer later, those who failed to ask for more men did so for broader strategic reasons, not because they had no aspirations to expand.)

Agency heads, then, periodically articulate manpower demands that threaten to push personnel costs upward. How does the manager respond to their challenge?

The Manager's Budget Tactics[7]

In struggling to minimize position increases, the city manager relies on the finance office. Agency requests for support arrive in this office in January and February. Analysts then spend two to three months analyzing the department requests. To reduce decision uncertainty about manpower and other budgetary matters, the analysts will often visit the agencies and talk with officials there; but there are limits to the amount of information that can be accumulated in this and other ways. Time is short. Moreover all five analysts in 1970 had been with the office less than two years. Thus, they could not fall back on expertise born of seniority.

Standard decision rules help analysts cope with uncertainty. Although lacking knowledge concerning the precise consequences of their decisions, analysts make choices expeditiously through the use of orientation, trade-off, and slash rules. Orientation rules give initial cues as to how to approach the budget request; trade-off rules dictate that the analyst give up something in return for eliminating positions; slash rules lead the analyst to cut positions from requests without giving much in return. Chart 1 lists some manifestations of these types. The most basic of these rules is one which the manager repeatedly emphasizes: cut all requests for additional personnel. On occasion, analysts make exceptions to this norm, but overall it is the major factor molding their choices.

Once the analysts have made their recommendations, the finance director and the city manager may modify manpower outcomes slightly. By and large, however, the initial judgments of the analysts remain unchanged. This in large part reflects their adoption of some of the manager's values. The decision rules they use are those that the chief executive encourages.

Although the city council possesses ultimate authority over personnel expenditures, the body seldom challenges the city manager's recommendations.[8] The manager's expertise and prestige as a cost cutter give him considerable leverage over the budget's contents. The budget format (in use up to 1971) also helps him. Under this system, the council never learns what each department requests. Consequently, the city manager's recommendation comes across as representing a kind of unanimous bureaucratic decision, even though it is nothing of the sort.[9]

Of course, the council's basic commitment to holding the line on taxes does establish an expectation which the manager must meet. This, however, creates little tension for the city manager because he shares the council's value orientation. It is doubtful that the manager's choices would be much different if he suddenly had final authority over personnel allocations.

Expansionary Budget Tactics

Year after year, then, the manager plays Scrooge with personnel. How do agency heads respond to an executive so stingy with man-years? The answer is mainly by asking for more personnel. In doing so, department heads tend to

Chart 1:
Budget Analyst Decision Rules in Reviewing Personnel Requests

---

Orientation Rules – give initial cues as to how to approach the budget request.
1. Carefully scrutinize and cut low-status departments.
2. Disregard work-load data (analysts believe they are inflated and inaccurate and often have little significance because there are no good norms which establish proper workloads or manpower distributions).
3. Look for reference points and compare (e.g., the analyst reviewing the library knew that it had more book-binder positions that the Los Angeles library even though the latter was much larger).

Exchange or Trade-Off Rules – dictate that the analyst give up something in return for eliminating positions.
4. Trade position for position in a way that will cut costs.
5. Exchange positions for overtime allocations and vice versa.
6. Exchange positions for a promise that the slot will fund itself.
7. Cut positions and give machines in return.*
8. Get rid of positions for monetary contracts with private firms (e.g., hire a private firm to pick up garbage rather than having city employees do it).
9. Exchange a position at present for a departmental commitment to eliminate it later.

Slash Rules – lead the analyst to cut positions from requests without giving much in return.
10. Cut requests for new personnel.
11. Cut a little deeper than you actually feel is justified.
12. Eliminate vacant positions (the analyst reasons that if a department has been unable to fill a budgeted position throughout the previous fiscal year and has performed satisfactorily, this is an indicator that the department can get along without the slot).

Source: Oakland Finance Office
*See Judith May, "Budgeting in the Street and Engineering Department" (unpublished paper, University of California, Berkeley, 1968).

---

argue that work is increasing, that they have assumed new functions, or that manpower expansion will not cost more money.

We can't keep up with the load. The most typical department tactic is to contend that continued satisfactory performance of present duties necessitates adding personnel. One reason why agency heads keep work-load statistics is to make this expansionist argument more convincing. In their budget requests, agency officials will generally emphasize the statistics that most graphically illustrate a heavier work load. In 1967, for instance, the personnel director noted in his request that the number of positions in city hall had increased and that turnover would rise from 5 to 15 percent in the next two years. According to the director these increases meant that his staff would have to do more recruiting for line agencies; to keep up with the demand he would need three additional employees.

The finance office's response to the director's request suggests the common futility of claiming that work is increasing. In the year the director made this argument, the finance office not only rejected the plea for three new personnel staffers but cut one of the civil service office's regular employees as well. In general, budget analysts are suspicious of work-load data. They have little faith that agency statistics are accurate. Moreover, in the absence of clear norms concerning the amount of work an employee can do, analysts remain skeptical that such statistics demonstrate a need for more manpower.

We are doing something new. Another agency gambit is to claim that new responsibilities necessitate more manpower. Since Oakland City Hall seldom takes on new tasks, department heads rarely have the opportunity to use this tactic. If an agency does acquire a new function, however, officials will generally use the addition to justify a request for more slots. In making this kind of justification it helps the agency if the new function directly contributes to salient objectives of the manager and finance office. Thus, the head of the purchasing department, which contracts out for supplies and services, won a new position in order to "assist in a complete review of the entire purchasing system and to institute major changes which should be possible with new data processing capabilities."[10] The new data processing facility is a pet project of the manager and the finance director.

Let the manager have his cake and eat it too. At times the claim that work is increasing yields manpower payoffs for department heads. A surer means of getting more men is, however, the no-cost approach. This amounts to showing that positions will pay for themselves and, perhaps, raise revenue beyond cost. Use of the tactic, in a sense, represents a triumph for the city manager. Department heads keep an eye out for positions that will produce revenue. They become concerned with finding avenues toward fiscally costless personnel expansion.

Departments directly engaged in gathering fees for the city or ones dealing with functions which the federal government often subsidizes possess the greatest opportunity to use this approach. The traffic engineering and parking director, for instance, supervises the enforcement of parking laws, which is a money-making function for the city. In 1970, he justified a request for four new parking meter checkers on grounds that each would bring at least $35,000 to city coffers. He based his estimate on a study which showed that checkers wrote from nine to twenty-five tickets each hour. Assuming the tickets to be worth $2.00 each (the minimum fine), he estimated that each meter maid brought in $50,000 per year to the city. To be on the safe side, he reduced the figure to $35,000. The director and his assistant knew that beyond certain reasonable limits each checker could not produce this much revenue; but they believed the point of diminishing returns to be distant. They found support for this conviction in San Francisco which had twice as many meters as Oakland and almost four times as many checkers. Eventually the finance office gave them two new meter maids.

A request such as the traffic director's has appeal to budget analysts because they experience little uncertainty that the position will yield revenue. People parking in Oakland are unlikely to become more law abiding: the opportunity to write parking tickets will not dry up suddenly.

Work-load and no-cost approaches are among the most common tactics for personnel expansion. There are, however, other ploys which agency heads can use. Such tactics are most likely to emerge in a bureaucracy, like Oakland's, which has a strong anti-expansionist leadership.

Self-Inflicted Reductions

However strategically sophisticated the department head, he is unlikely to win more positions. Not surprisingly, this has caused agency officials to lower their expectations, but has not resulted in a parallel reduction of aspirations. It is important in this context not to equate expectations with aspirations. Expectations are beliefs about what will happen. Aspirations are goals or future levels of performance which the individual wants to attain. Despite the fact that Oakland agency heads do not expect to procure many more slots, they still aspire to enlarge their work force. By and large this aspiration finds expression in their budget manpower requests.

This is not always true, however. At times reduced expectations have prompted agencies to ask for smaller personnel increases, to hold the line entirely, or actually to seek fewer men. When they practice such self-denial, it is usually out of a desire to secure some compensating benefit.

Belt tighten to invest in future status. When defeat seems inevitable, some administrators will ask for smaller personnel increases in an effort to build reputations for being "no fat" agency heads. By showing a willingness to restrain himself, the official hopes to build his status for economizing with the city manager and, perhaps, cash in on this enhanced prestige at some future point. In extreme form this type of belt tightening leads the department head to seek no new slots. The personnel director, for example, employed a "shame them and wait 'til next year" theme in his request for fiscal 1968/69. After noting that over the years the responsibilities of his staff had increased, he wrote: "Because of these various factors we asked in the 1967/68 budget for an increase in the staff of three positions. They were turned down without comment. Although the same situation exists this year as it has in the past, we are not asking for additional personnel since indications are for various reasons that they would not be granted." The personnel director hoped that this approach would enhance his status and would permit him to win personnel concessions in the future. The next year, however, he asked for new slots but did not receive any. This points to one reason why agency heads seldom use this tactic. Even if the city manager acknowledges their efforts to economize, he still may not grant them concessions in future years.

Trade personnel cuts for other budgetary concessions. Another self-denial tactic that is endemic to bureaucracies with an economizing leadership is to trade slots for nonpersonnel concessions. The fire chief used this approach in 1970, exchanging personnel cuts for capital outlay. The veteran chief, who heads a force of 684 persons, had for several years sought a $110,000 utility building. He wanted the structure in order to provide suitable space for fire-department training and the storage of apparatus. Year after year the city manager and finance office denied the request. Finally in his submission for 1970/71 the chief argued that the excellence of his fire prevention unit permitted him to cut two hosemen slots from his base of positions. In return the chief wanted the utility house. Convinced that the chief had shown a willingness to compromise and had displayed respect for economizing goals, the finance office and manager agreed. That they were impressed with the approach is evident from a later council session in mid-June 1970. One of the councilmen, chagrined at the lack of council control over the budget, suggested that he and his colleagues vote to eliminate the expenditure for the utility building. But the city manager defended the structure as a high-priority item stating that the chief was the only department head to request a cut instead of an increase in personnel.[11]

Exchange expensive slots for cheaper ones. Another variant of self-denial occurs when department heads try to trade expensive positions for cheaper ones. An agency head is more likely to attempt this infrequently used tactic if he has had difficulties in recruiting qualified personnel for a high-level position. During fiscal 1969/70, for instance, the traffic engineering and parking director was unable to fill a budgeted engineering position which had become vacant. He prodded the civil service office, scanned the market himself, and placed ads in professional journals but could find no satisfactory applicant. The director valued the engineering position since it was essential for planning and gave the department a skills slack useful in meeting contingencies and boosting its professional status. At the same time, the director foresaw the problems of continuing with the unfilled position. Obviously the vacancy reduced the service his department provided; and even if he suddenly succeeded in filling the slot, the director believed that there would be persistent turnover in the future. More fundamentally he knew that the budget analysts tended to cut vacant positions. To avoid this eventuality and to ease future recruitment problems, the director reluctantly asked that finance eliminate the engineering position and substitute a subprofessional senior engineering aide for it. The aide position was less expensive and called only for a high-school degree with advanced mathematics and two years of experience. Subsequently, the budget analyst agreed to the exchange.

There are, of course, risks to the self-denial approach which make its use infrequent. Many smaller departments believe that they do not have men to give away. Furthermore an agency head has to present a plausible excuse for being able to concede a slot and then make a good case for receiving something in return. Otherwise, he may find himself in a quandary comparable to that which the museum director faced in 1970. He requested fewer man-years than he had

had the previous year in exchange for certain benefits; instead the budget analyst cut even more slots and refused to grant him any concessions. In short, pursuing self-denial tactics is an uncertain business. The department gives up something at the outset and risks getting little in return. Once a man is lost, it is difficult to get him back.

Low expectations can at times, then, lead departments to make more conservative requests—seeking smaller manpower gains, holding the line, or even giving up slots. From the manager's perspective this amounts to success. Responding to his pressure, departments cut themselves and do not force the finance office either to spend time evaluating their requests or to wield its authority. This triumph does, however, bear the potential cost of information blockage for the manager. A budget request is one way those at the top of a hierarchy learn about manpower needs at the bottom levels. If agency heads believe that it is futile to seek more men, the manager risks losing touch with their problems. Given the general propensity of Oakland's agencies to continue to make requests, however, this is not a major managerial difficulty.

These, then, are the values and behavioral patterns which shape manpower determination decisions made through the budgetary process. Department heads play the game primarily to win more slots; the manager primarily to hold down fiscal costs. As will become even more apparent when we assess outcomes, the city manager generally prevails.

The Manager's Concern with Classification

The city manager's interest in the number of different kinds of positions city hall will contain does not end with the budgetary process. He has also considered the bureaucracy's position classification process. City hall has more than 300 classes of positions (for example, semi-skilled laborer, intermediate typist clerk, zoo keeper). The Civil Service Commission is formally in charge of keeping this structure accurate. Whenever someone consistently works outside his assigned classification, this body is supposed to reclassify him. For example the commission might conclude that an engineer had been doing the work of a subprofessional engineering aide and therefore downgrade him. In so doing, commissioners would eliminate a professional position and substitute another for it.

The city manager has a twofold interest in accurate classification. First, if the labels describe behavior he has a shorthand way of knowing what personnel in the organization actually do; it reduces some internal uncertainty. Second, accurate classification means that no one receives more pay than he should. Since class label determines salary, a failure to keep classification up-to-date can result in an employee being overpaid or underpaid. The manager suspects that the former is the more frequent occurrence.

Although the city manager values accurate classification, the existing array of forces makes such precision unlikely. The Civil Service Commission holds the authority to reclassify individuals but depends on the personnel director to bring the need for such decisions to its attention; the personnel director and his staff, however, seldom have much knowledge concerning which positions are misclassified. Moreover, they have little incentive to increase their information. The director senses that his status among department heads will decline if he constantly acts as a spokesmen for accurate classification. Since more honor flows to him if he focuses on recruitment the personnel director naturally sees little sense in spending time doing unwelcome exploratory studies. Further more, the director knows that even if he finds a position that needs reclassification, the Civil Service Commission may not approve the action. The commission dislikes moving employees downward in the hierarchy because it means that their salaries will be cut. The director can count on commission support only if he recommends an upward classification which would increase wage costs.

City departments also have few incentives for reporting inaccuracies. The incumbent in a position sees little reason to notify civil service that he is improperly labeled particularly if it would lead to downgrading and a resulting pay cut. Similarly, the supervisor or department head sees no advantage in consuming time and suffering a loss of prestige among subordinates by zealously searching for misclassification. To the extent that department heads become involved at all, it is mainly to get an employee upgraded; such reclassification gives them a position that has more skills associated with it. In sum, the actors in the civil service office's environment communicate about classification in frequently and then primarily when it costs the city more money.[12]

Aware of the tendency toward inaccuracy and the overgrading of employees, the city manager in 1969 successfully advocated hiring the classification consultant, Griffenhagen-Kroeger, for $40,000. Examining all agencies except police and fire, this firm suggested that city hall reclassify from 10 to 20 percent of all civilian employees, the majority of them downward.

The incentives pattern which fosters misclassification remains untouched. But the hiring of the consultant serves to illustrate further the city manager's interest in and leverage over manpower decisions. His commitment to shaping such choices goes beyond the budgetary arena.

The Politics of Reorganizing Positions

City officials at times change the location of positions in the formal authority structure; often the reorganization shifts positions from one department to another. Such activities are an integral part of manpower politics. The problems endemic to relocating slots are complex. Is it wise to decentralize? Should officials allocate positions in a way that promotes conflict and redundancy among agencies?[13] What is the relationship between grouping certain positions together and productivity? Convincing answers to these questions are in short supply. Many can only conclude that there is no one best way.[14]

Yet Oakland's city manager experiences relatively little uncertainty about the best way to structure positions within the bureaucracy. To be sure it is easier for him to compute the fiscal impact of adding or subtracting manpower than of reshuffling positions. This does not, however, drive him toward an administrative agnosticism with respect to relocating slots. The city manager feels that over the long run, adherence to certain principles will foster economy and efficiency in city hall. At the core of his credo is the belief that centralizing authority and reducing overlap will have desirable consequences. In his view, gaining authority more commensurate with his responsibility, and making procedures and jurisdictions "neat and clean" are the essentials of sound management.

This attitude finds expression in his activities. On taking office in 1966, he was upset by the fragmented city bureaucracy which awaited him. At the time, there were over twenty departments, including five major ones run by semi-autonomous commissions (parks, recreation, museum, library, and civil service). Though his predecessor had warned him that efforts to place positions in these agencies directly under his authority would fail, the city manager soon set out to strip the commissions of their prerogatives. Emphasizing that reorganization would save the city $900,000, the city manager convinced the mayor, business leaders, the *Oakland Tribune,* and others to support a ballot proposition which would shift authority to him. In 1968, a narrow majority of the voters approved the proposition.

Position relocations involving charter revision are, of course, the exception rather than the rule. On other occasions the city manager has had an easier time fostering reorganizations. Using his authority, status, and expertise to good advantage, he has reduced the number of agencies by about one-third since 1968. Under his auspices, for example, parks and recreation departments merged and two superdepartments, the Office of Public Works and the Office of General Services, were created from smaller units. Through these mergers, the city manager hoped to reduce the overlap in functions among different agencies and improve coordination.

In arranging position shifts, the city manager has met no serious opposition. Unlike the president of the United States, the city manager has few worries about bureaucrats mobilizing outside constituencies or legislative committees to resist a reallocation of slots. Unless reorganizing positions involves charter change, the scope of conflict is usually limited to the manager and the agency heads. The city council seldom intervenes since it respects the manager as an administrative expert. Employee organizations abstain unless a move threatens the civil service office or increases the likelihood of layoffs. Citizen groups generally do not recognize the significance of transfers for broader policy questions.

It is, then, high-level department officials who believe that they have a direct stake in transfers. But how do they perceive these stakes? Taking a hint from Downs's contention that bureaucracies seek to expand, we might conclude that agency heads feel victorious whenever they gain positions. After all, securing more slots contributes to their prestige within the organization and increases their ability to provide services. In fact, however, department heads do not invariably view the acquisition of positions as a victory; an episode involving the Department of Traffic Engineering and Parking helps to illustrate this.

Agency heads may be reluctant manpower imperialists.[15] Prior to 1969 the traffic engineering department handled such routine functions as traffic surveys, curb and street lane painting, and the installation and maintenance of name signs, traffic signals, and parking meters. Then in 1968, the police chief gave the head of traffic engineering an opportunity to expand when he told the city manager that Oakland should employ meter maids rather than uniformed policemen to enforce parking regulations, and that the manager should remove this enforcement function from the police department. From the chief's perspective parking enforcement was a low-priority area that brought him hostile protests from ticketed drivers and businessmen who feared overzealous enforcement near their stores. By dropping this function, his department would suffer no actual loss in personnel and would rid itself of an activity that hurt police status.

The city manager, after discussion with the chief, tentatively decided to support the proposal. Shortly thereafter he suggested to the traffic director that his agency might supervise the activity. The city manager soon learned, however, that the traffic director had reservations about assuming the new duties even if it meant personnel expansion. While the director believed that planning and maintenance of meters belongs in his department's jurisdiction, he was uncertain about meter enforcement. He and his professional staff might pay opportunity costs in supervising the meter checkers; time for planning and professional duties was already scarce without taking on lower priority tasks. Moreover the traffic director was aware that absorbing the function would bring him the potentially hostile constituencies of parking violators and local businessmen. While the director believed that meter enforcement did relate to his agency's aspiration to promote traffic safety, he was chary of taking over the function.

Faced with a reluctant, uncertain traffic director, the city manager called for more study. He asked the agency head to survey other cities to determine the practices they used. This kind of study (which is standard procedure whenever Oakland officials contemplate nonroutine change) would not only increase city hall's information but provide the traffic director with time to reflect. The results of the research were far from conclusive. Analyzing the practices of cities Oakland's size on the West Coast, the director found that one-half of the sampled governments placed parking enforcement in the police department and that about one-fourth put it under traffic engineering.

In the end the study was only one factor that shaped the choice of the director. By the time of its completion the manager had offered the director the accident analysis function if he accepted parking enforcement. The director had long wanted to assume the former activity. Faced with this enticement, aware that a precedent existed for such a step in Seattle and Portland, and not wanting to damage his reputation with the manager by being troublesome, the director agreed to become responsible for the meter maids.

The behavior of Oakland's traffic director suggests that an agency head will view a transfer favorably if it provides him with personnel: (a) who perform functions closely tied to major agency goals; (b) who will not require substantial supervision by his present staff; and (c) who will not involve him with hostile external constituencies. Hence Oakland's traffic director felt reluctant to add meter enforcement because he did not believe it was as important as more basic traffic engineering, because the new employees would require considerable surveillance, and because outside groups were bound to complain about enforcement decisions.[16]

Taking factors like these into account, then, agency heads usually develop firm opinions about the desirability of a transfer. Whether these attitudes lead to action is another matter. As the case of the meter maids illustrates, resistance is difficult. Documenting a case against a proposed position shuffle is often impossible. If an agency head resists too emphatically, he risks developing a reputation for being uncooperative and uninterested in new responsibility.

Department imperialism succeeds if the manager approves. If transfers are often hard to resist, they are also perplexing to arrange. Many of Oakland's top bureaucrats are at least latent manpower imperialists. But acting on this disposition is difficult. For instance the traffic engineer would like to absorb street lighting and signal maintenance personnel from the Office of General Services. Despite this aspiration he has not attempted to obtain them. The traffic director feels that he lacks a good justification for imperialism since General Services has given his agency adequate support. A further barrier to action is his realization that the director of General Services enjoys considerable prestige with the city manager. (The chief executive at one point showed his faith in the director of General Services by making him his acting assistant.)

If, therefore, another agency head has preserved his status with the city manager, the imperialistic aspirations of an expansionist bureaucrat are likely to go unfulfilled. On the other hand, when the leadership of another agency has limited prestige with the city manager and the expansionist department head can appeal to the manager's basic organizing values (for example, centralization, reduction or overlap), the likelihood of a transfer increases. Thus the traffic director did persuade the city manager to shift five slots from the Off-Street Parking Commission to his agency.[17] The fact that commissioners received their appointments from the mayor undermined their status with the city manager. By shifting personnel away from the commission's control, the city manager reaffirmed his faith in centralized administrative authority.

Agency heads can, then, occasionally encourage a desirable transfer but only if they can convince the manager that such a move is sound. As in decision concerning how many of what type of manpower to employ, the manager is the dominant figure. His veto power is secure. Unless a move requires charter change, what he initiates or approves will prevail most of the time.

Outcomes

What have been the results of this control pattern for outcomes? By looking at shifts in position allocations to departments since the city manager took office, we can begin to grapple with the issue. In terms of the overall work force, Table 1 shows that over a five-year period the manager has kept the bureaucracy

Table 1
Man-Years Increase Slightly Each Year, 1965-1970

Fiscal year	Full-time man-years	Part-time man-years	Total man-years	Increase over previous year	Percentage of increase over previous year
1965-66	3194.0	235.0	3429.0	—	—
1966-67	3228.0	237.8	3465.8	+36.8	1.1
1967-68	3250.2	235.8	3486.0	+20.2	.6
1968-69	3253.7	232.9	3486.6	+.6	.0
1969-70	3353.6	216.1	3569.7	+83.1	2.4
1970-71	3396.7	226.9	3623.6	+53.9	1.5

Source: Oakland Preliminary Budgets.

from expanding rapidly. During this time the number of man-years rose by about 195, or 39 annually. This is an increase of only 5.7 percent, or slightly more than 1.1 percent per year. This rate is less than the national average for municipal governments, 2.9 percent.[18]

A focus on the particular agencies that have won or lost slots also provides insight into the manager's values. We can divide Oakland's departments according to whether they are expanding, maintaining, or contracting their work force. In Table 2 expanding departments are those that have increased their man-years by more than 10 percent over five years; maintaining departments have had man-year changes of from minus 10 percent to plus 10 percent; shrinking departments have lost more than 10 percent of their man-years. While the manager has initiated reorganizations during the period considered, most units have remained constant in identity. Consequently, while eight departments now fall into the larger Offices of Public Works and General Services, we can still identify the number of man-years allocated to the original department.

The changes indicated in Table 2 have occurred in part as a result of budgetary decisions and in part because of transfers. Of the six expanding departments, traffic engineering and parking, purchasing, and municipal buildings grew substantially through position shifts. The other agencies expanded by having portions of their budget requests granted. Another pattern is that, with the possible exception of the museum, changes are not a consequence of the city adding new functions or giving up old ones. Rather, they primarily reflect managerial reassessment of the number of men needed to perform long-standing activities.

In terms of more fundamental values, the patterns of growth and shrinkage reflect a desire to economize, to reduce internal organizational uncertainty for top management, and to minimize risk for Oakland citizens. The patterns also reveal a willingness to honor commitments that the manager's predecessor had made.

Reduce internal organization uncertainty and economize. The city manager's concern with reducing internal organizational uncertainty and with

Table 2
Personnel Expanding, Maintaining, and Shrinking
in Oakland City Departments, 1966/71

Type of department	Formal function	1966/67 Man-years	1970/71 Man-years	Differ-ence	Percentage of increase over 1966/67
Expanding					
Finance	Accounting and budget preparation	8.0	104.5	96.5	1206.2
Traffic Engineering and Parking	Traffic planning, traffic marking upkeep, meter repair and enforcement	34.1	63.0	28.9	84.8
Museum	Art, history, and science exhibits	61.0	87.6	26.6	43.6
Purchasing	Contracting for services and supplies	21.3	27.8	6.5	30.5
Municipal Buildings	City building main-tenance and security	107.9	135.0	27.1	25.1
Police	Crime prevention and law enforcement	909.9	1033.3	123.4	13.6
Maintaining					
City Attorney	Counsel and legal advice to the city	17.0	18.0	1.0	5.9
Equipment	Maintenance of city mobile equipment	49.0	51.0	2.0	4.1
Civil Service	Recruitment and selection, employee records	18.2	18.5	0.3	1.6
Parks	Operation of city parks	198.1	199.2	1.1	0.6
Recreation	Recreational programs and operation of recreational facilities	323.6	325.4	1.8	0.6
Fire	Fire prevention and firefighting	684.0	685.0	1.0	0.1
Electrical	Maintenance of city electrical facilities	72.0	70.0	-2.0	-2.8

Table 2
Personnel Expanding, Maintaining, and Shrinking
in Oakland City Departments, 1966/71

Type of department	Formal function	1966/67 Man-years	1970/71 Man-years	Differ-ence	Percentage of increase over 1966/67
Streets and Engineering	Construction and maintenance of streets, sewers and storm drains	450.6	428.4	-22.2	-4.9
Building and Housing	Housing, building, plumbing, mechanical and electrical inspections	89.3	84.0	-5.3	-5.9
Shrinking					
City Planning	Zoning, planning for future in city	26.2	23.3	-2.9	-11.1
Library	Collection and lend-ing of books and other media	250.5	205.0	-45.5	-18.2
City Auditor	Auditing of books, accounts, money, and securities of city	51.0	6.0	-45.0	-88.2

Source: Oakland Preliminary Budgets.

economizing accounts for the growth of at least three departments (finance, purchasing, and municipal buildings) and the contraction of two (library and city auditor). The finance office expanded because it is the manager's main weapon in his fight to control the rest of the organization. Among other things it is the arm that he uses to gather and synthesize information. In this capacity, its staff scrutinizes budget requests, carries out various studies aimed at saving the city money, and operates the new electronic data processing system. Some of finance's expansion came at the expense of the city auditor. Shortly after assuming office, the manager became convinced that the auditor's office had failed to supply him with necessary data. Moreover, since the auditor was an elected official, the manager exerted less power over the office than he wanted to wield. Consequently he persuaded the council to shift a net total of 45 positions from the auditor to the finance director. Finance has also gained 57.5 man-years in its own right, particularly for its electronic data processing unit, and for its other divisions as well.

His aspirations to economize caused the manager to enlarge the purchasing and municipal buildings divisions. Convinced that fragmentation had previously caused the hiring of more personnel than were necessary, he directed that the municipal buildings division take over janitorial services for the library branches and the new museum, and that purchasing absorb all duplicating functions in city hall. The purchasing unit also received new staff to analyze ways of enhancing efficiency in procurement and contract procedures.

The decline in library personnel resulted from the manager's belief that the department was inefficient. When outside and inside analysts confirmed the manager's suspicion, he and the finance department arranged to cut costs through reorganization and the elimination of professional positions through attrition.

The slight contraction of the city planning department also stemmed from a desire to economize, though in a different way. In 1964 the Area Redevelopment Administration of the U.S. Department of Commerce awarded city hall a grant for the preparation of a comprehensive development plan. With federal largesse coming in, the manager increased the staff of the city planning department. As the study neared completion and federal support began dwindling, the manager gradually eliminated slots from the agency.

Reduce risk for citizens. When a problem involves a serious risk to life and property, even fiscal conservatives become spenders. Thus, Oakland's police department, in an absolute sense, has increased its numbers more than any other agency. The reason for this expansion has been the manager's distaste for rising crime rates. The rate of serious crimes increased each year during the last half of the sixties, attaining a record 52 percent increase in 1968. Although uncertain about the precise causal relationship between more police manpower and safer streets, the manager believed that giving the police chief more positions was the most direct way to tackle the problem. Faced with a high-risk problem and the absence of persuasive, less expensive alternatives, the manager will add personnel. To modify Downs's theory,[19] then, remoteness and uncertainty of benefits need not necessarily produce an unwillingness to invest in a program. When dealing with high-risk areas such as defense or police work, the fear of doing too little may actually lead to an exaggeration of the return on an investment.

Commitment to an attack on major crime indirectly led the traffic engineering and parking department to expand. As indicated earlier, the city manager became convinced that police officers should concentrate on more serious criminal investigation and consequently shifted responsibility for enforcing parking regulations to the traffic engineering director.

Past commitments shape expansion. The traffic engineering department also has expanded because of commitments made before the present city manager took office. Dissatisfied with deteriorating traffic control, faced with new federal requirements for traffic planning, and concerned about the impact of the new Bay Area Rapid Transit system, the council in 1964 agreed to support traffic engineering expansion. Respecting this pledge, the city manager allowed the department six full-time positions his first year in office. The growth of the museum also stemmed from decisions made before the present manager took office. Voters approved a bond issue for a new museum in the early sixties and the manager felt obliged to expand services and maintain a high-status operation.

Conclusion

The city manager has shaped manpower trends in Oakland more than any other single actor. Wielding his authority and status, he regularly beats back department efforts to expand through the budgetary process. He is also the pivotal figure in most reorganizations. The city manager's considerable leverage, his widely understood commitments, and the presence of scorecards help reduce decision uncertainty. With leverage centralized, others have less to consider when anticipating the consequences of their tactics; agency heads, for example, need not ponder how elected officials will respond to their gambits. The city manager's persistent commitment to economizing also reduces uncertainty. Department heads need not wonder whether this year the manager will be pro- or anti-expansion; the manager consistently opposes increases in personnel. Scorecards also help players get their bearings. Changes in personnel expenditures and changes in the number of different kinds of manpower within city hall help players gauge the payoffs of their tactics.

Given the objectives of Oakland officials, manpower decision making poses few uncertainties for officials. The city manager believes that he knows how to resist bureaucratic expansion; department heads sense that they will win few positions regardless of what they do. By comparison, officials face more information deficits when they grapple with the politics of pay.

Notes

1. Harold Seidman, *Politics, Position and Power: The Dynamics of Federal Organization* (New York: Oxford University Press, 1970), p. 14.

2. During the same period, assessed valuation of property rose from $712,358,017 to $961,152,669, an increase of about 35 percent. Oakland, *City of Oakland Preliminary Budget,* 1971/72, p. A-10.

3. Anthony Downs, "Why the Government Budget Is Too Small in a Democracy," *World Politics* 12 (June 1960): 541-563.

4. The manager is not, of course, interested in peepetuating such slack as a hedge against uncertainty since it costs him money to do so.

5. C. Northcoate Parkinson, *Parkinson's Law* (New York: Ballantine Books, 1964).

6. Anthony Downs, *Inside Bureaucracy* (Boston: Little, Brown, 1967), p. 17.

7. For an overview of Oakland's budgetary process, see Arnold J. Meltsner and Aaron Wildavsky, "Leave City Budgeting Alone! A Survey, Case History and Recommendation for Reform." (Unpublished draft, University of California, Berkeley, 1969).

8. *Ibid.*, pp. 50-52.

9. On the importance of unanimity, see Charles R. Adrian and Charles Press, "Decision Costs in Coalition Formation," *American Political Science Review* 62 (June 1968): 559;

and Richard F. Fenno, *The Power of the Purse: Appropriations Politics in Congress* (Boston: Little Brown, 1966).

10. Oakland, *City of Oakland Preliminary Budget, Fiscal 1970/71,* p. B-131.

11. A check of the budget requests indicates that the museum department also asked for fewer positions in 1970 than it had in 1969.

12. For discussions of classification behavior, see Bernard H. Baum, *Decentralization of Authority in a Bureaucracy* (Englewood Cliffs, N.J.: Prentice Hall, 1961), pp. 89-129; and Jay M. Shafritz, *Position Classification: A Behavioral Analysis for the Public Service* (New York: Praeger Publishers, 1973).

13. For an excellent analysis of redundancy see Martin Landau, "Redundancy, Rationality and the Problem of Duplication and Overlap," *Public Administration Review* 29 (July/August 1969): 346-358.

14. See, for example, C. West Churchman, *The Systems Approach* (New York: Dell, 1968), p. 229.

15. For a general discussion of bureaucratic imperialism see Matthew Holden, Jr., "Imperialism in Bureaucracy," *American Political Science Review* 55 (December 1966): 943-951.

16. Morton H. Halperin, "Why Bureaucrats Play Games," *Foreign Policy* 2 (Spring 1971): 80, discusses a similar phenomenon.

17. Examples from the traffic engineering department in part come from interviews which Eric Sears conducted there in 1966 and 1967.

18. International City Managers Association, *Municipal Year Book, 1967*, p. 228. Since it does not give data for the same period I examined, a comparison must be treated cautiously. It notes that from 1958 to 1968, the number of full-time positions rose from 1,372,000 to 1,813,000.

19. Downs, *Inside Bureaucracy,* 1960.

4
Employee Power in the Federal Service

Hugh Heclo

. . . a government ill executed, whatever it may be in theory, must be, in practice, a bad government.

— Alexander Hamilton, *The Federalist,* no. 70

Nearly a century ago the civil service joined the other American political institutions largely as an afterthought. It has continued into the present era with much the same status. Americans have long expressed impatience with red tape and Washington bureaucrats, but few of the heavy demands they make on the federal government can be satisfied without some form of organized bureaucratic activity.[1] Sometimes more and sometimes less intense, this ambivalence is a persisting—if poorly defined—influence on the work of all civil servants.

A relatively small fraternity ("establishment" would be too strong a term) of specialized Washington participants concerns itself with the actual workings of the civil service—its rules, pensions, pay, organization, and well-being. Normally these overseers include the Civil Service Commission, government employee unions, several congressional subcommittees, a few civic groups such as the National Civil Service League, and an occasional aide in the Executive Office of the President.

While public criticism of big government and bureaucracy is often remote from the day-to-day realities of administration, the practitioners' efforts are often narrowly focused on the nuts and bolts of administering civil service procedures without much attention to the bureaucratic system as a whole. Often those critical of bureaucracy and those concerned with the civil service seem to be living in two different worlds, and in a sense they are.

In this chapter I assess the role of higher civil servants from a viewpoint midway between the two extremes, a perspective more detailed than stereotypes about the bureaucracy but more general than descriptions of particular programs and procedures. In fact, "The" bureaucracy can hardly be said to exist as a collective entity in Washington. Instead, a number of subbureaucracies are linked by what are best thought of as similar predilections. These tendencies could be discussed in many ways. Here, my emphasis will be on bureaucratic careers, protections, and dispositions. By trying to put our-

Reprinted with permission from *A Government of Strangers: Executive Politics in Washington,* (c) Washington, D.C., The Brookings Institution, 1977, pp. 113-133.

Hugh Heclo is a Brookings Institution Fellow and co-author of *Comparative Public Policy: The Politics of Social Change in Europe and America.*

selves in the shoes of higher civil servants, we will be able to understand something more about their power and the price it extracts from those who would use it.

The Higher Career System

Over the decades reformers' efforts have left behind a series of arrangements that combine to produce the civil service version of people in government. Taken as a whole the U.S. federal bureaucracy appears open and broadly representative of the American population in education, income, and social status (as indicated by father's occupation).[2] But the higher their civil service rank, the more U.S. officials approach the statistical elite qualities observed among political executives. For example, in 1975 almost one-half of higher civil servants, compared with 14 percent of the general population, had fathers who were professionals or business executives. Almost two-thirds of GS 14-18 officials, compared with only one-third of the general population, assessed their parents' situation to have been middle class. In fact, the degree of unrepresentativeness suggested by these social class indicators seems to be about as great for the higher U.S. civil service as it is for the supposedly elitist British administrative class.[3]

This and similar information casts considerable doubt on the frequently discussed suggestion of relying on demographic sampling to assure democratic responsiveness in the bureaucracy. The theory of "representative bureaucracy" implies counting on civil servants who are a cross section of the general population to mirror the many values of society. The simple fact is that such conditions do not apply at the highest, most influential levels of the federal bureaucracy and are even less likely to occur at the top of each separate government bureau. Moreover, without arbitrary quota requirements it is difficult to see how all top positions in the bureaucracy could ever encompass the many dimensions of social representation, which are as varied as social life itself.[4]

There is little need here to concentrate on the demographic data about civil servants since, as noted for political executives, it is a long and tenuous route from such background characteristics to actual behavior in office. Talking with two budget officers, one of whom is from a workingclass background and the other from the middle class, a researcher is likely to find more similarities than in talking with two working-class bureaucrats, one of whom is a budget officer and the other the head of a spending program. Large and immensely complex social systems that they are, government agencies have their own ways of incubating bureaucrats and particular dispositions on the job.

The term "bureaucrat" camouflages the lack of any strong group identity among federal civil servants as a whole. In a way this is not remarkable, given the astounding variety of jobs (over 2,000 different occupational categories) throughout the federal civil service. Even at the highest ranks, where bureaucrats have less specialized jobs and should presumably have more in common (commiseration and mutual protection if nothing else), there is little evidence of a common identity with anything that could be termed a governmentwide civil service. Instead, the senior officials interfacing with political appointees are usually de facto members of different civil "services," depending on their agency or professional specialty. The retired winner of a distinguished award for civil servants suggested a fundamental characteristic when he said:

> *I've never thought of myself as a career servant. . . . Ask a civil servant who he is and you'll probably find he'll say he is an economist who works for the Treasury Department, a manager for the Housing Department and so on. What he's not likely to say first is that he's a civil servant.*

A much younger man who had recently entered government work gave a timeless quality to the older man's words. "It's a great place to influence policy. . . . I hadn't planned on becoming a bureaucrat. I was joining the bureau, not the civil service."

Typically, effective direction over civil service careers is not located at the department level and only rarely in the major subdivisions within the department. The normal source of control over the development of career executives is centered in the bureaus and other subunits that lie below the department or agency level. In each case there is a particular culture or subculture associated with life in the bureau, and those tied together in this culture generally develop the bureaucratic leaders of the future from among their own kind. According to one personnel expert:

> *The ordinary civil servant comes into government being hired by a particular person in a bureau and right away he's got a sponsor. Then he'll probably have a training program and a set of promotion possibilities laid out in the bureau and pretty soon he's walking down the hall almost as if he had a badge out in front of him saying, "I'm a Bureau X man," or "I'm a Bureau Y man."*

Immobilities

It is at the bureau level that the real day-to-day management occurs over both government operations and civil service personnel. It is there that civil servants' careers are typically "tunneled through narrow organization tubes with the managers at the top husbanding and hoarding their best talent for the benefit of their part of the organization."[5] The bureau and office heads who are in effective charge of bureaucratic careers worry about homegrown talent that might become so visible as to gain promotions elsewhere and are skeptical about outsiders from other parts of the bureaucracy who have not grown up learning about the bureaucrats' organization and its ways.

Such impressions gained in talking with higher civil servants are borne out by information on mobility, tenure, and the filling of career jobs. Since 1967 the newly created Bureau of Executive Manpower in the Civil Service Commission has gathered executive personnel data that generally confirm the findings of previous studies—any evidence of a governmentwide civil service is marginal.

Looking first at movement within the executive branch, it appears that the bulk of career executive (i.e.,, the supergrade group that is mainly involved in direct dealings with higher political appointees) falls into one of two patterns. In 1975 approximately two-thirds could be termed nonmobile in the sense of having always worked in the same agency since reaching grade 13 in the general schedule or its equivalent (the threshold between middle and higher ranks). On the other hand, only 12 percent of supergrade executives were generalists in that they had worked in three or more agencies since grade 13.[6] Moreover, the small minority of higher career officials who do change their organizational home can usually expect salary increases that are well below the average for all supergrades in general and the less mobile supergrades in particular.[7]

Another way to look at the immobility of bureaucratic careers in Washington is to consider how vacancies in career executive positions are filled and why they occur. Before the 1967 reforms . . . went into effect to improve the situation, the Civil Service Commission chairman complained about career immobility in these terms: "Of 1,072 classification actions covering positions in the top three grades in a recent year, 964 (90 percent) were promotions or reassignments of agency personnel. Only 19 (2 percent) were transfers from other agencies! And only 39 (4 percent) were new hires."[8] Table 1 shows that civil service careers remain as agency-centered as ever. Similar conclusions hold if one considers how vacancies are created. In general it remains only a little more likely that an executive vacancy in the civil service will be created because the incumbent has moved to another agency (the reason for 7 percent of career executive vacancies in 1971) than because he or she has died in office (3 percent of vacancies in that year). Some officials would almost seem to prefer the latter over the former.

Table 1
*How Career Executive Positions Have Been Filled
before and after 1967 Reforms*

Percent

| | Career executive positions | | |
Period	Filled from within agency	Filled from another agency	Filled from outside government
Before 1967 reforms	90.0	2.0	4.0
1971	88.5	5.0	6.5
1972	91.5	3.7	4.8
1973	88.9	7.9	3.2
1974	92.6	3.8	3.6
1975	92.4	4.7	2.9

Source: U.S. Civil Service Commission, Bureau of Executive Manpower, *Executive Personnel in the Federal Service* (GPO, 1976), table 17, p. 17.

One study revealed that the organizational immobility of higher civil servants is roughly equivalent to a "term of office" of seventeen to twenty-five years, compared with about two years for assistant secretaries, five years for foreign service officers and, of course, eight years for a reelected President.[9] The only other participants in Washington with organizational attachments to match the higher civil servants are Supreme Court justices and seniority-rich congressmen; in 1975 House committee chairmen had an average tenure of 23 years and Senate chairmen 21 years.

Mobility between the bureaucracy and private sector is also not as great as one might expect, considering the commonly held beliefs about "in-and-outers" and about government offering an "open opportunity for all Americans to compete for all positions at all levels in the Federal civil service."[10] Only about 18 percent of the career supergrades are what the Civil Service Commission terms in-and-outers—executives who entered public service at various grade levels but left and returned one or more times to the executive branch. Even for these careerists the breadth of experience is restricted because only a minority of this minority work in more than one federal agency in the course of their in-and-out careers (i.e., internal and external mobility are not often combined). Since 1970 the Civil Service Commission has conducted a formal program to provide more opportunities for career executives to take positions in the private sector and for private executives to spend a year working in government jobs. Again, almost all civil servants return to their home agency, having been mainly interested to learn new management techniques in their own field. For the businessmen who participate, the main motivations appear to be to understand how government works and to increase the scope of their contacts. Defenders of the program point out the value of better understanding between government and the private sector. Critics suggest that it gives a further advantage to corporate enterprises, accentuating the tendency for private and public spheres to interpenetrate and develop vested interests in particular government activities.[11]

On the basis of available data, there is little reason to change the observation made by a leading analyst of the public service over three decades ago: "Historically the component parts of the federal administrative mechanism have tended to remain somewhat apart from each other. With respect to inter- and often intradepartmental employment opportunities, each employee has been on his own." Experts writing in each succeeding decade have reported the same theme, namely, the absence of any governmentwide career structure for civil servants.[12]

Thus the openly competitive, in-and-out image of Washington's permanent government can be misleading. That image is due, not to mobility in the civil service itself, but to those filling exempted positions, particularly the one-half to two-thirds of noncareer executive appointments that are not filled by de facto career-type employees. ... The confusing array of positions outside the competitive civil service system (presidential appointments, noncareer executive assignments, schedule Cs, and so on) does bring a large number of new people into government. Bringing in new categories of people, however, does not change the narrowness of civil service careers themselves. If there is a strategy involved in all this, it is that of the deodorizer rather than of the open window—a design for covering up rather than for refreshing the stale air inside.

Mechanics of the System

Given that circulation is rare in the bureaucratic atmosphere, how does the higher careerists' personnel system actually work? In large part it is a shadow process that does not appear in the five-foot shelf of instructions and guidance known as the *Federal Personnel Manual*. In formal outline the personnel process is threefold and simple: applicants and their qualifications; a job and its requirements; and a matching of the two through a competitive examination of the applicants' qualifications for a particular job. But despite all the references to examinations, scores, ratings, and so on, the fact is that for those seeking civil service positions at the middle level or above (i.e., GS 9-18), usually no examination in the sense of a written test is scored. Instead, the applicants' education and work experience is evaluated in a judgmental process with procedural rules that are complex and arcane to insiders as well as outsiders.

The starting point is the job. Specific qualifications required in a position are laid down by the supervisor doing the hiring, but a trained classification official in the agency or (for supergrade positions) in the Civil Service Commission will already have classified the job as having duties at a particular grade and pay level. At first it is difficult to understand the emphasis placed on the extraordinarily complicated technology of job classification in the civil service.[18] The answer lies in history. A detailed evaluation of the skills needed in a specific position were thought essential to the traditional idea of an open competition for all jobs; this in turn was bound up with the nineteenth century effort to replace political favoritism with selection based on merits. Thus in Washington's domestic bureaucracy, rank and pay are attached to a particular job, not to the civil servant.

Once a particular job has been created and classified, how do civil service procedures affect its being filled? An applicant who already has status in the competitive civil service can simply be offered the job as long as it is below the supergrade level. If for no other reason than to avoid the cumbersome personnel procedures, it thus becomes much easier to hire a civil servant who is already known within the agency. In cases of a supergrade position or where applicants are outside the competitive civil service, the procedures differ somewhat but the theme is the same: an intensely bureaucratized process overlaying the highly personalized realm of executive politics.

For mid- and senior-level positions (GS 9-15), an "examination" (also termed a "rating schedule" in the personnel business) is devised by a Civil Service Commission examiner in conjunction with a request from the hiring agency for a list of candidates to fill a particular job. The commission assesses the various qualifications evident on a federal job application. Job seekers are then assigned a "rating" (that is, a rating as eligible for a particular grade level in the type of job sought in the application) and are put on a register containing the names of other applicants who are rated as eligible for that grade and occupation. A competitive match-up of people and jobs occurs when the commission receives a request to fill a particular job opening. The commission examiner assigns scores to applicants on the register by comparing their qualifications with the requirements specified for that particular job. The commission then "certifies" the three highest scorers to the hiring official in the agency. It is left to his or her discretion to choose among the three, except that a veteran cannot be passed over to select a nonveteran and an applicant from a state that is overrepresented in its share of federal jobs cannot be selected ahead of an applicant from an underrepresented state.

For career supergrade positions (GS 16-18) the process is even more complex and judgmental. Figure 1 shows the procedure for hiring a career supergrade official. Even this account simplifies the picture by assuming that a number of preliminary steps have already been completed—that authority for a supergrade position has been obtained from the Civil Service Commission quota (or special congressional authorization), that the commission has agreed to a given job classification for the work, and that it has accepted a set of qualifications for the job. After all this has occurred, the hiring process is basically one of requiring that a number of procedural rules are followed so as to search for candidates both inside the hiring agency and in other agencies, with an optional process for looking outside government.

Experienced bureaucrats recognize that the system operates far less automatically than it might seem to from the preceding formal outlines. The personal factor in personnel inevitably intervenes in a multitude of ways.[14] Three of the most common are in the areas of referrals for special attention, personalized recruitment, and preferential evaluations.

Referrals. In or out of government, people have a habit of tagging each other for special attention. This happens throughout civil service personnel work for both legitimate and illegitimate reasons. Often only a fine line separates a personnel action that is expedited to provide more effective management from one that uses preferential treatment as a means to curry favor. In either case personnel officials are in a position to treat something or someone as non-routine. The paperwork moves faster; an otherwise worrisome hiring is facilitated. Usually it is not a question of one powerful figure coercing a weaker one to take action against the latter's will, but of people exchanging help with the procedures and thus making each other's lives a little easier. One of the most common operations is the sending and receipt of referrals for civil service jobs.

Personal referrals for federal career jobs are a legal, generally accepted part of the career personnel process, and they may or may not take on . . . politicizing overtones. . . . Political appointees, pressure groups, congressmen, other bureaucrats—in fact any citizen with knowledge of whom to contact—can recommend a job seeker to the attention of any government official. The *only* restrictions that apply are not on those doing the referring but on the examining and appointing officials. Since 1883 all executive branch officials with authority

Figure 1
Procedures for Hiring a Career Executive

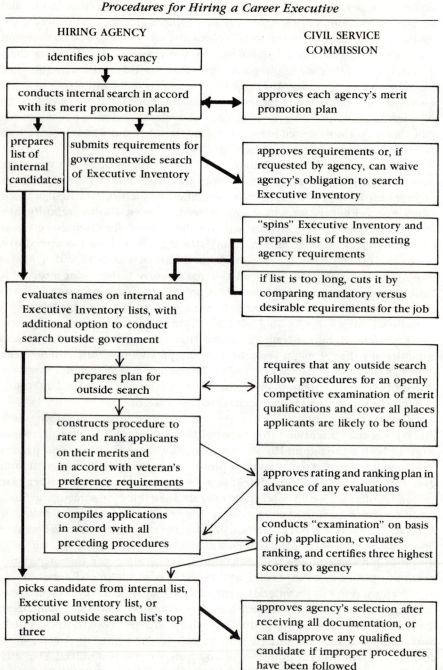

to take or recommend civil service personnel actions have been under presidential order (1) not to inquire into the political affiliations of job applicants, (2) to ignore such information if it is disclosed to them, and (3) to make civil service appointments only on the basis of merit and fitness without regard to political affiliation. In addition they cannot legally "receive or consider a recommendation of the applicant by a Senator or Representative, except as to the character or residence of the applicant."[15] In short, the entire responsibility for abiding by civil service rules is placed on those inside the system; it is not shared with outsiders who might seek preferential treatment.

Particularly for congressmen, inquiries about civil service jobs—up to 72,000 in a recent year—can be a valued link to constituents, even if it normally amounts to little more than the service of a public information bureau. But in practice congressmen can expect hiring agencies to do more than gratefully acknowledge their public information service. A congressman who writes a letter attesting to a job-seeker's character (and residence), according to Civil Service Commission officials, is entitled to a reply from the hiring agency, to a list of other positions for which the applicant might be qualified, and to the courtesy of an interview for the constituent.[16] Some hiring officials may understandably interpret such attention to job-seekers as going beyond the provision of neutral information, particularly if a sensitive position is involved or if the congressman has important leverage over the agency's budget and legislation.

Civil service procedures become similarly personalized by requests for special attention from political appointees or bureaucrats in the executive branch. To take a recent example (unusual only in that it is now part of the public record), between 1965 and 1974 the three Civil Service commissioners made at least thirty-five personal referrals to agencies on behalf of specific individuals seeking career jobs. In other cases the nonroutine interventions were more subtle, with a variety of commission officials involved in tagging some people for preferential treatment.[17] Of course, in all these instances it was the responsibility of the appointing officer in the agency to treat these and other applicants the same, whether they were commended by the chairman of the Civil Service Commission or the man on the street.

Personalized Recruitment. Outside referrals are only the most obvious and far from the most significant means of trying to personalize a supposedly automatic process of open competition and ranking of objective qualifications. Filling four-fifths of the 1,200 senior-level career vacancies each year has normally involved "name requests" by the hiring agency. This means that the Civil Service Commission, in preparing its lists of eligibles meeting the particular specifications of a job, is asked by the selecting official to certify a given individual as among those best qualified. At times, a chain of circumstances may suggest direct evidence of political intrusions—an outside referral, a name request for the same person, a highly specialized job description, and subsequently leaving the job unfilled if the name request is not certified.

Usually, however, more subtle questions of interpretation and motivation are involved. A name request combined with detailed job requirements laid down by the supervisor (so-called job tailoring) can mean that virtual preselection has occurred before any possibility of general competition could arise.[18] But a name request may also reflect the reality of how good people are found for high-level jobs. Traditional party spoils can undoubtedly be prevented by following anonymous procedures to process job applicants. However, to find high-caliber people for important bureaucratic jobs often requires a talent hunt, partly because such people are unlikely to be looking for jobs and filing applications and partly because capable professionals enter the job market by putting the word out among fellow professionals. Any efforts at active recruitment are likely to lead to name requests.

Thus there is often a fine line in the personnel process between helping a supervisor get the particular person he feels is needed and abusing the spirit of the civil service law with personal cronyism that is far more difficult to prove than political patronage. An experienced personnel director described how the doctrine of open competition for all jobs becomes diluted in practice.

> *Managers and professionals tend to figure they can tell who is qualified for a job better than the civil service system. You can find you're working the system backwards, from the guy the manager wants to the job description to get him. I suppose I'm guilty of several hundred violations. It's not that you're putting unqualified people in, but neither is it quite the full, open competition required by the rules. . . . Go too far and you;ll get into trouble because you don't necessarily know when, instead of an agency manager, some White House type or congressional administrative aide has slipped a name in. Then when it comes down to you it might seem like just the name of another guy the agency manager wants to hire, but it's actually a political hire.*

Evaluations. Finally, examinations to determine and rate qualifications for higher-level civil service positions are subject to various prejudices. In rating education and work experience outlined on job applications, commission examiners are compelled to make difficult, judgmental decisions with meager, second-hand information about both the candidate and the job. Yet such applications for mid- and senior-level jobs are assigned precise numerical scores and the three top-ranking candidates are certified to the agency for hiring. Typically, the sole source of information to be evaluated is the Personal Qualifications Statement, better known in the bureaucracy as form SF-171. Those who already know or are coached to use the right words and emphases in describing their experiences can go far in determining how their application will be evaluated by a harried examiner in the commission; others who do not know these folkways are at a disadvantage.[19]

Nongeneralist bureaucratic insiders have additional advantages in getting jobs. Despite all the civil service procedures, any evaluation of career personnel remains heavily dependent on the bureau's or agency's definition of what constitutes a civil service career. For outsiders trying to enter the higher career levels, "the thrust of the rating schedules . . . is on the specialized experience of the individuals."[20] Those already at work within an agency's specialized area are likely to have an advantage in gaining the particular experience in question, and the government careers of those selecting among the certified eligibles will also usually have followed the same specialized interests. For those who are already in the civil service and who are seeking positions up to the supergrade level, there is no requirement for the agency to look outside its own boundaries for hiring and advancing employees. The only outside evaluation will be a periodic inspection by the Civil Service Commission to see that procedures have been followed to provide a fair competition for jobs within the organization.

For all career supergrade positions there is, of course, the requirement for a search in other agencies, but few hiring officials depend very much on the lists provided from the commission's Executive Inventory. Any information provided by the commission is too sparse to count on in choosing people for important career jobs. The real evaluation process occurs by word-of-mouth among people who know each other, and such knowledge is naturally most likely among people within the same agency of subject area. What the commission evaluates is not people but whether or not a procedure has been followed. A seasoned bureaucrat with experience in the commission and several agencies accurately described the way things work:

> *Executive searches through the inventory and so on may help a little, but your own man is always likely to come out a little bit ahead. There's no magic in the civil service procedures. Especially, there's nothing in them offering a straight-up evaluation of the man's strengths and weaknesses. For that, everybody trusts his own judgment above all. So the first place you look is to the workmates you've had with you. . . . If that doesn't work out, you'll call up someone you know and ask for suggestions. Then you'll check out the names with other people you trust.*

None of the personalized referrals, recruitments, or evaluations mean that espousal of the merit system and the idea of civil service is empty rhetoric. It does mean that there is an inherent impracticality in the traditional mythology of an open opportunity for all Americans to compete for any civil service job. This is particularly true at the higher levels of the bureaucracy, where performance is almost impossible to measure and personal readings on people are all-pervasive. The rules and regulations of the competitive civil service do not, as some of their custodians like to suggest, constitute an impersonal system operating untouched by human hands, and those best able to lay their hands on it are those already operating from within. Given the extraordinary complexity of the rules, less experienced hands can quickly run into trouble from a Civil Service Commission jealous of its prerogatives. A personnel officer reflected on the recent case of a political executive who retired after having been charged with violating civil service regulations: "The trouble [with the appointee] wasn't that the people he wanted were unqualified but that he tried to ram it through and buck instead of use the established system. With patience he could have gotten everything he wanted."

Wider Horizons

The picture of a higher civil service based on agency career ladders needs to be filled in by three supplementary features: self-contained networks among bureaucrats in different agencies, occasional pockets of more mobile career development found in scattered parts of the executive branch, and non-civil service outlets for those at the top of their particular agency ladders. Considering these features as a whole, the senior officials' personnel system might be described as a system of parochialism tempered by accident.

Networks. Some of the personnel networks that cross government bureaus are a function of what academics have termed the professionalization of the civil service. [21] Significantly, this is a phrase used to identify professionals who happen to find themselves in the civil service rather than a development toward the civil service as a profession. Horizontal contacts exist both informally and through organized associations among people identified with particular technical specialties—statisticians, economists, public works engineers, and a host of others. Members of these groups have a shared need to protect their professional perquisites and standards. Indeed their common identity as professional specialists goes far in defining what in fact are the standards appropriate to their work in government. Thus, for example, a study of an agency's failure to implement presidential orders may have reflected adversely on that agency, but to a man within it who regards himself as "a professional management analyst," the catalogue of "delays and mixed signals didn't reflect badly" on him and his peers. "That's what we're supposed to find out about," he said.

Bureau chiefs and other program supervisors do not often need each other because they usually operate under different statutes with their own distinct constellations of constituents, pressure groups, and congressional committees.[22] Cross-agency networks, however, do frequently develop among officials who have similar staff positions in different bureaus (e.g., budget controllers, personnel experts, public information officers, accountants, and so on). At the base of their common identity is a custodianship over procedures that cut across many different agencies. Mobility is therefore somewhat more feasible for those in staff positions. Even if they do not move, staff bureaucrats have an incentive to get together because the procedures under their control are the one thing that central agencies (Office of Management and Budget, Civil Service Commission, General Services Administration) are constantly trying to coordinate. Staff work actually is one of the few common denominators in the bureaucracy that facilitates some movement between the particular departments and the central agencies with a governmentwide (or sometimes even a presidential) perspective. But career development is also arranged on a hit-and-miss basis, and staff bureaucrats are likely to have at least as much interest in ganging up to resist central coordination as they are in using their staff expertise to lessen departmental parochialism.

A vast number of other networks depend less on professional or staff identifications and more on particular individuals who see advantages in building and using personal contacts elsewhere in the bureaucracy. These idiosyncratic networks are apt to include people frequently drawn into interdepartmental committee work, analysts trying to forecast outsiders' reactions or hoping to learn what "really" lies behind the formal memoranda from another agency, and many other varieties of bureaucrat. Like political appointees, these officials will feel a strategic need to look outside the village life of their particular agency. The difference is that the bureaucratic network-builders, unlike political appointees, can expect to be around much longer and to establish contacts on a more stable and slowly evolving basis. The comment of one thirty-year Washington veteran about his "people to people relationships" in the bureaucracy can stand for many of its kind:

> *I need to be accepted over there [in another agency]. You have to go out, get introduced if necessary, so you know these people by name and who to contact. You need both the program and the budget people over there in order to get both sides of things. . . . Over the years it builds up. I joined this agency with Williams as my boss, and he had known his counterpart Miller over there, so we got used to dealing with each other with a lot of continuity—in fact from 1947 to 1960. Then both Williams and Miller left and I moved up, so did Miller's legislative counsel, so there was no problem. . . . Later you had the new deputy secretary who I knew from the Truman and Eisenhower years. Then with Johnson there was the new secretary and comptroller, who I didn't know, but their chief aide was Hudson who I'd known since he was a GS 12. . . . Experience is a big help in this job.*

Pockets. The networks across agencies are complemented by intra-agency pockets of broader career patterns. . . . a few officials in the Civil Service Commission and Office of Management and Budget have recently tried to encourage more mobile executive development. To date, the commitment of personnel and resources to these efforts has been meager. Moreover, . . . the ambitious initial experiment with a governmentwide career development program has retreated to a strategy of encouraging the traditional power centers—the bureaus—to launch internal programs to develop executive talent for their own use.

As a result, any effort to identify promising executive talent and to plan broadening assignments for bureaucratic leaders of the future is haphazard and depends on the particular official in charge. One official who made the effort said, "I learned from my boss that if you're in charge you've got a responsibility to the organization to get good young people, give them as much responsibility as they can handle, and stretch them with assignments outside their usual field." Following political scandals, the Internal Revenue Service in the 1950s created one of the most effective programs to develop career executives; other agencies with a strong collective identity have done the same—for example, the National Park Service, U.S. Geological Survey, Soil Conservation Service, and Federal

Aviation Administration, among others. But these programs are agency-centered, and in the domestic field only the Department of Transportation has anything approaching a departmentwide approach to planning civil service careers. Even here, where some success has been achieved in broadening career patterns, there is no mistaking the narrow interpretation of what is meant by a civil service career. As one of the officials in charge of the Transportation Department's program put it:

> We train our own people so they have to serve in every section of the department. You can say this substitutes departmental for bureau parochialism ... but I'm not training people to go to Health, Education, and Welfare or any other place. What interests me is this department.

The present personnel system does not preclude rapid advancement for some younger civil servants. Quite the contrary. When an agency is adding new duties or when it experiences rapid turnover in higher positions, the fact that rank is attached to a job and not the man means that younger specialists can advance quickly by moving into high-ranking jobs. Over two-fifths (44 percent) of civil service executives had attained their first supergrade position before they reached 45 years of age.[23] The point is that those who do advance quickly in the U.S. civil service can easily find that they have run up against the hazy ceiling dividing civil service and political appointments and that there is little chance to cross to the top of other agency ladders. One of the most widely respected and fastest risers in recent years described the decision facing such a bureaucrat:

> I was reluctant to take it [a political appointment], because it means I'll go when the administration goes, and I can't imagine anything in private business as interesting as government work. But when George Shultz offered me this job I looked at myself and at the people around here who had stayed on for a long time. At my age [38] I was at the top of my career. I had no place else to go.

Another department's personnel officer suggested why such dilemmas should be expected by young bureaucrats who "peak" early. "It is not unusual now to find a young supergrade in his late thirties or early forties who's gotten to the top of a GS 16 or 17. He's capped off his salary and in a way his career too. The question is where do they go for the next decade or so before retirement?"

Outlets. Obviously, there are outlets available in the growing congressional bureaucracy and in the particular interest groups operating close to the official's agency. ... within the executive branch a large number of political appointments are important sources of jobs for career bureaucrats. One-third to one-half of the 600 noncareer supergrade posts and anywhere from one-fifth to two-fifths of the higher political appointments are usually filled by career civil servants. That these outlets exist and are being used suggests mute acceptance of a significant role for bureaucrats in the higher reaches of the U.S. government.

For young bureaucrats confident of their own abilities, the insecure tenure may make little difference; for retiring civil servants with their government pensions assured, there may even be some advantage in a boost in retirement pay that is associated with the higher salaries of political executives. Yet is can hardly be called a strength of the bureaucratic personnel system that the price of mobility and challenge in government service is permanent exit from the civil service. The blunt fact is that officials who move into political appointments must accept the political reality that they are unlikely ever to return to a civil service job. One of the few who did move from career, to political, to career posts offered a fundamental lesson from his experience.

> *It's not something that I can recommend. Your credentials are always doubtful, both to civil service associates you rejoin and the political types in the department. I always felt as if I wasn't quite trusted. There's also something of the feeling that you're coming back at a lower level, with diminished prestige. . . . The result is that to compensate for the suspicion you become too eager to please. There are a couple of instances where I now feel ashamed I didn't make a bigger fight.*

For ambitious officials who want to remain civil servants and who do not happen to find themselves in a pocket of career development, what is the answer? Clearly there is little institutionalized help available when they want or need to move. The answer, once again, lies in the personalized networks that honeycomb the bureaucracy. The small minority of generalist civil servants who are mobile at the highest levels report essentially the same three features in their career patterns: far-flung personal contacts, a good reputation established within this network, and a large element of luck. Governmentwide career moves usually are worked out informally on a hit-and-miss basis by those who already know each other. Careerists in staff positions may be somewhat less constricted than line managers who have grown up with their programs, but even staff bureaucrats recognize the semifortuitous basis of their maneuverability. One imminent retiree described how there was "no systematic way of looking for other jobs" but added that

> *being displaced in one place has helped me elsewhere. Troubles in the State Department made me look acceptable at Interior and later, when the new administration didn't want me there, there were people in Treasury who respected my work and so I ended up a director there. The ability to move and land on your feet depends mostly on who you know and your reputation, and happening to be in the right place at the right time.*

A much younger bureaucrat who had just begun his career was drawing the same lessons early:

> *There is a fraternity of people around in this field and you know you're going to have to continue dealing with each other. Reputation counts. There are career people who can get a GS 15 or a supergrade slotted in with fifteen minutes of phone calls. So what they hear of me matters.*

Obviously no generalized configuration can capture all the personalized relations that go to make up the higher civil service personnel system. What is generalizable is the lack of relationship among configurations—the fact that agency ladders, horizontal networks, and outlets often are self-contained components. The chemistry of the higher civil service is that of a mixture rather than a compound. However comingled they may appear organizationally, officials retain separate identities that are derived from the characteristics of particular subgroups and not from being part of a government—or even departmentwide—civil service. The very diversity of this mixture can be an important resource for political leadership. But political executives seeking to use it will have to look more for an amalgamation of ingredients than for spontaneous fusion into one loyal team....

Notes

1. Public opinion polls show, for example, that the overwhelming majority of Americans agree that the federal government should control inflation; avoid depression; assure international peace; regulate (but not run) private business; and see to it that the poor are taken care of, the hungry fed, and every person assured a minimum standard of living. But a comparably large majority also agree that the federal government is so "big and bureaucratic" that it should return more taxes to subnational governments and count mainly on the states to decide what programs should be started and continued. See *Confidence and Concern: Citizens View American Government,* Committee Print. Subcommittee on Intergovernmental Relations of the Senate Committee on Government Operations. 93 Cong. 1 sess. (GPO, 1973), pt. 2, tables 026A, p. 111; 026, p. 117; 017, p. 118-19; 070A, p. 238.

2. James Fesler has compared the socioeconomic characteristics of bureaucracies in several countries in "Public Administration" (Yale University, 1975; manuscript).

3. Kenneth Jon Meier, "Representative Bureaucracy: An Empirical Analysis," *American Political Science Review,* vol. 69 (June 1975), tables 1 and 2, p. 534, and figures 5 and 6, p. 535.

4. This does not mean that affirmative action programs are undesirable—only that efforts to increase one dimension of demographic representativeness for a particular group of jobs will inevitably increase unrepresentativeness along other dimensions. For example, only 4.5 percent of civil service jobs GS 14 and above are filled by nonwhites, a figure far from representative since nonwhites constitute 14 percent of the population. But women, who hold only 3 percent of GS 14 and higher-grade jobs, are even more underrepresented. Yet these women in government are still less representative of the social class backgrounds of the general population than male bureaucrats are. Who, then, should have priority? Increasing representation for one combination of these dimensions (e.g., nonwhite women from poor backgrounds) will decrease it for another (nonwhite men from poor backgrounds). The various points in the debate on affirmative action and merit principles in the civil service can be traced over the last several years in the *Public Administration Review* and in Harry Kranz, *The Participating Bureaucracy* (Heath, 1976).

5. William A. Medina, "Factors Which Condition the Responses of Departments and Agencies to Centrally Mandated Management Improvement Approaches" (Ph.D. dissertation, American University, 1976), p. 202. See also pp. 203-04, 211-12, 217-18.

6. These are the definitions of generalist and nonmobile used in U.S. Civil Service Commission, Bureau of Executive Manpower, *Executive Manpower in the Federal Service* (GPO, 1972), table 22, p. 21. Data for 1975 are unpublished figures supplied by the Bureau of Executive Manpower.

7. Thomas E. Scism, "Employee Mobility in the Federal Service,"*Public Administration Review,* vol. 34 (1974) p. 232.

8. John Macy, "Assurance of Leadership," *Civil Service Journal,* vol. 7 (October-December 1966), p. 3.

9. Eugene B. MacGregor, Jr., "Politics and Career Mobility of Civil Servants," *American Political Science Review*, vol. 68 (1974), p. 24.

10. John Macy, *The Public Service* (Harper and Row, 1971), p. 46.

11. For a favorable evaluation, see President's Commission on Personnel Interchange. *Evaluation of the President's Executive Interchange Program, 1970-73* (GPO, 1974), especially table 1, p. 4. A more critical approach is in David Guttman and Barry Willner, *The Shadow Government* (Pantbeon Books, 19-6), p. 104.

12. The quotation is from Paul Van Riper, *History of the United States Civil Service* (Row and Peterson, 1958), p. 434. For more recent but similar appraisals, see David Stanley, *The Higher Civil Service* (Brookings Institution, 1964), p. 38; and Macy, *The Public Service,* p. 44.

13. For a detailed critique, see Jay M. Shafritz, *Position Classification: A Behavioral Analysis for the Public Service* (Praeger, 1973), pp. 13-34.

14. A large number of examples involving the Civil Service Commission and others are documented in *A Self-Inquiry into Merit Staffing,* Report of the Merit Staffing Review Team, U.S. Civil Service Commission, for the House Committee on Post Office and Civil Service, Committee Print 94-14, 94 Cong. 2 sess. (GPO, 1976); and in *Final Report on Violations and Abuses of Merit Principles in Federal Employment Together with Minority Views,* Subcommittee on Manpower and Civil Service of the House Committee on Post Office and Civil Service, Committee Print 94-28, 94 Cong. 2 sess. (GPO, 1976), pp. 1-138.

15. 5 U.S.C. 3303. See also Civil Service Rules 4.2 and 7.1 of 5 U.S.C. 330l.

16. *Violations and Abuses of Merit Principles in Federal Employment.* Hearings before the Subcommittee on Manpower and Civil Service of the House Committee on Post Office and Civil Service, 94 Cong. 1 sess. (GPO, 1975), pt. 1, pp. 29-30.

17. See *Final Report on Violations and Abuses,* pp. 6 ff. The commissioners denied that there was anything improper in such referrals. Nevertheless, following publicity about the referrals in 1974, the same commissioners concluded that the propriety of such special actions might be "misunderstood" and adopted a new standard of conduct prohibiting commission officers and employees from making referrals or recommendations for job applicants "unless requested by an agency, or specifically part of his or her official duties." (U.S. Civil Service Commission, Employee letter A-375. January 31, 1975.)

18. Because of what were viewed as persisting abuses in this area, the Civil Service Commission in 1974 established new rules to restrict name requests and to require supervisors to certify personally that job descriptions accurately portray the duties to be performed. The commission's aim, as the chairman expressed it, was "to put somebody's neck on the line." *Violations and Abuses of Merit Principles.* Hearings, pt. 1, p. 69.

19. *A Self-Inquiry into Merit Staffing,* p. 17. For GS 15 positions, the commission in 1975 began supplementing information on the SF-171 with questionnaires that are worked out between the agency and the commission and then sent to applicants before the examiner prepares a rating schedule.

20. *Violations and Abuses of Merit Principles,* Hearings, pt. 1, p. 127.

21. Frederick C. Mosher, *Democracy and the Public Service* (Oxford University Press, 1968), pp. 110-33.

22. Bureau chiefs do, of course, use intra-agency networks to meet their informational needs. For examples, see Herbert Kaufman, *Administrative Feedback* (Brookings Institution, 1973), pp. 33-37.

23. *Executive Manpower in the Federal Service* (1972), table 16b, p. 17.

Chapter Three

The Personnel Officer
and the Federal System

Introduction

The actions of other governments, the courts, and regulatory bodies have become major determinants of a variety of personnel policies. Keeping track of, evaluating, and influencing Congress, government agencies, and the courts are a major preoccupation of those in the public personnel field. This introductory essay and the selections that follow in this chapter deal with this important intergovernmental context.

Congress

Employment is a significant concern of legislators at all levels of government. Recent federal legislation bans discriminatory practices and requires certain safety standards in all occupations. The legislators have approved expenditure of funds for manpower programs which pay salaries of public employees in all levels of government. The passage of these measures has increased the federal role in state and local policymaking and the influence of Congress on personnel practices generally.

Members of Congress also investigate abuses of personnel systems in all levels of government and the actions of Congress have established regulatory bodies which directly influence personnel decisions. Grants in aid, which the legislature appropriates, often contain provisions of nondiscriminatory use which mandate certain personnel procedures.

The astute personnel officer must therefore watch the actions of Congress closely. He or she must become adept at reading pieces of legislation. More importantly, personnel specialists need to be involved in the writing of legislation. Contacts with congressmen and senators keep the officer posted about latest developments and offer the opportunity to affect the legislators' decisions. Interest groups such as the International Personnel Management Association, the American Society for Public Administration, and the International City Management Association are important sources of influence on Congress. The active personnel officer is a member of these and other similar organizations.

The 1964 Civil Rights Act has probably had a greater effect on public personnel policy than any piece of legislation since the Pendleton Act of 1887 which set up the national civil service system. The civil rights law outlawed employment discrimination and mandated federal enforcement efforts. Amendments have increased the level of enforcement and extended coverage to state and local governments.

This civil rights law is a specific piece of legislation which speaks directly to matters such as employment testing procedures. Portions of Title VII, which pertain to employment discrimination, are included here as Selection 5. It is an example of direct influence by Congress in personnel matters and should be read for its policy significance and as an example of legislation of this kind. A personnel officer needs to be familiar with relevant acts of legislation and aware of changes and additions that are made at later times.

The Role of the Courts

The judicial system can influence policymaking in several ways. Individual employees can sue public employers. Judicial victories by employees can be very costly to the organization of employment. Fired employees, for instance, have been reinstated and awarded back pay as a consequence of legal action. Precedents established in court may lead to similar judgments at little expense to the employee.

Courts can also invalidate general personnel procedures and order specific remedies. Recruitment procedures have been declared unconstitutional and agencies have been told to devise new tests, compile more inclusive records, advertise more extensively, and hire more members of minorities including women. The courts have also intervened to protect the political and organizational rights of employees, strike down grooming standards, and limit residency requirements. Thus, the jurisdiction of the court in personnel matters is very broad and major elements of policy have been affected.

Unlike other branches of government, the courts must give reasons for their actions. Each court decision contains a discussion of the relation between the acts in question and principles established in the Constitution, previous court cases, laws, or social practices. The courts change their policies in a given area of law, but the justices are obligated to do so by reinterpreting constitutional and legal principles. Consequently, knowledge of the rationale for previous decisions gives an indication of expected rulings. Assuming a consistent pattern of decision on the court, knowledge of the kinds of previous rulings may make the predictions of future decisions possible.

Understanding a judicial opinion is usually related to judicial interpretation of important constitutional provisions and laws. Several of these provisions are particularly important to decisions that affect the personnel area:

1. The commerce clause of the Constitution which states that Congress shall have the right to ". . . regulate commerce within foreign nations and among the several states and with Indian tribes" (Article 1, Section 8). This clause has often been used to expand the powers of the federal government by broadly interpreting "commerce among the states."

2. The Tenth Amendment of the Constitution. "The powers not delegated to the United States by the Constitution, nor prohibited by it to the States, are reserved to the States respectively and to the people." Interpretations of Amendment Ten have altered the relationship between the states and the national government. Proponents of the rights of the states tend to argue that the Tenth Amendment limits the extent to which the commerce clause can expand the role of the federal government.

3. The First Amendment of the Constitution. "Congress shall make no law respecting an establishment of religion or prohibiting the free exercise thereof; or abridging the freedom of speech, or the right of the people to peaceably assemble and petition the government for redress of grievances." This amendment has been used to challenge infringements of the freedom of government employees and controls on employee political behavior.

4. Section One of the Fourteenth Amendment which states that "No state shall make or enforce any law which shall abridge the privileges or immunities of citizens of the United States nor shall any state deprive any person of life, liberty or property without due process of law; nor deny to any person within its jurisdiction the equal protection of the laws." This provision permits the Supreme Court to rule on state actions that abridge individual rights. It has been particularly important in rulings dealing with discrimination.

The Supreme Court's role as an important actor in the personnel process is of recent origin. Before the 1950s, the Court tended to avoid public personnel cases. In these years the justices invoked the "doctrine of privilege" or the assumption that holding a government job was a privilege rather than a right of employment. Government could therefore place restrictions upon employees even if similar restrictions on those employed in the private sector were considered unconstitutional.[1]

Since several rulings of the Warren Court (1953-1969) called this doctrine into question the courts have become more active intervenors in the personnel process. Encouraging this more aggressive approach were a series of legislative enactments that expanded government's role in protecting individuals against discrimination. The most important of these was the Civil Rights Act of 1964. This Act and extensions of it have been used repeatedly to bring discrimination suits to court. The law also permits suits to be initiated by the Department of Justice.

The 1960s was a time of extensive judicial activism in the personnel area, bringing forth many of the specific decisions discussed later in this book. Actions of the present court suggest that some of the desire to affect personnel policy may be lessening. *The National League of Cities et al.* v. *Usery* (Selection 6) is a recent case which suggests that the future may see less judicial activism in the personnel field.

The Usery case is a good example of the application of conflicting laws and constitutional provisions to the personnel process. In question is an amendment to the Fair Labor Standards Act, a national law that mandated minimum wage and maximum hour provisions to state and local governments. At issue is a conflict between the commerce clause and the rights of states to regulate their own affairs (Amendment Ten). The justices must weigh the relative importance of each of these provisions and interpretations of the intent of the legislators in reaching a judicial decision. A personnel officer would want to examine a case like this closely to determine if all his or her employees are covered by it and if other cases are likely to narrow or broaden the scope of the ruling. Dissenting opinions may also be guides to future interpretations, particularly if there are several dissenters.

In reading the Usery case, note that the Court is changing its perspective on state-federal relations. Prior cases had tended to limit the role of the states. Justice Rhenquist's opinion emphasizes the Tenth Amendment and deemphasizes the power of Congress to regulate commerce. If this is a part of a more general trend, one may expect a decline in the influence of congressional acts on state and local matters. Only by following court decisions can the consequences of such rulings be understood and anticipated.

The Role of State and Federal Agencies

A personnel officer is never isolated from the influences of other agencies. Rulings of state and federal regulatory bodies and aid programs from other governments that require certain actions by the recipient affect numerous personnel actions at the state and local level. The federal personnel official is subject to similar influences from other parts of the federal government. Hence, knowledge of the functions and operations of the primary regulatory and funding agencies have become significant to the personnel officer's life.

There are two ways in which one agency influences another. One, grants can be awarded to an agency while the recipient in return agrees to conform to certain dictates of the donor. This process is referred to as the grant-in-aid system, and the conditions placed on the donor agency are called "strings."

Second, other agencies exert influence through regulation. Certain agencies are given the authority to enforce laws that affect the operation of other governments or agencies. The National Occupational Safety and Health Administration, for instance, has been delegated the power to enforce safety laws in all federal agencies. It may investigate possible violations of the law and take appropriate actions either independently or through legal action.

Both the grant-in-aid and regulatory processes may work toward similar goals, but the method of enforcement differs in each case. The grant process relies on the value of the financial incentive. An agency that finds the cost of complying greater than the perceived financial benefit can forego the grant and has no reason to alter the practices that might have been affected by the strings of the grant.

Regulatory bodies rely on respect for the law by those regulated and the regulator's ability to negotiate settlements, impose sanctions, or bring forth legal action. Respect, however, is the more important of the two types since investigations and legal actions are costly for the regulator as well as the agency that is regulated.

Federal Employment Regulation

The federal government contains a bewildering array of regulatory bodies that have some influence on the personnel process. All are the consequence of increasing pressure from women's and racial and ethnic minority groups for equal access to jobs in both the public and private sectors.

The personnel officer must be aware of the powers and actions of several agencies if he or she is to cope adequately with changes and new interpretations of the law. The major agencies that influence the personnel process are:

1. The Equal Employment Opportunity Commission (EEOC). The 1964 Civil Rights Act created the Equal Employment Opportunity Commission, a federal agency empowered to investigate charges of discrimination and attempt to resolve them through conciliation. The 1972 amendments expanded the powers of the EEOC to include the authority to file and prosecute law suits against respondents subject to its litigation jurisdiction where conciliation efforts fail, and extended its coverage to encompass state and local governments.

   Five commissioners who are appointed by the President with the advise and consent of the Senate for five-year terms govern the EEOC. No more than three commissioners may be of the same political party. It is thus designed to be relatively detached from presidential policy.

   The EEOC maintains a large central and regional staff. Most employee time is spent processing and resolving charges of discrimination. Complaints of discrimination are filed by individual employees or by organizations on their behalf. The Commission is empowered to investigate these complaints and seek remedies, if justified, through conciliation or legal methods. It also seeks to influence personnel agencies through the establishment of guidelines for acceptable practice.

2. The United States Office of Personnel Management (formerly a part of the Civil Service Commission). This agency is responsible for coordinating personnel functions of the federal government. It also implements equal

employment measures within that government. This includes revisions of recruitment and testing procedures and the handling of employee discrimination complaints. In 1977 this function was expanded to include class action complaints. The Office of Personnel Management also provides technical assistance to state and local governments.

3. The Department of Labor Office of Federal Contract Compliance (OFCC). This agency is responsible for equal employment compliance in organizations and firms holding government contracts. The power to enforce compliance in contracts is derived from a series of executive orders resulting in the creation of the present administrative agency in 1965. Equal opportunity clauses are required of all federal contractors. Two basic contractual commitments are expected: (1) not to discriminate in employment on the basis of race, color, sex, religion, or national origin, and (2) to undertake affirmative action to ensure that equal employment opportunity principles are followed in personnel practices at all company facilities, including those not engaged in a federal contract. Guarantees from subcontractors must also be obtained. State and local government agencies maintaining government contracts are also under OFCC jurisdiction.

The OFCC can impose sanctions on those in violation of equal opportunity clauses. This authority includes recommending that the Justice Department institute appropriate action to enforce the executive order, or cancel, terminate, or suspend any contract or portions of any contract and debar a contractor from future government work.

The OFCC maintains a central staff and delegates contract compliance responsibilities to representatives in agencies concerned with the type of contract in question.

4. The Department of Labor, Wage and Hour Division. This agency enforces the 1974 Fair Labor Standards Amendment which requires employees performing equal work to be paid equally regardless of sex. The amendment applies to state and local governments as well as private employers. The division employees investigate violations of the law, attempt to negotiate settlements, and litigate where efforts at compliance fail.

5. Department of Justice-Civil Rights Division-Employment Section. This agency is empowered to initiate discrimination suits against private employers and state and local governments. Its objectives are to develop a body of case law that enables employers, labor organizations, government agencies, and the public to understand what equal employment laws require and to provide relief for the greatest number of victims of discrimination. Hence, employees of the agency search for potential suits to accomplish these objectives.

6. State and Local Equal Employment Agencies. Many state and local governments maintain equal employment agencies. They are often aided by the EEOC and the Office of Personnel Management and are frequently

delegated authority by the EEOC. State and local laws may be more or less restrictive than federal statutes. Different rulings and policies may therefore come forth from these agencies.

The Practice of Personnel Regulation

The role of regulation in personnel matters is rapidly expanding. Its newness, coupled with changing judicial determinations, creates problems for personnel policymakers. Two of these difficulties deserve comment:

1. Conflict and Confusion. The regulatory agencies are designed to accomplish similar goals, but agreement on the means to achieve them is often lacking. Hence, different standards of compliance have been accepted by different agencies. These conflicts came clearly to light when these agencies attempted to develop common guidelines for employment testing.

   In 1971 the EEOC, OFCC, and the Civil Rights Division of the Department of Justice issued guidelines on test validation which were very much alike. The next year the Civil Service Commission issued instructions on employee selection standards which differed substantially from those of the other two agencies. The differences created much confusion for complying agencies and state and local governments. The matter was referred to the Equal Opportunity Coordinating Council, an intergovernmental body established to coordinate equal employment policy. The coordinating council devoted considerable staff time to the problem but could not get the various agencies to agree on a set of guidelines until 1978. Until that time, at least two sets of guidelines were in operation and enforcement depended upon which regulatory agency had adopted which set.

   Many agencies must deal with all of these regulating agencies. The Office of Revenue Sharing, for example, abides by the guidelines of the EEOC in determining state and local government compliance while Law Enforcement Assistance Administration recipients receiving funds under the Crime Control Act follow Office of Personnel Management policies. A local police department receiving funds from both sources has a problem.

2. Backlogs. The EEOC and the Wage and Hour Division were established as quasi-judicial agencies. Decisions are the product of individual complaints which are investigated by the agency staff. Decisions are reached through negotiations with the parties involved or through judicial action. The process is time consuming and expensive. The workload created by possible violations has been much greater than the staffs of these agencies can deal with and the backlog of cases has thus increased significantly each year. In 1977, over 130,000 cases were backlogged at the EEOC and over 33,000 were in a similar condition at the Wage and Hour Division. Hence, litigants may wait years for their cases to be adjudicated.[2]

Consequences and Future Prospects

The consequences of the practice of equal employment regulation for the personnel officer are much uncertainty and confusion. It is unclear what rules and regulations should be followed. If they are challenged, years may elapse before the agency will know if, in fact, its procedures are acceptable. Without agreement on the goals and means of compliance and resources to handle cases efficiently, the federal equal employment effort encourages confusion and evasion.

Alert to these problems, the Carter administration proposed a radical reorganization of these agencies in 1978. It advocated the establishment of a stronger EEOC, which would consolidate the services performed by the Civil Service Commission, the Wage and Hour Division, and the EEOC. The proposal would give this enlarged agency the power to impose sanctions directly on violators rather than referring such matters to the legal system. It also suggested that eventually the OFCC be directed by this new agency.

The Grant Process

Recipients of federal grants-in-aid are also subject to equal employment provisions. The mechanisms of enforcement and the standards employed are different from those of the regulatory agencies.

Title VII of the 1964 Civil Rights Act prohibits discrimination on grounds of race, color, and national origin in all federally-assisted programs. At least twenty-five agencies administer grant programs and each of them is responsible for its own Title VII compliance of the recipients. The Federal Programs Section of the Civil Rights Division of the Department of Justice is responsible for coordination of Title VII activities, which it carries out in a limited manner. Title VII, as written, does not include a sex discrimination provision, though Congress has added sex to Title VII coverage in most programs.

In addition, the courts have interpreted Title VII as applying only to the direct use of the granted funds. Grants for school libraries, for example, are contingent only upon lack of discrimination in the library. If discrimination persists in other facets of the school operation, the grant cannot be challenged.

Compliance with Title VII requires conformance with employment guidelines of federal departments which may include affirmative action programs, goals, and time tables for the employment of minorities and women if deficiencies are present. These requirements often differ from those expected by the federal employment regulatory commissions. Thus, a local official frequently finds several standards regulating his or her employment efforts.

Unfortunately, little is known about the effect of these provisions. Are agencies failing to seek grants because they do not conform to such guidelines? How frequently are grants rejected because of questionable employment procedures? How many grants are recalled because of such violations? A recent systematic study of revenue sharing compliance found that the anti-discriminatory provisions of the Act had a "significant effect" on the use of the funds in but one of sixty-five sampled cities. That city, however, was Los Angeles where funds, in fact, were temporarily withheld because of questions raised with regard to the affirmative action plan of that city's fire department.[8]

The history of the Comprehensive Employment and Training Act (CETA), a federally funded grant-in-aid program to assist the unemployed through job creation demonstrates the benefits and the problems of the grant process. CETA funds are used to hire the unemployed in nearly any relevant capacity. The entire range of public service occupations from refuse collection to the arts have added personnel through CETA funding. Its extensive use, however also increases the dependence of states, cities and school districts on the federal dollar. Some jurisdictions, for instance, employ as many as 20 percent of their work force through CETA funds. Selection 7 discusses some of the problems raised by this program.

Where Do We Go From Here?

One can view the courts, the grant system, and regulatory bodies as severe impediments to a sound personnel system. Personnel officials must spent much time reading rules, regulations, and court cases. They often need to confer with representatives of numerous agencies to determine the proper course of action. Even with the best of intentions, the efforts of one agency may be considered negligent though the directives of another agency are followed. The money, time, and skills required to conform fully with a request may be more than the local agency can bear.

Which would be preferable—a system where no regulation was present or where a single agency had clear enforcement powers over civil rights employment matters? The former perspective forces one to assume that no national effort to eliminate discrimination in employment is needed. To make such an assumption, one must reject the evidence of discrimination and the success our nation has experienced during the last twenty years in trying to create a more truly equal society. With no national efforts, the personnel officer could not become a part of the movement to change our government from being racist and sexist to one of genuine equal opportunity. Would local forces and clientele-oriented interest groups, in the absence of proddings from the courts and the Congress, encourage acts in conformity with equality? In some cases the answer would be positive, but certainly not in all. The commitment to equal opportunity in personnel matters was obviously much less before passage of the Civil Rights Act of 1964 and its resulting judicial interpretation than it is today.

To grant enforcement powers to a single body which would set all standards runs counter to American methods of problem solving. If we believe in a federal system and a decentralized democracy, we do not want a central body dictating the terms in a matter of such importance. To preserve a federal system, policy must result from the give and take of numerous actors and interests. Possibly a period of conflict, delay and confusion is needed to provide the time and experience to find a truly workable set of procedures. Out of such confusion may come policies that are less conflicting and more in keeping with the values of our system.

In this process of bargain and compromise, local autonomy may replace the move toward a national goal of equal opportunity. Or a more creative and workable policy may emerge. At this time we know only that our equal employment policies are in flux. For the personnel officer, this confusion may be as much a challenge as a frustration. The personnel policymaker can be a part of an attempt to make employment policies workable. Confusion and conflict provide access to the emerging changes in these policies. Dealing with these conflicts can be a creative effort all should welcome.

Notes

1. David H. Rosenbloom, "The Public Employee In Court: Implications for Urban Government," p. 58, in Charles H. Levine ed., *Managing Human Resources* (Beverly Hills, Ca., Sage, 1977).

2. See United States Commission on Civil Rights, *The Federal Civil Rights Enforcement Effort—1977: To Eliminate Employment Discrimination: A Sequel"* (Washington, D.C., United States Government Printing Office, 1977).

3. Robert Nathan and Charles Adams, *Revenue Sharing: The Second Round* (Washington, D.C., Brookings, 1977), p. 130.

5
Title VII, The Civil Rights Act, 1964, as Amended through 1975
United States Congress

Definitions

Sec. 70l. For the purposes of this title—

(a) The term "person" includes one or more individuals, governments, governmental agencies, political subdivisions labor unions, partnerships, associations, corporations, legal representatives, mutual companies, joint-stock companies, trusts, unincorporated organizations, trustees, trustees in bankruptcy, or receivers.

(b) The term "employer" means a person engaged in an industry affecting commerce who has fifteen or more employees for each working day in each of twenty or more calendar weeks in the current or preceding calendar year, and any agent of such a person, but such term does not include (1) the United States, a corporation wholly owned by the Government of the United States, an Indian tribe, or any department or agency of the District of Columbia subject by statute to procedures of the competitive service (as defined in section 2102 of title 5 of the United States Code), or (2) a bona fide private membership club (other than a labor organization) which is exempt from taxation under section 501(c) of the Internal Revenue Code of 1954, except that during the first year after the date of enactment of the Equal Employment Opportunity Act of 1972, persons having fewer than twenty-five employees (and their agents) shall not be considered employers.

(c) The term "employment agency" means any person regularly undertaking with or without compensation to procure employees for an employer or to procure for employees opportunities to work for an employer and includes an agent of such a person.

(d) The term "labor organization" means a labor organization engaged in an industry affecting commerce, and any agent of such an organization, and includes any organization of any kind, any agency, or employee representation committee, group, association, or plan so engaged in which employees participate and which exists for the purpose, in whole or in part, of dealing with employers concerning grievances, labor disputes, wages, rates of pay, hours, or other items or conditions of employment, and any conference, general committee, joint or system board, or joint council so engaged which is subordinate to a national or international labor organization.

(e) A labor organization shall be deemed to be engaged in an industry affecting commerce if (1) it maintains or operates a hiring hall or hiring office which procures employees for an employer or procures for employees opportunities to work for an employer, or (2) the number of its members (or, where it is a labor organization composed of other labor organizations or their representatives, if the aggregate number of the members of such other labor organization) is (A) twenty-five or more during the first year after the date of enactment of the Equal Employment Opportunity Act of 1972, or (B) fifteen or more thereafter, and such labor organization—

(1) is the certified representative of employees under the provisions of the National Labor Relations Act, as amended, or the Railway Labor Act, as amended;

(2) although not certified, is a national or international labor organization or a local labor organization recognized or acting as the representative of employees of an employer or employers engaged in an industry affecting commerce; or

(3) has chartered a local labor organization or subsidiary body which is representing or actively seeking to represent employees of employers within the meaning of paragraph (1) or (2); or

(4) has been chartered by a labor organization representing or actively seeking to represent employees within the meaning of paragraph (1) or (2) as the local or subordinate body through which such employees may enjoy membership or become affiliated with such labor organization; or

(5) is a conference, general committee, joint or system board, or joint council subordinate to a national or international labor organization, which includes a labor organization engaged in an industry affecting commerce within the meaning of any of the preceding paragraphs of this subsection.

(f) The term "employee" means an individual employed by an employer, except that the term "employee" shall not include any person elected to public office in any State or political subdivision of any State by the qualified voters thereof, or any person chosen by such officer to be on such officer's personal staff, or an appointee on the policy making level or an immediate adviser with respect to the exercise of the constitutional or legal powers of the office. The exemption set forth in the preceding sentence shall not include employees subject to the civil service laws of a State government, governmental agency or political subdivision.

(g) The term "commerce" means trade, traffic, commerce, transportation, transmission or communication among the several States; or between a State and any place outside thereof; or within the District of Columbia, or a possession of the United States; or between points in the same State but through a point outside thereof.

(h) The term "industry affecting commerce" means any activity, business, or industry in commerce or in which a labor dispute would hinder or obstruct commerce or the free flow of commerce and includes any activity or industry "affecting commerce" within the meaning of the Labor-Management Reporting and Disclosure Act of 1959, and further includes any governmental industry, business, or activity.

(i) The term "State" includes a State of the United States, the District of Columbia, Puerto Rico, the Virgin Islands, American Samoa, Guam, Wake Island, the Canal Zone, and Outer Continental Shelf lands defined in the Outer Continental Shelf Lands Act.

(j) The term "religion" includes all aspects of religious observance and practice, as well as belief, unless an employer demonstrates that he is unable to reasonably accommodate to an employee's or prospective employee's religious observance or practice without undue hardship on the conduct of the employer's business.

Exemption

Sec. 702. This title shall not apply to an employer with respect to the employment of aliens outside any State, or to a religious corporation, association, educational institution, or society with respect to the employment of individuals of a particular religion to perform work connected with the carrying on by such corporation, association, educational institution, or society of its activities.

Discrimination Because of Race, Color, Religion, Sex, or National Origin

Sec. 703. (a) It shall be an unlawful employment practice for an employer—

(1) to fail or refuse to hire or to discharge any individual, or otherwise to discriminate against any individual with respect to his compensation, terms, conditions, or privileges of employment, because of such individual's race, color, religion, sex, or national origin; or

(2) to limit, segregate, or classify his employees or applicants for employment in any way which would deprive or tend to deprive any individual of employment opportunities or otherwise adversely affect his status as an employee, because of such individual's race, color, religion, sex, or national origin.

(b) It shall be an unlawful employment practice for an employment agency to fail or refuse to refer for employment, or otherwise discriminate against, any individual because of his race, color, religion, sex, or national origin, or to classify or refer for employment any individual on the basis of his race, color, religion, sex, or national origin.

(c) It shall be an unlawful employment practice for a labor organization—

(1) to exclude or to expel from its membership or applicants for membership, or otherwise to discriminate against, any individual because of his race, color, religion, sex, or national origin;

(2) to limit, segregate, or classify its membership, or to classify or fail or refuse to refer for employment any individual, in any way which would deprive or tend to deprive any individual of employment opportunities, or would limit such employment opportunities or otherwise adversely affect his status as an employee or as an applicant for employment, because of such individual's race, color, religion, sex, or national origin; or

(3) to cause or attempt to cause an employer to discriminate against an individual in violation of this section.

(d) It shall be an unlawful employment practice for any employer, labor organization, or joint labor-management committee controlling apprenticeship or other training or retraining, including on-the-job training programs to discriminate against any individual because of his race, color, religion, sex, or national origin in admission to, or employment in, any program established to provide apprenticeship or other training.

(e) Notwithstanding any other provision of this title, (1) it shall not be an unlawful employment practice for an employer to hire and employ employees, for an employment agency to classify, or refer for employment any individual, for a labor organization to classify its membership or to classify or refer for employment any individual, or for an employer, labor organization, or joint labor-management committee controlling apprenticeship or other training or retraining programs to admit or employ any individual in any such program, on the basis of his religion, sex, or national origin in those certain instances where religion, sex, or national origin is a bona fide occupational qualification reasonably necessary to the normal operation of that particular business or enterprice, and (2) it shall not be an unlawful employment practice for a school, college, university, or other educational institution or institution of learning to hire and employ employees of a particular religion if such school, college, university, or other educational institution or institution of learning is, in whole or in substantial part, owned, supported, controlled, or managed by a particular religion or by a particular religious corporation, association, or society, or if the curriculum of such school, college, university, or other educational institution or institution of learning is directed toward the propagation of a particular religion.

(f) As used in this title, the phrase "unlawful employment practice" shall not be deemed to include any action or measure taken by an employer, labor organization, joint labor-management committee, or employment agency with respect to an individual who is a member of the Communist Party of the United States or of any other organization required to register as a Communist-action or Communist-front organization by final order of the Subversive Activities Control Board pursuant to the Subversive Activities Control Act of 1950.

(g) Notwithstanding any other provision of this title, it shall not be an unlawful employment practice for an employer to fail or refuse to hire and employ any individual for any position, for an employer to discharge any individual from any position, or for an employment agency to fail or refuse to refer any individual for employment in any position, or for a labor organization to fail or refuse to refer any individual for employment in any position, if—

(1) the occupancy of such position, or access to the premises in or upon which any part of the duties of such position is performed or is to be performed, is subject to any requirement imposed in the interest of the national security of the United States under any security program in effect pursuant to or administered under any statute of the United States or any Executive order of the President; and

(2) such individual has not fulfilled or has ceased to fulfill that requirement.

(h) Notwithstanding any other provision of this title, it shall not be an unlawful employment practice for an employer to apply different standards of compensation, or different terms, conditions, or privileges of employment pursuant to a bona fide seniority or merit system, or a system which measures earnings by quantity or quality of production or to employees who work in different locations, provided that such differences are not the result of an intention to discriminate because of race, color, religion, sex, or national origin, nor shall it be an unlawful employment practice for an employer to give and to act upon the results of any professionally developed ability test provided that such test, its administration or action upon the results is not designed, intended or used to discriminate because of race, color, religion, sex or national origin. It shall not be an unlawful employment practice under this title for any employer to differentiate upon the basis of sex in determining the amount of the wages or compensation paid or to be paid to employees of such employer if such differentiation is authorized by the provisions of section 6(d) of the Fair Labor Standards Act of 1938, as amended (29 U.S.C. 206(d)).

(i) Nothing contained in this title shall apply to any business or enterprise on or near an Indian reservation with respect to any publicly announced employment practice of such business or enterprise under which a preferential treatment is given to any individual because he is an Indian living on or near a reservation.

(j) Nothing contained in this title shall be interpreted to require any employer, employment agency, labor organization, or joint labor-management committee subject to this title to grant preferential treatment to any individual or to any group because of the race, color, religion, sex, or national origin of such individual or group on account of an imbalance which may exist with respect to the total number or percentage of persons of any race, color, religion, sex, or national origin employed by any employer, referred or classified for employment by any employment agency or labor organization, admitted to membership or classified by any labor organization, or admitted to, or employed in, any apprenticeship or other training program, in comparison with the total number or percentage of persons of such race, color, religion, sex, or national origin in any community, State, section, or other area, or in the available work force in any community, State, section, or other area.

Other Unlawful Employment Practices

Sec. 704. (a) It shall be an unlawful employment practice for an employer to discriminate against any of his employees or applicants for employment, for an employment agency, or joint labor-management committee controlling apprenticeship or other training or retraining, including on-the-job training programs, to discriminate against any individual, or for a labor organization to discriminate against any member thereof or applicant for membership, because he has opposed any practice made an unlawful employment practice by this title, or because he has made a charge, testified, assisted, or participated in any manner in an investigation, proceeding, or hearing under this title.

(b) It shall be an unlawful employment practice for an employer, labor organization, employment agency, or joint labor-management committee controlling apprenticeship or other training or retraining including on-the-job training programs, to print or publish or cause to be printed or published any notice or advertisement relating to employment by such an employer or membership in or any classification or referral for employment by such a labor organization, or relating to any classification or referral for employment by such an employment agency, or relating to admission to, or employment in, any program established to provide apprenticeship or other training by such a joint labor-management committee indicating any preference, limitation, specification, or discrimination, based on race, color, religion, sex, or national original, except that such a notice or advertisement may indicate a preference, limitation, specification, or discrimination based on religion, sex, or national origin when religion, sex, or national origin is a bona fide occupational qualification for employment.

6

The National League of Cities et al. v. W. J. Usery Jr., Secretary of Labor, June 24, 1976

United States Supreme Court

Mr. Justice Rehnquist delivered the opinion for the Court.

Nearly 40 years ago Congress enacted the Fair Labor Standards Act, and required employers covered by the Act to pay their employees a minimum hourly wage and to pay them at one and one-half times their regular rate of pay for hours worked in excess of 40 during a work week. By this act covered employers were required to keep certain records to aid in the enforcement of the Act, and to comply with specified child labor standards. This Court unanimously upheld the Act as a valid exercise of congressional authority under the commerce power in *United States* v. *Darby,* 312 U.S. 100 (1941), observing:

> *"Whatever their motive and purpose, regulations of commerce which do not infringe some constitutional prohibition are within the plenary power conferred on Congress by the Commerce Clause."* Id., *at 115.*

The original Fair Labor Standards Act passed in 1938 specifically excluded the States and their political subdivisions from its coverage. In 1974, however, Congress enacted the most recent of a series of broadening amendments to the Act. By these amendments Congress has extended the minimum wage and maximum hour provisions to almost all public employees employed by the States and by their various political subdivisions. Appellants in these cases include individual cities and States, the National League of Cities, and the National Governors' Conference; they brought an action in the District Court for the District of Columbia which challenged the validity of the 1974 amendments. They asserted in effect that when Congress sought to apply the Fair Labor Standards Act provisions virtually across the board to employees of state and municipal governments it "infringed a constitutional prohibition" running in favor of the States *as States.* The gist of their complaint was not that the conditions of employment of such public employees were beyond the scope of the commerce power had those employees been employed in the private sector, but that the established constitutional doctrine of intergovernmental immunity consistently recognized in a long series of our cases affirmatively prevented the exercise of this authority in the manner which Congress chose in the 1974 Amendments.

History of the Problem

In a series of amendments beginning in 1961 Congress began to extend the provisions of the Fair Labor Standards Act to some types of public employees. The 1961 amendment to the Act extended its coverage to persons who were employed in "enterprises" engaged in commerce or in the production of goods for commerce. And in 1966, with the amendment of the definition of employers under the Act, the exemption heretofore extended to the States and their political subdivisions was removed with respect to employees of state hospitals, institutions, and schools. We nevertheless sustained the validity of the combined effect of these two amendments in *Maryland* v. *Wirtz,* 392 U.S. 183 (1968).

In 1974, Congress again broadened the coverage of the Act. The definition of "employer" in the Act now specifically "includes a public agency," 29 U.S.C. Sec. 203 (d). In addition, the critical definition of "enterprises engaged in commerce or in the production of goods for commerce" was expended to encompass "an activity of a public agency," and goes on to specify that

> *"The employees of an enterprise which is a public agency shall for purposes of this subsection be deemed to be employees engaged in commerce, or in the production of goods for commerce, or employees handling, selling, or otherwise working on goods or materials that have been moved in or produced for commerce." 29 U.S.C. Sec. 203 (s)(5).*

Under the Amendments "public agency" is in turn defined as including

> *"the Government of the United States; the government of a State or political subdivision thereof; any agency of the United States (including the United States Postal Service and Postal Rate Commission), a State, or a political subdivision of a State; or any interstate governmental agency." 29 U.S.C. Sec. 203 (x).*

By its 1974 amendments, then, Congress has now entirely removed the exemption previously afforded States and their political subdivisions, substituting only the Act's general exemption for executive, administration, or professional personnel, 29 U.S.C. Sec. 213 (a)(1), which is supplemented by provisions excluding from the Act's coverage those individuals holding public elective office or serving such an officeholder in one of several specific capacities. 29 U.S.C. Sec. 203 (e)(2)(C). The Act thus imposes upon almost all public employment the minimum wage and maximum hour requirements previously restricted to employees engaged in interstate commerce. These requirements are essentially identical to those imposed upon private employers, although the Act does attempt to make some provision for public employment relationships which are without counterpart in the private sector, such as those presented by fire protection and law enforcement personnel. See 29 U.S.C. Sec. 207 (k).

Challenging these 1974 amendments in the District Court, appellants sought both declaratory and injunctive relief against the amendments' application to them, and a three-judge court was accordingly convened pursuant to 28 U.S.C. Sec. 2282. That court, after hearing argument on the law from the parties, granted appellee Secretary of Labor's motion to dismiss the complaint for failure to state a claim upon which relief might be granted. The District Court stated it was "troubled" by appellants' contentions that the amendments would intrude upon the States' performance of essential governmental functions. The court went on to say that it considered their contentions:

> *"substantial and that it may well be that the Supreme Court will feel it appropriate to draw back from the far-reaching implications of* [Maryland v. Wirtz, supra]; *but that is a decision that only the Supreme Court can make, and as a Federal district court we feel obliged to apply the Wirtz opinion as it stands."*

We noted probable jurisdiction in order to consider the important questions recognized by the District Court, 420 U.S. 906 (1975). We agree with the District Court that the appellants' contentions are substantial. Indeed upon full consideration of the question we have decided that the "far-reaching implications" of *Wirtz,* should be overruled, and that the judgment of the District Court must be reversed.

Constitutional Issues

It is established beyond peradventure that the Commerce Clause of Art. I of the Constitution is a grant of plenary authority to Congress. That authority is, in the words of Chief Justice Marshall in *Gibbons* v. *Ogden,* 9 Wheat. (21 U.S.) 1 (1824), ". . . the power to regulate; that is to prescribe the rule by which commerce is to be governed." *Id.,* at 196.

When considering the validity of asserted applications of this power to wholly private activity, the Court has made it clear that

> *"[e]ven activity that is purely intrastate in character may be regulated by Congress, where the activity, combined with like conduct by others similarly situated, affects commerce among the States or with foreign nations."* Fry *v.* United States, *421 U.S. 542, 547 (1975).*

Congressional power over areas of private endeavor, even when its exercise may pre-empt express state law determinations contrary to the result which has commended itself to collective wisdom of Congress, has been held to be limited only by the requirement that "the means chosen by [Congress] must be reasonably adapted to the end permitted by the Constitution." *Heart of Atlanta Motel, Inc.* v. *United States,* 379 U.S. 241, 262 (1964).

Appellants in no way challenge these decisions establishing the breadth of authority granted Congress under the commerce power. Their contention, on the contrary, is that when Congress seeks to regulate directly the activities of States as public employers, it transgresses an affirmative limitation on the exercise of its power akin to other commerce power affirmative limitations contained in the Constitution. Congressional enactments which may be fully within the grant of legislative authority contained in the Commerce Clause may nonetheless be invalid because found to offend against the right to trial by jury contained in the Sixth Amendment, *United States* v. *Jackson,* 390 U.S. 570 (1968), or the Due Process Clause of the Fifth Amendment, *Leary* v. *United*

States, 395 U.S. 6 (1969). Appellants' essential contention is that the 1974 amendments to the Act, while undoubtedly within the scope of the Commerce Clause, encounter a similar constitutional barrier because they are to be applied directly to the States and subdivisions of States as employers.

The Court has never doubted that there are limits upon the power of Congress to override state sovereignty, even when exercising its otherwise plenary powers to tax or to regulate commerce which are conferred by Art. I of the Constitution. In *Wirtz* for example, the Court took care to assure the appellants that it had "ample power to prevent . . . 'the utter destruction of the State as a sovereign political entity,'" which they feared. 392 U.S., at 196. Appellee Secretary in this case, both in his brief and upon oral argument, has agreed that our federal system of government imposes definite limits upon the authority of Congress to regulate the activities of the States as States by means of the commerce power. See, *e.g.,* Appellee's Brief, at 30-41; Tr. of Oral Arg. 39-43. In *Fry, supra,* the Court recognized that an express declaration of this limitation is found in the Tenth Amendment:

> *"While the Tenth Amendment has been characterized as a 'truism,' stating merely that 'all is retained which has not been surrendered,'* United States v. Darby, *312 U.S. 100, 124 (1941), it is not without significance. The Amendment expressly declares the constitutional policy that Congress may not exercise power in a fashion that impairs the States' integrity or their ability to function effectively in a federal system. . . ." 421 U.S., at 547.*

In *New York* v. *United States,* 326 U.S. 572 (1946), Chief Justice Stone, speaking for four Members of an eight-Member Court in rejecting the proposition that Congress could impose taxes on the States so long as it did so in a nondiscriminatory manner, observed:

> *"A State may, like a private individual, own real property and receive income. But in view of our former decisions we could hardly say that a general nondiscriminatory real estate tax (apportioned), or an income tax laid upon citizens and States alike could be constitutionally applied to the State's capitol, its State-house, its public school houses, public parks, or its revenues from taxes or school lands, even though all real property and all income of the citizen is taxed." 326 U.S., at 587-582.*

The expressions in these more recent cases trace back to earlier decisions of this Court recognizing the essential role of the States in our federal system of government. Chief Justice Chase, perhaps because of the particular time at which he occupied that office, had occasion more than once to speak for the Court on this point. In *Texas* v. *White,* 7 Wall. 700, 725 (1869), he declared that "[t]he Constitution, in all its provisions, looks to an indestructible Union, composed of indestructible States." In *Lane County* v. *Oregon,* 7 Wall. 71 (1869), his opinion for the Court said:

> *"Both the States and the United States existed before the Constitution. The people, through that instrument, established a more perfect union by*

substituting a national government, acting, with ample power, directly upon the citizens, instead of the Confederate government which acted with powers, greatly restricted, only upon the States. But in many Articles of the Constitution the necessary existence of the States, and, within their proper spheres, the independent authority of the States, is distinctly recognized." Id., at 76.

In *Metcalf & Eddy* v. *Mitchell,* 269 U.S. 514 (1926), the Court likewise observed that "neither government may destroy the other nor curtail in any substantial manner the exercise of its powers." *Id.,* at 523.

Appellee Secretary argues that the cases in which this Court has upheld sweeping exercises of authority by Congress, even though those exercises pre-empted state regulation of the private sector, have already curtailed the sovereignty of the States quite as much as the 1974 amendments to the Fair Labor Standards Act. We do not agree. It is one thing to recognize the authority of Congress to enact laws regulating individual businesses necessarily subject to the dual sovereignty of the government of the Nation and of the State in which they reside. It is quite another to uphold a similar exercise of congressional authority directed not to private citizens, but to the States as States. We have repeatedly recognized that there are attributes of sovereignty attaching to every state government which may not be impaired by Congress, not because Congress may lack an affirmative grant of legislative authority to reach the matter, but because the Constitution prohibits it from exercising the authority in that manner. In *Coyle* v. *Smith,* 221 U.S. 559 (1911), the Court gave this example of such an attribute:

"The power to locate its own seat of government and to determine when and how it shall be changed from one place to another, and to appropriate its own public funds for that purpose, are essentially and peculiarly state powers. That one of the original thirteen States could now be shorn of such powers by an Act of Congress would not be for a moment entertained." 221 U.S., at 565.

The Costs of Compliance

One undoubted attribute of state sovereignty is the States' power to determine the wages which shall be paid to those whom they employ in order to carry out their governmental functions, what hours those persons will work, and what compensation will be provided where these employees may be called upon to work overtime. The question we must resolve in this case, then, is whether these determinations are "functions essential to separate and independent existence," *Coyle* v. *Smith, supra,* at 580, quoting from *Lane County* v. *Oregon, supra,* at 76, so that Congress may not abrogate the States' otherwise plenary authority to make them.

In their complaint appellants advanced estimates of substantial costs which will be imposed upon them by the 1974 amendments. Since the District Court dismissed their complaint, we take its well-pleaded allegations as true, although it appears from appellee's submissions in the District Court and in this Court that resolution of the factual disputes as to the effect of the amendments is not critical to our disposition of the case.

Judged solely in terms of increased costs in dollars, these allegations show a significant impact on the functioning of the governmental bodies involved. The Metropolitan Government of Nashville and Davidson County, Tenn., for example, asserted that the Act will increase its costs of providing essential police and fire protection, without any increase in service or in current salary levels, by $938,000 per year. Cape Girardeau, Mo., estimated that its annual budget for fire protection may have to be increased by anywhere from $250,000 to $400,000 over the current figure of $350,000. The State of Arizona alleged that the annual additional expenditures which will be required if it is to continue to provide essential state services may total $2 1/2 million dollars. The State of California, which must devote significant portions of its budget to fire suppression endeavors, estimated that application of the Act to its employment practices will necessitate an increase in its budget of between $8 million and $16 million.

Increased costs are not, of course, the only adverse effects which compliance with the Act will visit upon state and local governments, and in turn upon the citizens who depend upon those governments. In its complaint in intervention, for example, California asserted that it could not comply with the overtime costs (approximately $750,000 per year) which the Act required to be paid to California Highway Patrol cadets during their academy training program. California reported that it had thus been forced to reduce its academy training program from 2,080 hours to only 960 hours, a compromise undoubtedly of substantial importance to those whose safety and welfare may depend upon the preparedness of the California Highway Patrol.

This type of forced relinquishment of important governmental activities is further reflected in the complaint's allegation that the City of Inglewood, California, has been forced to curtail its affirmative action program for providing employment opportunities for men and women interested in a career in law enforcement. The Inglewood police department has abolished a program for police trainees who split their week between on the job training and the classroom. The city could not abrogate its contractual obligations to these trainees, and it concluded that compliance with the Act in these circumstances was too financially burdensome to permit continuance of the classroom program. The city of Clovis, Cal., has been put to a similar choice regarding an internship program it was running in cooperation with a California State University. According to the complaint, because the interns' compensation brings them within the purview of the Act the city must decide whether to eliminate the program entirely or to substantially reduce its beneficial aspects by doing away with any pay for the interns.

Limits on Policy Making

Quite apart from the substantial costs imposed upon the States and their political subdivisions, the Act displaces state policies regarding the manner in which they will structure delivery of those governmental services which their citizens require. The Act, speaking directly to the States *qua* States, requires that they shall pay all but an extremely limited minority of their employees the minimum wage rates currently chosen by Congress. It may well be that as a matter of economic policy it would be desirable that States, just as private employers, comply with these minimum wage requirements. But it cannot be gainsaid that the federal requirement directly supplants the considered policy choices of the States' elected officials and administrators as to how they wish to structure pay scales in state employment. The State might wish to employ persons with little or not training, or those who wish to work on a casual basis, or those who for some other reason do not possess minimum employment requirements, and pay them less than the federally prescribed minimum wage. It may wish to offer part time or summer employment to teenagers at a figure less than the minimum wage, and if unable to do so may decline to offer such employment at all. But the Act would forbid such choices by the States. The only "discretion" left to them under the Act is either to attempt to increase their revenue to meet the additional financial burden imposed upon them by paying congressionally prescribed wages to their existing complement of employees, or to reduce that complement to a number which can be paid the federal minimum wage without increasing revenue.

This dilemma presented by the minimum wage restrictions may seem not immediately different from that faced by private employers, who have long been covered by the Act and who must find ways to increase their gross income if they are to pay higher wages while maintaining current earnings. The difference, however, is that a State is not merely a factor in the "shifting economic arrangements" of the private sector of the economy, *Kovacs v. Cooper,* 336 U.S. 77, 95 (1949) (Frankfurter, J., concurring), but is itself a coordinate element in the system established by the framers for governing our federal union.

The degree to which the FLSA amendments would interfere with traditional aspects of state sovereignty can be seen even more clearly upon examining the overtime requirements of the Act. The general effect of these provisions is to require the States to pay their employees at premium rates whenever their work exceeds a specified number of hours in a given period. The asserted reason for these provisions is to provide a financial disincentive upon using employees beyond the work period deemed appropriate by Congress. According to appellee,

> "[t]his premium rate can be avoided if the [State] uses other employees to do the overtime work. This, in effect, tends to discourage overtime work and to spread employment, which is the result Congress intended." Appellee's Brief, at 43.

We do not doubt that this may be a salutary result, and that it has a sufficiently rational relationship to commerce to validate the application of the overtime provisions to private employers. But, like the minimum wage provisions, the vice of the Act as sought to be applied here is that it directly penalizes the States for choosing to hire governmental employees on terms different from those which Congress has sought to impose.

This congressionally imposed displacement of state decisions may substantially restructure traditional ways in which the local governments have arranged their affairs. Although at this point many of the actual effects under the proposed Amendments remain a matter of some dispute among the parties, enough can be satisfactorily anticipated for an outline discussion of their general import. The requirement imposing premium rates upon any employment in excess of what Congress has decided is appropriate for a governmental employee's workweek, for example, appears likely to have the effect of coercing the States to structure work periods in some employment areas, such as police and fire protection, in a manner substantially different from practices which have long been commonly accepted among local governments of this Nation. . . .

Our examination of the effect of the 1974 amendments, as sought to be extended to the States and their political subdivisions, satisfies us that both the minimum wage and the maximum hour provisions will impermissibly interfere with the integral governmental functions of these bodies. We earlier noted some disagreement between the parties regarding the precise effect the amendments will have in application. We do not believe particularized assessments of actual impact are crucial to resolution of the issue presented, however. For even if we accept appellee's assessments concerning the impact of the amendments, their application will nonetheless significantly alter or displace the States' abilities to structure employer-employee relationships in such areas as fire prevention, police protection, sanitation, public health, and parks and recreation. These activities are typical of those performed by state and local governments in discharging their dual functions of administering the public law and furnishing public services. Indeed, it is functions such as these which governments are created to provide, services such as these which the States have traditionally afforded their citizens. If Congress may withdraw from the States the authority to make those fundamental employment decisions upon which their systems for performance of these functions must rest, we think there would be little left of the States' "separate and independent existence." *Coyle, supra.* Thus, even if appellants may have overestimated the effect which the Act will have upon their current levels and patterns of governmental activity, the dispositive factor is that Congress has attempted to exercise its Commerce Clause authority to prescribe minimum wages and maximum hours to be paid by the States in their capacities as sovereign governments. In so doing, Congress has sought to wield its power in a fashion that would impair the States' "ability to function effectively within a federal system," *Fry, supra,* at 547. This exercise of congressional authority does not comport with the federal system of government embodied in the Constitution. We hold that insofar as the challenged amendments operate to directly displace the States' freedom to structure integral operations in areas of traditional governmental functions, they are not within the authority granted Congress by Art. I, Sec. 8, cl. 3. . . .

7
CETA: Successful Job Program or Subsidy for Local Government?

Harrison H. Donnelly

Many members of Congress worry that a program originally intended to help the hard-core unemployed has become something very different—a new form of federal revenue sharing.

The issue will be an important one as Congress works on a reauthorization of the 1973 Comprehensive Employment and Training Act (CETA). The Carter administration is seeking a four-year extension of the act, which otherwise would expire Sept. 30.

CETA programs provide on-the-job and classroom training to the unskilled, operate Job Corps and summer job programs for disadvantaged youths, and put the unemployed to work in public service jobs.

Under the public service employment system, state and local governments get federal money to hire the unemployed to perform new services to the community. First created as a small-scale effort directed towards the severely disadvantaged, it was expanded during the 1974-75 recession to fight unemployment on a broad basis.

The problem is that many cities and counties are not using the money to hire additional workers. Instead they are paying for old jobs previously funded by local taxes. Known as "substitution," this tactic improves local fiscal standing, but gives little help to the millions of unemployed.

Moreover, many governments apparently are becoming "hooked" on CETA money. Some cities have a quarter or more of their employees on the CETA payroll; the ratio is even higher for many county governments. This suggests that in practice CETA has become a disguised form of federal subsidy for local government operations.

Some studies of public service employment have estimated that CETA money pays for four old jobs for every new one created. At that rate the cost of true job creation rises to astronomical levels.

Supporters of the program have been encouraged by release of a recent Brookings Institution study which found the levels of substitution to be much lower than previously estimated. These results were based in part on the idea that communities with fiscal problems would have had to lay off workers in essential positions without CETA help. If CETA was paying for a job that would not otherwise have been available, the argument goes, then the effect was the same as the creation of a new job.

Reprinted with permission from *Congressional Quarterly Weekly Report*, April 1, 1978, pp. 799-806.

Harrison H. Donnelly is a reporter for the *Congressional Quarterly*

Critics also charge that CETA has failed to serve the right people with the right kind of help. Set up to assist persons whose employment future was hurt by educational deprivation and racial and sexual discrimination, its participants are mostly white, male and educated. Meant to help people in the long run get permanent, unsubsidized jobs, it places only a fraction of its participants in regular positions.

In addition, the program has been buffeted by repeated charges of misuse of funds. Since its workers are hired outside of normal government hiring procedures, CETA is a tempting plum for local politicians who want to expand their patronage powers. In some areas investigators have found that political associates and relatives of politicians have been hired for programs meant for the needy. In other areas CETA workers have been found to be doing work for political parties or officeholders. . . .

Background

CETA developed out of the vast array of job and training programs spawned by Democratic "Great Society" legislation in the 1960s. It featured both centralization of the programs, concentrating overall supervision in the Labor Department, and decentralization, giving control of implementation to local governments.

Recent federal efforts to fight unemployment through job training began in 1962 with passage of the Manpower Development and Training Act (MDTA). Originally intended to provide retraining to workers who lost their jobs to automation, it was soon modified when it became clear that young workers with no training at all needed help much more than workers with outmoded skills.

The continuation of high minority unemployment rates during the boom periods of the 1960s led to further emphasis on training for groups with special employment problems. The Economic Opportunity Act of 1964 established the Job Corps, which provided training to disadvantaged youth in residential centers, and the Neighborhood Youth Corps, which helped high school dropouts and poor youths needing part-time or summer jobs to stay in school.

Another program sponsored by the Johnson administration, Job Opportunities in the Business Sector (JOBS), worked through the National Alliance of Businessmen to encourage employers to hire the disadvantaged. Funds were provided to help employers bear the additional training costs of hiring unskilled workers.

Studies of these and other employment programs showed that they had a substantial effect on participants' subsequent economic performance, though their effect on overall unemployment was limited. Participants in institutional and on-the-job programs increased their earnings on the average between $1,000 and $2,000 a year. The JOBS program was successful beyond initial expectations, with many employers forgoing available government assistance of hiring.

But the programs were difficult to administer, scattered as they were through various government offices. Agencies were forced to make separate contracts with thousands of training centers, making oversight difficult.

Nixon Approach

The Nixon administration preferred a different approach. In concert with his plans for revenue sharing, Nixon proposed that manpower funds be given directly to local governments to run their own programs.

Until enactment of CETA in 1973, Nixon and Congress engaged in a running battle over another aspect of manpower policy, public service jobs. Since the mid-1960s congressional liberals had pushed for public service jobs to put the unemployed to work. In 1970 Nixon vetoed a manpower bill providing $2.5 billion for public service employment, saying "WPA-type jobs are not the answer." But in 1971 he did consent to the Emergency Employment Act, authorizing $2.25 billion for public service jobs.

Passage of CETA in 1973 was a compromise between Nixon, who wanted to turn administration of manpower programs over to localities, and the Democratic majority in Congress, which wanted public service jobs.

Title I of the act consolidated most of the various manpower programs into a single system of block grants to local governments. Funds were provided by formula to city, county or state "prime sponsors."

Public Service Jobs

Title II established a limited program of public service jobs. It addressed problems of "structural" unemployment by providing jobs for those with long-term employment difficulties. Only persons unemployed for more than a month were allowed to participate. Assistance was provided by formula to areas with unemployment of more than 6.5 percent.

As the recession deepened in the mid-1970s, congressional leaders saw in CETA a vehicle for fighting increasing unemployment. In 1974 Congress added a new Title VI to CETA, authorizing $2.5 billion for public service jobs, allocated on the basis of unemployment rates. But in contrast to the structural emphasis of Title II, Title VI was a "countercyclical" measure attacking unemployment caused by recession.

In 1976 Congress extended and expanded the Ttile VI public service employment program. In addition to increasing the numbers of positions available, the extension bill contained provisions designed to limit substitution and focus programs on the poor. It required that new positions be used in community projects that could be finished within a year, and be limited to persons unemployed for more than 15 weeks who had low incomes.

In 1977 a new CETA Title VIII, designed to aid disadvantaged youth, was added. Title VIII established a Young Adult Conservation Corps and funded various experimental projects.

Also in 1977, Congress passed a simple one-year extension of CETA, authorizing the program through the end of fiscal 1978. The Carter administration requested a short-term extension in order to gain time to thoroughly study the program and propose substantive changes, as it did in 1978.

CETA in Action

The backbone of the CETA system are some 450 "prime sponsors" who administer employment and training programs in their areas. Cities and counties with populations over 100,000, or groups of smaller units, can qualify as prime sponsors. State governments handle the areas not covered by local prime sponsors.

Under Title I of CETA, prime sponsors in fiscal 1977 provided job training to 1,415,000 persons. Programs include classroom training, on-the-job experience, and some public service employment. Prime sponsors may contract with community groups to operate services.

Public service employment under Titles II and VI reached early in 1978 the goal of 725,000 jobs set by the Carter economic stimulus plan; the total was 753,000 by the first week of March. Jobs funded range from police and firefighting positions to park workers and arts instructors.

As originally conceived, Title II was to provide structural public service employment—for those with long-term employment problems, while Title VI was to concentrate on those out of work because of an economic downturn. But in practice the distinction between the two programs has been blurred. Shifting eligibility requirements and prime sponsor reluctance to divide up their employment programs into separate parts has made the distinction difficult to enforce. "Prime sponsors have not heavily weighted the distinction," according to Jon Weintraub, associate director of the National Association of Counties. Statistics show that the two titles serve substantially similar target groups.

One distinction that is applied divides public service jobs into sustainment and project positions. The 1976 CETA expansion required that new Title VI funds go first to sustain the level of public service jobs already in operation. The remaining funds were to be used in projects, defined as related undertakings which could be completed within one year and would not otherwise have been started.

Impact on Cities

Whatever the type of jobs, public service funds have become a vital factor in county and municipal finance. In Buffalo, N.Y., for example, CETA workers account for 32.8 percent of the city government work force, while in Hartford, Conn., they make up 25.8 percent.

Those statistics are disturbing to regular government employees. Municipal workers feel threatened by CETA workers, according to Nanine Meiklejohn of the American Federation of State, County and Municipal Employees, because they are hired outside of normal procedures designed to protect permanent workers. Regular workers dislike the creation of special job titles for CETA workers, who are paid less than regular workers, and fear in general that the program will result in a "gradual replacement of workers and a lowering of labor standards," she said.

Substitution

In addition to providing jobs for those out of work, public service employment offers to local governments the possibility of a substantial reduction in labor costs. If the federal government is willing to pay CETA workers to do jobs that the local government would otherwise have had to pay for, then the city or county will be able to use the savings to provide other services or cut taxes.

The CETA funds can either create new jobs, or pay for old ones. But the line between created and substituted jobs is very difficult to draw. The existence of fiscal problems in many local governments blurs the distinction. For governments that for budgetary reasons have had to lay off permanent, essential workers such as police and firefighters may be reluctant to use CETA funds to pay for dance instructors.

One type of job creation, then, occurs when a local government uses CETA funds to fill a position that would have been vacant because of lack of local money. These jobs are considered created jobs because they would not have been available without CETA. Other types of job creation occur when a government begins new programs, or expands old ones, or undertakes a special project that can be completed within a year.

An obvious case of substitution occurs when a government lays off employees and then rehires them, after the minimum period of unemployment, back to their old jobs with CETA funds. Solvent governments that allow the permanent work force to decline through attrition, while hiring CETA workers to fill vacancies, are also substituting. Another type of substitution occurs when governments use CETA workers to perform tasks traditionally contracted out.

Although CETA prohibits substitution, most observers agree that some substitution is taking place. But estimates of its exact extent vary tremendously.

The first studies of substitution showed very high rates, particularly in the Public Employment Program of 1971. Estimates of substitution ranged from 39 to 90 percent. A 1977 Congressional Budget Office study found that substitution reached 100 percent after two years.

A recent study, however, argues that these estimates are questionable because of the inherent limitations of the "econometric" methodology on which they are based. An analysis of past substitution studies, written by Michael Borus and Daniel Hamermesh for the National Commission for Manpower Policy, found that estimates of the same situation could be vastly different depending on the statistical assumptions on which they were based. "We can't be sure of what really is going on," observed one congressional analyst.

Brookings Study

Another study for the Manpower Commission, conducted by the Brookings Institution, used an entirely different method and came to strikingly different results. Instead of working from a mathematical model, Brookings researchers contacted a network of academics in selected areas around the country. These analysts examined public service programs in their own areas. They interviewed officials, looked at data on employment and the fiscal state of the area governments, and made independent estimates on the extent of substitution.

The Brookings study found that substitution accounted for 20 percent of all public service positions. Sustainment positions were found to be 21 percent substituted, while the newer project approach had a rate of 8 percent. Contrary to past assumptions, the study found that substitution positions did not go only to experienced workers; minority and disadvantaged participation rates were about the same as in other public service jobs.

One reason that the substitution rate was low was that the researchers found a high level (31 percent) of program maintenance, in which CETA funds were used to continue positions that otherwise would have been discontinued for fiscal reasons. Thus the low rate of substitution rested in part on the individual perceptions of researchers that the prime sponsors were in difficult financial situations. Taken together the results show that jobs formerly paid for by local government accounted for about half of all public service jobs.

'Red Herring'?

Whatever its exact extent, substitution raises serious questions as to the efficacy of public service employment. Sen. Gaylord Nelson, D-Wis., chairman of the Human Resources Employment Subcommittee, said that substitution even at the lowest estimates still involves "a very substantial amount in dollar terms." Sen. John H. Chafee, R-R.I., raised the common complaint that "CETA has become in effect a revenue sharing for the communities—even in the school systems CETA is carrying a tremendous load."

Critics of the program argue that the existence of substantial substitution raises the costs of new job creation to unacceptable levels. For example, at an 80 percent substitution rate the government would have to pay for five jobs in order to create one new one. Rep. Bill Frenzel, R-Minn., ruefully observed that this would mean that each new job would cost more than the salaries of members of Congress.

But others contend that substitution is infrequent and probably not so bad after all. Greg Wurzburg, executive director of the National Council on Employment Policy, called substitution "a red herring—a nonissue," peripheral to the real problems of municipal finance. Weintraub questioned "whether substitution is that dirty a word," because the eligibility requirement for CETA workers has had "very positive effects on affirmative action needs" of local governments. Substitution also can have local stimulative effects if CETA funds permit governments to cut taxes.

Ernest Green, head of the Labor Department's Employment and Training Administration (ETA), testified Feb. 23 that the administration had already stepped up its monitoring of substitution violations, leading to the recovery of $1.4 million from prime sponsor violators. To supplement this the administration bill provides for limits on salaries and lengths of time worked. Public Service employee salaries would be held below $10,000, with the recommended average wage set at $7,800. Prime sponsors would be prohibited from supplementing salaries by more than 10 percent of all public service funds received. Participants could stay in the program only up to 18 months.

Green argued that the effect of the limits would be to make "[CETA] jobs inappropriate for permanent substitution." But critics predicted that the measures would hurt participants without checking the practice. A spokesman for the Conference of Mayors said that the proposals were "totally inappropriate. The net effect impacts on workers—they're the ones that pay the price." A $10,000 limit could pose problems in some high-priced cities, where even entry-level workers often get more.

Targeting

A frequent criticism of CETA programs is that they fail to target on those who need assistance most—the economically disadvantaged and long-term unemployed. "We're not coping with the hard core," observed Sen. Thomas F. Eagleton, D-Mo. Instead of being made up mostly of the disadvantaged, argued Rep. Barber B. Conable Jr., R-N.Y., "the characteristics of CETA workers show that they are the most skilled of the unemployed."

The figures on CETA participation tend to back up Conable. Workers in public service programs are largely white, male and high school graduates. Only 15 percent come from welfare families. Critics contend that the figures show a persistent tendency by prime sponsors to "cream" the labor market—skim off the most skilled of the unemployed.

The struggle over the means for distributing CETA funds arises from the high difference between the scope of the programs and the number of people conceivably eligible. Eli Ginzberg, chairman of the National Commission for Manpower Policy, estimated that as many as 22 million people could be eligible for CETA assistance—a "colossal discrepancy" with the number that could be served. "We're holding this program out to 22 million people," observed Sen. Donald W. Riegle Jr., D-Mich., "but we can only reach a minor fraction of those in need."

CETA assistance can basically be distributed in three ways—to individuals who meet income and unemployment standards, to areas on the basis of unemployment and economic hardship rates, or to special groups that Congress is especially interested in helping.

Focus on Individuals

Current individual eligibility standards are confusing and contradictory, making program coordination by prime sponsors difficult. Applicants for Title II jobs, which were originally intended for the economically disadvantaged, have no income limit—they have only to have been unemployed for 30 days. But the largest part of Title VI, meant to help those laid off by temporary changes in the economy, is now limited to persons unemployed for more than 15 weeks, with a family income below 70 percent of the lower living standard—the poor. Other programs have different criteria. This proliferation of eligibility standards, argue prime sponsors, creates administrative headaches and makes it difficult to transfer participants to appropriate programs.

The administration bill would limit participation to the economically disadvantaged—defined as those below 70 percent of the lower living standard—who had been unemployed for five or more weeks.

Prime sponsors argue that the emphasis on tightened eligibility standards reflects a suspicion that, given the chance, prime sponsors will ignore the needs of the poor—a charge they feel is not borne out by the facts. Too tight standards will also exacerbate social tensions and "stigmatize" CETA workers, Wurzburg said. Opening CETA jobs only to the poorest would amount to creating "a separate kind of job for a separate kind of people," he said, further causing "too much isolation from the mainstream of the labor market."

Focus on Areas

Another way to distribute funds is to areas on the basis of local unemployment or poverty rates. Under existing law, Title I training funds are distributed to prime sponsors according to the following formula: 50 percent on the basis of the previous year's allotment, 37.5 percent on unemployment rates, and 12.5 percent on the number of poor families. Title II funds are allotted only to areas that had unemployment rates of 6.5 percent for more than three months. Half of the Ttiel VI funds available to prime sponsors are allotted on the basis of unemployment rates in all areas; one quarter is reserved for areas with more than 6.5 percent unemployment; the remainder is distributed on the basis of the number of unemployed in areas with over 4.5 percent unemployment.

The administration bill did not propose to change the allocation formulas. Administration representatives said that the uncertain nature of the recent changes in methods for determining local area unemployment rates made alteration of formulas problematic. But they left open the possibility of new formulas once the impact of the methodological changes could be evaluated.

Representatives of areas hard hit by unemployment argue that changes in allocation formulas are needed to give extra help to the areas that face the greatest problems. Sen. Jacob K. Javits, R-N.Y., who had introduced legislation to change the formulas, said that changes were essential to help older cities facing chronic unemployment caused by an exodus of jobs to the "sunbelt" regions. His bill would give greater weight in the formulas to the relative severity of unemployment and poverty. diverting more funds to areas with the worst structural employment problems. Supporters of giving more weight to poverty in allocating training funds say that the change would concentrate assistance in areas with long-term problems, rather than on areas with cyclical unemployment, where workers might not need more training.

Focus on Groups

Finally, special consideration can be given to selected groups within the eligible population. Current Labor Department regulations require prime sponsors to give special consideration to veterans, welfare recipients, former manpower trainees and teachers.

But many prime sponsors dislike the imposition of special consideration. One city representative pointed out that there were hundreds of different population sub-groups that could be selected, in disregard to local conditions. "Prime sponsors don't want to be dictated to," he said. Joan Wills, director of employment programs for the National Governors' Conference, disputed the idea that special quotas help the groups that seek them. "They're such a sham for the people who need the services the most," she said, since "there's just not enough to go around" for every group that could push for special consideration.

Transition

Critics of CETA worry that the employment and training programs are failing to meet the stated ultimate goal—preparing people to take unsubsidized, permanent jobs. If participants fail to make the transition to regular jobs, it is questionable how much benefit they have obtained from a temporary, stopgap solution to their long-term problems.

Green conceded that "the current CETA program is not yet successful enough in moving workers from unsubsidized employment to the private sector." Labor Department statistics show that 39 percent of participants in Title I training programs transfer to unsubsidized jobs; 17.7 percent of Title II and 34.0 percent of Title VI public service employees make the transition. Labor Department regulations set a goal, but not a requirement, of 50 percent annual transition.

Problems

One problem with achieving high rates of transition is that it sometimes works in opposition to other desirable goals of the program. One Brookings analyst said that "it appears to me that attempts to maximize the transition rates are frequently in conflict with other goals of the program, such as minimizing displacement and reaching social targeting objectives." An urban spokesman observed that "the more placement standards you have the more creaming you get," since prime sponsors trying to meet high transition goals were likely to "recruit the folks that are more apt to find jobs."

Other reasons for the low transition rates were general economic conditions and the way the program was operated. CETA was just getting off the ground when the 1974-75 recession struck. Employers who were forced to lay off old employees were not likely to go to prime sponsors seeking new people to hire. "Anytime you have an employers' market," said Wills, "why shouldn't the employer take the better qualified?" Furthermore, critics contend, public service jobs provide very little training to make participants more employable.

Prime sponsors and others say that many of the transition problems stem from the confusing and irritating bureaucratic aspects of the program. Private employers participating in programs must fulfill substantial record-keeping requirements—"there are too many administrative headaches and too much red tape" for the private sector to want to get involved, Wurzburg said.

Public Sector Jobs

Prime sponsors have been most successful in transferring CETA participants to permanent jobs in the public sector. This makes some people worry that training and public service programs will end up preparing workers only for the limited public sector. Chafee said that "the problem I have is that these CETA jobs are the ones that have a very limited private sector outside requirement." He cited the example of a fireman hired under CETA—"after 18 months, that person's marketability is very limited" in the private sector. ...

Chapter Four

Labor, Management, and Personnel Policy

Introduction

No personnel topic generates more fervor in current meetings of government practitioners than the increase in numbers and militancy of organized employees. A growth industry of public sector collective bargaining specialists, consultants and instructors, is with us. Scores of publications depict dire consequences ranging from higher taxes to creeping fascism as the numbers of organized employees multiply and the incidence of militant activities increase.

And the change in the numbers and activities of organized employees has indeed been significant. The American Federation of State, County and Municipal Employees reports that its membership more than doubled from 1960 to 1977. There were more than twenty times the number of strikes and work stoppages in government in 1975 than fifteen years earlier. Over three million days were idled due to labor activities in governments in 1975 compared with less than 200,000 in 1967.

Changes of such magnitude significantly affect the process of management. Unionization and collective bargaining may mean that new interests are added to the decisionmaking process, disturbing the balance of power and resources and demanding different skills and resource allocations from management. Wage and salary determination requires negotiators and arbitrators, and employers and employees need to be trained in techniques of labor management. State and federal labor law and court rulings have become a more relevant component of governmental actions at all levels.

Union influence in policy seems to turn the political system upside down. In a democracy elected officials are supposed to direct appointed employees. The proposed influence of unions on policymaking seems to imply the opposite. Some therefore find the influence of organized employees fundamentally undemocratic and therefore an unmitigated evil.

This introduction and the accompanying selections in this chapter examine the current state of knowledge of employer-employee relations in government.

The arguments advocating stern measures to control employee organization are assessed in light of empirically based analyses and cases of the process and outcomes of collective negotiations.

Need We Fear Unions?

Some of those who have looked at union-management relations in government have assumed that employee unionization presents management with a fundamental problem. They have argued that employee unions are a new, well organized actor, added to a system of representative interests. The consequence is a change in the balance of power leading to unrestrained union influence in public policy. Wellington and Winter, (Selection 8) make this point in an articulate manner. Transplanting collective bargaining to the public sector would, they believe, ". . . institutionalize the power of public employee unions in a way that would leave competing groups in the political process at a permanent and substantial disadvantage."[1] Their argument should be studied closely because it lucidly represents an important viewpoint echoed or amplified by others. Their inferences are also supported in their book from which Selection 8 is taken by court cases, numerous statements of public managers, and their own experience as law professors.

Horton, Lewin, and Kuhn (Selection 9) challenge some of the arguments made by Wellington and Winter. They contend that the impact of public employee organizations depends upon different environmental conditions and will vary from city to city or state to state. It is therefore difficult to determine the overall impact of collective bargaining.

What influence have organized employees really had on wages, disruptive activities, and changes in policy? The presence and absence of unions and organizations in different settings permit analysts to account for the impact of employee organizations. Both quantitative and qualitative methods of research have been used in various settings and with many different kinds of employees. Although the variety of techniques and samples prevents definitive generalizations, a summary of these studies does reveal similar findings.[2] Very little impact on salaries, working conditions, or decisionmaking can be attributed to unionization or collective bargaining.

Powers of Management

Assuming the validity of these studies, an explanation of the effects of collective bargaining on the public sector policy different from the arguments of Wellington and Winter is required. If unionization does not affect policy drastically, either management has more significant resources of support than previous analyses have recognized or the potential power of organized employees has been greatly exaggerated.

A number of conditions can be cited as potential aids to management in its desire to curb the influence of organized employees. One is led to look initially at the public itself which, in many cities, has reacted to unions in a very hostile way. Recent referenda in San Francisco, for instance, ratified a roll-back of employee salaries and approved several anti-union measures including a required public vote in the case of negotiation impasse. Voters in both San Diego and San Francisco recently approved propositions calling for the automatic firing of illegally striking workers.[3]

These and other direct examples of the public acting to control the influence of unions may be responses to specific abuses, or they may reflect a general hostility to public employee organizations. In general, the public's support of the labor movement in the private sector has been high only on the principal of trade unionism. Specific labor-supported positions in the private sector such as the advocacy of the closed shop, the right to strike, and opposition to compulsory arbitration have been opposed by the majority of the public.[4] Thus it is reasonable to assume that in many jurisdictions the public is a potential ally of management in its desire to prevent or control union excesses. Recent efforts to open up the bargaining process to the public, and the increased use of the referendum to finalize collective bargaining agreements therefore may be an effective device to control union influence.

It is also likely that among city councils, mayors, and city managers, a management perspective is common. A survey of city managers' attitudes toward organized employees revealed that a vast majority of managers tend to be hostile to unionization.[5] The background and socialization of city managers would also suggest a conservative position in labor-management matters.[6] The prevalence of at-large elections, part-time city council members, and nonpartisanship, all of which coincide with the council-manager plan, may also act to lessen the influence of union concerns on city policymaking. Recruitment to such city councils emphasizes the upper class.[7] As population continues to grow in the West and South and in suburbs, and decline in the Northeast and in central cities, more and more people will be ruled by cities with the "reformed" governmental structure. The rise of more conservative mayors in cities such as Philadelphia and the effects of the fiscal crisis in New York City and Cleveland suggest that policy in mayor-council cities may also be contrary to the short-run concerns of organized employees.

Lastly, rulings of the Supreme Court have provided management with significant support in its efforts to control the influence of unionization. The most significant of such rulings, the Usery case (Selection 6 in Chapter Three), where the court struck down amendments to the Fair Labor Standards Act that extended minimum wage coverage to state and local governments.

Problems of Government Unions

In 1977 unions of government employees in San Francisco called a strike to prevent the rolling back of the wages of skilled workers. By and large, the effort was a failure, because many of the unskilled members saw no reason to support the efforts of their better paid colleagues. Union solidarity among American workers has always been more of a goal than a reality, and this seems to be particularly true among government employees who are divided into numerous occupations, and often work in different locations. Those who fear union power have tended to exaggerate the extent of union solidarity.

Likewise, union goals may have been overstated by some of the critics.

Stanley, for one, notes that union power has generally been restrained because of a lack of desire on the union's part to alter the traditional management-labor relationship. "Constitutions, charters, laws, and political traditions require that governments be run by officials chosen by citizens should be responsible for results. Unions recognize this. They need an adversary—"someone to make demands of, to criticize, to push against."[8]

In summary, the environment of the governmental political process surrounding collective bargaining contains many potential sources of support for management. The immediate environment of most governments contains interests that are hostile to the efforts of organized employees. Legislators and administrators are more likely to be sympathetic to a management perspective. The public can be a potential ally of management if it is mobilized. The courts have adopted a stance favorable to management and undoubtedly its rulings give support to those who wish to limit the power of employee organizations. Only where the union's political influence is unusually strong, as may have been the case in pre-1973 New York City, should one expect significant power of organized employees to be present.

Living with Organized Employees

Regardless of who gains or loses, the influence of organized employees in government has changed the game. Wage and salary decisions require new procedures. State laws and court rulings have become an integral part of personnel decisions. Lobbying and electoral activity by both labor and management are now facts of life in many cities and states. The final two selections are case studies of labor-management policymaking under different kinds of collective bargaining statutes.

Greer (Selection 10) demonstrates the interaction between the state collective bargaining law in Oklahoma and strike activity. He concludes that the adequacy of legislation and its administration contribute significantly to the kinds of organized activities that followed. He implies that inclusive laws and fair administration may provide solutions which are acceptable to both parties.

The diversity of public labor law is demonstrated by Helburg and Barnum (Selection 11) who analyze Texas cities, where law requires local referenda before granting collective bargaining rights for police and fire employees. Their analysis casts doubt on the wisdom of this method.

The changes in the policymaking process brought on by organized employees coincide with other changes in the American political system. Employees have often had influence in the making of public policy. Crouch, for instance, argues that the efforts of organized employees are a consequence of the search for access to the political process that is characteristic of all successful interest groups. Employees were an important component of state and local political machines. When progressive reforms destroyed the machines, employees exerted influence through involvement in electoral politics, lobbying and referenda.[9] The militancy of the 1960s and 1970s, then, may be a consequence of the increased legitimacy of direct confrontation. With the added importance of state and national legislative and judicial actions, employee organizations have attempted to exert influence in these arenas. When the methods of influence and points of access change, one can expect alterations in personnel policies. Thus, the kinds of conflicts in labor-management relations will change as different facets of the political system affect personnel policy. Today, therefore, labor, management, and the public need to be alert to the ever-changing arenas of public policy.

Employer-employee relations are, at best, an unstable truce. Those who suggest that efforts on both sides can lead to lasting harmony ignore the fundamental economic issues that divide the "haves" from the "have-nots" in American society. One can hope, however, that a more detailed understanding of the aims, goals and methods of both parties, and more regularized and legitimate methods of conference will lead to a more stable relationship.

Notes

1. Harry H. Wellington and Ralph K. Winter, Jr., *The Unions and the Cities* (Washington, D.C.: The Brookings Institution, 1961), p. 30. Reprinted in Selection 9 of this book.

2. These studies are summarized in Alan Saltzstein, "Organized Public Employees and Political Power," paper presented at the American Society for Public Administration Convention, 1977. Examples of these works are: Donald E. Frey, "Wage Determination in Public Schools and the Effects on Urbanization" in Daniel Hamermesh, ed., *Labor in the Public and Nonprofit Sectors,* (Princeton, N.J.: Princeton University Press, 1975), Hervey Juris and Peter Feuille, *Police Unionism,* (Boston: Heath, 1973), and David T. Stanley *Managing Government Under Union Pressure,* (Washington, D.C.: Brookings, 1972). A lucid summary of ths literature with several examples is found in chapter six of *Public Sector Labor Relations: Analysis and Readings* by David Lewin, Peter Feuille, and Thomas A. Kochan (Glen Ridge, N.J.: Thomas Horton and Daughters, 1976).

3. See Daryl L. Simbke, "How Labor Lost the San Francisco Strike," *California Journal,* (July, 1978) and James W. Singer, "Public Employee Unionism Groping for Light in 'Season of Darkness'"*National Journal,* July 24, 1976.

4. Rita James Simon, *Public Opinion in America: 1936-1970* (Chicago: Markham, 1970), pp. 21-22.

5. Alan Saltzstein, "Can Urban Management Control the Organized Employee?" *Public Personnel Management,* July-Aug. 1974.

6. Lloyd M. Wells, "Social Values and Political Organization of City Managers: A Survey Report" *Social Science Quarterly,* December, 1967.

7. See Heinz Eulau and Kenneth Prewitt, *Labyrinths of Democracy: Adaptations, Linkages, Representation and Policies* (Indianapolis: Bobbs Merrill, 1973) and Robert L. Lineberry and Edmund Fowler, "Reformism and Public Policies in American Cities," *American Political Science Review* 61 (Sept. 1967), pp. 701-716.

8. Stanley, *op. cit.* p. 145.

9. Winston W. Crouch, *Organized Civil Servants: A Study of the Development of State Policy Concerning Public Employer-Employee Relations in California* (Berkeley: University of California Press, 1978).

8
The Limits of Collective Bargaining in Public Employment
Harry Wellington and Ralph K. Winter

Writing in the March 1969 issue of the *Michigan Law Review,* Mr. Theodore Kheel, the distinguished mediator and arbitrator, placed the weight of his considerable authority behind what is fast becoming the conventional wisdom. In the public sector, as in the private, Mr. Kheel argues, "the most effective technique to produce acceptable terms to resolve disputes is voluntary agreement of the parties, and the best system we have for producing agreements between groups is collective bargaining—even though it involves conflict and the possibility of a work disruption." Clearly for Kheel, as for others, the insistence upon a full extension of collective bargaining—including strikes—to public employment stems from a deep commitment to that way of ordering labor-management affairs in private employment. While such a commitment may not be necessary, a minimal acceptance of collective bargaining is a condition precedent to the Kheel view. Those skeptical of the value of collective bargaining in private employment will hardly press its extension. But even if one accepts collective bargaining in the private sector . . . the claims that support it there do not, in any self-evident way, make the case for its full transplant. The public sector is *not* the private, and its labor problems *are* different, very different indeed.

The Claims for Collective Bargaining in the Private Sector

Four claims are made for private-sector collective bargaining. First, it is said to be a way to achieve industrial peace. The point was put as early as 1902 by the federal Industrial Commission:

> *The chief advantage which comes from the practice of periodically determining the conditions of labor by collective bargaining directly between employers and employees is that thereby each side obtains a better understanding of the actual state of the industry, of the conditions which confront the other side, and of the motives which influence it. Most strikes and lockouts would not occur if each party understood exactly the position of the other.*

Second, collective bargaining is a way of achieving industrial democracy, that is, participation by workers in their own governance. It is the industrial counterpart of the contemporary demand for community participation.

Reprinted from *The Unions and the Cities,* (c) 1971 The Brookings Institution, Washington, D.C., pp. 7-32. Footnotes omitted.
Harry H. Wellington and Ralph K. Winter are professors at Yale University Law School.

Third, unions that bargain collectively with employers represent workers in the political arena as well. And political representation through interest groups is one of the most important types of political representation that the individual can have. Government at all levels acts in large part in response to the demands made upon it by the groups to which its citizens belong.

Fourth, and most important, as a result of a belief in the unequal bargaining power of employers and employees, collective bargaining is claimed to be a needed substitute for individual bargaining. Monopsony—a buyer's monopoly, in this case a buyer of labor—is alleged to exist in many situations and to create unfair contracts of labor as a result of individual bargaining. While this, in turn, may not mean that workers as a class and over time get significantly less than they should—because monopsony is surely not a general condition but is alleged to exist only in a number of particular circumstances—it may mean that the terms and conditions of employment for an individual or group of workers at a given period of time and in given circumstances may be unfair. What tends to insure fairness in the aggregate and over the long run is the discipline of the market. But monopsony, if it exists, can work substantial injustice to individuals. Governmental support of collective bargaining represents the nation's response to a belief that such injustice occurs. Fairness between employee and employer in wages, hours, and terms and conditions of employment is thought more likely to be ensured where private ordering takes the collective form.

There are, however, generally recognized social costs resulting from this resort to collectivism. In the private sector these costs are primarily economic, and the question is, given the benefits of collective bargaining as an institution, what is the nature of the economic costs? Economists who have turned their attention to this question are legion, and disagreement among them monumental. The principal concerns are of two intertwined sorts. One is summarized by Professor Albert Rees of Princeton:

> *If the union is viewed solely in terms of its effect on the economy, it must in my opinion be considered an obstacle to the optimum performance of our economic system. It alters the wage structure in a way that impedes the growth of employment in sectors of the economy where productivity and income are naturally high and that leaves too much labor in low-income sectors of the economy like southern agriculture and the least skilled service trades. It benefits most those workers who would in any case be relatively well off, and while some of this gain may be at the expense of the owners of capital, most of it must be at the expense of consumers and the lower-paid workers. Unions interfere blatantly with the use of the most productive techniques in some industries, and this effect is probably not offset by the stimulus to higher productivity furnished by some other unions.*

The other concern is stated in the 1967 Report of the Council of Economic Advisers:

> *Vigorous competition is essential to price stability in a high employment*

> *economy. But competitive forces do not and cannot operate with equal strength in every sector of the economy. In industries where the number of competitors is limited, business firms have a substantial measure of discretion in setting prices. In many sectors of the labor market, unions and managements together have a substantial measure of discretion in setting wages. The responsible exercise of discretionary power over wages and prices can help to maintain general price stability. Its irresponsible use can make full employment and price stability incompatible.*

And the claim is that this "discretionary power" too often is exercised "irresponsibly."

Disagreement among economists extends to the quantity as well as to the fact of economic malfunctioning that properly is attributable to collective bargaining. But there is no disagreement that at some point the market disciplines or delimits union power. As we shall see in more detail below, union power is frequently constrained by the fact that consumers react to a relative increase in the price of a product by purchasing less of it. As a result any significant real financial benefit, beyond that justified by an increase in productivity, that accrues to workers through collective bargaining may well cause significant unemployment among union members. Because of this employment-benefit relationship, the economic costs imposed by collective bargaining as it presently exists in the private sector seem inherently limited.

The Claims for Collective Bargaining in the Public Sector

In the area of public employment the claims upon public policy made by the need for industrial peace, industrial democracy, and effective political representation point toward collective bargaining. This is to say that three of the four arguments that support bargaining in the private sector—to some extent, at least—press for similar arrangements in the public sector.

Government is a growth industry, particularly state and municipal government. While federal employment between 1963 and 1970 increased from 2.5 million to 2.9 million, state and local employment rose from 7.2 to 10.1 million, and the increase continues apace. With size comes bureaucracy, and with bureaucracy comes the sense of isolation of the individual workers. His manhood, like that of his industrial counterpart, seems threatened. Lengthening chains of command necessarily depersonalize the employment relationship and contribute to a sense of powerlessness on the part of the worker. If he is to share in the governance of his employment relationship as he does in the private sector, it must be through the device of representation, which means unionization. Accordingly, just as the increase in the size of economic units in private industry fostered unionism, so the enlarging of governmental bureaucracy has encouraged public employees to look to collective action for a sense of control over their employment destiny. The number of government employees, moreover, makes it plain that those employees are members of an interest group that can organize for political representation as well as for job participation.

The pressures thus generated by size and bureaucracy lead inescapably to disruption—to labor unrest—unless these pressures are recognized and unless existing decision-making procedures are accommodated to them. Peace in government employment too, the argument runs, can best be established by making union recognition and collective bargaining accepted public policy.

Much less clearly analogous to the private model, however, is the unequal bargaining power argument. In the private sector that argument really has two aspects. The first, just adumbrated, is affirmative in nature. Monopsony is believed sometimes to result in unfair individual contracts of employment. The unfairness may be reflected in wages, which are less than they would be if the market were more nearly perfect, or in working arrangements that may lodge arbitrary power in a foreman, that is, power to hire, fire, promote, assign, or discipline without respect to substantive or procedural rules. A persistent assertion, generating much heat, relates to the arbitrary exercise of managerial power in individual cases. This assertion goes far to explain the insistence of unions on the establishment in the labor contract of rules, with an accompanying adjudicatory procedure, to govern industrial life.

Judgments about the fairness of the financial terms of the public employee's individual contract of employment are even harder to make than for private sector workers. The case for the existence of private employer monopsony, disputed as it is, asserts only that some private sector employers in some circumstances have too much bargaining power. In the public sector, the case to be proved is that the governmental employer ever has such power. But even if this case could be proved, market norms are at best attenuated guides to questions of fairness. In employment as in all other areas, governmental decisions are properly political decisions, and economic considerations are but one criterion among many. Questions of fairness do not centrally relate to how much imperfection one sees in the market, but more to how much imperfection one sees in the political process. "Low" pay for teachers may be merely a decision—right or wrong, resulting from the pressure of special interests or from a desire to promote the general welfare—to exchange a reduction in the quality or quantity of teachers for higher welfare payments, a domed stadium, and so on. And the ability to make informed judgments about such political decisions is limited because of the understandable but unfortunate fact that the science of politics has failed to supply either as elegant or as reliable a theoretical model as has its sister discipline.

Nevertheless, employment benefits in the public sector may have improved relatively more slowly than in the private sector during the last three decades. An economy with a persistent inflationary bias probably works to the disadvantage of those who must rely on legislation for wage adjustments. Moreover, while public employment was once attractive for the greater job security and retirement benefits it provided, quite similar protection is now available in many areas of the private sector. On the other hand, to the extent that civil service, or merit, systems exist in public employment and these laws are obeyed, the arbitrary exercise of managerial power is substantially reduced. Where it is reduced, a labor policy that relies on individual employment contracts must seem less unacceptable.

The second, or negative, aspect of the unequal bargaining power argument relates to the social costs of collective bargaining. As has been seen, the social costs of collective bargaining in the private sector are principally economic and seem inherently limited by market forces. In the public sector, however, the costs seem economic only in a very narrow sense and are on the whole political. It further seems that, to the extent union power is delimited by market or other forces in the public sector, these constraints do not come into play nearly as quickly as in the private. An understanding of why this is so requires further comparison between collective bargaining in the two sectors.

The Private Sector Model

Although the private sector is, of course, extraordinarily diverse, the paradigm is an industry that produces a product that is not particularly essential to those who buy it and for which dissimilar products can be substituted. Within the market or markets for this product, most—but not all—of the producers must bargain with a union representing their employees, and this union is generally the same throughout the industry. A price rise of this product relative to others will result in a decrease in the number of units of the product sold. This in turn will result in a cutback in employment. And an increase in price would be dictated by an increase in labor cost relative to output, at least in most situations. Thus, the union is faced with some sort of rough trade-off between, on the one hand, larger benefits for some employees and unemployment for others, and on the other hand, smaller benefits and more employment. Because unions are political organizations, with a legal duty to represent all employees fairly, and with a treasury that comes from per capita dues, there is pressure on the union to avoid the road that leads to unemployment.

This picture of the restraints that the market imposes on collective bargaining settlements undergoes change as the variables change. On the one hand, to the extent that there are nonunion firms within a product market, the impact of union pressure will be diminished by the ability of consumers to purchase identical products from nonunion and, presumably, less expensive sources. On the other hand, to the extent that union organization of competitors within the product market is complete, there will be no such restraint and the principal barriers to union bargaining goals will be the ability of a number of consumers to react to a price change by turning to dissimilar but nevertheless substitutable products.

Two additional variables must be noted. First, where the demand for an industry's product is rather insensitive to price—that is, relatively inelastic—and where all the firms in a product market are organized, the union need fear less the employment-benefit trade-off, for the employer is less concerned about raising prices in response to increased costs. By hypothesis, a price rise affects unit sales of such an employer only minimally. Second, in an expanding industry, wage settlements that exceed increases in productivity may not reduce union employment. They will reduce expansion, hence the employment effect will be experienced only by workers who do not belong to the union. This means that in the short run the politics of the employment-benefit trade-offs do not restrain the union in its bargaining demands.

In both of these cases, however, there are at least two restraints on the union. One is the employer's increased incentive to substitute machines for labor, a factor present in the paradigm and all other cases as well. The other restraint stems from the fact that large sections of the nation are unorganized and highly resistant to unionization. Accordingly, capital will seek nonunion labor, and in this way the market will discipline the organized sector.

The employer, in the paradigm and in all variations of it, is motivated primarily by the necessity to maximize profits (and this is so no matter how political a corporation may seem to be). He therefore is not inclined (absent an increase in demand for his product) to raise prices and thereby suffer a loss in profits, and he is organized to transmit and represent the market pressures described above. Generally he will resist, and resist hard, union demands that exceed increases in productivity, for if he accepts such demands he may be forced to raise prices. Should he be unsuccessful in his resistance too often, and should it or the bargain cost him too much, he can be expected to put his money and energy elsewhere.

What all this means is that the social costs imposed by collective bargaining are economic costs; that usually they are limited by powerful market restraints; and that these restraints are visible to anyone who is able to see the forest for the trees.

The Public Sector Model: Monetary Issues

The paradigm in the public sector is a municipality with an elected city council and an elected mayor who bargains (through others) with unions representing the employees of the city. He bargains also, of course, with other permanent and ad hoc interest groups making claims upon government (business groups, save-the-park committees, neighborhood groups, and so forth). Indeed, the decisions that are made may be thought of roughly as a result of interactions and accommodations among these interest groups, as influenced by perceptions about the attitudes of the electorate and by the goals and programs of the mayor and his city council.

Decisions that cost the city money are generally paid for from taxes and, less often, by borrowing. Not only are there many types of taxes but also there are several layers of government that may make tax revenue available to the city; federal and state as well as local funds may be employed for some purposes. Formal allocation of money for particular uses is made through the city's budget, which may have within it considerable room for adjustments. Thus, a union will bargain hard for as large a share of the budget as it thinks it possibly can obtain, and even try to force a tax increase if it deems that possible.

In the public sector, too, the market operates. In the long run, the supply of labor is a function of the price paid for labor by the public employer relative to what workers earn elsewhere. This is some assurance that public employees in the aggregate—with or without collective bargaining—are not paid too little.

The case for employer monopsony, moreover, may be much weaker in the public sector than it is in the private. First, to the extent that most public employees work in urban areas, as they probably do, there may often be a number of substitutable and competing private and public employers in the labor market. When that is the case, there can be little monopsony power. Second, even if public employers occasionally have monopsony power, governmental policy is determined only in part by economic criteria, and there is no assurance, as there is in the private sector where the profit motive prevails, that the power will be exploited.

As noted, market-imposed unemployment is an important restraint on unions in the private sector. In the public sector, the trade-off between benefits and employment seems much less important. Government does not generally sell a product the demand for which is closely related to price. There usually are not close substitutes for the products and services provided by government and the demand for them is relatively inelastic. Such market conditions are favorable to unions in the private sector because they permit the acquisition of benefits without the penalty of unemployment, subject to the restraint of nonunion competitors, actual or potential. But no such restraint limits the demands of public employee unions. Because much government activity is and must be, a monopoly, product competition, nonunion or otherwise, does not exert a downward pressure on prices and wages. Nor will the existence of a pool of labor ready to work for a wage below union scale attract new capital and create a new, and competitively less expensive, governmental enterprise.

The fear of unemployment, however, can serve as something of a restraining force in two situations. First, if the cost of labor increases, the city may reduce the quality of the service it furnishes by reducing employment. For example, if teachers' salaries are increased, it may decrease the number of teachers and increase class size. However, the ability of city government to accomplish such a change is limited not only by union pressure but also by the pressure of other affected interested groups in the community. Political considerations, therefore, may cause either no reduction in employment or services, or a reduction in an area other than that in which the union members work. Both the political power exerted by the beneficiaries of the services, who are also voters, and the power of the public employee union as a labor organization then combine to create great pressure on political leaders either to seek new funds or to reduce municipal services of another kind. Second, if labor costs increase, the city, like a private employer, may seek to replace labor with machines. The absence of a profit motive, and a political concern for unemployment, however, may be deterrents in addition to the deterrent of union resistance. The public employer that decides it must limit employment because of unit labor costs will likely find that the politically easiest decision is to restrict new hirings rather than to lay off current employees.

Where pensions are concerned, moreover, major concessions may be politically tempting since there is no immediate impact on the taxpayer or the city budget. Whereas actuarial soundness would be insisted on by a profit-seeking entity like a firm, it may be a secondary concern to politicians whose conduct is determined by relatively short-run considerations. The impact of failing to adhere to actuarial principles will frequently fall upon a different mayor and a different city council. In those circumstances, concessions that condemn a city to future impoverishment may not seem intolerable.

Even if a close relationship between increased economic benefits and unemployment does not exist as a significant deterrent to unions in the public sector, might not the argument be made that in some sense the taxpayer is the public sector's functional equivalent of the consumer? If taxes become too high the taxpayer can move to another community. While it is generally much easier for a consumer to substitute products than for a taxpayer to substitute communities, is it not fair to say that, at the point at which a tax increase will cause so many taxpayers to move that it will produce less total revenue, the market disciplines or restrains union and public employer in the same way and for the same reasons that the market disciplines parties in the private sector? Moreover, does not the analogy to the private sector suggest that it is legitimate in an economic sense for unions to push government to the point of substitutability?

Several factors suggest that the answer to this latter question is at best indeterminate, and that the question of legitimacy must be judged not by economic but by political criteria.

In the first place, there is no theoretical reason—economic or political—to suppose that it is desirable for a governmental entity to liquidate its taxing power, to tax up to the point where another tax increase will produce less revenue because of the number of people it drives to different communities. In the private area, profit maximization is a complex concept, but its approximation generally is both a legal requirement and socially useful as a means of allocating resources. The liquidation of taxing power seems neither imperative nor useful.

Second, consider the complexity of the tax structure and the way in which different kinds of taxes (property, sales, income) fall differently upon a given population. Consider, moreover, that the taxing authority of a particular governmental entity may be limited (a municipality may not have the power to impose an income tax). What is necessarily involved, then, is principally the redistribution of income by government rather than resource allocation, and questions of income redistribution surely are essentially political questions.

For his part, the mayor in our paradigm will be disciplined not by a desire to maximize profits but by a desire—in some cases at least—to do a good job (to implement his programs), and in virtually all cases by a wish either to be reelected or to move to a better elective office. What he gives to the union must be taken from some other interest group or from taxpayers. His is the job of coordinating these competing claims while remaining politically viable. And that coordination will be governed by the relative power of the competing interest groups. Coordination, moreover, is not limited to issues involving the level of taxes and the way in which tax moneys are spent. Nonfinancial issues also require coordination, and here too the outcome turns upon the relative power of interest groups. And relative power is affected importantly by the scope of collective bargaining.

The Public Sector Model: Nonmonetary Issues

In the private sector, unions have pushed to expand the scope of bargaining in response to the desires of their members for a variety of new benefits (pension rights, supplementary unemployment payments, merit increases). These benefits generally impose a monetary cost on the employer. And because employers are restrained by the market, an expanded bargaining agenda means that, if a union negotiates an agreement over more subjects, it generally trades off more of less for less of more.

From the consumer's point of view this in turn means that the price of the product he purchases is not significantly related to the scope of bargaining. And since unions rarely bargain about the nature of the product produced, the consumer can be relatively indifferent as to how many or how few subjects are covered in any collective agreement. Nor need the consumer be concerned about union demands that would not impose a financial cost on the employer, for example, the design of a grievance procedure. While such demands are not subject to the same kind of trade-off as are financial demands, they are unlikely, if granted, to have any impact on the consumer. Their effect is on the quality of life of the parties to the agreement.

In the public sector the cluster of problems that surround the scope of bargaining are much more troublesome than they are in the private sector. The problems have several dimensions.

First, the trade-off between subjects of bargaining in the public sector is less of a protection to the consumer (public) than it is in the private. Where political leaders view the costs of union demands as essentially budgetary, a trade-off can occur. Thus, a demand for higher teacher salaries and a demand for reduced class size may be treated as part of one package. But where a demand, although it has a budgetary effect, is viewed as involving essentially political costs, trade-offs are more difficult. Our paradigmatic mayor, for example, may be under great pressure to make a large monetary settlement with a teachers' union whether or not it is joined to demands for special training programs for disadvantaged children. Interest groups tend to exert pressure against union demands only when they are directly affected. Otherwise, they are apt to join that large constituency (the general public) that wants to avoid labor trouble. Trade-offs can occur only when several demands are resisted by roughly the same groups. Thus, pure budgetary demands can be traded off when they are opposed by taxpayers. But when the identity of the resisting group changes with each demand, political leaders may find it expedient to strike a balance on each issue individually, rather than as part of a total package, by measuring the political power of each interest group involved against the political power of the constituency pressing for labor peace. To put it another way, as important as financial factors are to a mayor, political factors may be even more important. The market allows the businessman no such discretionary choice.

Where a union demand—such as increasing the disciplinary power of teachers—does not have budgetary consequences, some trade-offs may occur. Granting the demand will impose a political cost on the mayor because it may anger another interest group. But because the resisting group may change with each issue, each issue is apt to be treated individually and not as a part of a total package. And this may not protect the public. Differing from the private sector, nonmonetary demands of public sector unions do have effects that go beyond the parties to the agreement. All of us have a stake in how school children are disciplined. Expansion of the subjects of bargaining in the public sector, therefore, may increase the total quantum of union power in the political process.

Second, public employees do not generally produce a product. They perform a service. The way in which a service is performed may become a subject of bargaining. As a result, the nature of that service may be changed. Some of these services—police protection, teaching, health care—involve questions that are politically, socially, or ideologically sensitive. In part this is because government is involved and alternatives to governmentally provided services are relatively dear. In part, government is involved because of society's perception about the nature of the service and society's need for it. This suggests that decisions affecting the nature of a governmentally provided service are much more likely to be challenged and are more urgent than generally is the case with services that are offered privately.

Third, some of the services government provides are performed by professionals—teachers, social workers, and so forth—who are keenly in-terested in the underlying philosophy that informs their work. To them, theirs is not merely a job to be done for a salary. They may be educators or other "change agents" of society. And this may mean that these employees are concerned with more than incrementally altering a governmental service or its method of delivery. They may be advocates of bold departures that will radically transform the service itself.

The issue is not a threshold one of whether professional public employees should participate in decisions about the nature of the services they provide. Any properly run governmental agency should be interested in, and heavily reliant upon, the judgment of its professional staff. The issue rather is the method of that participation.

Conclusions about this issue as well as the larger issue of a full transplant of collective bargaining to the public sector may be facilitated by addressing some aspects of the governmental decision-making process—particularly at the municipal level—and the impact of collective bargaining on that process.

Public Employee Unions and the Political Process

Although the market does not discipline the union in the public sector to the extent that it does in the private, the municipal employment paradigm, nevertheless, would seem to be consistent with what Robert A. Dahl has called the "'Normal' American political process," which is "one in which there is a high probability that an active and legitimate group in the population can make itself heard effectively at some crucial stage in the process of decision," for the union may be seen as little more than an "active and legitimate group in the population." With elections in the background to perform, as Mr. Dahl notes, "the critical role . . . in maximizing political equality and popular sovereignty," all seems well, at least theoretically, with collective bargaining and public employment.

But there is trouble even in the house of theory if collective bargaining in the public sector means what it does in the private. The trouble is that if unions are able to withhold labor—to strike—as well as to employ the usual methods of political pressure, they may possess a disproportionate share of effective power in the process of decision. Collective bargaining would then be so effective a pressure as to skew the results of the "'normal' American political process."

One should . . . make plain that the strike issue is not simply the importance of public services as contrasted with services or products produced in the private sector. This is only part of the issue, and in the past the partial truth has beclouded analysis. The services performed by a private transit authority are neither less nor more important to the public than those that would be performed if the transit authority were owned by a municipality. A railroad or a dock strike may be more damaging to a community than "job action" by police. This is not to say that governmental services are not important. They are, both because the demand for them is inelastic and because their disruption may seriously injure a city's economy and occasionally impair the physical welfare of its citizens. Nevertheless, the importance of governmental services is only a necessary part of, rather than a complete answer to, the question: Why be more concerned about strikes in public employment than in private?

The answer to the question is simply that, because strikes in public employment disrupt important services, a large part of a mayor's political constituency will, in many cases, press for a quick end to the strike with little concern for the cost of settlement. This is particularly so where the cost of settlement is borne by a different and larger political constituency, the citizens of the state or nation. Since interest groups other than public employees, with conflicting claims on municipal government, do not, as a general proposition, have anything approaching the effectiveness of the strike—or at least cannot maintain that relative degree of power over the long run—they may be put at a significant competitive disadvantage in the political process.

The private sector strike is designed to exert economic pressure on the employer by depriving him of revenues. The public employee strike is fundamentally different: its sole purpose is to exert political pressure on municipal officials. They are deprived, not of revenues but of the political support of those who are inconvenienced by a disruption of municipal services. But precisely because the private strike is an economic weapon, it is disciplined by the market and the benefit/unemployment trade-off that imposes. And because the public employee strike is a political weapon, it is subject only to the restraints imposed by the political process and they are on the whole less limiting and less disciplinary than those of the market. If this is the case, it must be said that the political process will be radically altered by wholesale importation of the strike weapon. And because of the deceptive simplicity of the analogy to collective bargaining in the private sector, the alteration may take place without anyone realizing what has happened.

Nor is it an answer that, in some municipalities, interest groups other than unions now have a disproportionate share of political power. This is inescapably true, and we do not condone that situation. Indeed, we would be among the first to advocate reform. However, reform cannot be accomplished by giving another interest group disproportionate power, for the losers would be the weakest groups in the community. In most municipalities, the weakest groups are composed of citizens who many believe are most in need of more power.

Therefore, while the purpose and effect of strikes by public employees may seem in the beginning designed merely to establish collective bargaining or to "catch up" with wages and fringe benefits in the private sector, in the long run strikes may become too effective a means for redistributing income; so effective, indeed, that one might see them as an institutionalized means of obtaining and maintaining a subsidy for union members.

As is often the case when one generalizes, this picture may be considered overdrawn. In order to refine analysis, it will be helpful to distinguish between strikes that occur over monetary issues and strikes involving nonmonetary issues. The generalized picture sketched above is mainly concerned with the former. Because there is usually no substitute for governmental services, the citizen-consumer faced with a strike of teachers, or garbage men, or social workers is likely to be seriously inconvenienced. This in turn places enormous pressure on the mayor, who is apt to find it difficult to look to the long-run balance sheet of the municipality. Most citizens are directly affected by a strike of sanitation workers. Few, however, can decipher a municipal budget or trace the relationship between today's labor settlement and next year's increase in the mill rate. Thus, in the typical case the impact of a settlement is less visible—or can more often be concealed—than the impact of a disruption of services. Moreover, the cost of settlement may fall upon a constituency much larger—the whole state or nation—than that represented by the mayor. And revenue sharing schemes that involve unrestricted funds may further lessen public resistance to generous settlements. It follows that the mayor usually will look to the electorate that is clamoring for a settlement, and in these circumstances the union's fear of a long strike, a major check on its power in the private sector, is not a consideration. In the face of all of these factors other interest groups with priorities different from the union's are apt to be much less successful in their pursuit of scarce tax dollars than is the union with power to withhold services.

With respect to strikes over some nonmonetary issues—decentralization of the governance of schools might be an example—the intensity of concern on the part of well-organized interest groups opposed to the union's position would support the mayor in his resistance to union demands. But even here, if the union rank and file back their leadership, pressures for settlement from the general public, which may be largely indifferent as to the underlying issue, might in time become irresistible.

The strike and its threat, moreover, exacerbate the problems associated with the scope of bargaining in public employment. This seems clear if one attends in slightly more detail to techniques of municipal decision making.

Few students of our cities would object to Herbert Kaufman's observation that:

> *Decisions of the municipal government emanate from no single source, but from many centers; conflicts and clashes are referred to no single authority, but are settled at many levels and at many points in the system: no single group can guarantee the success of any proposal it supports, the defeat of every idea it objects to. Not even the central governmental organs of the city—the Mayor, the Board of Estimate, the Council—individually or in combination, even approach mastery in this sense.*
>
> *Each separate decision center consists of a cluster of interested contestants, with a "core group" in the middle, invested by the rules with the formal authority to legitimize decisions (that is to promulgate them in binding form) and a constellation of related "satellite groups" seeking to influence the authoritative issuances of the core group.*

Nor would many disagree with Nelson W. Polsby when, in discussing community decision making that is concerned with an alternative to a "current state of affairs," he argues that the alternative "must be politically palatable and relatively easy to accomplish; otherwise great amounts of influence have to be brought to bear with great skill and efficiency in order to secure its adoption."

It seems probable that such potential subjects of bargaining as school decentralization and a civilian police review board are, where they do not exist, alternatives to the "current state of affairs," which are not "politically palatable and relatively easy to accomplish." If a teachers' union or a police union were to bargain with the municipal employer over these questions, and were able to use the strike to insist that the proposals not be adopted, how much "skill and efficiency" on the part of the proposals' advocates would be necessary to effect a change? And, to put the shoe on the other foot, if a teachers' union were to insist through collective bargaining (with the strike or its threat) upon major changes in school curriculum, would not that union have to be considerably less skillful and efficient in the normal political process than other advocates of community change? The point is that with respect to some subjects, collective bargaining may be too powerful a lever on municipal decision making, too effective a technique for changing or preventing the change of one small but important part of the "current state of affairs."

Unfortunately, in this area the problem is not merely the strike threat and the strike. In a system where impasse procedures involving third parties are established in order to reduce work stoppages—and this is common in those states that have passed public employment bargaining statutes—third party intervention must be partly responsive to union demands. If the scope of bargaining is open-ended, the neutral party, to be effective, will have to work out accommodations that inevitably advance some of the union's claims some of the time. And the neutral, with his eyes fixed on achieving a settlement, can hardly be concerned with balancing all the items on the community agenda or reflecting the interests of all relevant groups.

The Theory Summarized

Collective bargaining in public employment, then, seems distinguishable from that in the private sector. To begin with, it imposes on society more than a potential misallocation of resources through restrictions on economic output, the principal cost imposed by private sector unions. Collective bargaining by public employees and the political process cannot be separated. The costs of such bargaining, therefore, cannot be fully measured without taking into account the impact on the allocation of political power in the typical municipality. If one assumes, as here, that municipal political processes should be structured to ensure "a high probability that an active and legitimate group in the population can make itself heard effectively at some crucial stage in the process of decision," then the issue is how powerful unions will be in the typical municipal political process if a full transplant of collective bargaining is carried out.

The conclusion is that such a transplant would, in many cases, institutionalize the power of public employee unions in a way that would leave competing groups in the political process at a permanent and substantial disadvantage. There are three reasons for this, and each is related to the type of services typically performed by public employees.

First, some of these services are such that any prolonged disruption would entail an actual danger to health and safety.

Second, the demand for numerous governmental services is relatively inelastic, that is, relatively insensitive to changes in price. Indeed, the lack of close substitutes is typical of many governmental endeavors. And, since at least the time of Marshall's *Principles of Economics,* the elasticity of demand for the final service or product has been considered a major determinant of union power. Because the demand for labor is derived from the demand for the product, inelasticity on the product side tends to reduce the employment-benefit trade-off unions face. This is as much the case in the private as in the public sector. But in the private sector, product inelasticity is not typical. Moreover, there is the further restraint on union power created by the real possibility of nonunion entrants into the product market. In the public sector, inelasticity of demand seems more the rule than the exception, and nonunion rivals are not generally a serious problem.

Consider education. A strike by teachers may never create an immediate danger to public health and welfare. Nevertheless, because the demand for education is relatively inelastic, teachers rarely need fear unemployment as a result of union-induced wage increases, and the threat of an important nonunion rival (competitive private schools) is not to be taken seriously so long as potential consumers of private education must pay taxes to support the public school system.

The final reason for fearing a full transplant is the extent to which the disruption of a government service inconveniences municipal voters. A teachers' strike may not endanger public health or welfare. It may, however, seriously inconvenience parents and other citizens who, as voters, have the power to punish one of the parties—and always the same party, the political leadership—to the dispute. How can anyone any longer doubt the vulnerability of a municipal employer to this sort of pressure? Was it simply a matter of indifference to Mayor Lindsay in September 1969 whether another teachers' strike occurred on the eve of a municipal election? Did the size and the speed of the settlement with the United Federation of Teachers (UFT) suggest nothing about one first-rate politician's estimate of his vulnerability? And are the chickens now coming home to roost because of extravagant concessions on pensions for employees of New York City the result only of mistaken actuarial calculations? Or do they reflect the irrelevance of long-run considerations to politicians vulnerable to the strike and compelled to think in terms of short-run political impact?

Those who disagree on this latter point rely principally on their conviction that anticipation of increased taxes as the result of a large labor settlement will countervail the felt inconvenience of a strike, and that municipalities are not, therefore, overly vulnerable to strikes by public employees. The argument made here, however—that governmental budgets in large cities are so complex that generally the effect of any particular labor settlement on the typical municipal budget is a matter of very low visibility—seems adequately convincing. Concern over possible taxes will not, as a general proposition, significantly deter voters who are inconvenienced by a strike from compelling political leaders to settle quickly. Moreover, municipalities are often subsidized by other political entities—the nation or state—and the cost of a strike settlement may not be borne by those demanding an end to the strike.

All this may seem to suggest that it is the strike weapon—whether the issue be monetary or nonmonetary—that cannot be transplanted to the public sector. This is an oversimplification, however. It is the combination of the strike and the typical municipal political process, including the usual methods for raising revenue. One solution, of course, might well be a ban on strikes, if it could be made effective. But that is not the sole alternative, for there may be ways in which municipal political structures can be changed so as to make cities less vulnerable to strikes and to reduce the potential power of public employee unions to tolerable levels. (The relative merits of these alternatives are weighed in Part IV.)

All this may also seem to suggest a sharper distinction between the public and private sectors than actually exists. The discussion here has dealt with models, one for private collective bargaining, the other for public. Each model is located at the core of its sector. But the difference in the impact of collective bargaining in the two sectors should be seen as a continuum. Thus, for example, it may be that market restraints do not sufficiently discipline strike settlements in some regulated industries or in industries that rely mainly on government contracts. Indeed, collective bargaining in such industries has been under steady and insistent attack.

In the public sector, it may be that in any given municipality—but particularly a small one—at any given time, taxpayer resistance or the determination of municipal government, or both, will substantially offset union power even under existing political structures. These plainly are exceptions, however. They do not invalidate the public-private distinction as an analytical tool, for that distinction rests on the very real differences that exist in the vast bulk of situations, situations exemplified by these models. On the other hand, in part because of a recognition that there are exceptions that in particular cases make the models invalid, we shall argue that the law regulating municipal bargaining must be flexible and tailored to the real needs of a particular municipality....

9
Some Impacts of Collective Bargaining on Local Government: A Diversity Thesis

Raymond Horton, David Lewin, and James W. Kuhn

In recent years, government has grown faster than any other sector of the American economy. This growth has been accompanied by a major expansion of public employee unionism and collective bargaining. Consequently, widespread scholarly interest has developed in public sector labor relations, particularly the structure of collective bargaining and the process by which bargaining decisions are reached. Relatively little attention, however, has been paid to the impacts of collective bargaining on governmental management. Utilizing a diversity-of-impacts theory, this paper discusses some of the conceptual and methodological approaches useful in an impact analysis of labor relations decisions in the public sector.[1] Central to the theory is the notion that the impacts of public sector labor relations decisions on governmental management reflect sharp differences that exist among and even within governments with respect to structural, political, organizational, and union variables.

Reprinted from *Administration and Society,* Vol. 7 No. 4 (February 1976), pp. 497-516 by permission of the Publisher, Sage Publications, Inc.
At the time of this writing, the authors were affiliated with the Graduate School of Business, Columbia University.

Trends in Government Employment, Pay, and Unionism

Between 1960 and 1972, public employment in the United States grew by more than 60% or approximately 25% faster than employment in the private nonfarm sector of the economy.[2] The increase was especially sharp in state and local government where employment rose almost 78% over this 13-year period. Employment advanced more rapidly in state than in local government (89 versus 74%), but more than two and one-half times as many persons, 8.3 million, were employed in the latter sector than in the former in 1972. Employment growth rates varied substantially among state and local government functions, with the largest increases recorded in public welfare (161%), health (120%), education (102%), corrections (91%),[3] general control (72%), hospitals (63%), and police (57%). However, growth rates were large in virtually all public categories compared to the overall growth rate in the private economy (35%).

While the number of government employees has grown rapidly since 1960, public payrolls have risen even faster. For example, average monthly earnings of full-time employees of state and local governments increased 112.3% during the 1960-1973 period. Average hourly earnings in the private nonfarm sector rose three-fourths as much, 86.1%, and manufacturing earnings increased but 79.6%. Government workers who enjoyed the largest earnings increases over this period were employed in hospitals (132%), fire protection (123%), general control (119%), police protection (119%), health (115%), and highways (115%). These increases were all greater than earnings changes in the high-wage private construction sector (110%). So rapid and large have been the earnings increases for public employees that many of them now are paid more than their private sector counterparts (Perloff, 1971; Fogel and Lewin, 1974). These rates of pay increase may help explain why payroll costs represent well over half of all state and local government expenditures, and also why state and local governments accounted for more than 61% of all government purchases of goods and services in 1973, compared to 49.6% just six years earlier (Joint Economic Committee, 1974: 2). Government compensation expenditures now are claimed by some (Kuhn, 1972) to be an important element of modern inflation in the United States.

Finally, government workers continue to join unions and employee associations in record numbers, and to push for collective bargaining rights in public employment. In the federal sector, 52% of all employees were members of labor organizations in 1970, although much of this membership was concentrated in the postal service (Goldberg, 1972). More important, by 1972, slightly more than half of the 8.3 million full-time state and local government employees had enrolled in unions and employee associations (Labor Management Relations Service, 1975:1; hereafter, LMRS).[4] The extent of employee organization in the public sector is particularly impressive when compared with private industry, where about 25% of all wage and salary workers belong to unions and employee associations, and 30% in the nonagricultural sector (U.S. Department of Labor, Bureau of Labor Statistics, 1972:72).

In response to the heightened organizational activity of public employees, governments at all levels have attempted to formalize and treat labor relations as a functional specialty. In the federal government, the framework for labor relations was established in 1962 by President Kennedy's Executive Order 10988, and was subsequently modified by Executive Orders 11491 and 11616 in 1969 and 1972, respectively (see Taylor and Witney, 1975: 545-556). By 1973, two-thirds of American states had enacted legislation providing for some form of collective negotiations in their respective public sectors (U.S. Department of Labor, 1973), and in every one of the 50 states at least some governments engaged in such negotiations (LMRS, 1975: 1). In summary, government has been a major source of growth in the American economy since 1960 and an important arena of labor relations activity.

Assumptions about the Public and Private Sectors

The aforementioned developments raise major questions about the role of collective bargaining in the public sector and the impacts of unionism and collective bargaining on various dimensions of governmental management and operations. In addressing these issues, both scholars and policymakers generally have emphasized the peculiarities of the public sector; specifically, their analyses stress essential differences between the private and public sectors. Representative of this view are Wellington and Winter (1971: 8), who claim that "the public sector is *not* the private, and its labor problems *are* different, very different indeed." Differences indeed do exist, though to us some are not as pronounced as they appeared initially and others are more important than usually recognized.[5]

The difference identified earliest and to which the most attention has been paid concerns the legal position of government. Elected officials possess or are delegated rights that did not, at first glance, easily mesh with the concept and practice of collective bargaining. The problems of introducing collective bargaining and of adjusting legal perspectives to produce a tolerable fit with the "sovereignty" doctrine have been examined closely, and we have little to add to this literature. Suffice it to say that the sovereignty doctrine is withering away as the practice of collective bargaining continues to grow in government.

A second celebrated difference between the public and private sectors is the monopoly aspect of governmental services (Wellington and Winter, 1971).[6] Often, consumers have no, or few, alternatives; even if they choose not to avail themselves of a publicly provided service, they nevertheless must pay for it through taxes. However, not all state and local governmental services occupy a monopoly position. For example, alternative private services are typically available in sanitation and transportation. Some consumers have purchased protective services in the private market to supplement police protection. Given time for adjustment through relocation, some consumers can escape a government's high taxes. The costs and feasibility of alternatives to local government services cover a wider range than has been recognized and deserve further exploration, for they may be important determinants of manpower utilization and collective bargaining outcomes in the public sector. The diversity of government services needs to be emphasized, rather than being considered monolithic simply because they are publicly provided.

A third difference between public and private employment pertains to personnel administration. Civil service and the practices characteristic of it form a more common and broader personnel system than ever existed in private industry before, and probably even after, workers employed in that sector turned to collective bargaining. However, civil service systems vary markedly in operation from one government to another. The interaction of collective bargaining with civil service systems appears to produce a variety of outcomes that can be delineated, although much more work in this area is required.[7]

A fourth difference between the public and private sectors, only recently mentioned in the literature (see Fogel and Lewin, 1974; Lewin, 1974), but appearing to be one of signal importance, is governments' egalitarian pay structure: pay differentials between high and low positions are narrower in the public than in the private sector. Individuals in low positions—unskilled, blue-collar, and entry level white-collar jobs—enjoy higher pay in public than in private employment, while the opposite appears to be true for those in high positions—professionals, managers, and executives. Significantly, these pay patterns antedate the development of unions and collective bargaining in the government sector. The egalitarian pay structure in government also provides a set of constraints and opportunities for negotiators on both sides of the bargaining table not present for bargainers in the private sector. The effects of relatively well-paid public employees working in various capacities, directed by managers who are relatively poorly paid, deserve careful scrutiny by those concerned with collective bargaining in government.

A Diversity Model

Certainly as a consequence of the four major differences mentioned above, labor relations and patterns of manpower utilization in the public service display some features not found in the private sector. To focus on these differences as a key to understanding governmental labor problems, however, may mislead both scholars and policy-makers. It implies that government officials face unique problems and can expect little or no help from examining the solutions devised in the private sector. Similarly, it is unwise to assume that collective bargaining processes and solutions to industrial relations problems developed in the private economy provide "the answer" for public managers. In fact, managers and union leaders in private employment have elaborated a wide variety of roles, styles, procedures, and approaches to labor and manpower problems. They respond in many different ways because the situations in which they find themselves and the purposes they pursue are widely different.

Too often, observers of the labor scene implicitly assume a model of private sector labor relations and manpower management that describes only the manufacturing sector—and, more precisely, a model descriptive of large production firms and large industrial unions. In it, managers retain the initiative in directing employees, while the union concentrates its activities through grievance procedures on deflecting or modifying the thrust of managerial decisions. Alternatively, in other models, such as those provided by organized musicians and workers in the building trades and garment industry, union leaders have assumed a number of functions in decision-making areas usually regarded as strictly managerial, such as hiring, layoffs, and discipline. In some of these industries as well as in others, workers' representatives play important roles in strategic decisions affecting plant location, investment, subcontracting policy, and accounting methods, as well as wages, hours, and working conditions. Grievance handling plays a far less important part in labor relations patterned after the second model than the first.

If differences in labor relations and patterns of manpower utilization *within* the private sector are as wide and significant as suggested here, imputed differences, *between* the public and private sectors may well be exaggerated and even misleading. For example, public employees not only bargain for benefits over the negotiating table, but through voting and other political activities may also punish or reward their employing managers. In the private sector, some unions occupy an analogous position. The coal miners' union, as a large stockholder in several coal-producing and transportation companies, has "sat" on both sides of the bargaining table; the garment unions and the Teamsters in local trucking are powerful enough in their respective industries to influence small employers directly as well as through collective bargaining.

Exaggeration of the differences between the public and private sectors arises not only from assuming more uniformity in private industry than actually exists, as noted above, but also from ignoring the diversity in the public sector with respect to control devices, organizational structures, services, and occupational work groups. We believe this diversity, which is rooted in historical, legal, functional and political features of government, contains several implications for public sector labor relations. There may be no a priori reason to assume that labor relations in New York City ever will closely resemble those in Chicago or Los Angeles, even after formal collective bargaining has been introduced in Chicago and has matured in Los Angeles.[8]

The foregoing discussion suggests, then, that to conceive of governmental labor relations as sui generis and to hypothesize that only one pattern of union impact on public sector management will occur, overlooks the diversity of organizations, relationships, and impacts that may occur even within a single jurisdiction. Thus, a diversity model of public sector labor relations and collective bargaining impacts seems especially appropriate.

The Impacts of Collective Bargaining on Governmental Management

All but the most inconsequential political decisions produce impacts, latent as well as manifest, that change some patterns of relationships in the political system. The most important evidence in analyzing the impact of political decisions concerns the exchange or redistribution of resources that usually (but not always) accompanies a political decision. The process leading up to a political decision and the decision itself may permit hypotheses about decisional impacts, but observation of actual resource exchanges is necessary to translate hypotheses into findings (see Horton, 1974).

As noted earlier, labor relations and collective bargaining decisions appear to be playing an increasingly important allocative or redistributive role in American government, especially at the local government level. While some evidence and much speculation has surfaced concerning the impact of public employee labor relations on government, little systematic, comparative research has been conducted.[9] Five impact areas warrant particular analytical concern: compensation, service production and delivery, personnel administration, formal governmental structure, and informal politics.

Compensation. The level of wages (or, more accurately, total compensation) which induces or maintains employment in a given organization represents perhaps the most important labor relations exchange. This is true in public or private organizations, and it is true whether or not employees are organized and bargain collectively with management to establish wages.[10]

Popular opinion is divided over the cause of the relatively rapid increase in public employee wages that has occurred in the United States during the last two decades. One school of thought emphasizes the emerging political strength of public workers, including their organization and, in some jurisdictions, the introduction of collective bargaining, while another branch of opinion interprets public sector wage developments as essentially economic phenomena whereby intersectoral wage differentials were erased or even reversed by exceedingly strong demand for public services (see Wellington and Winter, 1971; Hayes, 1972; and Ehrenberg, 1973).

Our inclination, at present, is to view both explanations, standing alone or in conjunction, as overly simplistic and incapable of explaining what appears to be an extremely diverse pattern of wages and wage development—not only within and between the aggregate private and public sectors, but within and between private and public industries.

There are, to be sure, considerable data which suggests that for certain occupations in the public sector wages are higher than for comparable positions in the private sector,[11] but this neither establishes the political explanation based on emerging public sector bargaining nor disproves the explanation centered around market considerations. That the causal scenario is more complex is indicated by the fact that some public workers were paid as much, if not more, than comparable private employees *before* public sector unionization and bargaining and *before* the strong demand for public services that emerged in the 1960s (see Smith, 1975).

Service Provision and Delivery.

Here we refer to collective bargaining impacts on work rules and procedures (broadly defined), manning schedules, job assignments, and the like.

According to some industrial relations theorists (Kuhn, 1968: 284-309), organized workers in the private sector of the American economy are concerned primarily with protecting their "property in work" as reflected in the detailed provisions of collective agreements and the informal working rules of the ship, office, and factory. While this claim may be accurate as a generalization, it covers a wide variety of practices and relationships—ranging from a situation in which bargaining occurs only over wages and fringe benefits to one in which the union plays a major role in production, marketing, and financial decisions.

It has been argued (Wellington and Winter, 1971: 137-153) that workers in the public sector seek to negotiate over a broad range of employment-related issues, and that the impact of bargaining upon governmental management policy and decision-making will be greater than in industry. (For a contrary view, see Gerhart, 1969). Alternatively, however, our diversity thesis suggests major differences among and within local governments in the extent to which unions endeavor to bargain over or "control" so-called management rights. For example, in Chicago's local government, where formal collective bargaining does not exist outside of the educational sector, some public employee unions—the building trades, Teamsters, and Service Employees International Union (SEIU)—to a considerable degree control access to city jobs. None of the labor organizations in cities with more "developed" labor relations systems (for example, New York and Los Angeles) exercises similar control. In New York City, several important unions, including firemen, police, teachers, and municipally employed interns and residents, negotiate over hours of work and job assignments, but other unions limit their concerns to grievance procedures and/or compensation. In Los Angeles, public employee labor organizations are also differentially concerned with service production and delivery issues; however, in response to the bargaining efforts of these organizations, the city and county governments now are attempting to identify more accurately public managers, devise incentive systems appropriate to their functions, and hold them more closely accountable for the performance of their departments, bureaus, and agencies. Further empirical work is necessary, of course, to fully identify the impacts of collective bargaining on governmental service production and delivery, but preliminary evidence supports the view that these impacts will be diverse rather than singular.

Personnel Administration

Most students of the governmental labor relations-personnel interface see substantial conflict between the emergence of collective bargaining and traditional civil service (i.e., "merit") rules.[12] We neither see nor predict inherent pervasive conflict between collective bargaining decisions and merit rules, but, rather, diverse impacts on merit administration resulting in some instances in a strengthening and in other instances in a weakening of traditional merit rules.

Our central hypothesis is that labor relations conflict in this area is concerned not with merit rules per se, but with deep-seated divisions between labor and management regarding control over the rules by which employees are selected, promoted, and disciplined (see Lewin and Horton, 1975). Thus, where merit rules are supportive of control over the personnel process, management will assert and unions will attack traditional merit concepts in collective bargaining; but where management's personnel goals are inconsistent with merit rules, the positions of labor and management with respect to the validity or lack thereof of merit rules will be reversed.

This hypothesis appears to rationalize much of the seemingly contradictory discussion of union impacts on personnel administration recorded in the literature. Seniority, for example, clearly is not a merit rule, but it is gradually being implanted in personnel systems where unions possess substantial bargaining power. Many unions that have succeeded with respect to seniority also have succeeded in instituting the rule-of-one, an appointment procedure clearly more consistent with the merit concept than the rule-of-three, management's generally preferred position.

Adding additional validity to this diversity thesis is the fact that public managers and public unions appear to have differing degrees of allegiance to the merit principle.[13] Finally, we suspect that differences in the scope of bargaining and in bargaining power among and within jurisdictions further weaken the notion that collective bargaining and unionism in the public sector will lead to "zero-sum" impacts on merit rules.

Government Structure

In order to promote and administer the public policy of collective bargaining, most governments have instituted structural as well as legal changes in their institutional make-up. In some instances, existing agencies such as personnel boards have been charged with the responsibility for representing management in collective bargaining, but for the most part new labor relations departments have been created specifically for this purpose. Furthermore, many collective bargaining programs create independent or quasi-independent agencies responsible for administering labor relations and providing third-party assistance in conflict resolution.

In addition to structural additions, accretions of power and responsibility to new agencies from traditional overhead and line agencies are likely to occur when formal collective bargaining programs are instituted in government. Personnel commissions, budget bureaus, line agencies, and even legislative bodies quite often lose authority (sometimes not reluctantly) to new administrative agencies.

The structural impacts of unionism and collective bargaining on government have received relatively little scholarly attention. Most academics (for example, Burton, 1972) who have studied this phenomenon have concluded that the impact of new labor relations programs has tended to centralize previously fragmented personnel decision-making systems.[14]

While fragmentation of managerial structure and authority is, in our opinion, an impediment to the development of effective labor relations in the public sector, for a variety of reasons we are not as sanguine as others about the presumed centralizing effects of new labor relations programs and institutions. First, the formal dispersion of political power, particularly at the local governmental level in American cities, is so well-advanced that political "end-runs" around newly designated labor relations agencies and actors remain possible. Second, and closely related to the above point, one must distinguish between formal and informal power structures. The mere act of creating new labor relations institutions and delegating to them responsibilities to make decisions previously reached elsewhere in government does not mean, in fact, that the locus of control over decision-making also changes. Third, in certain cities where public employees are well-organized and politically strong, formal bargaining programs may result in a redistribution of power from public officials to municipal unions. This may represent a form of centralization, but not of the kind customarily anticipated by academics or public officials.

Again, we return to a more plausible hypothesis than the centralization thesis—namely, that diverse impacts on governmental structure will result from the promulgation of formal collective bargaining systems. In a sense, our focus here shifts from the concerns of industrial relations and economic analysis to those of political science and public administration.

Politics.

One rationale for the introduction of formal collective bargaining programs into government has been to insulate labor relations from the unwholesome reach of "politics," but we are struck with the vigorous and often successful attempts of political actors, particularly mayors, to use emerging labor relations systems for their own political purposes. This has occurred despite the wide differences in politics and public employee labor relations among New York, Los Angeles, and Chicago.[15]

At first glance, it might be assumed that the rapid growth of public employment and public employee organizations virtually dictates that mayors pursue policies of accommodation rather than conflict over not only the introduction of formal bargaining into government but also over bargaining itself. Collective bargaining settlements would appear to be a rich source of "patronage" for mayors seeking wider political constituencies.

Closer examination of the politics of municipal labor relations, however, discloses a number of quite varied mayoral reactions to public employee unionism. In Chicago, where a centralized party apparatus works closely with powerful private sector unions, Mayor Daley has vigorously opposed the formalization of bargaining. He has sustained this position by pursuing a high-wage policy under that city's "prevailing rate" system. In New York, however, where party organizations are fragmented, Mayors Wagner and Lindsay were influential proponents of extending bargaining rights to municipal workers, though not entirely for the same reasons. Both mayors reaped important electoral benefits from civil service unions during critical election campaigns. The Los Angeles situation is more complex, in part because of the chief executive's more diffuse governing responsibilities in that city; but it appears that Mayor Bradley, unlike his predecessor, Samuel Yorty, realizes both the potential managerial problems and political opportunities posed by public employee unionism. Bradley is emerging as a key actor in that city's youthful labor relations program.

Policy and Research Implications

Public policies designed to regulate state and local government labor relations are in flux. To date, these policies largely have been constructed in the absence of impact analysis—a sequence which violates the policy scientist's admonition that policy-making should reflect, rather than precede, analysis of various policy options and their consequences.

While several policy implications ranging from the macro to the micro level are suggested by the aforementioned diversity thesis and discussion of collective bargaining impacts on government management, only two will briefly be considered here. The first is the issue of comprehensive labor relations. If, as the present analysis indicates, divergent labor relations processes and impacts reflect functional adaptations to the peculiarities of state and local governments, it is questionable whether a comprehensive federal law should be enacted to regulate labor relations at the state and local level. Instead, federal legislation based on the "minimum standards" concept may be preferable either to extending the National Labor Relations Act to the public sector or to instituting a "model" public sector labor relations law.[16]

A second important policy issue germane to this paper concerns public employee strikes. For various reasons, we are skeptical about the dominant (though not exclusive) view that favors blanket no-strike laws in the public sector. Once again, recognition of clearly disparate political and bargaining relationships within and among governments argues for a more sophisticated approach to the admittedly serious problem of public sector strikes than simply (and often unsuccessfully) prohibiting them. Similar difficulties are raised by the use of compulsory arbitration as a substitute for public sector strikes. The rationale for a no-strike/arbitration law may be far stronger in one jurisdiction than another, and applicable only to some, not all, employee groups within a single jurisdiction.

With respect to research implications of the present study, perhaps the key point is that collective bargaining impacts on governmental management must be examined longitudinally, if they are to be understood and properly evaluated. This is particularly true in those impact areas which are at best only partially amenable to quantitative analysis—for example, service production and delivery, personnel administration, and government structure. This is not to gainsay that importance of cross-sectional studies or survey data in the examination of public sector labor relations; indeed, these methodologies dominate the current literature on this subject. Rather, it is to emphasize the special value of the longitudinal method in analyzing the dynamics of a public sector labor relations system.

Finally, the diversity thesis and the accumulating evidence regarding public sector labor relations, especially the impacts of collective bargaining on governmental management, could well be used as a basis for reexamining labor relations in (and public policies governing) the private sector of the American economy. Much of what we presume to know about the latter sector has taken on connotations of the conventional wisdom and rests, in part, on old evidence. The aforementioned reexamination not only would challenge this conventional wisdom, it also would represent a "revised sequence" of research in this field—i.e., using the accumulating knowledge about *public sector labor relations* to better understand those in industry.

Notes

1. This paper is based on an as yet uncompleted study of public sector labor relations in New York City, Chicago, and Los Angeles which is being supported by the Ford Foundation and U.S. Department of Labor and conducted under the auspices of the Conservation of Human Resources Project, Columbia University. The larger study relies on a variety of research methodologies and data sources to analyze the diversity-of-impacts thesis outlined in the paper. The central empirical concern, the impact of labor relations decisions on the five areas described in this paper, is being analyzed longitudinally through data collected in on-site research and cross-sectionally through a survey of 2,200 American cities. The survey questionnaire is designed by the authors and administered by the International City Management Association.

2. Unless otherwise indicated, all data presented in this section were obtained from U.S. Department of Commerce, Bureau of the Census (1961 and 1974).

3. For corrections, the change reported is for the 1961-1973 period; 1960 data for this function were not available.

4. Previous estimates had placed state and local membership at only about 33%. See Steiber (1973) and U.S. Department of Labor (1971).

5. Assumption of major differences between the public and private sectors leads to another familiar theme:prediction of dire outcomes resulting from collective bargaining in government. For a critique of these assumptions and additional insights into the approach followed in the present study, see Lewin (1973).

6. Wellington and Winter (1971) feel that the existence of such monopoly requires the imposition of restrictions on the bargaining activities of organized public employees.

7. A framework for analyzing these impacts is provided in Lewin and Horton (1975).

8. The development of collective bargaining in New York City government is reviewed in Horton (1973 and 1971). Chicago has received little analysis in terms of its municipal labor relations system, but see Derber (1968) and Jones (1972). The Los Angeles experience is analyzed in Lewin (1976).

9. For a general critique of the literature of public sector labor relations, see Lewin (1973).

10. It should be kept in mind, despite the heavy attention paid to the impact of collective bargaining on wages in both sectors, that wages of a substantial majority of private workers (75%) and more than half of public workers are not established by collective bargaining.

11. Publications of the regional offices of the Bureau of Labor Statistics comparing salaries and benefits of municipal workers with those of private sector counterparts show that in most metropolitan areas public workers are better compensated. These comparative surveys, unfortunately, were not begun until 1970.

12. For a thorough review of the literature, see U. S. Department of Labor, Labor Management Services Administration (1972). See also Morse (1973) and Stanley with Cooper (1971: 32-59).

13. For instance, the Lindsay administration in New York City for eight years attempted through a variety of administrative initiatives to circumvent certain strictures of the "civil service" system. One of Mayor Beame's first formal acts upon succeeding Lindsay in 1974 was to issue an executive order replacing the rule-of-three with the rule-of-one. Civil service unions also display divergent attitudes toward merit rules. Unions based on departmental rather than citywide units often favor closed rather than open promotional exams.

14. For a different viewpoint emphasizing the fragmentation theme, see Kochan (1971), Horton (1973), and Lewin (1976).

15. New York City represents a "mature" system—that is, one in which the institutional and legal structures surrounding formal collective bargaining are well-entrenched (see Horton, 1975). Los Angeles, including both the City and County, may be characterized as a "transitional" system moving from an informal to a formal labor relations system (see Lewin, 1976). Chicago's public sector labor relations system for the most part remains underdeveloped. For a description of the Chicago system, see Jones (1972: 195-226).

16. A discussion of the minimum standards concept and various types of federal labor legislation for public employees is contained in Bureau of National Affairs (1974: B12-19 and F1-9).

References

Bureau of National Affairs (1974) Government Employees Relations Report 575 (October).

BURTON, J. F., Jr. (1972) "Local government bargaining and management structure." Industrial Relations 11 (May): 133-139.

DERBER, M. R. (1968) "Labor-management policy for public employees in Illinois: the experience of the Governor's Commission, 1966-67." Industrial & Labor Relations Rev. 21 (July): 541-558.

EHRENBERG, R. G. (1973) "The demand for state and local government employees." Amer. Econ. Rev. 3(June): 366-379

FOGEL, W. and D. LEWIN (1974) "Wage determination in the public sector." Industrial & Labor Relations Rev. 27 (April): 410-431.

GERHART, P. F. (1969) "Scope of bargaining in local government labor negotiations." Labor Law J. 20 (August): 545-553.

GOLDBERG, J. P. (1972) "Public employee developments in 1971." Monthly Labor Rev. 95(January):56.

HAYES, F. O. (1972) "Collective bargaining and the budget director," pp. 89-100 in S. Zagoria (ed.) Public Workers and Public Unions. Englewood Cliffs, N.Y.: Prentice-Hall.

HORTON, R. D. (1975) "Reforming the municipal labor relations process in New York City." Study prepared for the State Charter Revision Commission for New York City (January).

--- (1974) "Public employee labor relations under the Taylor Law," pp. 172-174 in R. H. Connery and G. Benjamin (eds.) Governing New York State: The Rockefeller Years. New York: Academy of Political Science.

--- (1973) Municipal Labor Relations in New York City: Lessons of the Lindsay-Wagner Years. New York: Praeger.

--- (1971) "Municipal labor relations: the New York City experience." Social Sci. Q. 52 (December): 680-696.

Joint Economic Committee, Council of Economic Advisers (1974) Economic Indicators, February 1975. Washington, D.C.: Government Printing Office.

JONES, R. T. (1972) "City employee unions in New York and Chicago." Ph.D. dissertation, Harvard University.

KOCHAN, T. A. (1971) City Employee Bargaining with a Divided Management. Madison: University of Wisconsin, Industrial Relations Institute.

KUHN, J. W. (1972) "The riddle of inflation: a new answer." Public Interest 27 (Spring): 63-77.

--- (1968) "Business unionism in a laboristic society," pp. 284-309 in I. Berg (ed.) The Business of America. New York: Harcourt, Brace & World.

Labor Management Relations Service (1975) Labor Management Relations Service (1975) Labor Management Relations Service Newsletter, Vol. 6, No. 3. Washington, D.C.: Labor Management Relations Service.

LEWIN, D. (1976) "Local government labor relations in transition: the case of Los Angeles." Labor History 16.

--- (1974) "Aspects of wage determination in local government employment." Public Administration Rev. 34 (March-April): 149-155.

--- (1973) "Public employment relations: confronting the issues." Industrial Relations 12 (October): 309-321.

--- and R. D. HORTON (1975) "Evaluating the impacts of collective bargaining on personnel administration in government." Arbitration J. 30 (September): 199-211.

MORSE, M. M. (1973) "Should we bargain away the merit principle?" Public Personnel Rev. (October): 233-243.

PERLOFF, S. H. (1971) "Comparing municipal salaries with industry and federal pay." Monthly Labor Rev. 94(October): 46-50.

SMITH, S. P. (1975) "Wage differentials between federal government and private sector workers." (unpublished manuscript)

STANLEY, D. T. with the assistance of C L. Cooper (1971) Managing Local Government Under Union Pressure. Washington, D.C.: Brookings.

STEIBER, J. (1973) Public Employee Unionism: Structure, Growth, Policy; Studies of Unionism in Government. Washington, D.C.: Brookings.

TAYLOR, B. J. and F. WITNEY (1975) Labor Relations Law (second ed.). Englewood Cliffs, N.J.: Prentice-Hall.

U.S. Department of Commerce, Bureau of the Census (1974) Public Employment in 1973. Washington, D.C.: Government Printing Office.

--- (1961) State Distribution of Public Employment in 1960. Washington, D.C.: Government Printing Office.

U.S. Department of Labor (1973) Summary of State Policy Regulations for Public Sector Labor Relations: Statutes, Attorney Generals' Opinions and Selected Court Decisions. Washington, D.C.: Government Printing Office.

--- (1972) Directory of National Unions and Employee Associations. Washington, D.C.: Government Printing Office.

--- Bureau of Labor Statistics (1971) "Labor union and employee association membership." New Release (September 13).

U.S. Department of Labor, Labor Management Services Administration (1972) Collective Bargaining and the Merit System. Washington, D.C.: Government Printing Office.

WELLINGTON, H. H. and R. K. WINTER, Jr. (1971) The Unions and the Cities, Studies of Unionism in Government. Washington, D.C.: Brookings.

10
Public Sector Bargaining Legislation and Strikes: A Case Study
Charles R. Greer

The rapid growth of public sector unions has created problems for state and local governments. States have reacted to this trend for unionization in a variety of ways. Some states have passed relatively comprehensive labor legislation while others have no such legislation.[1] A question which has been the subject of recent research efforts concerns the relationship between public sector labor relations legislation and the incidence of strikes. The purpose of this article is to contribute to the body of knowledge by analyzing the relationship between Oklahoma's public employee labor relations legislation and a serious failure in employer and employee relations. This failure was the Oklahoma City police strike in 1975. Before analyzing Oklahoma's public sector labor legislation and the strike experience, a review of the literature regarding legislation and public sector strikes is in order.

Some students of industrial relations have maintained that states may prevent some strikes and work interruptions by the adoption of collective bargaining and impasse resolution procedures. Bakke has argued for giving public sector employees the right to bargain collectively while requiring both

Reprinted with permission from The Labor Law Journal, Vol. 29, No. 4 (April, 1978).

Charles R. Greer is Assistant Professor of Management, College of Business Administration, Oklahoma State University.

unions and employers to bargain in good faith. This procedure prevents employees from pursuing strikes and other such tactics as their only alternative for obtaining desired results.[2]

A similar conclusion is reached by Seidman. "While there are differences of opinion over the most desirable type of legislation, and while no legislation will solve all problems, in the absence of legislation the parties must depend on *ad hoc* procedures, with their rights and duties in doubt, the scope of bargaining uncertain, and no agency to determine bargaining units or conduct elections . . . Union-management relationships are likely to be most satisfactory where the law establishes exclusive bargaining rights for the majority union rather than a system of proportional representation and where the employing agency has a duty to bargain rather than merely to meet and confer."[3]

The adoption of public sector collective bargaining legislation would be expected to reduce the number of strikes due to recognitional disputes. Such reductions, however, might be offset by increases in strikes which could be expected to occur in a system of collective bargaining.[4] Which effect is dominant has been the subject of recent empirical research. These empirical investigations, however, provide evidence of the dominance of both effects.

Perry conducted a cross-sectional study utilizing strike data from 1973. The number of years since passage of a state's first public sector legislation was found positively correlated to strike frequency and strike duration for teachers. No similar relationship was found, however, for local employees (other than teachers, police and firefighters) and state employees. The comprehensiveness of public sector collective bargaining legislation was also found positively correlated to strike frequency and duration and an index of man-days idle for teachers. Similar correlations were found only between the comprehensiveness of such legislation and strike duration for other local employees. No such correlations were found for state employees.[5]

In a comprehensive empirical study of strikes in local government, during the years from 1968 to 1971, Burton and Krider found that, " . . the statutory prohibition on strikes has little apparent impact on the incidence of strikes, nor does the enactment of a law either prohibiting or encouraging collective bargaining by public employees appear to affect materially the number of local government strikes . . . Those states that encourage collective bargaining because they believe this is a meritorious way to determine working conditions for public employees do not incur a rash of strikes as a result."[6]

In another empirical study, Kochan found states' environmental characteristics (economic, social, political and industrial relations subenvironment) to be related to their public policies (such as public employee labor relations legislation). Therefore, studies of the effects of such policies (such as public sector strikes) should control for environmental characteristics.[7] Kochan's findings seem to imply the following: It would make little sense to compare the incidence of public sector strikes in two states having different public sector labor relations legislation without controlling for the fact that those states may vary widely in environmental characteristics.

It can be concluded from this review of the literature that the relationship between legislation and public sector strikes is complex. It cannot be assumed, as have some politicians, that passage of such legislation must result in more public sector strikes. In order to obtain additional information concerning the legislation and strike relationship, a case study approach is employed in this analysis. The case study application has the advantage of allowing consideration of some of the environmental characteristics which may affect the relationship. Before examining the police strike experience in Oklahoma City, it is necessary to review Oklahoma's public employee labor relations legislation.

The Legislative Environment

On March 11, 1971, the Oklahoma Firefighters' and Policemen's Arbitration Act became effective.[8] In its initial version,[9] the law provided firefighters and policemen the right to bargain collectively. Municipal authorities were required to meet and confer in good faith. There was provision for interest arbitration. If agreement on a contract could not be reached within 30 days after the commencement of negotiations, unresolved issues were to be submitted to arbitration if either party requested. The arbitration provision specified that the arbitration panel's ruling would be binding on the union if the municipal authorities adopted the decision but that the municipal authorities would not be bound by the ruling.

Unions were denied the right to strike. Penalties were provided for municipal authorities found in violation of the good faith bargaining requirements.

In 1972, the law was amended[10] to include coverage of other municipal employees. In addition, a Public Employees Relations Board was created to administer the Act. The Board was granted authority to "adopt, promulgate, amend or rescind such rules and regulations as it deems necessary and the Provisions . . ."[11] of the Act.

Unfair labor practices applicable to the municipal authorities were: 8. a. (1) interfering with, restraining, intimidating or coercing employees exercising their rights: (2) domination of or interference with the union; (3) interference with the selection of employee bargaining agents; (4) discriminatory treatment of employees giving testimony under the Act or electing to be represented by a bargaining agent; (5) refusal to bargain in good faith; and (6) locking out employees.

Unfair labor practices applicable to unions were: 8. b. (1) interfering with, restraining, intimidating or coercing employees exercising their rights; (2) interfering with the selection of the employer's collective bargaining representatives; and (3) refusal to bargain in good faith.

Since passage and amendment of the Act, it has been subjected to several court decisions that have narrowed its scope.[12] The bargaining agent for the Midwest City police charged the city with an unfair labor practice, failure to bargain in good faith over salaries.[13] The *Midwest Civy v. Cravens*[14] case, which was eventually decided by the Oklahoma Supreme Court, marked the demise of the Act as a comprehensive law governing public sector labor relations. The court rules that the Oklahoma Public Public Employees Relations Board had no authority to adjudicate the unfair labor practice charge because of an unconstitutional delegation of legislative authority to the board. Furthermore, the court ruled that since the 1972 amendment had not met requirements of re-enactment and publication at length, the 1972 amendment did not confer collective bargaining rights to municipal employees other than police and firefighters.

The aftermath of the *Midwest City v. Cravens* decision is that "the authority and duties of the Oklahoma Public Employees Relations Board have been reduced to overseeing the selection and election of bargaining agents for firemen and policemen."[15] The date of the Midwest City decision was February 14, 1975. Within nine months, Oklahoma City experienced a police strike.

The Oklahoma City Police Strike

Although public sector unionization is not as prevalent in Oklahoma[16] as in some other states, the state has not been immune from public sector strikes. The Oklahoma City policemen were involved in a strike which began on October 23, 1975.[17] A review of events leading up to the strike and its eventual resolution provides insight into the relationship of these events to Oklahoma's legislation governing public sector labor relations.

The strike represented the culmination of events related to arbitration of police wage demands. The policemen's bargaining agent (the Fraternal Order of Police (FOP), Lodge 123) had bargained for a 10 percent wage increase retroactive to August 1, 1975.[18] Earlier in the year, the police had engaged in a traffic ticket slowdown in order to persuade the city to request arbitration of the matter.[19] The city eventually requested arbitration, although it was not obligated to accept the arbitration panel's ruling.[20] The tripartite arbitration panel recommended that the police be given a 10 percent wage increase retroactive to August 1, 1975; however, the city refused to accept the panel's ruling. Accounts of the city council's response to the panel's ruling indicated a feeling that police raises could not be instituted without giving comparable raises to other municipal employees and because of the city's inability to pay.[21]

Prior to the work stoppage, the city had made an offer of a wage increase of 7 to 7.3 percent.[22] The policemen charged that the city was morally obligated to accept the panel's recommendation since the city had requested arbitration.[23] A day before the work stoppage the police had initiated a work slowdown.[24] The work slowdown involved failures to investigate traffic accidents or answer non-emergency calls.[25]

When the work slowdown failed to cause the city to accede to the FOP's demands, the police began a work stoppage. In a show of force, the policemen filed in to turn in their badges in the city manager's office. The FOP lodge president said the policemen were "suspending themselves" rather than striking, while the FOP's attorney termed the action "mass resignations."[26] In a dramatic event, an officer recovering from a gunshot wound was carried in on a stretcher to turn in his badge.[27] According to accounts of the work stoppage, 582 of the police department's 598 officers participated in the walkout.[28]

Police duties during the strike were performed by Oklahoma state highway patrolmen and sheriff's department deputies. The troopers and sheriff's deputies had been on standby status and assumed the duties of the police immediately following the walkout.[29] Oklahoma City faced no apparent onslaught of criminal activity as a result of the police strike. During the first night of the strike a lower than normal number of calls for police assistance were received.[30]

Nevertheless, the transition of police replacements into the regular officers' duties was not without problems. According to one source, the main problem of the emergency replacements was their lack of familiarity with Oklahoma City streets.[31] Although a serious situation, accounts of some of the problems faced by replacements provide insight as well as some humor. One reporter's account of some incidents follows:

" 'Now, on what authority do I make this arrest?' a trooper asked.

"The sergeant gave his name and the trooper wrote it on the palm of his hand for quick reference . . .[32]

"While troopers were receiving instructions in the field from Oklahoma City police supervisors, they were also being guided by drunks at the city jail.

" 'Now be sure and put me on five (cell floor),' an inebriate cautioned an arresting trooper.

" 'I usually get beat up if they put me on three,' he explained."[33]

These quotations, although humorous, indicate that the replacements constituted a police force which was probably not prepared to deal with any real crisis. Oklahoma City was spared the misfortunes of other cities where police strikes have occurred, such as Boston in 1919 and Montreal in 1969. As Burton and Krider conclude from the experiences of such strikes, "In the case of strikes by essential employees, such as policemen, the deterioration of public order occurs almost immediately."[34]

Three days after the strike began, it ended when the FOP accepted the city's offer of a 9 percent across the board wage increase. The increase applied to all positions except entry levels, and was retroactive to August 1, 1975. Educational incentive pay was reduced; the officers involved in the strike would not be paid for the three days during the walk-out, and would be penalized another two days' pay for "improper action."[35]

Upon conclusion of the strike, several statements were made regarding the experience. The city manager concluded that the city should not have gone to arbitration.[36] *The Daily Oklahoman* concluded that, "Arbitration has no valid place in public employee bargaining . . ."[37] One councilman predicted tyranny through the following causal chain: "To succumb to these illegal acts (the strike) is to contribute to the eventual destruction of our society. Disrespect for the law leads to anarchy, and anarchy always leads to tyranny . . ."[38] Another councilman predicted the death of his conscience before he would vote for giving the union benefits gained by a work stoppage.[39] It almost goes without saying that these are extreme statements, but ones that may convey a notion of the emotion of those dealing with the union and a major newspaper in the state.

Emotion and inexperience on the part of negotiators probably contributed to occurrence of the strike, but the failure of the law is apparent. The power of the Public Employee Relations Board to administer the law had been eliminated. The law had no provision for final resolution of impasses. The arbitration provision served only to intensify the dispute by allowing the city to refuse to abide by the panel's ruling. Unfavorable views of the present arbitration procedure seem warranted, but not for arbitration in which the award is binding on both parties. In this case, legislation contributed to a strike but more comprehensive legislation with a compulsory arbitration provision could have eliminated the cause for the strike.

Conclusion

Arbitration is not the cure for all labor problems. The Oklahoma City experience is perhaps better explained by an alternative view of the value of arbitration. This view would be that arbitration serves a valuable purpose in public sector bargaining, particularly compulsory arbitration as an alternative to public sector strikes in essential services. According to this explanation, the Oklahoma City police work slowdown could have been prevented if arbitration of the dispute had been effectively mandated. Furthermore, the strike could probably have been prevented if the arbitration panel's ruling had been binding on all parties. Instead, the city's refusal to accept the panel's ruling caused the police to feel they had been treated unfairly.

Whether collective bargaining legislation leads to more strikes is a yet unresolved question. One study indicates some tendency among certain employee groups to strike more frequently after passage of such legislation. A comprehensive study indicates that such legislation is not associated with a higher incidence of strikes. A third study indicates that environmental characteristics are important determinates of how such legislation is related to strike incidence.

The present analysis provides evidence that inadequate legislation and administration of such legislation may have contributed to a serious strike in an essential service. Conversely, legislation providing for final resolution of impasses would probably have eliminated the cause of the strike. Without such legislation, given the somewhat mild penalties assessed of police officers participating in the strike, a recurrence of a similar work stoppage may be more than a remote possibility.

Notes

1. Rehmus, Charles M. "Labor Relations in the Public Sector in the United States," *International Labor Review,* Vol. 109 (March 1974), pp. 199-216.

2. Bakke, E. Wight. "Reflections on the Future of Bargaining in the Public Sector," *Monthly Labor Review,* Vol. 93 (July 1970),pp. 21-25.

3. Seidman, Joel. "State Legislation on Collective Bargaining by Public Employees," *Labor Law Journal,* Vol. 22 (January 1971), p. 21.

4. Burton, John F., Jr. and Krider, Charles E. "The Incidence of Strikes in Public

Employment," in Hamermesh, Daniel S., ed. *Labor in the Public and Nonprofit Sectors,* Princeton, New Jersey: Princeton University Press, 1975, pp. 135-177.

5. Perry, James L. "Public Policy and Public Employee Strikes," *Industrial Relations,* Vol. 16 (October 1977), pp. 273-282.

6. Burton and Krider, *op. cit.,* p. 171.

7. Kochan, Thomas A. "Correlates of State Public Employee Bargaining Laws," *Industrial Relations,* Vol. 12 (October 1973), pp. 322-337.

8. SR 115. A summary of the act appears in the *Oklahoma Law Review,* Vol. 27 (Summer 1974), pp. 528-533.

9. 11 O. S. 1971.

10. 11O. S. Supp. 1972.

11. O. S. Supp. 1972, 548.4-1 subparagraph (D).

12. Barnett, James R., Assistant Attorney General, State of Oklahoma, letter dated June 27, 1977.

13. *Ibid.*

14. *Midwest City v. Cravens,* Okl., 532 P. 2d 829 (1975).

15. Barnett, cited at note 12, p. 8.

16. Oklahoma is somewhat unique with respect to unionization in the private sector in that it is one of the few states in the region that does not have a right-to-work law.

17. Dryden, Dave and Teyington, Andrew. "City Police Go on Strike," *The Daily Oklahoman.* October 24, 1975, pp. 1-2.

18. Dryden, Dave. "Raises Could Mean Cut in City Jobs, Officials Say," *The Daily Oklahoman.* October 11, 1975, pp. 1-2.

19. *Ibid.*

20. Tevington, Andrew. "City Officers Air Threats in Pay Rift," *The Daily Oklahoman.* October 12, 1975, pp. 1-2.

21. Dryden, Dave, cited at note 18.

22. McCarthy, Tom. "Police Pay Bid Faces Rejection," *The Daily Oklahoman.* October 20, 1975, pp. 1-2 and Dryden, Dave "Docking Strikers, Pay Probably Won't Show," *The Daily Oklahoman.* October 28, 1975, p. 12.

23. Dryden, Dave. "Council Pair Urge Firings in Walkout," *The Daily Oklahoman.* October 14, 1975, pp. 1-2

24. Tevington, Andrew. "Police Start Slowdown to Protest Wage Vote," *The Daily Oklahoman.* October 22, 1975, pp. 1-2

25. Donovan, Kevin and McCarthy, Tom. "Police Chiefs Deny Men Ignore Nonemergency Calls," *The Daily Oklahoman.* October 22, 1975, pp. 1-2.

26. Dryden, Dave and Tevington, Andrew; cited at note 17, and Dryden, Dave, "Talks Bring No Changes in Situation" *The Daily Oklahoman.* October 25, 1975, pp. 1-2.

27. Dryden, Dave and Tevington, Andrew; cited at note 17.

28. McCarthy, Tom and Donovan, Kevin. "Emergency Forces Find Task Routine," *The Daily Oklahoman.* October 24, 1975, pp. 1-2.

29. Dryden, Dave and Tevington, Andrew; cited at note 17.

30. McCarthy, Tom and Donovan, Kevin; cited at note 28.

31. *Ibid.*

32. Donovan, Kevin, "Duties Trying for Busy Troopers," *The Daily Oklahoman.* October 26, 1975, p. 1.

33. *Ibid.,* p. 2.
34. Burton, John F., Jr. and Krider, Charles E. "The Role and Consequences of Strikes by Public Employees," *The Yale Law Journal,* Vol. 79 (January 1970), p. 434.
35. McCarthy, Tom, "Strike Ends; Police on Job," *The Daily Oklahoman.* October 27, 1975, pp. 1-2.
36. *Ibid.*
37. Editorial. *The Daily Oklahoman,* October 30, 1975, p. 8.
38. Dryden, Dave. "City Officials Hint at Vote on Sales Tax," *The Daily Oklahoman,* October 29, 1975, p. 15.
39. *Ibid.*

11
Making Personnel Decisions by Public Referenda: Campaigns for Police and Fire Fighter Collective Bargaining in Texas

I. B. Helburn and Darold T. Barnum

In many political jurisdictions across the nation voters can participate directly in public personnel decisions through various initiative and referendum procedures. A conspicuous example of this was Anita Bryant's crusade to change the Dade County, Florida, policy regarding homosexuals via a public vote. The Dade County procedure is not unique however. In Texas, police and/or fire fighters in home rule cities have forced votes on changes in wages and hours of work.[1] The Texas civil service law and collective bargaining law for police and fire fighters apply in a political jurisdiction only after adoption by a local vote.[2] In Florida, a statewide vote was held in November, 1976 on a constitutional amendment which limited the number of full-time state employees to one percent of the population and the number of part-time employees to ten percent of the full-time group.[3] Also in November, 1976, San Francisco voters adopted an ordinance requiring a public vote on a pay plan based on the last demand of the employee organization, in the event negotiations reached impasse.[4] Since 1973 the city of Englewood, Colorado, has had a local labor relations ordinance that provides for the resolution of contract impasses by local referendum.[5]

Reprinted with permission from *Public Personnel Management,* Vol. 7, No. 2 (March-April, 1978), pp. 119-126.

I. B. Helburn is Associate Professor, Graduate School of Business, University of Texas at Austin. Darold T. Barnum is Associate Professor, Division of Business Administration, Indiana University Northwest.

Whether such processes result in optimal personnel decisions however is open to question, especially where the issue is a complex one. Such matters as adoption of the comprehensive civil service or collective bargaining law involve so many complexities that an extensive and in-depth education process would seem necessary before the voters could make an intelligent decision. Even in more simple cases such as determining a "fair wage," there are many factors to be considered, as any fact finder or interest arbitrator could testify.

One way to assess the workability of local referenda is to examine the campaigns themselves. Campaigns conducted so as to provide voters with adequate information on an issue argue for the acceptability of this method, just as due process rather than the verdict itself is often important in trials of law.

This article will examine public referenda concerning adoption of the Texas Fire and Police Employee Relations Act (FPERA), which, as already noted, provides that collective bargaining for public safety workers will be legal only after the Act has been adopted by a local referendum. Emphasis is on the campaign process preceding the vote, with a view of the process as an instrument of rational decision-making.

Material on which the analysis is based was drawn from 28 referenda held in 28 Texas cities between August 1973 and September 1976.[6] There were 25 adoption referenda and three repeal elections. In most cases we were able to interview an employee organization official and a municipal official in the city concerned. These interviews were supplemented with newspaper accounts of the campaigns, published advertisements and, where available, financial reports filed by pro and anti-bargaining groups.

The following section summarizes the legal environment, after which the experience under the FPERA is reviewed. Finally, the arguments used by proponents and opponents of public employee bargaining are discussed, as are the implications of this particular process for decision-making.

FPERA and Related Law

Prior to the passage of the FPERA all public employees in Texas fell under the provisions of law passed in 1947. Employees were free to join or refrain from joining "labor organizations" which represented employees for purposes of presenting grievances over wages and other conditions of work. Public employers were not permitted to recognize employee organizations for the purpose of collective bargaining, negotiated agreements were unenforceable, and employees were discouraged from striking by penalties including loss of job and accrued benefits.[7]

In addition to the above law, relations between police and fire fighters and public employers have been affected by The Firemen's and Policemen's Civil Service Act.[8] This much amended act, the result of intensive bargaining and lobbying with the legislature by police and fire fighters, contains provisions for "wages, longevity pay, severance pay, classifications, educational incentive pay, hours of work, extra hours, exchange of hours, overtime, vacations, holidays, paid sick leave, leave of absence, and—as would be expected—procedures for promotion, discipline and dismissal."[9]

The Civil Service Law authorizes but does not require cities with a population of 10,000 or more to adopt civil service on a local option basis, and thus not all cities have elected coverage. A 1975 report listed 43 cities that had adopted state civil service law and eight additional cities having local civil service provisions,[10] with local benefits generally equal to those provided by state law.

> *The FPERA is a significant departure from the 1947 law, stating that "collective bargaining is deemed to be a fair and practical method for determining wages and other conditions of employment for employees who comprise the paid fire and police departments of the cities, towns, and other political subdivisions within this state. A denial to such employees of the right to organize and bargain collectively would lead to strife and unrest, with consequent injury to the health, safety, and welfare of the public."[11]*

In brief, the FPERA provides collective bargaining rights for police and/or fire fighters if such rights are granted in a local option referendum. Political subdivisions are then required to bargain with an exclusive representative of the employees over "wages, hours, working conditions, and all other terms and conditions of employment,"[12] with compensation and other conditions of employment to be "substantially the same" as those in "comparable private sector employment."[13] Both strikes and lockouts are prohibited, with interest arbitration encouraged as a means of resolving disputes arising over the negotiation of agreements. However, if there is no agreement to arbitrate, the local district court is empowered to enforce the prevailing wage and working conditions requirements. Bargaining is to be conducted in conformance with state open meetings or "sunshine law" requirements.

The FPERA legislation was prepared and introduced into the House of Representatives at the request of The Texas State Association of Fire Fighters. This version did not include the open meeting language, the strike penalties contained in the final version, nor the local option provision. The local option provision was included in the final version of the bill at the insistence of the Governor. It is, however, consistent with approaches to other legislation in this state. As noted above, there is a local option provision in the civil service law. Local option has also been written into legislation regarding liquor by the drink, the one percent municipal sales tax and exemptions for the elderly from *ad valorem* taxes.

The local option provision of FPERA requires interested employee associations to gather signatures from 5% or 20,000 (whichever is less) of the qualified voters voting in the last general election in the political subdivision concerned.[14] The petition containing the signatures is to be filed with the governing body of the political subdivision (normally the city council or commission), with the governing body responsible for certifying the validity of the petition and setting an election date within 60 days of the date on which the petition was filed. Section 5(b) requires the following proposition to be put on the ballot:

"For or against the following: Adoption of the state law applicable to

*'firefighters and policemen' or 'firefighters' or 'policemen', (whichever shall
be applicable), which establishes collective bargaining when a majority of
the affected employees favor representation by an employees' association
and which preserves the prohibition of strikes and lockouts and provides
penalties therefore."*

If the referendum passes, the governing body is required to place the Act
into effect within 30 days after the beginning of the first fiscal year following the
election.

Section 5(c) contains procedures for repeal of the Act, a process that is
essentially the same as the one leading to the granting of bargaining rights. The
governing body is not required to put the repeal proposition on the ballot within
a specified period of time. However, repeal petitions cannot be submitted and
thus an election could not be held, for one year from the date of a previous
adoption or repeal election. If repeal is passed, the Act becomes null and void
immediately upon certification of the vote. The question to be voted upon shall
read: "For or against the following: Repeal of the adoption of the state law . . ."

Supporters and Opponents of the Act

The Act may be adopted for only one of the two groups or for both jointly.
Of the 25 adoption referenda, the election applied to police only in four cities, to
fire fighters only in eleven, and to both groups in the remaining ten. In every case
the primary proponents of the Act were the fire and/or police associations
directly involved. When only one association went, the other gave no help. In
fact, there was little active support for the Act from any organization other than
the involved association(s). To be sure, in nine of the 25 cases the city's
organized labor movement (generally a central labor council) endorsed the
measure, as did some individual union locals, but they typically provided no
active support in terms of campaign workers or money. (The presence of an
endorsement was not related to the community's private sector unionization
rate however, since half were in cities above and half below the sample's mean
rate of 10.2%). Additionally the Catholic Church supported the Act from the
pulpit in El Paso, and a newspaper supported the Act in Texas City.

Arrayed against passage of the Act was a somewhat more diverse set of
opponents, although in eleven referenda there was no active opposition. In the
remaining fourteen cases however, active opposition was present. The active
opposition effort originated from either the governing body (city council or
commission), an ad hoc group formed specifically to oppose the Act, or both.
Where both were present the ad hoc groups often had been formed at the behest
of the governing body, and often had support from the business sector. In the
two cases with ad hoc groups but no governing body opposition, it appears that
the ad hoc groups were formed and funded primarily through activities of the
business community. In addition, eleven chambers of commerce and nine
newspapers opposed the Act, with active opposition in Baytown from volunteer
fire fighters and in Houston from the Republican Party and Right-to-Work
organizations.

Campaign expenditures by proponents varied from a low of $100 to a high of $100,000, or from 1.1 to 33.3 cents per registered voter. Opponents who spent money had expenses ranging from $136 to $52,951 or from 1.2 to 10.5 cents per registered voter. In those cases where heavy expenditures occurred, they were the result of heavy use of newspaper, radio and television advertising.

Influencing Voters

The most common method used to get the message to the voters was press releases, with 60 percent of both proponents and opponents indicating that they employed this method. Next in frequency was radio advertising, followed by newspaper advertising, direct mail letters to voters, and speakers. The number of methods used varied from one to twelve for the associations, the most common number being six. The Act's opponents generally used two to four different methods.

The Message

The major arguments advanced by proponents of bargaining are listed in Table 2. There is considerable overlap in these arguments, out of which emerge four areas of concern. First, employees are obviously concerned with wages and wage-related fringe benefits. Second, there are a series of defensive arguments, either anticipating or in response to public anti-bargaining positions. These arguments include the "illegal strikes" or "no employee desire" to strike, and the "no adverse financial impact" notions. Third, employees are concerned with the quality and quantity of communications between themselves and the administration. This is reflected in the third argument listed in Table 2 as well as other arguments noting desires for better communications, talk with management, and a voice in decisions. Finally, there is the notion that collective bargaining will lead to improvements in the protective service in such areas as equipment, training, manpower and safety.

Table 3 contains a listing of anti-bargaining arguments. There are both positive and negative thrusts to these positions, with the negative dominating. Opponents concentrated on publicizing the perceived negative impact of public employee bargaining on the city—higher taxes, loss of local control to outside arbitrators, resulting losses in efficiency or increases in personnel needed. Additionally, there were a series of arguments that can be labeled "anti-union," with the spector of strikes, "disguised" public sector bargaining and private sector unionization as examples. Finally, there were the more positive arguments that benefits and treatment were currently good and that collective bargaining was unlikely to improve effectiveness or safety.

Obviously, in those cities where bargaining was first approved and later repealed, the anti-bargaining arguments were more effective after actual negotiations began than before. The concern with higher taxes seemed to dominate, since city management was likely to break off negotiations and express the concern that employee demands were unreasonable in the light of the city's financial position.

In pro-bargaining campaign advertising, issues were not explored in any depth, a comment which may be generally applied. Further, some of the statements tend to distort reality. Ads were written to convey the impression that for the first time strikes would be prohibited, while in fact the 1947 law outlawing public employee bargaining provided for dismissal in the event of a strike. The assurance of no interruption rang hollow in some areas in the face of anti-bargaining ads that noted police and/or fire fighter work stoppages in other communities with no-strike laws. Many of the statements could only be taken on faith since no proof was offered that, for example, improved morale and professionalism or a better quality force would result.[15]

Anti-bargaining advertising also included partial truths and assertions that had to be accepted on faith, there being no hard evidence to support the contention. There is evidence suggesting that public employee bargaining has not had a major impact on wages,[16] thus leaving open the question of higher taxes. While under the FPERA, an "outside arbitrator" could rule on wages and working conditions only with the consent of the municipality. Furthermore, given the evidence that passage of public employee bargaining law has not led to an increase in strikes,[17] there is no reason to believe that the threat of a strike is greater under the FPERA.

The commonalities between the approaches used by both sides are unfortunate. It appears that the referenda campaigns generated far more heat than light. In an area where relatively few people are knowledgeable to begin with, campaigns were designed to appeal to already-existing biases rather than to win votes by truly educating the public.

Almost unanimously, municipal officials felt the voting public had a good grasp of the issues when bargaining was defeated; employee organization officials felt the public understood the issues when the referenda were approved. Conversely, the defeated parties consistently expressed concern that the issues were not understood. Without pre- and post-referenda interviews of voting populations, conclusions cannot be drawn. However, a review of the campaigns does not suggest the achievement of real knowledge and understanding of the complex issues associated with public employee bargaining in general and such activity under the FPERA in particular. Even worse, only a handful of the local interviewees seemed to have an adequate understanding of the Act and its consequences.

The Decision: Voter Participation

Voter turnout for the referenda elections generally was low. Less than 10% of the registered voters voted in twelve of the 25 adoption referenda. The turnout exceeded 20% only in those six cases where the bargaining referenda occurred concurrently with city council or commission elections.

The Decision: Referenda Outcomes

Although election *processes* rather than *outcomes* are the primary concern of this article, a brief discussion of the latter may be of interested.[18] Of the 25 adoption referenda, 12 passed and 13 failed (with both the first and second attempts failing in Galveston). Two of the three repeal attempts succeeded, with the Act being retained in the third city. These results, however, had little if anything to do with the nature and quality of the arguments put forth in the campaigns. Although beyond the scope of this article, the key influences were the organizations and institutions involved on each side of the issue, their level of campaign activity, and environmental factors such as income levels and unionization rates. These influences explain 98.8% of the differences in election outcomes, with no recourse possible or necessary to what should have made a major impact, namely the issue itself and the quality of the campaigns. Thus we return to our original concern, the usefulness of the referendum process as a method of making personnel and labor relations decisions.

An Evaluation of the Process

Generally, an electorate directly determines governmental policies of only the most general nature, thereby providing guidance on major policy issues, but not being involved in the means by which these policies will be implemented. Rightly so, for the typical voter has neither the interest, time, nor ability to adequately evaluate the complexities of alternative methods of achieving objectives. This is the job of elected officials and appointed professional

Table 1
Referendum Campaign Methods, by Type Used

Method	Proponents No.	%	Opponents No.	%
Press Releases	15	60	15	60
Radio Ads	19	76	8	32
Newspaper Ads	12	48	10	40
Letters to Voters	9	36	9	36
Speakers	9	36	9	36
Brochures or Handbills	14	56	1	4
Posters or Billboards	14	56	1	4
Television Ads	10	40	4	16
Window or Bumper Stickers	13	52	0	0
Telephoning	9	36	3	12
Panels or Debates	5	20	3	12
Door-to-Door	7	28	0	0
Word of Mouth	5	20	2	8
Yard Signs	6	24	0	0
Letters to Other Employees	0	0	3	12
Rides to Polls	3	12	0	0
Public Address Advertising	2	8	0	0
Displays	2	8	0	0
Letters to Editor	1	4	1	4

Table 2
Major Official Arguments Used by Proponents of the Act

| | Referenda | |
Argument	No.	%
Means of achieving a "living wage," parity, etc.	13	52
Strikes illegal under Act and/or employees have no desire to strike	12	48
Provides an effective, fair and/or democratic method for setting terms and conditions of employment	11	44
Need better employee-management communications	9	36
Will improve efficiency and effectiveness of departments	9	36
Want to "talk" to city management	8	32
Need better working conditions	8	32
Need better equipment	7	28
Want voice in decisions affecting workers	6	24
Will not cause increase in costs or taxes	6	24
Vote "For" your local fire fighters and/or police	5	20
Need better safety	3	12
Need more and/or better manpower	3	12
Local control will be retained	2	8
Need more fringe benefits	2	8
Need better hours of work	1	4
Need more training	1	4

Source: Interviews with management and union representatives, newspapers, ads, and newspaper articles.
Note: Percentages based on 25 referenda (e.g., 13/25 = 52 percent) because there were official proponents in all cases.

Table 3
Major Official Arguments Used by Opponents of the Act

| | Referenda | |
Argument	No.	%
Will result in loss of control over budgets and/or taxes by local elected representatives	17	85
Higher Taxes: Will result 11		
May result 6		
Total	17	85
Strikes: Will result 4		
May result 7		
Total	11	55
Current benefits and/or employee treatment is good	9	45
"Outsiders will take over" city	8	40
Unfair to other city employees because of equal treatment	7	35
Act is disguised "unionism" and/or "collective bargaining"	3	15
Will not improve efficiency and effectiveness of departments	3	15
Will slow administrative process and/or increase personnel needed to deal with employee relations	3	15
Safety will not be improved	1	5
Will increase unionization of private sector workforce	1	5

Source: Interviews with management and union representatives, newspaper ads and newspaper articles.
Note: Percentage based on only those 20 referenda where there was public opposition (e.g., 17/20 = 85 percent). In the remaining 5 referenda there were no opposing arguments made publicly.

managers.[19] The electorate is ill-equipped to make rational decisions on complex issues unless impractically large resources are devoted to public education.

Faced with this situation, the opposing parties, each desiring to win, tend to conduct campaigns based on gross oversimplification, half-truths and known voter biases. Then the voters, equipped with no hard information on which to make a rational decision, either do not vote at all or vote on half-baked opinions. This is exactly what has happened in the Texas campaigns.

Although public management can sometimes benefit from a situation where the cry of higher taxes or loss of citizen control automatically brings out a large conservative vote, this is a two edged sword. If the socioeconomic character of the electorate favors primarily with the workers, for example, then city management may be forced to adopt resolutions that professionals would never have made. Based on the Texas experience, therefore, we feel that issues involving complex personnel and labor relations decisions should be made by professionals.

Notes

1. John Larkin Matthews, "The Initiative Referendum and Its Use by the Texas Fire Fighters: 1947-1974," unpublished professional report, Graduate School of Business, The University of Texas at Austin, 1977.

2. Vernon's Tex. Rev. Civ. Stat. Ann. art 1926m, section 27(a)(1971). (Hereafter abbreviated as V.A.C.S.)

3. Douglas R. Sease, "Efficiency or Chaos? Floridians Expected to Vote Limit on Number of State's Employees; Impact of Move Debated," *The Wall Street Journal,* October 8, 1976, p. 26.

4. "San Francisco adopts referendum; Eugene sets new plan," *LMRS Newsletter,* No. 7 (December 1976), p. 4.

5. Andy McCowan, "Referendum impasse plan works in Englewood, Colo.," *LMRS Newsletter,* No. 8, (June 1977), pp. 2-3.

6. A more extensive review and analysis of the referenda may be found in Darold T. Barnum and I. B. Helburn, *Local Option Recognition and Bargaining: The Texas Fire Fighter and Police Experience* (Lubbock, TX: College of Business Administration, Texas Tech. University, 1976).

7. V.A.C.S. art. 5154c (1971).

8. V.A.C.S. art. 1269m-r (supp. 1974).

9. Charles J. Morris, "Everything You Always Wanted to Know About Public Employee Bargaining in Texas—But Were Afraid to Ask," *Houston Law Review* No. 13, p. 301.

10. Texas Municipal League, *Fringe Benefits of Texas Municipal Employees* (Austin: Texas Municipal League, 1975), pp. 171-172.

11. V.A.C.S. art 5152c-1, section 2(b)(1).

12. *Ibid.,* sec. 5(a).

13. *Ibid.,* sec. 2(a) and 4.

14. *Ibid.,* sec. 5(b).

15. Ronald G. Ehrenberg, "Municipal Government Structure, Unionization, and the

Wages of Fire Fighters," *Industrial and Labor Relations Review,* No. 27 (October 1973), pp. 36-48.

16. John F. Burton, Jr. and Charles E. Krider, "The Incidence of Strikes in Public Employment," *Labor in the Public and Nonprofit Sectors* (edited by Daniel S. Hammermesh) (Princeton, NJ: Princeton University Press, 1975), pp. 135-172.

17. For a detailed analysis of the reasons for the outcomes, see Helburn and Barnum, *Local Option Recognition and Bargaining,* Ch. V.

18. The most extensive study to date of questions of public employee bargaining in Texas was undertaken by the Public Employees Study Commission, an interim study committee created by the 1972 Legislature. I. B. Helburn, one of the 18 members of the Commission, has observed that even this inquiry into public employee bargaining lacked both breadth and depth. See I. B. Helburn, "Public Employee Labor Relations in Texas: The Widening Gap," *Labor Law Journal,* No. 27 (February 1976), pp. 112-116.

Chapter Five

Employment Discrimination
and the Personnel Administrator

Introduction

Naively, many of us think that the passage of laws and the rendering of court decisions lead directly to sound administration of the leaders' intent. We would like to assume that court rulings such as *Brown* v. *The Board of Education* and laws such as the Civil Rights Act of 1964 solve important societal problems. We see the application of these rulings and laws as simple and nondiscretionary processes. Administrators are thought to know how to apply the laws fairly and accurately and the public is assumed to accept the change without resistance.

Often, however, good rulings and laws do not result in clearly articulated policy. Controversial acts , in fact, sometimes leave important questions of implementation unanswered and administrators must try to cope with the meaning of a law while lacking the knowledge, skills, or resources to carry out its intent.

Nowhere are these problems more evident than in the attempt to implement Title VII of the 1964 Civil Rights Act. While employment discrimination was forbidden by this law, the means to carry out its provisions still remain unclear. The burden of relating legislative and judicial intent with the realities of organizational life rests with the personnel policymaker. The problems of policy implementation are greater here than in other areas of concern because the societal commitment has been limited, governments have allocated few resources to the problem, and conflicts between discrimination and other rights are unresolved. The personnel specialist therefore becomes a decisionmaker where few solid guidelines for action are present.

Why is Ending Employment Discrimination a Problem?

The passage of the 1964 Civil Rights Act did not change personnel practices immediately. In fact many would argue that little has been accomplished in spite of numerous court cases and regulatory actions, much expense, and considerable commitment from leaders at all levels of government. The reasons for the slowness in ending discrimination are related in part to the magnitude of the problem and naive assumptions about the power of the law.

1. Ending discrimination affects the wealth and well being of those who are advantaged as well as the disadvantaged. Therefore, it is in the self-interest of some to resist.
2. Removing legal barriers may have little effect on practice unless daily activities are monitored closely. Rarely are enforcement resources sufficient for close scrutiny of ongoing activities.
3. Influencing the aspects of discrimination that are the result of acts that have biased effects demands a sophisticated understanding of how social processes operate. The unconscious effects of discrimination influence matters such as how schools select students for advancement and how people learn the accepted dress and speech in a particular setting. Social scientists are only beginning to understand these processes and how they influence employment discrimination.

Because discrimination is deeply ingrained in our way of life, eradicating it requires profound changes in many social practices. The efforts in the personnel field to enforce the Civil Rights Act attempt to alter radically many established personnel policies.

1. Questions have been raised about standard merit system practices such as personnel tests, seniority systems, and in-house promotions.
2. The courts and regulatory agencies have become frequent interveners in personnel matters by assisting those experiencing discrimination. The personnel system is thus no longer isolated from the influence of those outside of the organization.
3. A variety of new concerns have been added to the tasks of personnel administration. Training programs to lessen the amount of discrimination in an organization have become common. Agencies have developed outreach programs to attract new minority and female employees.

Creating Equal Employment

The selections in this chapter discuss several different aspects of the problems associated with equal employment efforts. The first three (Selections 12, 13, 14) document and consider problems associated with creating equal employment for several major disadvantaged groups—blacks, Hispanics, and women.

Stewart and Williams (Selections 12 and 13) look closely at the problems related to employment of women and blacks respectively. Both selections emphasize the sociological reasons for failures to gain increased employment of these people. They also suggest some important internal problems often faced by public organizations when women and blacks attempt to reach positions of importance within the organization.

Much that has been written about increased employment of racial and ethnic minorities and women assumes that a common set of policies will work effectively for all deprived groups. Increased training and outreach and educational counseling are among the most frequently suggested techniques. Saltzstein and Saltzstein examine black, Spanish surnamed and women's employment in Texas cities. The patterns they find suggest that different strategies for each group may lead to greater employment success.

New Procedures

The second group of readings in this chapter (Selections 15-18) show the extent to which basic personnel procedures have been changed by equal employment policies. Most important in this regard is testing, which has come under close scrutiny in recent years. This has forced analysts to deal with statistical properties of employment tests such as reliability and validity. Consequently, agencies often use forms of employment screening drastically different from the traditional civil service test.

Most instrumental in this change is the Supreme Court. The two cases included here (Selections 15 and 16) reveal that the justices have become much more involved in the practices of personnel agencies.

The Duke Power Company required a high school diploma or the passing of an intelligence test as a condition of employment. The test had no relationship to the jobs performed, but was not a blatantly discriminatory test. Griggs and others were black plant employees who sued the company, arguing that the discriminatory impact of the test was contrary to the 1964 Civil Rights Act.

In the Griggs case (15) the Court ruled that employment tests that have a discriminatory impact on who is hired or promoted are forbidden unless those tests are, in fact "... a reasonable measure of job performance." All civil service examinations are thus subject to question if, in fact, the consequence of the test is a disproportionate number of minorities or women hired or promoted.

The precedent established by the Griggs case was applied by numerous lower court decisions. It resulted in the banning of practices such as the use of arrest records in evaluating prospective employees, reliance on "word of mouth" contracts by unions and employers as a means of recruiting, and the use of minimum height and weight requirements for various positions. According to this case, such requirements are valid only if the employer can clearly show that the traits are job related.

The case is also a superb example of the coordination between legislative acts and the court system. The relevant portions of the 1964 Civil Rights Act (Selection 5) should be reviewed in reading this case.

The ruling in the second case, *Washington* v. *Davis* (Selection 16) may alter many policies established by the Griggs case. At issue is a written personnel test of the Washington, D.C., police department which had eliminated a disproportionate number of blacks from membership.

Here the Court takes a more lenient position regarding the obligation of the employer. The justices argue that evidence of differential impact is not a sufficient reason for remedial action, and they are less definitive about the need for job relatedness. The decision thus significantly weakens the potential power of those who feel discriminated. It is also an example of how the Court sometimes alters previous rulings when new cases are brought to it.

Quotas and Reverse Discrimination

Removing discriminatory barriers has often meant changing basic personnel processes. The courts and regulatory bodies have, on occasion, had to apply remedies which appear to some people to be drastic in nature. To avoid prosecution or loss of funds, agencies themselves have often imposed hiring quotas for disadvantaged groups. The granting of special preference in employment to disadvantaged groups has raised a fundamental conflict for the American political system. Does it deny equal rights to the majority?

Bakke v. *California* is a Supreme Court decision concerning the conflict between the effort of a university to improve opportunities for the disadvantaged and the rights of the majority to equal treatment. The issues in this case are analyzed by Bert Buzan (Selection 17), followed by a portion of the text of the Supreme Court decision (Selection 18).

The case and the commentary do not provide an answer to this important conflict. In fact, the argument is made that an harmonious solution to the "quota" controversy may never come forth. The personnel policymaker then must grapple with these problems daily without definitive guidance. The only approach to dilemmas of this sort is to be acquainted thoroughly with the relevant issues and recent rulings, and to try to act with a sense of fairness. These three readings should be seen as serious attempts to come to grips with the problem. It is the task of the administrator to take such material and deal with the practical issues at hand.

12
Women in Top Jobs:
An Opportunity for Federal Leadership
Debra Stewart

The year 1976 finds American women firmly entrenched in the country's labor force. With nine out of ten women having worked during their lifetime and 46 per cent of all American women currently engaged in salaried employment, the female worker is no longer a deviant case.[1] This trend toward large-scale participation is mirrored in the public sector. There females constitute some 41.7 per cent of the white collar work force and, in certain cases, occupy up to 63 per cent of all agency slots.[2] Accordingly, policy objectives, congruent with

---

Reprinted with permission from the *Public Administration Review,* Vol. 36, No. 4 (July-August, 1976), pp. 357-364.
Debra Stewart is Assistant Professor of Political Science, North Carolina State University.

emerging national needs in this sphere, relate less to mere participation of women in the labor force and more to the character of that participation. Focusing specifically on government as employer, the issue becomes not how many women will be employed in the public service of the future, but rather in what capacity they will be employed.

This article is grounded in the assumption that expansion of employment opportunities for women in American society calls for a focus, not on jobs per se, but rather on job stratification. National occupational data reveals small numbers of women have indeed gained acceptance in the most prestigious occupations: 9.8 per cent of the physicians, 7 per cent of the lawyers and judges, 9.4 per cent of the full professors, and 2.3 per cent of highest level (GS16-18) federal civil servants.[3] Yet the pattern of mobility parallels that recently identified in Great Britain. There women's entry into top slots has gone from breakthrough in earlier decades to acceptance, but now remains fixed on a plateau.[4] The public policy question is simply: "how might these percentages be increased?" Through an analysis of obstacles to full participation in the upper echelons of private and public bureaucracy, this article aims to bring change direction into sharp relief and, in the process, to illuminate the special leadership role for the federal public service.

Obstacles to Change

In the plethora of recent works on women in American society three broad explanations for the blockage of female entry into high-level decision-making positions are found: the political, the biological, and the sociological.[5] Each type of explanation contains elements of the others, the sociological in particular having pronounced biological and political dimensions. Nevertheless, these labels do function to locate the core of each explanation as well as to allow for some demarcation of boundary lines. Critical examination of each explanatory model, and its implications, in conjunction with data on public and private sector employment patterns serves to highlight that set of factors best explaining the barrier to movement beyond the current threshold. Only through such isolation of the "problem," will the solution in the form of a change strategy emerge.

The Political Thesis

In the most extreme form the political thesis posits that men constitute the ruling class of the world and are determined to stay in power. In the words of one author, male-female relations reflect ". . . the oldest, most rigid class/caste system in existence, the class system based on sex—a system consolidated over thousands of years, lending the archtypal male and female roles an undeserved legitimacy and seeming permanence."[6] This analysis points out that characteristically "feminine" traits are nothing more than the traits of any oppressed class. While emphasizing the historical similarity between the condition of women as an oppressed class in American society and the condition of blacks, this mode of analysis stresses the ubiquitous character of the sexual class system.

To the extent that this thesis is correct, only a rigorously enforced quota system would facilitate the movement of significant numbers of women into top jobs in American society. And yet, if this analysis does capture reality, the possibility of gaining the political clout to make such a quota system effective, even in government employment, is highly problematic. But, before subscribing to an analysis which yields only the alternatives of subjection or revolution, elements of federal service experience, challenging the political thesis, should be brought forward.

While at one level the class/power explanation fits with the picture of women clustering in the low pay and low status jobs, it is contradicted by formal government action endorsing EEO for women, as well as by the pattern of employment variation across agencies within the federal government. With respect to the formal endorsement of EEO, which may go as far as requiring affirmative action, one could simply respond that this is just a move in the symbolic politics game. Such moves are necessary to feign compliance with the formal American "equality of opportunity" ideology. Indeed we know from cross-national studies that formal ideology may account for little in explaining the position of women in modern society.[7] The debate on formal vs. real opportunity is not easily resolved, for it gets into the motivations of EEO rule makers. Fortunately, we need not await such resolution before pronouncing judgment on the political thesis.

The pattern of employment within and across government agencies clearly flies in the face of this class/power analysis. If, in fact, there were a conscious male conspiracy, bent on keeping women in low status jobs, then one would expect to find little variation in opportunity for distaff advancement across agencies. This expectation is, however, not borne out by the data. On the contrary one is struck by the apparent variation in opportunity across agencies. Table 1 illustrates this point.

These agencies are selected for examination because they exhibit substantial variation. While the percentage of women in GS grades 1-6 ranges from an adequate 54.1 per cent in Agriculture, to an expansive 84.1 per cent in HUD, variation in the percentage employed in GS grades 7-12, and 13+ is truly striking. In the middle-range grades, GS 7-12, women account for a high 55.6 per cent in HEW, and a low 9.4 per cent of the total in Transportation. Differences become even more pronounced in grades GS 13 through GS 18. Here, if figures reflect real opportunity, HEW stands out as the agency where women have made greatest strides, with the percentages in grades 14-15-16 appearing as 14.3, 9.2, and 8 respectively. While admittedly there remains room for opportunity expansion in HEW, these percentages seem quite favorable when juxtaposed to the NASA figures of 8 per cent (GS 14), .5 per cent (GS 15), and 0 per cent (GS 16). The point verified by even a cursory glance at Table 1 is that advancement for women has varied by agency. Since men have traditionally been the guardians of the gates in all agencies, the variation calls into question the political thesis itself.

Table 1

Women as Percent of Total Employed by Grade,
within Selected Federal Agencies, 1974[8]

Grade(s)	HEW	HUD	Agri-culture	NASA	Transpor-tation
1-6	81.0%	84.1%	54.1%	77.9%	77.5%
	(49,447)*	(4,417)	(14,776)	(3,928)	(7,438)
7-12	55.6%	29.6%	9.8%	14.2%	9.4%
	(24,212)	(2,311)	(4,628)	(1,314)	(3,084)
13	18.3%	10.4%	3.9%	1.8%	1.3%
	(1,227)	(177)	(212)	(98)	(169)
14	14.3%	6.1%	3%	.8%	1.1%
	(641)	(66)	(72)	(25)	(53)
15	9.2%	5.2%	1.1%	.5%	.7%
	(268)	(31)	(13)	(9)	(13)
16	8%	1.4%	1.7%	0%	2.1%
	(22)	(1)	(3)	(0)	(4)
17	5.5%	0%	0%	**	1.2%
	(5)	(0)	(0)		(1)
18	3.8%	0%	0%		0%
	(1)	(0)	(0)		(0)

*N=(49,447)
**NASA shows no personnel in 17 and 18 grades in the GS and equivalent pay plan.

The Biological Thesis

As distinct from the political thesis, which blames men, the biological thesis blames evolution for the dearth of women in positions of power. The thrust of the "biology is destiny" argument is not simply that certain mental or behavior traits may be sex linked and hence physiologically determined , but that presence of some traits and absence of others act directly on the fitness of women for high-level decision-making positions. One variation of this argument fixes on the concept of leadership. Leadership, seen here as the major activity of the high-level decision makers, is not merely associated with an official position, but must be granted to a would-be leader by a follower. Yet, as Lionel Tiger, the major proponent of this position, would argue, it is just this trait, the capacity to compel followership, that women do not have and, furthermore, can not have because of their physiological makeup.[9] Adapting such an argument to organizational life, one would say that underlying regularities in the species explain the paucity of women in top jobs. Women have not laid claim to leadership roles in the bureaucracy chiefly because they are women, and not because of limited opportunity. Should an aggressively enforced affirmative action program put a woman into formal leadership position, male colleagues will, on any issue of great significance, be strongly disposed to form an all-male group and accordingly to exclude the interloper from decision making on that issue.

A second variation of the "biology is destiny" thesis attributes the sparseness of women in positions of power to the functioning female sex hormones. The very facts of menstrual cycle and menopause limit a woman's capacity for leadership because these biological conditions lead inevitably to periodically impaired judgment. Put most practically by Dr. Edgar Berman, physician and advisor to former Vice-President Hubert Humphrey, "If you had an investment in a bank, you wouldn't want the president of your bank making a loan under these raging [female] hormonal influences at that particular period."[10]

To the extent that the "biology destiny" thesis is correct, we may simply be wrong headed in trying to move women up into high-level decision-making positions in American society. Whether the explanation is rooted in an inability to command followership or to control raging hormones, the public policy implication is obvious. No realistic conception of the "public interest" could be served by moving boldly against "nature."

The popular appeal of this kind of argument is unquestionably limited, since it goes against the grain of a fundamentally egalitarian ethos in U.S. political culture. One can as well question the character of research that supports these conclusions.[11] For our purposes, however, it is sufficient to examine this explanation in light of both our own national experience and empirical data on trends in female employment.

As was suggested at the very beginning of this article, the fact that some women have made it into top jobs is indisputable. They are found, albeit in small number, in the most prestigious of occupations. Particularly in the Executive Branch of government where merit weighs heavier toward promotion than family relationships[12] numerous women have held top positions and have unquestionably "commanded" followership.[13] At one level this may constitute prima facie evidence of the fatuousness of the "biology is destiny" explanation. If biological considerations set the limits of possible achievement, how does one explain these loophole women?

Furthermore, to the extent that biological considerations hold sway, one would expect little variation in the general pattern of labor force participation over time. We would expect the life-cycle pattern, conventionally identified with the female labor force, to remain constant, i.e., "taking a job when first out of school, withdrawing from the labor force for marriage and motherhood, and returning to paid work in later years when children are in school or on their own."[14] Yet Labor Department statistics suggest that a dramatic shift has occurred in participation rates among women in the 25 to 34 age bracket. Participation rates of this cohort, traditionally thought most intensely constrained by their biological stage of life, jumped from 34 per cent in 1950 to 52 per cent by 1974.[15] While such a pattern does not directly refute the biological determinant thesis, as far as top jobs are concerned, it does make one skeptical of broad generalizations rooted in biological makeup.

The Sociological Thesis

From a sociological perspective, the concept of role differentiation holds the key to the difficulties faced by women when entering high-level positions in the organizational world. As formally defined, the term role refers to "a position in a social structure, involving a pattern of specific expectations, privileges, responsibilities, including attitudes and behaviors, and codified to some recognizable degree by norms, values, and sanctions."[16]

Using this framework, the thesis holds that while for men role differentiation within the family complements occupational role achievement, it frustrates such "outside" role achievement for women. The role conflict phenomenon is highlighted in discussion of both the functions of the women in the family and the personal qualities deemed necessary for adequate performance.

Motherhood, as distinct from fatherhood, has traditionally been viewed as a full-time job. Women report spending 60 hours a week in their housewife role; even when employed outside the home, women tend to remain responsible for both the mothering and general housekeeping functions.[17] These essentially caring and cleaning functions are best carried out by one who exhibits conventional female traits of understanding, helpfulness, solicitousness, and passivity.

Obviously, the role conflict stems from the fact that top jobs in government and elsewhere demand both a full-time commitment, irrespective of family obligations, and a strength in personality traits diametrically opposed to those cultivated by the mother role. For women, goals set by the occupational role and the family role are at worst mutually exclusive and at best only partially reconcilable. As stated in an earlier study of role contradiction: "the full realization of one role threatens defeat in the other."[18] In short, the major obstacle to enlarging the percentage of women in top government jobs is that society is organized so as to discourage larger numbers of female contestants for those jobs.[19]

Having said all this, one might still raise the question: why must this be? What is it that in fact sustains a pattern of action which results in differential access to top jobs based on sex? Role differentiation, it can be argued, is rooted in gender differentiation which encompasses dimensions of both the political and biological theses elaborated above. It is from the biological fact of sex that gender differences are inferred. To view the woman as passive, solicitous, understanding, and nonachievement oriented is to say nothing of her biology and everything about her gender. Gender as a cultural phenomenon reinforces family and occupational role choices insofar as it sanctions those choices. The political dimension of gender differentiation intrudes with the realization that those attributes commonly associated with the "feminine" are also the attributes generally associated with ruled classes.[20]

Hence, while neither the biological nor political thesis stands on its own, dimensions of each fit when viewed in conjunction with the gender-based analysis of role differentiation. In a recent work, Kenneth Boulding effectively

weaves these competing explanations together in the concept of role prejudice.[21] Role prejudice is viewed as a product of a false social learning process
by which certain biological or genetic characteristics of individuals come to be
associated with certain roles. According to Boulding, role prejudice develops
when there are genetic differences in the human population which are visible,
but not significant for role performance. The political implication is that such
role prejudice translates into discrimination against individuals who strive to
achieve outside of their socially defined role set. It is this "role prejudice," a
prejudice shared by women and men alike, that accounts for the political reality
of few top spots for women.

If the analysis is correct, the question then becomes how to dissolve role
prejudice. Is it possible, given the grounding of role prejudice in the psychocul-
tural phenomenon of gender differentiation, that women as a percentage of top
job holders in the federal service or elsewhere will ever surpass the single digit
mark? In order to answer this question one must probe the attitudinal and the
structural supports for role prejudice.

The Response of the Private Sector:
Role Prejudice as Attitude

At first glance the term role prejudice suggests a problem of individual
attitude. In conventional usage, prejudice suggests an inner tendency to
respond unfavorably to persons on the basis of their group membership.[22] This
inner tendency is essentially a problem of attitude and hence is susceptible to
modification through innovative techniques of organizational development.
Accordingly, the response of private industry to the role prejudice phenomenon
has been to employ various kinds of awareness training programs in the service
of an "integration" objective. Recognizing that career advancement for women
is blocked by organizational "scripts" that discourage women from aiming high,
concerned private firms are trying to develop new scripts that facilitate female
adaptation to the existing career system.[23]

To be sure, this direction promises to improve the organizational climate
for women already competing for top slots in American industry. Just as federal
equal opportunity legislation mandated the elimination of formal barriers to
advancement for women, awareness training programs undermine those informal obstacles to change that stem from individually held sex role stereotypes.
Still, given this thrust, the question from an analytical perspective remains: will
this combination of legal and organizational development measures facilitate
substantial movement beyond current threshold?

Admittedly the data is not yet in to answer this question definitively. Still,
there is reason to believe the answer to the question will be no. That negative
response emerges from a more probing consideration of the role prejudice
concept, a consideration stressing the structural dimension of the role prejudice
phenomenon.

From decades of research in the field of social psychology we know that
individual attitudes can in fact be modified. Yet role prejudice as it resides in the

very structure of the career system may account to a far greater degree for the dearth of women at the top. I would argue that this is indeed the situation we now face in the consideration of equal opportunity for women. Through understanding the symbiotic relationship between gender differentiation and career systems the road for public service action is illuminated.

The Nature of Career Systems

In advanced industrial societies the career system is biased in favor of the "two-person, single career."[24] This two-person, single career option is played out through an organization which places a combination of formal and informal demands on both members of a married couple, while formally employing only the man. To insure success in this single endeavor the wife role requires meeting fully the stereotype definition of "feminine," e.g., to be the supporter, the comforter, the child rearer, the housekeeper, and the entertainer.[25] Her achievement is vicarious; achievement needs are met either completely or predominantly in her husband's accomplishments.[26]

The two-person, single career pattern that has received the most popular attention is that associated with corporate executives,[27] but the analysis applies equally well to any high-level organizational decision-making position. Since reputation in high-level executive careers is measured against time, and recognition for achievement is frequently a function of age, the supportive role played by the wife is a key element in success.[28] A recent analysis of career executive marriages stresses the importance of this supportive female role by pointing out that the substantially lower divorce rate among executives could be attributed to the dampening effect such separation would have upon a man's career.[29] This two-person, single career route to success has become so institutionalized that even those observers concerned with the potentially dehumanizing aspects of contemporary bureaucracy eulogize the traditional wife for her shelter-giving qualities.[30]

Those women who do try to achieve nonvicariously within the modern career system tend to start later and may proceed more slowly in large part because they are acting out a single-person, rather than two-person career. Most succinctly summed up in a recent study by Hochschild (1975) the essential problem with the career systems of the modern world is that their guiding rules are made to suit men. The traditional family functions as the service agency supporting the organization in which the male career is conducted.[31] Role prejudice resides thus in the very structure of modern careers systems, not merely in the attitudes of individuals towards members of the opposite sex.

If this analysis of role prejudice as inherent in the structure of modern career systems is correct, it casts serious doubt on the feasibility of private industry's integration strategy. The burgeoning literature on private sector opportunity expansion glorifies the aspiring female executive in terms of the extent to which she magnifies her male counterpart.[32] Debate centers largely on the effectiveness of alternative mechanisms for integrating females into the male career system. One analyst assures us that although a time lag is inevitable until women change individual role expectations, amalgamation is clearly down the road.[33] Little attention is paid to the less tractable obstacles blocking the way.

Yet if the analysis presented above accurately describes the bias in modern career systems, "making it" within that system is simply not feasible for most women. Only women who enjoy the services of a full-time house-husband will start out in the race on equal footing with their male colleagues. Even with all other things being equal, structural factors will assign women to a competitive disadvantage in the push for top jobs. Nothing in the career histories of top executives in the United States suggests that the structural characteristics of the modern career system will change in a more favorable direction. On the contrary, if any change has occurred in recent years it has been in the direction of intensification.[34] Hence we must challenge the feasibility of this method for moving beyond the current level of accomplishment. We can as well question on normative grounds the desirability of a change strategy which accepts as given a requirement that women desirous of "public" success give up family life while men continue to enjoy the family life option. This seems to be the practical outcome of the private sector approach.

It is against this backdrop that a new direction for public sector equal opportunity can be set and strategies for implementation considered. The time has come for the public service to bring a new orientation to the very concept of career and accordingly to go beyond the now traditional "modern" career system.

A Leadership Role for the Federal Service

The federal service historically has taken the initiative in removing formal barriers to female participation in the labor market.[35] Nonetheless, it is now time to probe deeper into the barriers to further advancement. To the extent that the career system blocks further advancement, it is necessary to attack that system directly. Quite naturally questions arise as to the shape of an alternative career system. Here only in broad strokes can the vital dimensions of this ideal be sketched.

The hallmark of a career system free of role prejudice is formal recognition of employees as whole people. In terms of the shape of the alternative career system this suggests that organizations themselves must assume the responsibility for meeting many needs now met by the family-*qua* service agency. Further, it implies that we must develop and institutionalize new models for measuring achievement. Such models should take into account success in broad life experience as well as in "service to the agency" as narrowly defined. Finally, we must cultivate an organizational ethos that balances the conventional "male" value of competition with the traditional "female" value of cooperation.[36]

Today the federal service could move toward this ideal by acting on any or all of the following: the further development of flexible work schedules and the institutionalization of permanent, part-time, promotion track slots for men and women; the de-emphasis of "freedom of movement" as a criterion for advancement; the exploration of job splitting possibilities for husbands and wives, and the conscious development of career tracks for such couples; the establishment of government career counseling, advertising, and legitimizing these options; and finally, the securing of government support for comprehensive quality child care.

In reaction to this alternative future for the public organization, one might protest that such "reform" strikes at values close to the heart of modern public management—the values of excellence and of productivity.

To recommend the transformation of the modern career system is not to gainsay the importance of excellence, but rather to recognize that excellence as a concept relates to the quality of personnel and not to the organization of work itself. With attention focused on people and the quality of their contribution, one might stress that excellence in this sphere resides neither in numbers of hours worked, nor in the distribution of those hours. Indeed, research suggests that excellence can be achieved under varying conditions.[37] For those who cling to measuring performance by the totality of commitment to a job, it need be stressed that individuals choosing to define personal achievement in that way would remain free to make that choice, just as many ambitious women have done, per force, under today's rules of the game. What this new vision of the public service promises is simply multiple career routes to excellence, within the organizational structure, including one which views the human being as a multifaceted creature.

But what of the more pressing issue of productivity? Few would deny that productivity is on the mind of most public managers today. Improved productivity management means simply getting more out of all available resources. Thus, on one level at least, little conflict is generated when productivity needs are juxtaposed to important dimensions of the alternative career structure. Some advocates of the alternative career model might even argue that the part-time employment strategy would yield a dividend in enhanced productivity per employee.[38] The least that can be said is that there is no compelling reason for believing in an inverse relationship between productivity and the modification of the work environment suggested above.

Conclusion

This article began with the posing of a dilemma. Why, when women constitute nearly 40 per cent of America's labor force, have so few women made it to the top? While the political and biological explanations both hold some appeal, the sociological explanation casts the most revealing light on this phenomenon. Specifically, it has been argued that the concept of role prejudice, as it resides not merely in attitudes, but more significantly in the structure of contemporary career systems, holds the key to understanding the dearth of women at the top. To the extent that this analysis is correct, success via the concerned private sector's "integration" approach becomes problematic, while a new direction for public service leadership emerges. That direction implies movement toward the alternative career system ideal, and preliminary steps along the road have been suggested.

Since the federal government has long set the tone for employment practice in the equal opportunity area, the impact of its response to the current dilemma will resonate far beyond the immediate federal employee population.[39] Presently, the impulse for expansion of opportunity for women at the top of government service is strong. This thrust need not flounder on the shoals of organizational myopia. If the history of federal service leadership in an earlier era holds a vision of the future, we might rest confident that it will not.

Notes

1. "International Women's Year . . . More Women Focus on a Career," *Monthly Labor Review,* Vol. 98, No. 11 (November 1975), p. 2; and U.S. Department of Labor, Women's Bureau, "Facts on Women workers" (February 1973).

2. U.S. Civil Service Commission, *Study of Employment of Women in the Federal Government, 1974,* GS and Equivalent Pay Plan. Women occupy 63 per cent of all full-time slots in the Department of HEW.

3. Stuart H. Garfinkle, "Occupations of Women and Black Workers, 1962-74, *Monthly Labor Review,* Vol. 98, No. 11 (November 1975), p. 28; for university professors see "Making Affirmative Action Work in Higher Education," Carnegie Council on Policy Studies in Higher Education (July 1975), p. 26; for federal civil servants, GS 16-18, see U.S. Civil Service Commission, *op. cit.*

4. Michael P. Fogarty, R. Rapoport, and R. N. Rapoport, *Sex, Career, and Family* (Beverly Hills: Sage, 1971), p. 20. Also see Elizabeth Waldman and Beverly J. McEaddy, "Where Women Work—An Analysis by Industry and Occupation," *Monthly Labor Review,* Vol. 97, No. 5 (May 1974), p. 3.

5. For an analysis of similar constraints on women in state legislative politics see Jean J. Kirkpatrick, *Political Women* (New York: Basic Books, 1974), ch. 1.

6. Shulamith Firestone, *The Dialectic of Sex* (New York: William Morrow, 1970), p. 19. Also reflecting this perspective are: Gunnar Myrdal, "A Parallel to the Negro Problem," in *An American Dilemma* (New York: Harper and Row, 1962), Appendix 5; Helen Hacker, "Women are a Minority Group," *Social Forces,* Vol. 30, No. 1 (October 1959),, pp. 60-68; Kirsten Amundsen, *The Silenced Majority* (Englewood Cliffs, N.J.: Prentice-Hall, 1971).

7. Elena Haavio-Mannela and Veronica Stolte-Heiskanen, "The Position of Women in Society: Formal Ideology vs. Everyday Ethic," *Social Science Information,* Vol. VI (December 1967), p. 171.

8. U.S. Civil Service Commission, *op. cit.*

9. Lionel Tiger, *Men in Groups* (New York: Random House, 1969), ch. 4.

10. Nancy L. Ross, *Washington Post,* July 29, 1970, cited by Judith Hole and Ellen Levine, *Rebirth of Feminism* (New York: Quadrangle Books, 1971), p. 174.

11. *Ibid.,* pp. 172-174.

12. Martin Gruberg reports that family relationship has been traditionally a major access route to elected political office for women. Martin Gruberg, *Women In American Politics* (Oshkosh, Wis.: Academia Press, 1968), p. 121.

13. For an abbreviated review of such women see *ibid.,* pp. 134-144.

14. U.S. Department of Labor, Women's Bureau, *Handbook of Women Workers* (Washington, D.C.: U.S. Government Printing Office, 1969), p. 18.

15. Deborah Pisetizner Klein, "Women in the Labor Force: The Middle Years," *Monthly Labor Review,* Vol. 98, No. 11 (November 1975), p. 11.

16. Jean Lipman-Blumen, "Role De-Differentiation as a System Response to Crisis," *Sociological Inquiry,* Vol. 43, No. 2, p. 106.

17. Kenneth M. Davidson, Ruth Bader Binsburg, and Herma Kay Hill, "Marriage and Family Life," in *Sex-Based Discrimination: Text, Cases and Materials* (St. Paul, Minn.: West Publishing Company, 1974), p. 188. See also Janice Neepert Hedges and Jeanne K. Barnett, "Working Woman and the Division of Household Tasks," *Monthly Labor Review,* Vol. 95, No. 4 (April 1972), pp. 9-14, which reports results of one study indicating that wives, employed more than 30 hours a week, spend an average of 34 hours a week on household tasks. Women not employed report spending 57 hours a week on household tasks. Husbands' contribution to household jobs averaged to 1.6 hours a day, whether or not their wives worked.

18. Mirra Komarovsky, "Cultural Contradictions in Sex Role," *American Journal of Sociology,* Vol. 52, No. 3 (November 1946), p. 184.

19. Recent research suggests that the domestic role differentiation phenomenon is reified in the response of managers to employees. Managers expect male employees to give top priority to jobs when career demands and family obligations conflict; yet they expect female employees to sacrifice their careers to family responsibilities. See Benson Rosen and Thomas H. Jerdee, "Sex Stereotyping in the Executive Suite," *Harvard Business Review,* Vol. 52, No. 2 (March/April 1974), p. 47.

20. Hacker, *op. cit.*

21. Kenneth Boulding, "Role Prejudice as an Economic Problem," *Monthly Labor Review,* Vol. 97, No. 5 (May 1974), p. 40.

22. See Milton Yinger, "Prejudice," *International Encyclopedia of the Social Sciences* (New York: Macmillan Company, 1968), p. 449.

23. For a discussion of the need for and operation of such programs, see Rosalind Loring and Theodora Wells, *Breakthrough: Women into Management* (New York: Van Nostrand Reinhold, 1972), pp. 57-64; and Dorothy Jongeward and Dru Scott, *Affirmative Action for Women: A Practical Guide* (Reading Mass: Addison-Wesley, 1973), ch. 7-10.

24. Hanna Papanek, "Men, Women, and Work: Reflections on the Two-Person Career," *American Journal of Sociology,* Vol. 78, No. 4 (January 1973), pp. 852-872. The term "two-person, single career' was coined by Papanek, whose work informed this analysis. The concept of "two-person, single career" needs to be distinguished from the "dual career" in which the husband and wife are each gainfully employed in their own individual careers.

25. *Ibid.,* pp. 856-864.

26. For a recent study of the correlates of vicarious achievement orientations, see Jean Lipman-Blumen, "How Ideology Shapes Women's Lives," *Scientific American,* Vol. 226, No. 1 (January 1972).

27. William H. Whyte (tr.), *The Organization Man* (New York: Anchor Books, 1957), pp. 286-291.

28. For analysis of the same phenomenon in the academic world, see Arlie R. Hochschild, "Inside the Clockwork of Male Careers," in Florence Howe (ed.), *Women and the Power to Change* (New York: McGraw-Hill, 1975), pp. 47-80.

29. Signs by the early 1970s that even the executive divorce rate is on the rise have generated substantial concern among personnel specialists in the private sector. See "The High Cost of Executive Divorce," *Duns Review,* Vol. 98 (October 1971), pp. 52-54.

30. Warren Bennis warns the aspiring executive that ". . . living in temporary systems . . . [of the future organization] . . . augur[s] social strains and tensions . . . To be a good wife in this era will be to undertake the profession of providing stability and continuity," "Changing Organizations" in William Scott (ed.), *Organizational Concepts and Analysis* (Belmont, Calif.: Dickenson Publishing Co., 1969), p. 154.

31. Hochschild, *op. cit.,* p. 59.

32. This point is well illustrated in recent issues of the *MBA* magazine. See "The Woman MBA," *MBA,* Vol. 9, No. 2 (February 1975), pp. 25-41; and "The Struggle for Status," *MBA,* Vol: 10, No. 2 (February 1976), pp. 25-40.

33. Victor Fuchs, "Women's Earnings: Recent Trends and Long-Run Prospects," *Monthly Labor Review,* Vol. 97, No. 5 (May 1974), pp. 23-26.

34. "The New Youth Movement," *Dun's Review,* Vol. 98 (August 1971), p. 47. This article reports a trend toward putting younger men in top slots of old line as well as new companies and predicts "In five years or so you will find the top men in business are going to be in their forties."

35. For discussion of specific measures taken, see Samuel Krislov, *Representative Bureaucracy* (Englewood Cliffs, N. J.: Prentice-Hall, 1974), p. 114.

36. Hochschild, *op. cit.,* p. 28.

37. *Exploitation From 9 to 5: Report of the Twentieth Century Fund Task Force On Women and Employment* (Lexington, Mass.: D.C. Heath and Company, 1975), p. 80.

38. *Ibid.,* p. 79.

39. *Ibid.,* p. 72.

13
Employing the
Black Administrator

Cortez H. Williams

Fredrick Case and many other blacks also agree that the educational programs for producing trained black administrators do not address themselves to the problems of either white administrators and the ethnic minorities or black administrators and their white peer groups. From the aspects of a cost-benefit

Reprinted with permission from *Public Personnel Management,* Vol. 6, No. 2 (March-April, 1972), pp. 76-83. Footnotes omitted.

At the time of this writing, Cortez H. Williams was a teacher of Afro-American history and a Ph.D. candidate in public administration at the University of New Mexico.

analysis system, Case sees a great shortage in the development of ready-to-function minority administrators. However, as we shall see later, these individuals, when they are ready to function, really do not have anywhere to go. They are limited in the availability of positions and the mobility of positions. The rationale behind such actions will be discussed later under the heading, "Problem Areas."

In offering some insight into the problems, some solutions are also offered; however, the social, economic, and political impact must be given careful analytical scrutiny if we are to avoid Eric Sevareid's cliche, "The chief causes of problems are solutions." Surely we can agree that there are problems in dealing with minorities from an administrative standpoint, but there is also sincere doubt as to what the solutions should be. In 1968, Robert F. Kennedy saw the problem not as black versus white, but rather as poor versus rich. In January 1974, the editor of *Black Enterprise* agreed with Kennedy:

> ... *Not just black issues, but the same issues affecting millions of Americans, who suffer the agonies of our systems without ever sharing in their abundance.*

Mahlon T. Puryear, in *The Economics of Black America,* attempted to nail down specific points that might be conceived as giving impetus to the ethnic minority problems. Puryear attacked the educational system, which is supposed to provide these minorities with the necessary tools and expertise to occupy administrative positions. However, it is ironic that blacks have been graduating from these same institutions of higher education for more than 100 years; however, other than black colleges, the same institutions, with all their prestige and influence, have not produced more than one black university or college president. Not only are blacks eliminated from the top administrative positions, but they are also limited in the middle management positions in the same institutions that are training them. A survey of the major universities (those with 25,000 or more students) revealed the limited number of black deans and department heads. Puryear reiterated this point:

> *The opportunity to learn, to acquire meaningful experiences, to explore, to make mistakes and recover from them, to be a part of the whole and not just a segment, to be understood as having desires, aspirations, ambitions and feelings for America has not typically been the lot of (our minority citizenry).*

The question now is, "If the minorities have the tools, skills, education and expertise, where do they go?" An attempt to answer this question will be made in the sections dealing with top-level jobs and the training of black administrators.

Problem Areas

It is an important fact that people live and work in organizations over periods of time during which relationships are established, grow, continue, blow up or decline, and the existence and state of these relationships have a great effect on how we behave toward one another.

Cornog has recognized that problems in dealing with human behavior are of a multitudinal nature. Like most authors writing about administrative theory, however, he limits the spectrum of cultural diversity on the behavioral patterns that they elicit. Cornog appears to assume that there is no difference between a minority administrator supervising whites and a white administrator supervising whites or a mixed group. It is not how we behave toward one another that needs total comprehension, but why we behave toward one another as we do.

The answer to this is not a simple one, but Frank Angel provides some very interesting concepts. Angel points out that the lack of inter-group interaction among the various members of the community, including all racial groups, is the result of identifiable and unidentifiable forces, creating a multitude of conflicts that lead to alienation—characteristic of a great deal of our behavior. Therefore, the attempt to resolve ethnic problems by the use of furtive, crippling, or disruptive mechanisms—confrontations, threats, annihilation of the weaker party, compromises, coalitions, group dynamics that work toward the exclusion of others, and the appeals to narrow ethnic loyalties—creates a continuing vicious cycle that resolves nothing. Instead, it provides impetus for more hate, prejudice, disharmony, and waste.

The astute administrator must be able to recognize these facets, which create negative interaction among his organizational members, and then develop effective conflict-management mechanisms to make communication and positive interaction feasible. The administrator must also be astute enough to recognize the fine lines of distinction between ethnocentrism, dogmatic ethnocentrism, and cultural fanaticism, if he is to make effective use of conflict-management mechanisms. Ethnocentrism implies that an individual tends to center his perceptions and behavior on his own culture and to exclude all others, which is nothing more than the usual tendency among all cultural groups to consider their own culture and customs the true and correct ones, and all others to be strange and unacceptable. However, as we move toward the extreme end of ethnocentrism, we overlap into dogmatic ethnocentrism, which carries with it separatism, narrow-mindedness, hate, and other correlates that tend to approach racism. At the extreme end of the spectrum we find cultural fanaticism, which illegitimatizes all cultural behavior other than one's own.

Labeling and stereotyping are other mechanisms which are used that prevent perceiving individuals as human beings. Such mechanisms exist simply because human beings tend to perceive and interpret the actions of others through culturally prescribed lenses of their own ethnic groupings. This is nothing more than lack of knowledge concerning other ethnic groups of our pluralistic society. A critical analysis of our current ethnic studies programs and departments strongly indicates that administrative planning in this area is very poor. The emphasis is always on a separatism for the groups involved, while at the same time catering to only a small percentage of the campus population. Very few courses are ever offered above the freshman and sophomore levels, and very few courses are ever taught above the indoctrination approach, which tends to breed dogmatic ethnocentrism.

To be tolerant of a person's cultural behavior, there must be an understanding of that culture's values—the determinants of that behavior. On the other hand, the prevention of misunderstanding of culturally determined actions or intentions requires some knowledge of the other culture. In order to survive the forces of racism, the modern-day administrator must understand that culture manifests itself overtly and covertly, and a more complete understanding of culturally determined behavior would include the covert aspects as well as the overt aspects. The sum total of this particular behavior is that:

> ... people tend to behave toward each other in terms of why they think the others act as they do, regardless of what the actual truth is. It is important to know and understand the way in which culture affects behavior.

The behavior problems discussed above also have their effects in the area of personnel administration. The employment test has been a great obstacle in the path of black employment for years, and major board examinations, such as the law board and medical board, have provided obstacles as well.

In Richmond, Virginia, there are 14 black lawyers in the secondary school system as teachers, because they failed to pass the bar examination. In 1972, a black Ph.D. graduate from the University of New Mexico failed to pass the New Mexico State Civil Service Examination for an entry-level position in Albuquerque, New Mexico. The student then went to New York, where he took New York's Civil Service Examination and achieved an extremely high score. Today, many blacks feel that jobs open when quotas open.

In 1972, a group of top-level administrators was brought together to form the Equal Employment Opportunity Coordinating Council (EEOCC). It was this group that provided the testing guidelines implemented by the Equal Employment Opportunity Commission (EEOC), which have had a tremendous impact on the hiring and promotions of blacks. It was the 1971 Supreme Court case, *Griggs* v. *Duke Power Company* which gave impetus to the formation of the Council. The court decided against the Duke Power Company and prohibited testing that excludes minorities and does not yield some demonstrably reasonable measures of job performance. Discriminatory testing has also shown its ugly face in the federal sector, as well. In the case of *Douglas* v. *Hampton,* Douglas, a former black intern of the Department of Housing and Urban Development, failed the Federal Service Entrance Examination (FSEE) in 1973. Douglas sued the U.S. Civil Service Commission (CSC), charging that FSEE illegally discriminates against blacks. Douglas was supported by the EEOC, which claimed that the FSEE did not meet the EEOC guidelines for test validation. The CSC won this case; however, the case was won on procedural grounds and is currently being appealed. If this case is won during the appeal, all Civil Service examinations at the federal level will be revised, which could lead to the revision of state civil service examinations.

Yet, on the other hand, there is the interview, which plays a key role for blacks seeking high-level jobs. To solve the interview problem, the EEOC requires that statistics be produced showing that unscored interviews work to the advantage of minority applicants.

Jonathan Bramwell views the black administrator's problems in a two-fold dimension that could be the catalyst for numerous problems that the black administrator must deal with. The first of the problems stems from the "quota system" and/or tokenism. The second involves black administrators' constantly having to prove themselves. The battle against tokenism and the quota system, described in the March 1974 issue of *Black Enterprise,* involves the necessity for black administrators to resist such outmoded titles as "Urban Affairs Specialists" and "Community Affairs Specialists." Such titles and token positions to fill a black-quota system only demean the functional responsibilities of black administrators, as they will surely find themselves the keepers of their people with marginal clerical responsibilities. There is some correlation between tokenism and limited promotional opportunities for an individual who is hired to fill a quota; however, the empirical data available at this time are limited, therefore making validations of this correlation infeasible.

To further enlighten the reader about the difficulties of the black administrator, it is necessary to scan the reactions of the employers toward their black employees. This material will be covered in two sections.

Employers' Reactions to Black Administrator

In 1971, the Department of Labor interviewed a number of corporation presidents to discuss their policies in hiring minorities. The discussions, however, appeared to center directly around the hiring of blacks. Those who had the most experience with blacks reported that blacks were average, neither significantly better nor significantly worse than comparable groups of white workers. Here the normal assumption would be that blacks are neither superior nor inferior in carrying out their administrative responsibilities. It also appears that what the corporate presidents were looking for as an administrator was not the average black, but the black who had superior qualifications. Even blacks with superior qualifications could create serious morale problems among the white employees, and above all would make it very difficult for the next black employee.

Where to place new black administrators also appeared to be a matter of great concern among the corporate presidents. Some suggested that they be placed where they would be highly visible, but this could be regarded as tokenism. However, there was a general agreement among the group that the new black administrator should not be placed in a position where promotions would be limited.

The whole interview suggested that the hiring of a black administrator involved administrative and personnel problems of great magnitude. The acceptance of such a suggestion is not difficult, but the magnitude of the problem is, indeed, overly exaggerated. This particular group of corporate presidents also implied that there were problems involving supervision, special preparation of the white employees, whether or not to place the new black in an intern buddy system, and whether or not there should be double standards in promoting blacks.

On the other extreme of the spectrum we find Jonathan Bramwell expounding on the ideology that blacks are really paranoiac in their job relations. Yet, he later counters this ideology by placing the blame on the white professionals, who feel that professional blacks encounter very little racism in moving up the ladder. Nonetheless, there is no doubt that problems do exist in the administrative relationships of black administrators and white employees. However, a greater understanding of the spectrum of the problem could be eliminated through an educational process, if the white executive and/or white administrator were completely cognitive of the ethnic cultures that they are to interact with in their daily administrative duties. This would also eliminate some of the controls from outside the organizational structures. There are times when such mechanisms of control as the government, special interest groups, and influential individuals can create havoc within an organization. In the next section, we will survey the power of the government as an outside control mechanism.

The Effects of the Federal Government

With the implementation of equal opportunity laws by the federal government, many doors have been opened for the minorities. From a moral stand-point, this is good; but from an administrative and personnel standpoint, it provides the possibility of having undesirables forced upon an organization. In other words, it takes away the right of an organization to select whom it wants. Even though such an option has been deleted, it is understandable, considering the history of employment discrimination in this country. Today, there are numerous ways of forcing the employer to hire the minority, such as equal opportunity clauses in defense contracts, union contracts, and building contracts.   But there are also numerous ways, which appear to tax one's ingenuity, in cutting down on the hiring of minorities, as well. Who is the victor in this case? In reality, there is no victor, because the hiring agency loses by turning its back on potential manpower which could effectuate maximum efficiency and profit in both the public and private sectors, and the employee loses from both a psychological and physiological standpoint, losing the opportunity to fulfill personal needs, which would lead to fulfilling the needs of society.

Many blacks still see the mandates of the equal opportunity laws as the catalyst which provides the basic opportunity for financial security in America. However, what is not known is that many of America's large corporations provided the impetus for the hiring of qualified blacks to fill some of the administrative positions that were open to blacks in the federal government at the beginning of the integration era. In some minor or major way, 137 corporations participated in providing blacks with the necessary tools and skills to fill administrative positions in the public and private sectors. For those who recognized the potentials in developing the manpower of a pluralistic society, they should be commended; but for those who have not nor do not care to develop the potentials of a pluralistic society, then let them feel the weight of the equal opportunity laws.

In 1964, the Johnson Administration got the ball rolling in the right direction with the passing of the Civil Rights Act, with its Title VII provisions that outlawed job discrimination. The act also established a weak, but an effective administrative tool, the EEOC. The weakness of the EEOC can be identified in its inability to enforce the Title VII provision of the Civil Rights Act of 1964. To enforce this act, the EEOC could do nothing more than to ask a conference, a counciliation, or attempt to persuade the individuals violating the Act. The end result of all this was that by 1971, more than 60,000 cases were backlogged in the Attorney General's office.

By 1972, job discrimination had become a civil offense; therefore, it could be tried in court. It was through the implementation of this law that EEOC partnered with the Justice Department and the Labor Department to reach a settlement with American Telephone and Telegraph for $38 million to pay policy and wage adjustments. AT&T then became a generous employer of minorities, and placed a number of blacks in administrative positions. The question now is "Was it worth the price for AT&T to close the doors on the development of our pluralistic manpower, and also, was it a good administrative policy?"

EEOC did not stop at AT&T, but continued to attack such large corporations as General Motors, General Electric, and Sunshine Biscuit Company, as well as unions representing the auto and aerospace industries. But, again, the government failed the minorities when the chairman of the EEOC, William H. Brown, III, was forced to resign. Rumors in Washington among the blacks as to why he resigned had it that Brown went about his work more vigorously than was expected of him, and that he was rocking too many boats.

Even though the EEOC made some headway, it remains to be seen whether or not black administrators will come above the national percentage mark of 6.1 in both the private and public sectors.

Training of Black Administrators

Even though decisionmaking is done by an individual, it cannot be taught; however, education and experience are sincerely needed. Universities could serve better in their preparation of the administrator if they departed from traditional concepts of methodology and developed more flexibility in their programs. This is to say that the training skills are only supplementary, as most good administrators are excellent practitioners. The university training grounds for the up-coming administrators have provided specific programs with numerous weaknesses. The basics of the programs usually include history, theory, landmark authors, practical laboratory situations, and problem analysis which are covered on a survey basis. It appears that more detailed study is necessary. The major weaknesses of black administrators have been the lack of detail in theory and in the practical laboratory situation. However, Haddad and Pugh assumed that the failure of conventional employment can be traced to technical and administrative problems rather than to the concept of administrative training procedures, which appears to imply that practical applications are more important than theory. Black administrators get very few opportunities to comprehend the theory applications, which in the long run weakens their ability to comprehend the technical and administrative problems. What usually occurs when they encounter the technical and administrative problems is that they attack the problems with the idea of changing the problem situations without ever considering the ripple effects.

At this point, it must be understood that there is no set methodology for producing an instant administrator, black or white. At times, it seems that the process is not clearly understood by the people involved in such training, and even less understood among the people being trained. The accelerated training programs and the hiring of the trainees will only be a temporary palliative unless these individual trainees can compete effectively for promotions within the organization, thus showing the true effects of the program(s) that trained them. This is why entry-level administrative positions do not provide an adequate picture of the effectiveness of an administrative program, because, as Frederick Case sees it, there are many weaknesses in many of the educational programs in turning out minority trained, ready-to-function administrators. This could be a probable cause for the fact that most minorities must take entry-level positions as trainees, interns, or glorified clerks. However, at the same time, we must recognize the fact that racial barriers do exist. As we shall see in the following section on government employees, the majority of the high-ranking administrators acquired at least 10 to 15 years or more of job experience to reach their current positions.

Blacks in Top-Level Government Jobs

In 1971, blacks in General Schedule grades 12 to 13 rose 3.4 percent from 5.7 percent in the federal government, with most of them concentrated in the Departments of Health, Education, and Welfare and the State. Out of 11,000 positions (as of December 1, 1973), there were 240 blacks holding top-level positions in the Executive Branch of the federal government, which is just a little over 2 percent; however, on the whole, blacks constitute about 20 percent of the federal bureaucracy. The picture here is that the top-level positions are occupied by veterans of 10 to 15 years service, and, as one top-level (black) official put it:

Whether you like it or not, people advance in the civil service grades by putting in time on the job ...

The question now is, "Where are the young blacks who complete the educational administrative programs going to go, and how long is it going to take them to get there?" It is a known fact that most of the top-level positions are held by older whites who are only going to vacate these positions by dying, and when you get beyond GS-15, the White House determines the promotions which

Table 1
Blacks with Rating of GS 15-18 in the Federal Government

Federal Areas	No. of Blacks
White House Office	2
Department of Defense	2
Department of the Air Force	2
Department of Agriculture	8
Department of State	48
Department of the Army	15
Department of Justice	8
Department of Commerce	3
Department of the Treasury	8
Department of the Navy	5
Department of the Interior	2
Department of Labor	8
Department of Housing and Urban Development	12
Department of Health, Education, and Welfare	32
Department of Transportation	18
ACTION	3
Atomic Energy Commission	1
Civil Service Commission	1
Cost of Living Council	1
Consumer Product Safety Commission	2
Board of Governors of the Federal Reserve System	2
Environmental Protection Agency	3
Equal Employment Opportunity Commission	11
Federal Communications Commission	1
Federal Trade Commission	1
Foreign Claims Settlement Commission	1
General Services Administration	2
National Aeronautics and Space Administration	1
National Science Foundation	1
Office of Economic Opportunity	4
Office of Management and Budget	3
Renegotiation Board	1
Securities and Exchange Commission	1
Small Business Administration	3
Smithsonian Institute	1
Tennessee Valley Authority	1
U.S. Commission on Civil Rights	4
U.S. Information Agency	4
U.S. Postal Service	6
Veterans Administration	12

differ with each administration. An example of the latter was the increased positions for blacks above the GS-15 level with the Johnson Administration, and the decrease of these same positions in the Nixon Administration.

In the supergrades (GS-16, -17, and -18), there are approximately 194 blacks, with 29 in appointed positions, and 16 of these are generals and 2 admirals. Table 1 indicates the number of blacks in the supergrades and the federal areas they are associated with. There is no doubt that inequities exist in both the private and public sectors of administration, but the problem cannot be solved on an equity basis, either. To attempt to secure equality in this country would breed reverse racism due to the political aspects involved. This would be nothing more than using a political process for establishing or implementing a means to an end, while at the same time passing over the residual effects of the entire situation. An individual must be judged outside of a particular cultural frame of reference on such essential human qualities as character, honor, decency, intelligence, dependability, common sense, humor, and perception, which are randomly dispersed in the population and do not necessarily depend upon the amount of one's education. Until we are able to judge another person on these essentials and areas of competence regardless of that person's skin pigmentation, we will always live in a world of "pigmentocracy."

14
The Reality of Equal Employment Compliance in Municipalities
Alan Saltzstein and Grace Hall Saltzstein

Concern for equal employment in municipal government has heightened recently as a consequence of increased pressure from minority and women's organizations and the passage of the 1972 Equal Employment Opportunity Act. Such pressures have been a part of federal level personnel concerns for years, and a small body of knowledge dealing with resulting problems that personnel managers face is present.[1] Application of these same concerns to the city scene, however, presents personnel policy makers with a set of different and more perplexing problems.

City governments are more directly involved in the daily lives of minority residents than are most state and federal agencies. Hence, pressures upon these

A revision of a paper prepared for the American Society for Public Administration Convention, 1976. Alan Saltzstein is Professor of Political Science and Coordinator of Public Administration programs at California State University, Fullerton. Grace Hall Saltzstein is a doctoral candidate in political science at the University of California, Riverside.

governments for altered hiring patterns may be more intense than those at higher levels. Yet pressure from the community to hire certain kinds of employees, may vary from community to community depending on the kind of city, the representation of various minority groups within the city, and the extent of political activity on the part of each group. In addition, the success of municipal governments in attracting more women and minorities to municipal employment may depend upon factors beyond their control, such as the proximity of the city hall to the living areas of various groups.

Similarly, attempts to hire minorities and women may be hindered by factors embedded in the histories of different ethnic and racial groups and racial and sexual biases within the white majority community. While authors tend to assume that the problems of minority and women's recruitment are similar, a substantial body of literature suggests that one ought to expect pronounced hiring differences among different groups. Grebler *et al.,* for instance, has noted that the relative employability of Mexican Americans and blacks in federal and local service varies considerably in different states.[2] A recent study by Rosenbloom also implies that competition among minority groups may result in certain agencies being dominated by one group at the expense of others.[3]

If different patterns of employment for various groups occur, personnel policies leading to equal employment would require different procedures and practices for each group. Personnel managers must know what these patterns are to effectively maximize employment opportunities for any specific group. To determine the presence of differing employment patterns, numerous questions must be answered. We must know whether some groups are more readily recruited through normal personnel processes than others, if some groups are more frequently hired for certain types of employment than others, and whether existing personnel practices encourage the "capture" of an agency or department by one group to the exclusion of others. Any one of these patterns could easily hinder the effective allocation of personnel resources to improve minority and female employment in a municipality.

In an attempt to examine some of these questions, various kinds of data were collected concerning black, Spanish-surnamed, and female employment in 26 of the 27 Texas cities larger than 50,000 in population. This paper summarizes the findings of several studies, based on these data sources.[4] The studies were limited to Texas cities for various reasons, primarily concerning source availability.[5] The details of the individual studies are available elsewhere; we are concerned here with summarizing the central conclusions and discussing their implications.

What is the nature of minority and women's employment in these cities? The representation of women and minorities in municipal government was depicted through the construction of several indicators. These included 1) a use index combining measures of minority representation in an organization and their distribution across salary levels, 2) the percentage of professional employees, 3) the percentage of maintenance employees which are black or Spanish-surnamed, and 4) the percentage of clerical employees which are female.

Inspection of the percentage breakdowns revealed a more complex picture than much of the personnel literature suggests (Table 1). The use indices and percent professional measures demonstrate that women are most heavily disadvantaged while the Spanish-surnamed minority is least disadvantaged in terms of representation. Women's indices are lower and rather consistently low from one city to the next. There is also an indication that significant differences in the rates of employment for blacks and Spanish-surnamed members are present. This is most evidently demonstrated in Table 2 where several indicators of representation are totaled for all the cities. Here, all indicators show a higher Spanish-surnamed representation.

What accounts for differences in employment rates? Given the diversity of cities in the survey it is possible that the employment differences between the groups is a function of differences in the size of the work force of each community, the pool of available and qualified potential minority and women employees, or particular traits of the cities themselves.[6] To test for explanations of this kind, we hypothesized that three basic kinds of variables were plausible sources of explanation for varying employment patterns:

A. *Group characteristics* which include indicators of the minority or women's population such as the percent minority or women in the workforce, the percentage minority and women's professional employment in the total city population and the median school years completed for each group.

B. *City characteristics* which include indicators of communities such as population increases or decreases, the percent of manufacturing jobs, the percent of the population living in the same house for the last five years, and the city's classification as suburb or central city.

Data Analysis

To test the hypothesized relationships between group and city characteristics and city employment of minorities and women, correlation and regression analyses were performed. Equations were designed and tested to analyze the aggregate effect of each group of variables and the relative influence of each variable in the several employment indicators. The basic findings of these analyses were as follows:

Characteristics of the individual group are more closely associated with Spanish-surnamed employment than is the case for blacks or women. Much of the variation in Spanish-surnamed employment, particularly in the professional categories, can be explained by factors such as the percent of the Spanish-surnamed workforce and percent professional of the workforce. These kinds of factors are less useful in explaining black employment and of no value in explaining employment of women.

City characteristic variables do explain significant amounts of variation in the percent of Spanish-surnamed professionals and in the Spanish-surnamed use index, though in both cases, the variance explained is considerably less than that explained by the indicators of workforce characteristics.

For blacks, on the other hand, population characteristics explain roughly the same amount of variance in both indicators as do workforce qualities. Hence,

Table 1

City-wide Use Indices, a) Workforce Representation, b) and Percentage Professional c) for Blacks and Spanish-surnamed Individuals in 26 Texas Cities: 1973

(As of October 31. Covers employment in all city departments except hospitals and sanatoriums, health, corrections, or employment security.)

City	Black			Spanish-surnamed		
	% Work-force Rep.	Use Index	% Pro-fessional	% Work-force Rep.	Use Index	% Pro-fessional
Abilene	5.2	.67	0	7.5	.66	0
Amarillo	4.2	.42	0	4.9	.41	0
Arlington	10.4	.10	0	4.9	.30	0
Austin	10.4	.63	4.68	12.3	.62	5.66
Beaumont	22.8	.15	1.60	4.1	.33	1.60
Brownsville	1.0	.00	**	70.0	.97	61.60
Corpus Christi	5.1	.67	1.43	35.8	.85	16.47
Dallas	15.1	.58	3.92	5.6	.58	1.79
El Paso	3.1	.45	.81	49.4	.92	36.56
Ft. Worth	10.4	.60	7.28	4.9	.54	2.01
Galveston	18.6	.75	8.18	10.1	.79	6.46
Grand Prairie	13.5	.17	1.48	5.4	.67	1.57
Houston	18.8	.54	6.58	9.0	.35	2.43
Irving	15.1	.09	1.36	5.6	.38	2.52
Laredo	*	**	**	78.9	.86	82.06
Lubbock	6.5	.40	0	12.9	.51	2.06
Mesquite	15.1	.16	0	5.6	.25	0
Midland	10.2	.39	3.16	8.9	.52	4.81
Odessa	4.9	.51	0	10.2	.61	0
Pasadena	18.8	.01	0	9.0	.61	25.0
Port Arthur	22.8	.57	4.33	4.1	.36	1.72
San Angelo	4.1	.40	1.89	14.1	.59	3.67
San Antonio	7.0	.67	4.62	37.2	.90	28.6
Tyler	22.4	.47	0	1.6	.48	2.8
Waco	14.9	.58	3.87	5.8	.75	2.9
Wichita Falls	7.6	.57	1.82	4.9	.72	0
		X=.42	X=2.38		X=.59	X=11.24
		S=.224	S=2.64		S=.218	S=27.1

a. Measure of employment status combining salary levels and representation levels of a given group. (See text, p. 1)
b. Percentage of total employment in the city which is comprised of teach minority group.
c. Percentage of all professionals employed by the municipal government which belong to each minority group.
* Workforce representation less than 1.0
66 Cannot be computed; no minority group members employed by the city.
Sources: Workforce representation figures computed for each city and supplied by Texas Employment Commission, 1973 data. Measures of employment status computed from Equal Employment Opportunity Commission Local Government Information Form EEO-4, collected individually from cities; 1973 data.

Table 2

Indicators of Rates of Employment for Blacks and Mexican Americans

| | Blacks | | Mexican Americans | |
	Mean	St. Dev.	Mean	St. Dev.
All departments use index	*.397	.242	.585	.227
Public works departments use index	*.590	.350	.881	.224
Finance departments use index	*.351	.295	.522	.314
Fire departments use index	*.137	.217	.338	.334
Police departments use index	*.333	.264	.556	.313
Percent workforce	11.2	6.8	15.8	3.9
Percent of professional employees	2.1	2.4	11.2	21.2

*Difference of means test significance at .01.

city characteristics have a relatively greater effect than workforce characteristics on black employment than on the employment of Spanish-surnamed individuals.

The effect of city characteristics on employment differs for the black and Spanish-surnamed minorities. Black employment is positively related to population size and negatively related to suburbanization. Employment of the Spanish-surnamed minority, however, is more strongly related to such factors as the absence of manufacturing concerns in the city and less mobile populations.

Again, as was the case with group characteristic variables, city characteristic variables were not related to female employment in city government.

C. In the case of female employment, it was further hypothesized that attitudes and personal characteristics of individual department heads (hiring agents) might well account for variations in women's employment. Hence, separate interviews were conducted with department heads of four major departments in each city to obtain information about attitudes and personal characteristics, and the resulting measures were then correlated with female employment measures for these departments.

Basically, this analysis was not very fruitful, in that almost all of the variation in female employment in these departments proved to be accounted for by the number of jobs in the department which are clerical in nature. Hence, at the time of this study at least, women were seriously underrepresented in municipal employment generally, and those who were employed were functioning almost exclusively in clerical positions.

Yet certain attitudes and characteristics of department heads were related to actual female representation in these cities and did, however, suggest some avenues of explanation for variations in women's employment. Some relationship was found between department head's attitudes concerning the innate job abilities of females and actual female employment in that department. Thus there is some support for the frequently voiced assumption that hiring choices with regard to women may be in part a reflection of personal biases, at least in regard to women's job abilities, on the part of the hiring agent. Additionally, a positive correlation between female employment and previous experience working with women as peers was also recorded, which could suggest that on the job socialization may have a positive effect on women's employment.

Other measures of attitudes on the part of department heads were unrelated to female employment within departments. Hence, while most department heads viewed the federal government as being "very committed" to the equal employment opportunity program and as being "very likely" to impose sanctions on discriminating employers, these perceptions were not related to actual employment of females in a given department. It thus seems likely that city officials perceive a serious intent on the part of the EEOC but doubt their ability to impose severe sanctions. This notion is given further support by the fact that cities in the sample which had been involved in formal charges of discrimination had no better records in terms of female employment than did those which had not been involved in such litigation.

Implications

At least since the publication of the Kerner Report (1967), much thought and considerable governmental efforts have been spent to increase minority employment in city government. In recent years EEOC litigation and denials of federal funds have been employed to force municipalities to provide more and better jobs for Spanish-surnamed Americans and blacks. Concern for women's employment has been of more recent origin but the thrust has been similar. Although increased minority and women's hiring has been viewed as a cure for problems as far ranging and basic as social equity and domestic tranquility, little has been said concerning how changes in employment can come about or whether certain techniques or approaches might be more successful with certain groups than others. The proposals of the Kerner report and the annual President's manpower report, for instance, have a similar ring to them. The removal of discriminatory hiring and promotion practices, expansion of training efforts and more thorough recruitment efforts are generally cited as the primary tools. Our research suggests that some of these techniques ought to be more successful than others with certain minorities or in certain kinds of cities.

Because Spanish-surname employment in Texas cities is rather directly related to the Spanish-surname workforce and characteristics of that workforce, there is reason to assume that programs to increase the education and training of this group will lead to increased hiring. The high correlations of these indicators suggest that blockages between the supply of employable people and city employment needs are less severe for this group than others. Hence, the generation of employable people through education and training, particularly professionals and administrators, ought to result in a higher employment percentage.

A different picture emerges for blacks. The importance of community characteristics as determinants of employment implies that legal or administrative intervention from a higher level of government is needed if education and training programs are to be effective. Thus, without enforced affirmative action programs and the imposition of sanctions against employers with low numbers of blacks, manpower programs cannot be fully effective.

The case for women is similar to that of blacks but more severe. The low employment indicators probably reflect the problems of both employment prejudices and restrictions and a lack of supply of potential employees. Progress in women's employment in cities cannot be expected until prohibitions on discrimination against hiring in areas such as police and fire positions are removed. The supply of eligible applicants, however, may not increase sufficiently until these positions are viewed as legitimate work for women by the larger society. Hence, improved women's employment depends upon legal and administrative intervention, improved education and training, and a change in the socialization processes of the society at large. All of these processes are, of course, related. As more women successfully challenge sex-related job requirements and are admitted to employment or training programs, they serve as examples that may affect social norms and values.[7] It is likely, therefore, that legal and administrative intervention on behalf of able women applicants is the important triggering device for a larger social change.

Furthermore, the research suggests a need for a change of "image" on the part of the EEOC. The agency must have more substantial incentives to encourage compliance than is presently the case if the program is to be successful. Perhaps the most immediate need is for more rapid processing of cases, through increased staffing and/or preferential handling of class action suits as opposed to individual suits. The large backlog of cases is well known to personnel officers and openly discussed by federal officials in seminars with city officials. As a result, many public officials, in this survey at least, assume they can successfully avoid compliance.

A purely regulatory policy may never be completely successful. If employment opportunity is as complex a problem as this research indicates, upgrading minority and female employment in municipalities could be an extremely expensive proposition. Hence, compliance might be more likely if coupled with financial incentives, perhaps directly through manpower revenue sharing and grants-in-aid.

Notes

1. See N. Joseph Cayer, *Public Personnel Administration in the United States* (1975, St. Martins), pp. 128-138; "Mini-Symposium on Affirmative Action," *Public Administration Review,* (May/June, 1974), pp. 234-246; "Symposium on Social Equity and Public Administration," *Public Administration Review,* (Jan./Feb., 1974), pp. 1-50.

2. Leo Grebler, Joan Moore and Ralph C. Guzman, *The Mexican American People: The Nation's Second Largest Minority* (Fress Press, New York, 1970), pp. 222-226.

3. David H. Rosenbloom, "A Note on Interminority Competition for Federal Positions," *Public Personnel Management,* Jan.-Feb., 1973, pp. 43-48.

4. See "Equal Employment in Urban Government: The Potential Problem of Inter-Minority Competition," *Public Personnel Management* 4:6 (Nov.-Dec., 1975), "Dimensions of Women's Employment in City Governments: The Influence of Attitudes and

Intergovernmental Pressures on Personnel Policy" paper presented at the annual meeting of the American Political Science Association, 1975 and "Equal Opportunity for Minorities in Municipal Government Employment: Some Correllates and Implications for Public Policy" *Social Science Quarterly* (57:4 March 1977). Copies of any of these may be obtained from Alan Saltzstein, Department of Political Science California State University, Fullerton, California 92686.

5. The Equal Employment Opportunity Act of 1972 states that "It shall be unlawful for any officer or employee of the Commission to make public in any manner whatever any information obtained by the Commission pursuant to its authority ..." (Sec. 709(e)).

Texas House Bill 6 states that the following category of information be specifically made available to the public: "the names, sex, ethnicity, salaries, title, and dates of employment of all employees and officers of governmental bodies." All the data contained on the EEO4 forms falls within these boundaries and hence is open to public scrutiny. In spite of the law, however, some difficulty in securing the forms occurred. Several were obtained only after a site visit. Local contacts were also needed in a few of the cities. Thanks to our persistence, perserverance, and endurance, however, we collected forms for all but one city.

6. This study is limited to one state and one point in time, less than two years after municipalities were placed under the jurisdiction of the EEOC. Therefore, the lack of compliance noted here could be simply a reflection of insufficient time to respond to federal pressure to upgrade women's and minority employment. Compliance activities could have been underway at the time of the study but would not have effected employment for some time. However, it is also true that private enterprise has been under EEOC jurisdiction since 1964 and extension to municipalities could have been anticipated.

7. Women in non-traditional roles not only serve as an example to other women to aspire to such positions but also may serve to change the attitudes of male colleagues and superiors towards women in such capacities. Suzanne Saunders Taylor, "The Attitudes of Superintendents and Board of Education Members in Connecticut Toward the Employment and Effectiveness of Women as Public School Administrators," unpublished dissertation, University of Connecticut, 1971, found that attitudes of male school board members who have worked for female administrators are more favorable toward female administrators than attitudes of those who have never worked for a woman in an administrative capacity. Hence, exposure to females in non-traditional roles may provide an impetus to changing male attitudes.

15
Griggs et al. v. Duke Power Co., December 14, 1970

United States Supreme Court

Mr. Chief Justice Burger delivered the opinion of the Court.

We granted the writ in this case to resolve the question whether an employer is prohibited by the Civil Rights Act of 1964, Title VII, from requiring a high school education or passing of a standardized general intelligence test as a condition of employment in or transfer to jobs when (a) neither standard is shown to be significantly related to successful job performance, (b) both requirements operate to disqualify Negroes at a substantially higher rate than white applicants, and (c) the jobs in question formerly had been filled only by white employees as part of a longstanding practice of giving preferences to whites.

Congress provided, in Title VII of the Civil Rights Act of 1964, for class actions for enforcement of provisions of the Act and this proceeding was brought by a group of incumbent Negro employees against Duke Power Company. All the petitioners are employed at the Company's Dan River Steam Station, a power generating facility located at Draper, North Carolina. At the time this action was instituted, the Company had 95 employees at the Dan River Station, 14 of whom were Negroes; 13 of these are petitioners here.

The District Court found that prior to July 2, 1965, the effective date of the Civil Rights Act of 1964, the Company openly discriminated on the basis of race in the hiring and assigning of employees at its Dan River plant. The plant was organized into five operating departments: (1) Labor, (2) Coal Handling, (3) Operations, (4) Maintenance, and (5) Laboratory and Test. Negroes were employed only in the Labor Department where the highest paying jobs paid less than the lowest paying jobs in the other four "operating" departments in which only whites were employed. Promotions were normally made within each department on the basis of job seniority. Transferees into a department usually began in the lowest position.

In 1955 the Company instituted a policy of requiring a high school education for initial assignment to any department except Labor, and for transfer from the Coal Handling to any "inside" department (Operations, Maintenance, or Laboratory). When the Company abandoned its policy of restricting Negroes to the Labor Department in 1965, completion of high school also was made a prerequisite to transfer from Labor to any other department. From the time the high school requirement was instituted for the time of trial, however, white employees hired before the time of the high school education requirement

---

Footnotes omitted.

continued to perform satisfactorily and achieve promotions in the "operating" departments. Findings on this score are not challenged.

The Company added a further requirement for new employees on July 2, 1965, the date on which Title VII became effective. To qualify for placement in any but the Labor Department it became necessary to register satisfactory scores on two professionally prepared aptitude tests, as well as to have a high school education. Completion of high school alone continued to render employees eligible for transfer to the four desirable departments from which Negroes had been excluded if the incumbent had been employed prior to the time of the new requirement. In September 1965 the Company began to permit incumbent employees who lacked a high school education to qualify for transfer from Labor or Coal Handling to an "inside" job by passing two tests—the Wonderlic Personnel Test, which purports to measure general intelligence, and the Bennett Mechanical Comprehension Test. Neither was directed or intended to measure the ability to learn to perform a particular job or category of jobs. The requisite scores used for both initial hiring and transfer approximated the national median for high school graduates.

The District Court had found that while the Company previously followed a policy of overt racial discrimination in a period prior to the Act, such conduct had ceased. The District Court also concluded that Title VII was intended to be prospective only and, consequently, the impact of prior inequities was beyond the reach of corrective action authorized by the Act.

The Court of Appeals was confronted with a question of first impression, as are we, concerning the meaning of Title VII. After careful analysis a majority of that court concluded that a subjective test of the employer's intent should govern, particularly in a close case, and that in this case there was no showing of a discriminatory purpose in the adoption of the diploma and test requirements. On this basis, the Court of Appeals concluded there was no violation of the Act.

The Court of Appeals reversed the District Court in part, rejecting the holding that residual discrimination arising from prior employment practices was insulated from remedial action. The Court of Appeals noted, however, that the District Court was correct in its conclusion that there was no showing of a racial purpose or invidious intent in the adoption of the high school diploma requirement or general intelligence test and that these standards had been applied fairly to whites and Negroes alike. It held that, in the absence of a discriminatory purpose, use of such requirements was permitted by the Act. In so doing, the Court of Appeals rejected the claim that because these two requirements operated to render ineligible a markedly disproportionate number of Negroes, they were unlawful under Title VII unless shown to be job related. . . .

Intent of Title VII

The objective of Congress in the enactment of Title VII is plain from the language of the statute. It was to achieve equality of employment opportunities and remove barriers that have operated in the past to favor an identifiable group of white employees over other employees. Under the Act, practices, procedures, or tests neutral on their face, and even neutral in terms of intent, cannot be maintained if they operate to "freeze" the status quo of prior discriminatory employment practices.

The Court of Appeals' opinion, and the partial dissent, agreed that, on the record in the present case, "whites register far better on the Company's alternative requirements" than Negroes. . . . This consequence would appear to be directly traceable to race. Basic intelligence must have the means of articulation to manifest itself fairly in a testing process. Because they are Negroes, petitioners have long received inferior education in segregated schools and this Court expressly recognized these differences in *Gaston County* v. *United States,* 395 U. S. 285 (1969). There, because of the inferior education received by Negroes in North Carolina, this Court barred the institution of a literacy test for voter registration on the ground that the test would abridge the right to vote indirectly on account of race. Congress did not intend by Title VII, however, to guarantee a job to every person regardless of qualifications. In short, the Act does not command that any person be hired simply because he was formerly the subject of discrimination, or because he is a member of a minority group. Discriminatory preference for any group, minority or majority, is precisely and only what Congress has proscribed. What is required by Congress is the removal of artificial, arbitrary, and unnecessary barriers to employment when the barriers operate invidiously to discriminate on the basis of racial or other impermissible classification.

Congress has now provided that tests or criteria for employment or promotion may not provide equality of opportunity merely in the sense of the fabled offer of milk to the stork and the fox. On the contrary, Congress has now required that the posture and condition of the jobseeker be taken into account. It has—to resort again to the fable—provided that the vessel in which the milk is proffered be one all seekers can use. The Act proscribes not only overt discrimination but also practices that are fair in form, but discriminatory in operation. The touchstone is business necessity. If an employment practice which operates to exclude Negores cannot be shown to be related to job performance, the practice is prohibited.

On the record before us, neither the high school completion requirement nor the general intelligence test is shown to bear a demonstrable relationship to successful performance of the jobs for which it was used. Both were adopted, as the Court of Appeals noted, without meaningful study of their relationship to job-performance ability. Rather, a vice president of the Company testified, the requirements were instituted on the Company's judgment that they generally would improve the overall quality of the work force.

The evidence, however, shows that employees who have not completed high school or taken the tests have continued to perform satisfactorily and make progress in departments for which the high school and test criteria are now used. The promotion record of present employees who would not be able to meet the new criteria thus suggests the possibility that the requirements may not be needed even for the limited purpose of preserving the avowed policy of advancement within the Company. In the context of this case, it is unnecessary to reach the question whether testing requirements that take into account capability for the next succeeding position or related future promotion might be utilized upon a showing that such long-range requirements fulfill a genuine business need. In the present case the Company has made no such showing.

The Court of Appeals held that the Company had adopted the diploma and test requirements without any "intention to discriminate against Negro employees." . . . We do not suggest that either the District Court or the Court of Appeals erred in examining the employer's intent; but good intent or absence of discriminatory intent does not redeem employment procedures or testing mechanisms that operate as "built-in headwinds" for minority groups and are unrelated to measuring job capability.

The Company's lack of discriminatory intent is suggested by special efforts to help the undereducated employees through Company financing of two-thirds the cost of tuition for high school training. But Congress directed the thrust of the Act to the *consequences* of employment practices, not simply the motivation. More than that, Congress has placed on the employer the burden of showing that any given requirement must have a manifest relationship to the employment in question.

Inadequacy of Testing

The facts of this case demonstrate the inadequacy of broad and general testing devices as well as the infirmity of using diplomas or degrees as fixed measures of capability. History is filled with examples of men and women who rendered highly effective performance without the conventional badges of accomplishment in terms of certificates, diplomas, or degrees. Diplomas and tests are useful servants, but Congress has mandated the commonsense proposition that they are not to become masters of reality.

The Company contends that its general intelligence tests are specifically permitted by Sec. 703(h) of the Act. That section authorizes the use of "any professionally developed ability test" that is not "designed, intended *or used* to discriminate because of race. . . ." (Emphasis added.)

The Equal Employment Opportunity Commission, having enforcement responsibility, has issued guidelines interpreting Sec. 703(h) to permit only the use of job-related tests. The administrative interpretation of the Act by the enforcing agency is entitled to great deference. . . . Since the Act and its legislative history support the Commission's construction, this affords good reason to treat the guidelines as expressing the will of Congress.

Section 703(h) was not contained in the House version of the Civil Rights Act but was added in the Senate during extended debate. For a period, debate revolved around claims that the bill as proposed would prohibit all testing and force employers to hire unqualified persons simply because they were part of a group formerly subject to job discrimination. Proponents of Title VII sought throughout the debate to assure the critics that the Act would have no effect on job-related tests. Senators Case of New Jersey and Clark of Pennsylvania, comanagers of the bill on the Senate floor, issued a memorandum explaining that the proposed Title VII "expressly protects the employer's right to insist that any prospective applicant, Negro or white, *must meet the applicalbe job qualifications.* Indeed, the very purpose of Title VII is to promote hiring on the basis of job qualifications, rather than on the basis of race or color." 110 Cong. Rec. 7247. (Emphasis added.) Despite these assurances, Senator Tower of Texas introduced an amendment authorizing "professionally developed ability tests." Proponents of Title VII opposed the amendment because, as written, it would permit an employer to give any test, "whether it was a good test or not, so long as it was professionally designed. Discrimination could actually exist under the guise of compliance with the statute." 110 Cong. Rec. 13504 (remarks of Sen. Case).

The amendment was defeated and two days later Senator Tower offered a substitute amendment which was adopted verbatim and is now the testing provision of Sec. 703(h). Speaking for the supporters of Title VII, Senator Humphrey, who had vigorously opposed the first amendment, endorsed the substitute amendment stating: "Senators on both sides of the aisle who were deeply interested in title VII have examined the text of this amendment and have found it to be in accord with the intent and purpose of that title." 110 Cong. Rec. 13724. The amendment was then adopted. From the sum of the legislative history relevant in this case, the conclusion is inescapable that the EEOC's construction of Sec. 703(h) to require that employment tests be job related comports with congressional intent.

Nothing in the Act precludes the use of testing or measuring procedures; obviously they are useful. What Congress has forbidden is giving these devices and mechanisms controlling force unless they are demonstrably a reasonable measure of job performance. Congress has not commanded that the less qualified be preferred over the better qualified simply because of minority origins. Far from disparaging job qualifications as such, Congress has made such qualifications the controlling factor, so that race, religion, nationality, and sex become irrelevant. What Congress has commanded is that any tests used must measure the person for the job and not the person in the abstract.

16
Walter E. Washington etc. et al. Petitioners v. Alfred E. Davis et al., June 7, 1976

United States Supreme Court

Mr. Justice White delivered the opinion of the Court.

This case involves the validity of a qualifying test administered to applicants for positions as police officers in the District of Columbia Metropolitan Police Department. The test was sustained by the District Court but invalidated by the Court of Appeals. We are in agreement with the District Court and hence reverse the judgment of the Court of Appeals.

The Facts of the Case

This action began on April 10, 1970, when two Negro police officers filed suit against the then Commissioner of the District of Columbia, the Chief of the District's Metropolitan Police Department and the Commissioners of the United States Civil Service Commission. An amended complaint, filed December 10, alleged that the promotion policies of the Department were racially discriminatory and sought a declaratory judgment and an injunction. The respondents Harley and Sellers were permitted to intervene, their amended complaint asserting that their applications to become officers in the Department had been rejected, and that the Department's recruiting procedures discriminated on the basis of race against black applicants by a series of practices including, but not limited to, a written personnel test which excluded a disproportionately high number of Negro applicants. These practices were asserted to violate respondents' rights "under the due process clause of the Fifth Amendment to the United States Constitution, under 42 U. S. C. Sec. 1981 and under D. C. Code Sec. 1-320." Defendants answered, and discovery and various other proceedings followed. Respondents then filed a motion for partial summary judgment with respect to the recruiting phase of the case, seeking a declaration that the test administered to those applying to become police officers is "unlawfully discriminatory and therefore in violation of the Due Process Clause of the Fifth Amendment ..." No issue under any statute or regulation was raised by the motion. The District of Columbia defendants, petitioners here, and the federal parties also filed motions for summary judgment with respect to the recruiting aspects of the case asserting that respondents were entitled to relief on neither constitutional nor statutory grounds. The District Court granted petitioners' and denied respondents' motions.

According to the findings and conclusions of the District Court, to be accepted by the Department and to enter an intensive 17-week training program, the police recruit was required to satisfy certain physical and

---

Footnotes omitted.

character standards, to be a high school graduate or its equivalent and to receive a grade of at least 40 on "Test 21," which is "an examination that is used generally throughout the federal service," which "was developed by the Civil Service Commission not the Police Department" and which was "designed to test verbal ability, vocabulary, reading and comprehension.". . .

The validity of Test 21 was the sole issue before the court on the motions for summary judgment. The District Court noted that there was no claim of "an intentional discrimination or purposeful discriminatory actions" but only a claim that Test 21 bore no relationship to job performance and "has a highly discriminatory impact in screening out black candidates.". . . Petitioners' evidence, the District Court said, warranted three conclusions: "(a) The number of black police officers, while substantial, is not proportionate to the population mix of the city. (b) A higher percentage of blacks fail the Test than whites. (c) The Test has not been validated to establish its reliability for measuring subsequent job performance." *Ibid.* This showing was deemed sufficient to shift the burden of proof to the defendants in the action, petitioners here; but the court nevertheless concluded that on the undisputed facts respondents were not entitled to relief. The District Court relied on several factors. Since August 1969, 44% of new police force recruits had been black; that figure also represented the proportion of blacks on the total force and was roughly equivalent to 20-29-year-old blacks in the 50-mile radius in which the recruiting efforts of the Police Department had been concentrated. It was undisputed that the Department had systematically and affirmatively sought to enroll black officers many of whom passed the test but failed to report for duty. The District Court rejected the assertion that Test 21 was culturally slanted to favor whites and was "satisfied that the undisputable facts prove the test to be reasonably and directly related to the requirements of the police recruit training program and that it is neither so designed nor operated to discriminate against otherwise qualified blacks.". . . It was thus not necessary to show that Test 21 was not only a useful indicator of training school performance but had also been validated in terms of job performance—"the lack of job performance validation does not defeat the test, given its direct relationship to recruiting and the valid part it plays in this process." The District Court ultimately concluded that "the proof is wholly lacking that a police officer qualifies on the color of his skin rather than ability" and that the Department "should not be required on this showing to lower standards or to abandon efforts to achieve excellence."

Having lost on both constitutional and statutory issues in the District Court, respondents brought the case to the Court of Appeals claiming that their summary judgment motion, which rested on purely constitutional grounds, should have been granted. The tendered constitutional issue was whether the use of Test 21 invidiously discriminated against Negroes and hence denied them due process of law contrary to the commands of the Fifth Amendment. The Court of Appeals, addressing that issue, announced that it would be guided by *Griggs* v. *Duke Power Co.,* 401 U. S. 424 (1971), a case involving the interpretation and application of Title VII of the Civil Rights Act of 1964, and held that the statutory standards elucidated in that case were to govern the due process question tendered in this one. . . . The court went on to declare that lack of discriminatory intent in designing and administering Test 21 was irrelevant; the critical fact was rather that a far greater proportion of blacks—four times as many—failed the test than did whites. This disproportionate impact, standing alone and without regard to whether it indicated a discriminatory purpose, was held sufficient to establish a constitutional violation, absent proof by petitioners that the test was an adequate measure of job performance in addition to being an indicator of probable success in the training program, a burden which the court ruled petitioners had failed to discharge. That the Department had made substantial efforts to recruit blacks was held beside the point and the fact that the racial distribution of recent hirings and of the Department itself might be roughly equivalent to the racial makeup of the surrounding community, broadly conceived, was put aside as a "comparison[not] material to this appeal.". . . The Court of Appeals, over a dissent, accordingly reversed the judgment of the District Court and directed that respondents' motion for partial summary judgment be granted. We granted the petition for certiorari, 423 U. S. 820 (1975), filed by the District of Columbia officials.

Constitutional Issues

Because the Court of Appeals erroneously applied the legal standards applicable to Title VII cases in resolving the constitutional issue before it, we reverse its judgment in respondents' favor. . . .

As the Court of Appeals understood Title VII, employees or applicants proceeding under it need not concern themselves with the employer's possibly discriminatory purpose but instead may focus solely on the racially differential impact of the challenged hiring or promotion practices. This is not the constitutional rule. We have never held that the constitutional standard for adjudicating claims of invidious racial discrimination is identical to the standards applicable under Title VII, and we decline to do so today.

The central purpose of the Equal Protection Clause of the Fourteenth Amendment is the prevention of official conduct discriminating on the basis of race. It is also true that the Due Process Clause of the Fifth Amendment contains an equal protection component prohibiting the United States from invidiously discriminating between individuals or groups. . . . But our cases have not embraced the proposition that a law or other official act, without regard to whether it reflects a racially discriminatory purpose, is unconstitutional *solely* because it has a racially disproportionate impact.

Almost 100 years ago, *Strauder* v. *West Virginia,* 100 U. S. 303 (1879), established that the exclusion of Negroes from grand and petit juries in criminal proceedings violated the Equal Protection Clause, but the fact that a particular jury or a series of juries does not statistically reflect the racial composition of the community does not in itself make out an invidious discrimination forbidden by the Clause. "A purpose to discriminate must be present which may be proven by systematic exclusion of eligible jurymen of the prescribed race or by an unequal application of the law to such an extent as to show intentional discrimination." *Akins* v. *Texas,* 325 U. S. 398, 403-404 (1945). A defendant in a criminal case is entitled "to require that the State not deliberately and systematically deny to the members of his race the right to participate as jurors in the administration of justice."

The school desegregation cases have also adhered to the basic equal protection principle that the invidious quality of a law claimed to be racially discriminatory must ultimately be traced to a racially discriminatory purpose. That there are both predominantly black and predominantly white schools in a community is not alone violative of the Equal Protection Clause. The essential element of *de jure* segregation is "a current condition of segregation resulting from intentional state action ... the differentiating factor between *de jure* segregation and so-called *de facto* segregation ... is *purpose* or *intent* to segregate." *Keyes* v. *School District No. 1,* 413 U. S. 189, 205, 208 (1973). See also *id.,* at 199-211- 213. The Court has also recently rejected allegations of racial discrimination based solely on the statistically disporportionate racial impact of various provisions of the Social Security Act because "the acceptance of appellant's constitutional theory would render suspect each difference in treatment among the grant classes, however lacking the racial motivation and however rational the treatment might be." *Jefferson* v. *Hackney,* 406 U. S. 535, or 548 (1972).

This is not to say that the necessary discriminatory racial purpose must be express or appear on the face of the statute, or that a law's disproportionate impact is irrelevant in cases involving Constitution-based claims of racial discrimination. A statute, otherwise neutral on its face, must not be applied so as invidiously to discriminate on the basis of race. ... It is also clear from the cases dealing with racial discrimination in the selection of juries that the systematic exclusion of Negroes is itself such an "unequal application of the law ... as to show intentional discrimination.". ...

Necessarily, an invidious discriminatory purpose may often be inferred from the totality of the relevant facts, including the fact, if it is true, that the law bears more heavily on one race than another. It is also not infrequently true that the discriminatory impact—in the jury cases for example, the total or seriously disproportionate exclusion of Negroes from jury venires—may for all practical purposes demonstrate unconstitutionality because in various circumstances the discrimination is very difficult to explain on nonracial grounds. Nevertheless, we have not held that a law, neutral on its face and serving ends otherwise within the power of government to pursue, is invalid under the Equal Protection Clause simply because it may affect a greater proportion of one race than of another. Disproportionate impact is not irrelevant, but it is not the sole touchstone of an invidious racial discrimination forbidden by the Constitution. Standing alone, it does not trigger the rule, ... that racial classifications are to be subjected to the strictest scrutiny and are justifiable only by the weightiest of considerations.

There are some indications to the contrary in our cases. In *Palmer* v. *Thompson*, 403 U. S. 217 (1971), the city of Jackson, Miss., following a court decree to this effect, desegregated all of its public facilities save five swimming pools which had been operated by the city and which, following the decree, were closed by ordinance pursuant to a determination by the city council that closure was necessary to preserve peace and order and that integrated pools could not be economically operated. Accepting the finding that the pools were closed to avoid violence and economic loss, this Court rejected the argument that the abandonment of this service was inconsistent with the outstanding desegregation decree and that the otherwise seemingly permissible ends served by the ordinance could be impeached by demonstrating that racially invidious motivations had prompted the city council's action. The holding was that the city was not overtly or covertly operating segregated pools and was extending identical treatment to both whites and Negroes. The opinion warned against grounding decision on legislative purpose or motivation, thereby lending support for the proposition that the operative effect of the law rather than its purpose is the paramount factor. But the holding of the case was that the legitimate purposes of the ordinance—to preserve peace and avoid deficits— were not open to impeachment by evidence that the councilmen were actually motivated by racial considerations. Whatever dicta the opinion may contain, the decision did not involve, much less invalidate, a statute or ordinance having neutral purposes but disproportionate racial consequences. . . .

Another Side to the Issue

Both before and after *Palmer* v. *Thompson,* however, various Courts of Appeals have held in several contexts, including public employment, that the substantially disproportionate racial impact of a statute or official practice standing alone and without regard to discriminatory purpose, suffices to prove racial discrimination violating the Equal Protection Clause absent some justification going substantially beyond what would be necessary to validate most other legislative classifications. The cases impressively demonstrate that there is another side to the issue; but, with all due respect, to the extent that those cases rested on or expressed the view that proof of discriminatory racial purpose is unnecessary in making out an equal protection violation, we are in disagreement.

As an initial matter, we have difficulty understanding how a law establishing a racially neutral qualification for employment is nevertheless racially discriminatory and denies "any person equal protection of the laws" simply because a greater proportion of Negroes fail to qualify than members of other racial or ethnic groups. Had respondents, along with all others who had failed Test 21, whether white or black, brought an action claiming that the test denies each of them equal protection of the laws as compared with those who had passed with high enough scores to qualify them as police recruits, it is most unlikely that their challenge would have been sustained. Test 21, which is administered generally to prospective government employees, concededly seeks to ascertain whether those who take it have acquired a particular level of verbal skill; and it is untenable that the Constitution prevents the government from seeking modestly to upgrade the communicative abilities of its employees rather than to be satisfied with some lower level of competence, particularly where the job requires special ability to communicate orally and in writing. Respondents, as Negroes, could no more successfully claim that the test denied them equal protection than could white applicants who also failed. The conclusion would not be different in the face of proof that more Negroes than whites had been disqualified by Test 21. That other Negroes also failed to score well would, alone, not demonstrate that respondents individually were being denied equal protection of the laws by the application of an otherwise valid qualifying test being administered to prospective police recruits.

Nor on the facts of the case before us would the disproportionate impact of Test 21 warrant the conclusion that it is a purposeful device to discriminate against Negroes and hence an infringement of the constitutional rights of respondents as well as other black applicants. As we have said, the test is neutral on its face and rationally may be said to serve a purpose the government is constitutionally empowered to pursue. Even agreeing with the District Court that the differential racial effect of Test 21 called for further inquiry, we think the District Court correctly held that the affirmative efforts of the Metropolitan Police Department to recruit black officers, the changing racial composition of the recruit classes and of the force in general, and the relationship of the test to the training program negated any inference that the Department discriminated on the basis of race or that "a police officer qualifies on the color of his skin rather than ability.". . .

Under Title VII, Congress provided that when hiring and promotion practices disqualifying substantially disproportionate numbers of blacks are challenged, discriminatory purpose need not be proved, and that it is an insufficient response to demonstrate some rational basis for the challenged practices. It is necessary, in addition, that they be "validated" in terms of job performance in any one of several ways, perhaps by ascertaining the minimum skill, ability or potential necessary for the position at issue and determining whether the qualifying tests are appropriate for the selection of qualified applicants for the job in question. However this process proceeds, it involves a more probing judicial review of, and less deference to, the seemingly reasonable acts of administrators and executives than is appropriate under the Constitution where special racial impact, without discriminatory purpose, is claimed. We are not disposed to adopt this more rigorous standard for the purposes of applying the Fifth and the Fourteenth Amendments in cases such as this.

A rule that a statute designed to serve neutral ends is nevertheless invalid, absent compelling justification, if in practice it benefits or burdens one race more than another would be far reaching and would raise serious questions about, and perhaps invalidate, a whole range of tax, welfare, public service, regulatory, and licensing statutes that may be more burdensome to the poor and to the average black than to the more affluent white.

Given that rule, such consequences would perhaps be likely to follow. However, in our view, extension of the rule beyond those areas where it is already applicable by reason of statute, such as in the field of public employment, should await legislative prescription.

As we have indicated, it was error to direct summary judgment for respondents based on the Fifth Amendment.

A Final Question

We also hold that the Court of Appeals should have affirmed the judgment of the District Court granting the motions for summary judgment filed by petitioners and the federal parties. Respondents were entitled to relief on neither constitutional nor statutory grounds.

The submission of the defendants in the District Court was that Test 21 complied with all applicable statutory as well as constitutional requirements; and they appear not to have disputed that under the statutes and regulations governing their conduct standards similar to those obtaining under Title VII had to be satisfied. The District Court also assumed that Title VII standards were to control the case, identified the determinative issue as whether Test 21 was sufficiently job related and proceeded to uphold use of the test because it was "directly related to a determination of whether the applicant possesses sufficient skills requisite to the demands of the curriculum a recruit must master at the police academy.". . . The Court of Appeals reversed because the relationship between Test 21 and training school success, if demonstrated at all, did not satisfy what it deemed to be the crucial requirement of a direct relationship between performance on Test 21 and performance on the policeman's job.

We agree with petitioners and the federal respondents that this was error. The advisability of the police recruit training course informing the recruit about his upcoming job, acquainting him with its demands and attempting to impart a modicum of required skills seems conceded. It is also apparent to us, as it was to the District Judge, that some minimum verbal and communicative skill would be very useful, if not essential, to satisfactory progress in the training regimen. Based on the evidence before him, the District Judge concluded that Test 21 was directly related to the requirements of the police training program and that a positive relationship between the test and training course performance was sufficient to validate the former, wholly aside from its possible relationship to actual performance as a police officer. This conclusion of the District Judge that training-program validation may itself be sufficient is supported by regulations of the Civil Service Commission, by the opinion evidence placed before the District Judge and by the current views of the Civil Service Commissioners who were parties to the case. Nor is the conclusion foreclosed by either *Griggs* or *Albemarle Paper Co.* v. *Moody,* 422 U. S. 405 (1975); and it seems to us the much more sensible construction of the job relatedness requirement.

The District Court's accompanying conclusion that Test 21 was in fact directly related to the requirements of the police training program was supported by a validation study, as well as by other evidence of record; and we are not convinced that this conclusion was erroneous.

The federal parties, whose views have somewhat changed since the decision of the Court of Appeals and who still insist that training-program validation is sufficient, now urge a remand to the District Court for the purpose of further inquiry into whether the training program test scores, which were found to correlate with Test 21 scores, are themselves an appropriate measure of the trainee's mastership of the material taught in the course and whether the training program itself is sufficiently related to actual performance of the police officer's task. We think a remand is inappropriate. The District Court's judgment was warranted by the record before him, and we perceive no good reason to reopen it, particularly since we were informed at oral argument that although Test 21 is still being administered, the training program itself has undergone substantial modification in the course of this litigation. If there are now deficiencies in the recruiting practices under prevailing Title VII standards, those deficiencies are to be directly addressed in accordance with appropriate procedures mandated under that section.

The judgment of the Court of Appeals accordingly is reversed.

So ordered.

17
Bakke and Beyond:
The Future of Affirmative Action
Bert C. Buzan

This essay is addressed to the disappointed practitioner or student of personnel administration who anticipated a quick and unambiguous judicial resolution of the affirmative action controversy. The central thesis of this essay is that the widely publicized *Bakke* case should not have been expected to sweep affirmative action into the historical dustbin as easily and neatly as the anti-affirmative action forces presumed, nor could the case have delivered a clear justification for affirmative action programs everywhere. Without taking the equally simplistic position that *Bakke* decided nothing but the admission of a single aspirant to medical school, this essay views the case as the first in a long line of upcoming litigation concerning the legal basis for affirmative action, the significance of complex factual determinations in this area, and the implementation problems raised by *Bakke* itself.

By now, the facts of the *Bakke* case should be familiar to everyone not marooned on an uncharted desert island in the South Pacific. Allan Bakke, a

An original essay prepared for this book.

Bert C. Buzan is Assistant Professor of Political Science, California State University, Fullerton white male applicant was denied admission to the University of California, Davis medical school. The school had reserved sixteen of its one hundred admissions for minority applicants. Bakke's attorneys argued that this "special admissions" program violated the Equal Protection Clause of the 14th Amendment[1] to the Constitution and Title VI of the 1964 Civil Rights Act.[2] The California Supreme Court accepted Bakke's Equal Protection argument and broadened its ruling to prohibit any use of racial criteria in university admissions programs. The University appealed to the U. S. Supreme Court. The High Court ruled 5 to 4 in favor of Bakke's admission but (also by the narrowest margin) reversed the California Supreme Court's total ban on any consideration of race as a factor in admissions.

The Bakke case had become a *cause celebre* among opponents of (so-called) "reverse discrimination." Organizations filing *amicus curiae* (friend of the court) briefs on Bakke's behalf include local bar associations, police organizations and white ethnic interest groups representing Jews, Poles, Italians, Greeks and Ukranians. Various labor unions are to be found on either side of the question, while civil rights organizations such as the American Civil Liberties Union, the National Association for the Advancement of Colored People, the Mexican American Legal Defense Fund and the Urban League filed *amicus curiae* against Bakke's position.

Judicial Politics

In symbolic terms, at least, the Bakke case has represented judicial politics at its most dramatic. American liberals, in particular, have been appalled at the sight of labor leaders, prominent academics and representatives of the Jewish community squaring off against old allies in the black, Chicano and civil libertarian communities. The issues are complex, emotional and divisive: exactly the sort of issues that courts are ill-suited to handle in a manner that everyone can live with. As a result, both sides entered the case with a grim determination, reinforced by dire prophecies of the inevitable consequences of a defeat for "their" side. The pro-Bakke forces claimed that "special admissions" and "preferential hiring" of minorities pose an evil as great as the old days of racial segregation. The anti-Bakke forces feared a return to precisely those "bad old days" of racial injustice had the sweeping "color blindness" rhetoric of the California Court's decision prevailed.

Neither side won total victory or suffered total defeat in the U. S. Supreme Court's Bakke decision. Both sides can find grounds for consolation. Likewise, both should be apprehensive about the future course of "special admissions" and other "affirmative action" programs in the United States. The anti-affirmative action forces can find comfort in the Court's condemnation of flat quotas in college admissions, but they are fearful that the Court's approval of less obtrusive minority recruitment programs may lead to the same result as an overt quota system. The pro-affirmative action forces can take heart at the Court's reaffirmation of the basic principle of affirmative action, but they fear that Bakke's admission may prove to be a crushing symbolic defeat and that administrators will use the case's complexity as an excuse for abandoning affirmative action altogether. Finally, both sides realize that the *Bakke* decision narrowly focused its attention on the unique character of the college admissions process and left "preferential hiring" and the "setting aside" of contracts for minority businesses for another session.

What should the practicing administrator make of all this forbidding complexity? He or she should prepare for a lifetime of conflict and uncertainty concerning the entire affirmative action controversy. The *Bakke* decision did not resolve the legal and factual muddle surrounding this titanic public conflict. There is a maxim in law that "difficult cases make bad law." *Bakke* was just such a difficult case, and "bad" law is law that raises more questions than it answers.

The *Bakke* case is difficult at several levels of analysis. At the level of constitutional law it raises questions about the jruisprudential rationale behind the 14th amendment's Equal Protection Clause. At a statutory level it raises numerous questions of Congressional intent behind the passage of the 1964 Civil Rights Act. At a factual level it turns on an unclear distinctions between forbidden "quotas" and permissible uses of race as well as "remedial" and "voluntary" affirmative action programs. Moreover, the decision largely ignores complex factual problems concerning the meaning of "qualifications" and "merit" in a wide variety of contexts. At an administrative level, it implicates questions of agency autonomy. Finally, the case—like any controversial court decision—raises, at every turn, delicate questions concerning the proper role of the judicial branch in a nation that prides itself on decentralization and electoral democracy.

In sum, the case raises so many inter-related issues that it is difficult, even unreasonable, to expect a quick, politically acceptable resolution of them by judicial *fiat.*

Given this, all that can be attempted in a short essay is a thumbnail sketch of the positions taken by the two "majorities" (one against quotas, the other against requiring "color blind" admissions) and a brief discussion of some of the potential problems raised by the *Bakke* decision.

The Legal Dilemma

Nearly everyone concedes that *Bakke* represents no clear-cut legal "total victory" for either side in the affirmative action controversy. But this should not lead one to jump to the conclusion that *Bakke* decided nothing more than the fate of one aspiring medical student. Before *Bakke* there was total confusion about the applicability of the Equal Protection Clause in so-called "reverse discrimination" cases.

The phrase "equal protection" sounds simple, but its constitutional application has been most complex.[3] No law treats everyone equally. A cursory glance at the tax codes, for instance, reveals lower income tax rates for the poor, homeowner deductions that benefit the middle class and exclusion on the sale of corporate stocks for the rich. Courts normally strain to find some "rational basis" for unequal classifications of this sort, and judges routinely reject legal challenges to them under the Equal Protection Clause.

Racial classifications, on the other hand, are immediately "suspect," and the courts have invalidated these classifications unless the state can survive "strict judicial scrutiny" by overcoming an overpowering burden of proof. A mere "rational basis" for the classification will not survive strict judicial scrutiny. The state must show a "compelling interest" that cannot be attained by any "less burdensome means" than imposing a racial classification and treating these "classes" differently. Since the 1960s the Supreme Court has employed this logic of strict judicial scrutiny to strike down a host of discriminatory state laws designed to keep non-white in positions of legally-sanctioned inferiority.

Bakke's more ardent supporters insist that this taboo on racial classifications constitutionally mandates a state posture of absolute "color blindness." They consider the Davis medical school's admission program perfectly analogous to an 1880 West Virginia law forbidding blacks to serve on juries[4] or a wartime action placing the Japanese in concentration camps.[5] This analogy rejects any compromise with the notion that there is any difference between affirmative action and the historic racial discrimination imposed upon non-whites on the basis of longstanding color prejudice. In this view, a classificatory scheme that works to the detriment of whites is forbidden because constitutional rights are conferred on individuals, not groups. This argument is generally buttressed by claims that certain white ethnic groups, chiefly Jews and East Europeans, have been discriminated against, too. Moreover, the proponents of this view argue that the civil rights legislation of the 1960s, such as Title VI, was designed to promote a "color-blind" equality of opportunity without regard to any inequality of condition past patterns of discrimination may have imposed upon blacks, Chicanos and Indians.

Like all attractive legal arguments, the rhetoric of "color-blindness" contains powerful emotional appeals grounded in the national experience. It appeals to individualism, impartiality, inclusiveness, self-help and a rough hewn frontier egalitarianism.

This argument has been countered by another theory of the meaning of "equal protection" and "non-discrimination", a theory that deals with the 14th Amendment, Title VI, and the nation's tragic racial legacy in quite a different manner. In this second view, all racial distinctions made by the states are not immediately suspect. The 14th Amendment was designed originally in 1868 to protect the rights of newly freed blacks. Since then, the courts have departed from their normal posture of straining to find some rational basis for state classifications only in cases involving "discrete and insular minorities"[6] historically denied full access to the political process by popular bigotry and prejudice.

In this way of thinking the political powerlessness of racial minorities has provided the jurisprudential rationale for the extraordinary judicial intervention into "normal" legislative and administrative procedures that the courts have undertaken on behalf of non-whites. Racial minorities, like unpopular religious groups and political dissenters, often have "negative political power."[7] It is often more expedient for elected officials to attack them than to defend their rights or even to ignore them. As a result, the routine processes of American democracy break down where these "discrete and insular minorities" are concerned. Therefore, the federal courts, mindful of their position as the "unelected" branch in an electoral democarcy, justify the extraordinary exercise of judicial power through "strict scrutiny" by referring to the legacy of systematic state abuse imposed upon persecuted and historically powerless minorities. Turning this "discrete and insular minorities" rationale around to protect the white majority from itself represents a major departure in judicial policy, at least in the minds of the adherents of this theory of the meaning of the 14th Amendment.

The proponents of this perspective, unlike the adherents of the "color-blindness" theory, do not consider the sort of racial distinctions the Davis medical school made to be the same as the old "invidious" (or "stigmatizing") labels imposed upon non-whites throughout American history. The school's action implied no racial slur: Bakke was not rejected because the admissions board thought white folks were lousy people. As legal philosopher Ronald Dworkin put it, "since discrimination supposes prejudice, he (Bakke) was not the victim of discrimination."[8] In short, if no connection to a legacy of prejudice can be made, no *racial* discrimination exists. To quote Dworkin again:

> *It seems natural to say that a black actor has been excluded from a social club on racial grounds, but odd to say that he is not permitted to play Hamlet, in a conventional production, on grounds of race.*[9]

Thus, Bakke was excluded, in this view, from the Davis medical school for the "benign" purposes of reversing past patterns of societal discrimination, providing better medical care in minority communities, and providing a more diverse educational experience for Davis medical students. Like the white actor who gets the part of Hamlet over the black aspirant to the role, the non-white applicant serves the purposes of the institution better than Allan Bakke. To sum it up: when the Anglo majority denies one of its own the reason may not be "good", but racial bigotry cannot be one of the "bad" reasons for doing so. Thus, the staunchest opponents of the "color-blindness" theory of non-discrimination insist that the more lenient "rational basis" test, rather than strict judicial scrutiny should be applied in cases like *Bakke*.

The Court's Response

Neither the "color-blindness" theory nor the theory that only "discrete and insular minorities" are protected from racial classifications received total, unqualified acceptance in *any* of the six opinions written in Bakke. The Court resolved itself into two "blocs" of four Justices each, with Justice Powell casting a deciding "split vote" agreeing in part with each of the two blocs. Justice Powell, plus a bloc speaking through Justice Stevens ruled that Bakke should be admitted to the Davis medical school. But Powell also voted with a "pro-quota" bloc, speaking primarily through Justice Brennan, to reverse the California Supreme Court's uncompromising ban on the use of race in admissions programs.

The "color-blindness' theory received qualified support from the four-man "Stevens bloc":

> *the meaning of Title VI is crystal clear: Race cannot be the basis of excluding anyone from participation in a federally funded program.*[10]

This endorsement of "color blindness" was restrained in two respects. First, Stevens took pains to point out that his opinion applied only to Bakke and the Davis medical school. ("This is not a class action," he cautioned). Second, the opinion aimed for a minimal judicial impact on the entire affirmative action controversy by ignoring the "equal protection" arguments and, instead, deciding on statutory grounds. Had this viewpoint attracted a decisive fifth vote, then minorities *would have* retained the option of lobbying Congress for a revision of Title VI that would specifically permit the reimplementation of "quotas."In contrast, a pro-Bakke ruling on Constitutional grounds would have been virtually irreversible.

As the vote on the Court turned out, the "Stevens bloc" did little more than provide four of the five votes Bakke needed to get into medical school. The other five Justices rejected Stevens' "color blind" reading of the Congressional intent behind Title VI, arguing, instead that Congress deliberately left the legal definition of "discrimination" to the courts. Moreover, a majority of the Court disagreed with Stevens attempt to narrow the scope of the decision to Bakke's solitary case. In the view of five Justices, the California Supreme Court decision had justified Bakke's admission with an unqualified (and erroneous) endorsement of the "color blindness" theory of the Equal Protection Clause.

The "Anti-Bakke" Position

An "anti-Bakke" bloc of four, speaking primarily through Justice Brennan, emphatically rejected the "color blindness" theory, but did not embrace the view that allegedly "benign" racial classifications need only pass the lenient "rational basis test." The "Brennan bloc" accepted the distinction between "remedial" and "stigmatizing" racial classifications, but concluded that judicial review of even "remedial" racial classifications should be "strict and searching." Remedial quotas are dangerous because they

> *...may promote racial separation and reinforce the views of those who believe that racial minorities are incapable of succeeding on their own.*

Second, race, like sex, is an "immutable characteristic"; people cannot readily change their color or their gender. Therefore, classifications based on race or gender, while not presumptively invalid, run the risk of allocating legal burdens without regard to individual responsibility. In this context, Brennan points out that preferential programs for "non-whites" may single out the most discrete and insular whites to bear the brunt of the "benign" discrimination. Finally, respect for individual rights demands a closer examination of *"any"* racial classification than the weak "rational basis" test provides.

Nonetheless, Brennan makes it clear that these considerations are relevant only because all racial classifications are potentially "stigmatizing." Traditional forms of discrimination against non-whites blatantly stigmatize and are *ipso facto* invalid. "Benign" classifications may subtly stigmatize either non-whites or powerless whites. Therefore, a state employing such a "benign" racial classification must defend it by demonstrating "an important and articulated purpose for its use . . ."

This is clearly more than a "rational basis." As applied by the "Brennan bloc," however, it seems a standard less strict than the "compelling state interest" demanded in cases involving discrimination against non-whites. It is not altogether clear whether or not Brennan is establishing a "middle tier" standard of review for "reverse discrimination" cases. At any rate, Brennan concludes that

> *Davis' articulated purpose of remedying the effects of past societal discrimination is . . . sufficiently important to justify the use of race-concious admissions programs . . . (because) minority under-representation is substantial and chronic, and . . . the handicap of past discrimination is impeding access of minorities to the medical school.*

In the view of Brennan and three other Justices, no "color blind" remedy will correct this minority under-representation. "Economic deprivation" cannot substitute for race, since poor whites greatly outnumber minority applicants. Moreover, non-whites tend, overall, to possess lower grades and standardized test scores than the average applicant while lower class whites do not.

The Powell Opinion

This plea for a racial remedy to racial problems provided four of the five votes needed to reverse the state court ruling that "color blindness" was a constitutional mandate. The "Brennan bloc" was unsuccessful, however, in attracting the fifth vote necessary to uphold the Davis quota. The crucial fifth vote for each "majority" in the *Bakke* case, Justice Powell, insisted on traditional strict scrutiny in all race cases, considered the question of "stigma" hopelessly subjective, accepted the promotion of educational diversity (but not the remedying of societal discrimination) as a compelling state interest, and, most importantly, made a constitutional distinction between quotas and "less burdensome" methods of considering race in the admissions process.

Powell addresses the applicability of the Equal Protection Clause to *Bakke* by attacking the "discrete and insular minorities" theory:

> *This rationale has never been invoked in our decisions as a prerequisite to subjecting racial or ethnic distinctions to strict scrutiny . . . These characteristics may be relevant in deciding whether or not to add new types of classifications to the list of "suspect" categories or whether a particular classification survives close examination . . . Racial and ethnic classification, however, are subject to stringent examination without regard to these additional characteristics.*

Conceding that the original purpose of the Fourteenth Amendment was the protection of blacks, Powell pointed out that since the end of the Civil War "the United States had become a nation of minorities." This "nation of minorities" view apparently is central to Powell's legal assessment of American ethnic relations. In Powell's view there is no "white majority." Whites are a diverse lot and frequently discriminate against one another on ethno-cultural grounds. Thus, there is no clear ground for reserving the protection of "strict scrutiny" for non-whites. On this presumption, the notion of "stigma", so crucial to the anti-*Bakke* argument, becomes hopelessly subjective and diffuse.

Turning to the Davis quota itself, Powell finds the remediation of "societal discrimination" against non-whites to be too vague a basis for showing of "compelling state interest." Racial quotas can only be justified as a remedy for "ameliorating ... the disabling effects of identified discrimination," as in the school desegregation cases, where the school boards themselves were found guilty of "constitutional or statutory violations." In such instances

...the governmental interest in preferring members of the injured groups at the expense of others is substantial, since the legal rights of the victims must be vindicated.

At this point in Powell's opinion, questions of administrative autonomy and purpose occupy a crucial position.

Without such findings of constitutional or statutory violations, it cannot be said that the government has any greater interest in helping one individual than in refraining from harming another ... (The Davis medical school) is in no position to make ... such findings. Its broad mission is education, not the formulation of legislative policy or the adjudication of particular claims of illegality.

In Powell's view, schools have no capacity to undertake the task of remedying past discrimination. Equal Protection is a personal—not a group—right and only courts and legislatures, after a proper showing of specific (not "amorphous" *societal*) discrimination, can impose racial quotas that deny whites benefits in the name of remedying injuries done to non-whites.

This position puts Powell in sharp contradiction with the "Brennan" position that educational institutions may impose racial quotas to remedy societal discrimination. It does not, however, place Powell in support of the "color blindness" theory of "equal protection." The medical school's stated goal of attaining

a diverse student body ... clearly is a constitutionally permissable goal for an institution of higher education. Academic freedom ... long has been viewed as a special concern of the First Amendment. The freedom of a university to make its own judgments as to education includes the selection of its student body. The atmosphere of "speculation, experiment and creation"—so essential to the quality of higher education—is widely believed to be promoted by a diverse student body. (This argument) invokes a countervailing constitutional interest, that of the First Amendment.

The thrust, of Powell's opinion is clear: the promotion of "diversity" in education is a component of academic freedom sufficiently "compelling" to justify some sort of racial consideration. But a state must also show that its "suspect" classification is necessary to the attainment of the "compelling state interest" that justifies it. It is at this point that Powell draws a line between "quotas" and "less burdensome" schemes aimed at educational diversity. In Powell's view, Davis' argument that its quota

> *is the only effective means of serving the interest of diversity is seriously flawed ... The diversity that furthers a compelling state interest encompasses a far broader array of qualifications and characteristics of which racial or ethnic origin is but a single though important element ... (Davis' program), focused* solely *on ethnic diversity, would hinder ... attainment of genuine diversity.*

Powell then contrasts Davis' forbidden "quota" with a Harvard admissions program that awards a "plus" or varying weight to applicants who might contribute to the school's "diversity" by virtue of their race, geographical origin, or special interests and skills. Such a program

> *... does not insulate the individual from comparison with all other candidates ... (Harvard's program) is flexible enough to consider all pertinent elements of diversity ... (yet) treats each applicant as an individual.*

The line between the Davis and Harvard programs may be thin but it is constitutionally crucial to Powell. Quotas (in the absence of specific findings of past discrimination) are clear evidence of an intent to discriminate, thus they violate the Equal Protection Clause "on their face" (i.e., by their very existence). More "flexible" affirmative action admissions programs *may* be operated in a racially discriminatory fashion, Powell acknowledges, but the Court must assume the "good faith" of the academic community "in the absence of a showing to the contrary."

Powell's opinion may be re-stated as follows: flat racial quotas cannot be justified by anything short of a "proper" showing of specific violations of the *legal* rights of non-whites, but absolute "color blindness" is not required by the Constitution as long as race is only one factor in an admissions program designed to promote a "diverse" educational experience for its students.

The Practical Implications of Litigation Strategies

Powell's "swing-vote" opinion was crucial to the resolution of the Bakke case despite the fact that none of the other Justices concurred in his views. Moreover, it provides the best available guide to future policy-making in the affirmative action field, assuming that the Court's composition and internal divisions remain constant. Given this, the ambiguous distinctions in Powell's opinion, the problems of generalizing from the facts in *Bakke* to other college admissions procedures and, indeed, Powell's narrow focus on the educational dimension of the affirmative action conflict all combine to make *Bakke* a very poor guide to future policy-making. One clear implication of this uncertainty is that personnel administrators, along with the rest of us, should prepare for an embittered, protracted struggle over affirmative action. The battle lines are drawn, neither side feels that it can accept a substantial defeat, the Supreme Court seems a peculiarly ill-suited forum for effecting a workable compromise, and the "elected" branches show little willingness to step into the breach.

One primary *Bakke* outcome, the distinction between the "Harvard" and "Davis" models of affirmative action, should please no one for very long. If the "Harvard" approach results in the admission of significant numbers of minorities with grades and test scores lower than those of the average white applicant, the anti-affirmative action forces will formulate litigation strategies aimed at attacking the "good faith" of admissions committees across the nation. One can easily imagine a half-generation of litigation answering the question: "when does a 'Harvard-type' program function as a 'quota' under the meaning of *Bakke*?"

If administrators respond to this intimidating barrage of litigation by substantially reducing minority admissions, minorities have no *legal* recourse under *Bakke*. Affirmative action programs are purely voluntary unless findings of specific discrimination against non-whites are uncovered by the courts or by the "proper" administrative authorities. This puts the anti-affirmative action forces on the offensive in the absence of such findings. *Bakke* reinforced this advantage by apparently rejecting *societal* discrimination as a justification for any affirmative action program and by ruling that educational institutions are limited to "academic freedom" as a justification for racially sensitive "diversity" in admissions programs. These apparent restrictions present another avenue of anti-affirmative action litigation. If societal discrimination does not justify affirmative action, and agencies must possess a particular "competence" to make findings of specific discrimination, then what is the justification for purely voluntary affirmative action hiring programs? "Academic freedom" provides no clear analogues outside an educational context. Hence, voluntary affirmative action programs in non-educational public institutions are now open to the challenge that they serve no "permissible" purpose analogous to the university's need for a diverse student body.

This is not to argue that a parks and recreation department, for instance, could not come up with some reason why it must "diversify" its workforce or clientele. The point, rather, is that this sort of vulnerability invites litigation strategies that, conceivably, could intimidate administrators (besides college admissions officers) into a general retreat from affirmative action.

Should this combined legal attack on the "good faith" of administrators and "permissible purpose" of voluntary affirmative action programs prove extremely successful, minorities and civil libertarians may look back at *Bakke* as the starting point of a "Second Betrayal" of non-whites analogous to the federal government's post-Reconstruction abandonment of the black race to lynch-law and racial caste segregation. This would be an extreme outcome, to be sure, perhaps it is also an unlikely one. But the symbolic significance for non-whites of a systematic, slow judicial dismantling of voluntary affirmative action programs is not a consequence policy-makers should take lightly. The analogy to the nineteenth century "betrayal" of blacks to "Jim Crow" would not be wholly inexact, for any future decisions tending to place "color blindness" on a constitutional footing would deny non-whites any peaceful recourse short of the arduous, extra-majoritarian process of constitutional amendment! The last time the courts decided (gradually) that coping with minority demands was more trouble than it was worth, the abandoned black race became the passive object of white violence. If there is a "Second Betrayal", the violence quite likely will be "fully integrated."

This apocalyptic scenario, is, by no means, pre-ordained. The courts are likely to assume "good faith" on the part of affirmative action admissions programs. Moreover, the next session of the Supreme Court may produce another series of "compromise" decisions on employment and contracting that sufficiently differentiates them from college admissions to avoid the narrow emphasis on "academic freedom" that presently menaces minority aspirations. Finally, there is a factual controversy brewing within the overall affirmative action maelstrom that either side could turn to its future advantage.

The factual controversy permeating nearly every aspect of the affirmative action conflict concerns an ambiguous notion of "qualifications" in admissions and employment. The staunchest supporters of affirmative action argue that measures such as standardized tests are culturally biased, systematically under-state the "qualifications" of minorities and are discriminatory *per se*. The court has rejected this view in the absence of a sharing of "discriminatory intent" in the testing process.[11] On the other hand, the most vocal adherents of "color blindness" rewrite history a bit (a valuable skill for which lawyers and interest group leaders are handsomely rewarded) when they insist that standardized scores and grade point averages were the only criteria employed as "qualifica-tions" before affirmative action came along. No court need refute this view; it is simply incorrect. Athletes, the children of generous or influential alumni, "hardship cases" and persons who "diversify" the program have been the historic beneficiaries of non-quantitative considerations, as the opinions of Justices Powell and BLackman clearly acknowledge in *Bakke*. There is nothing in *Bakke* that precludes an admissions committee from asking the questions:

Are this applicant's low grades/scores due to a) the obstacles imposed by inferior schooling?, b) cultural bias in standardized testing?

The very openess of Davis' sixteen percent minority quota prevented this sort of factual justification for affirmative action from receiving a full judicial hearing. The Davis medical school had (rather impatiently) replaced the consideration of such subtleties with its quota system. Thus, the opportunity remains open for minorities to defend so-called "preferential" admissions (and, by analogy, hiring) with a justification much broader than "academic freedom": the remediation of systematic biases in standardized testing and measures of past educational attainment. The anti-affirmative forces, on the other hand, will certainly attempt to counter this justification with arguments that grades and tests are valid predicters of performance in school or on the job and that the agencies attempting to "remediate" the disparate racial impact of these measures are incompetent to do so. These arguments over "objective" notions of "qualifications" are the objects of great controversy within educational and industrial psychology. Somewhere along the line, these factual considerations will be tried in court. The civil rights groups will see to that. Thus, it is unlikely that the courts will resolve the affirmative action controversy without someday considering mountains of expert testimony. Until these facts have been considered, personnel administrators will have to make decisions in the face of grave uncertainties, while outraged whites threaten litigation, and minorities demand that the administrator withstand these intimidating pressures.

Thus, American society is faced with two possible long-range outcomes: a gradual, *de facto* judicial enshrinement of "color blindness" that virtually invites non-whites to take their grievances to the streets, or a succession of re-endorsements of the basic principle of affirmative action that eventually exhausts its determined opponents. Either way, personnel administrators face a protracted ordeal of case-by-case adjudication that will leave them in the dark about the legal status and political acceptability of their next move.

Courts have seldom been capable of dispensing "quick fixes" that resolve divisive social questions. Moreover, racially-tinged conflicts have traditionally frustrated our best efforts at compromise. Elected officials tend to run for cover at the sound of racial conflict in the distance, leaving to administrators and judges the nasty choice of resolving these problems. Given this legacy, there is little reason to expect that we will not be grappling with affirmative action—or the aftermath of its gradual abandonment—for the rest of our lives.

Notes

1. "No state shall make or enforce any law which shall . . . deny to any person within its jurisdiction the equal protection of the laws."

2. "No person in the United States shall, on the ground of race, color or national origin, be denied the benefit of, or be subjected to discrimination under any program or activity receiving federal financial assistance."

3. For a succinct review of the massive body of literature and cases on equal protection, see J. Norvak, R. Rotunda, and J. N. Young, *Constitutional Law* (West Pub. Co., 1978), pp. 517-688.

4. *Strauder* v. *West Virginia,* 100 U.S. 303.

5. *Korematsu* v. *U.S.,* 323 U.S. 214 (1944).

6. *U.S.* v. *Carolene Products Co.,* 304 U.S. 144, 152, n. 4 (1938).

7. L. Frantz, "The First Amendment in the Balance", in W. Lockhart, Y. Kamisar, J. Choper (eds.) *The American Constitution,* (West Pub. Co., 1975), p. 556.

8. R. Dworkin, *New York Review of Books,* January 26, 1978.

9. *Ibid.*

10. *Regents* . . . v. *Bakke* (76-811), reprinted in full in *Los Angeles Daily Journal,* June 30, 1978. (All *Bakke* quotes are derived from this source.)

11. *Washington* v. *Davis,* 96 S.Ct. 2040 (1976).

18
Regents of the University of California v. Alan Bakke

United States Supreme Court

Opinion by Justice Powell

[Mr. Justice Powell delivered the opinion of the Court. Powell voted with the Chief Justice and with Justices Stevens, Stewart, and Rehnquist to declare the University of California, Davis Medical School's "special admissions program" unlawful and to order Bakke's admission. Powell also voted with Justices Brennan, Marshall, Blackmun and White to reverse the California Supreme Court's ruling that college admissions programs may not consider race in their evaluations of applicants. In his opinion, Justice Powell outlines the reasons supporting his crucial "swing" votes on each of these issues.]

This case presents a challenge to the special admissions program of the petitioner, the Medical School of the University of California at Davis, which is designed to assure the admission of a specified number of students from certain minority groups...

The Supreme Court of California affirmed those portions of the trial court's judgment declaring the special admissions program unlawful and enjoining petitioner from considering the race of any applicant...

For the reasons stated in the following opinion, I believe that so much of the judgment of the California court as holds petitioner's special admissions program unlawful and directs that respondent be admitted to the Medical School must be affirmed. For the reasons expressed in a separate opinion, my Brothers the Chief Justice, Mr. Justice Stewart, Mr. Justice Rehnquist, and Mr. Justice Stevens concur in this judgment.

I also conclude for the reasons stated in the following opinion that the portion of the court's judgment enjoining petitioner from according any consideration to race in its admissions process must be reversed. For reasons expressed in separate opinions, my Brothers Mr. Justice Brennan, Mr. Justice White, Mr. Justice Marshall, and Mr. Justice Blackmun concur in this judgment.

Affirmed in part and reversed in part...

Inapplicability of Title VI

In this Court the parties neither briefed nor argued the applicability of Title VI of the Civil Rights Act of 1964. Rather, as had the California court, they focused exclusively upon the validity of the special admissions program under the Equal Protection Clause. Because it was possible, however, that a decision on Title VI might obviate resort to constitutional interpretation . . . we requested supplementary briefing on the statutory issue.

At the outset we face the question whether a right of action for private parties exists under Title VI. Respondent argues that there is a private right of action. . . . He contends that the statute creates a federal right in his favor, that legislative history reveals an intent to permit private actions, that such actions would further the remedial purposes of the statute, and that enforcement of federal rights under the Civil Rights Act generally is not relegated to the States. . . . Petitioner denies the existence of a private right of action. . . . In its view, administrative curtailment of federal funds under that section was the only sanction to be imposed upon recipients that violated S. 601. [Section 601 of Title VI of the 1964 Civil Rights Act.] . . .

We find it unnecessary to resolve this question in the instant case . . . We therefore do not address this difficult issue. Similarly, we need not pass upon petitioner's claim that private plaintiffs under Title VI must exhaust administrative remedies. We assume only for the purposes of this case that respondent has a right of action under Title VI . . .

The language of s. 601, like that of the Equal Protection Clause, is majestic in its sweep: "No person in the United States shall, on the ground of race, color, national origin, be excluded from participation in, be denied the benefits of, or be subjected to discrimination under any program or activity receiving Federal financial assistance."

The concept of "discrimination," like the phrase "equal protection of the laws," is susceptible to varying interpretations, for as Mr. Justice Holmes declared, "(a) word is not a crystal, transparent and unchanged, it is the skin of living thought and may vary greatly in color and content according to the circumstances and the time in which it is used.". . .

Examination of the voluminous legislative history of Title VI reveals a congressional intent to halt federal funding of entities that violate a prohibition of racial discrimination similar to that of the Constitution. Although isolated statements of various legislators, taken out of context, can be marshalled in support of the proposition that S. 601 enacted a purely color-blind scheme, without regard to the reach of the Equal Protection Clause, these comments must be read against the background of both the problem that Congress was addressing and the broader view of the statute that emerges from a full examination of the legislative debates.

The problem confronting Congress was discrimination against Negro citizens at the hands of recipients of federal moneys. Indeed, color-blindness pronouncements . . . generally occur in the midst of extended remarks dealing with the evils of segregation in federally funded programs. Over and over again, proponents of the bill detailed the plight of Negroes seeking equal treatment in such programs. There simply was no reason for Congress to consider the validity of hypothetical preferences that might be accorded minority citizens. . . .

In addressing that problem, supporters of Title VI repeatedly declared that the bill enacted constitutional principles. . . .

Further evidence of the incorporation of a constitutional standard into Title VI appears in the repeated refusals of the legislation's supporters precisely to define the term "discrimination." Opponents sharply criticized this failure, but proponents of the bill merely replied that the meaning of "discrimination" would be made clear by reference to the Constitution or other existing law. In view of the clear legislative intent, Title VI must be held to proscribe only those racial classifications that would violate the Equal Protection Clause or the Fifth Amendment.

Standards of Review

Petitioner does not deny that decisions based on race or ethnic origin by faculties and administrations of state universities are reviewable under the Fourteenth Amendment. For this part, respondent does not argue that all racial or ethnic classifications are per se invalid. . . .

The parties do disagree as to the level of judicial scrutiny to be applied to the special admissions program. Petitioner argues that the court below erred in applying strict scrutiny, as this inexact term has been applied in our cases. That level of review, petitioner asserts, should be reserved for classifications that disadvantage "discrete and insular minorities." Respondent, on the other hand, contends that the California court correctly rejected the notion that the degree of judicial scrutiny accorded a particular racial or ethnic classification hinges upon membership in a discrete and insular minority and duly recognized that the "rights established (by the Fourteenth Amendment) are personal rights." . . .

En route to this crucial battle over the scope of judicial review, the parties fight a sharp preliminary action over the proper characterization of the special admissions program. Petitioner prefers to view it as establishing a "goal" of minority representation in the medical school. Respondent, echoing the courts below, labels it a racial quota.

This semantic distinction is beside the point: the special admissions program is undeniably a classification based on race and ethnic background. To the extent that there existed a pool of at least minimally qualified minority applicants to fill the 16 special admissions seats, white applicants could compete only for 84 seats in the entering class rather than the 100 open to minority applicants. . . .

The guarantees of the Fourteenth Amendment extend to persons. . . . The guarantee of equal protection cannot mean one thing when applied to one individual and something else when applied to a person of another color. If both are not accorded the same protection, then it is not equal. . . .

Nevertheless, petitioner argues that the court below erred in applying strict scrutiny to the special admissions programs because white males, such as respondent, are not a "discrete and insular minority" requiring extraordinary protection from the majoritarian political process. . . . This rationale, however, has never been invoked in our decisions as a prerequisite to subjecting racial or ethnic distinctions to strict scrutiny. . . . These characteristics may be relevant in deciding whether or not to add new types of classifications to the list of "suspect" categories or whether a particular classification survives close examination. . . . Racial and ethnic classifications, however, are subject to stringent examination without regard to these additional characteristics. . . .

Racial and ethnic distinctions of any sort are inherently suspect and thus call for the most exacting judicial examination.

A "Nation of Minorities"

This perception of racial and ethnic distinctions is rooted in our Nation's constitutional and demographic history. The Court's initial view of the Fourteenth Amendment was that its "one pervading purpose" was "the freedom of the slave race, the security and firm establishment of that freedom, and the protection of the newly-made freeman and citizen from the oppressions of those who and formerly exercised dominion over him. The Equal Protection Clause, however, was "(v)irtually strangled in its infancy by post-civil-war judicial reactionism." It was relegated to decades of relative desuetude while the Due Process Clause of the Fourteenth Amendment, after a short germinal period, flourished as a cornerstone in the Court's defense of property and liberty of contract ... In that cause, the Fourteenth Amendment's "one pervading purpose" was displaced. ...

During the dormancy of the Equal Protection Clause, the United States had become a nation of minorities. Each had to struggle—and to some extent struggles still—to overcome the prejudices not of a monolithic majority, but of a "majority" composed of various minority groups of whom it was said—perhaps unfairly in many cases—that a shared characteristic was a willingness to disadvantage other groups. As the Nation filled with the stock of many lands, the reach of the Clause was gradually extended to all ethnic groups seeking protection from official discrimination. ...

Although many of the Framers of the Fourteenth Amendment conceived of its primary function as bridging the vast distance between members of the Negro race and the white "majority," *Slaughter-House Cases, supra,* the Amendment itself was framed in universal terms, without reference to color, ethnic origin, or condition of prior servitude. ...

Over the past 30 years, this Court has embarked upon the crucial mission of interpreting the Equal Protection Clause with the view of assuring to all persons "the protection of equal laws," ... Because the landmark decisions in this area arose in response to the continued exclusion of Negroes from the mainstream of American society, they could be characterized as involving discrimination by the "majority" white race against the Negro minority. But they need not be read as depending upon that characterization for their results. ...

Petitioner urges us to adopt for the first time a more restrictive view of the Equal Protection Clause and hold that discrimination against members of the white "majority" cannot be suspect if its purpose can be characterized as "benign." The clock of our liberties, however, cannot be turned back to 1868....

... the difficulties entailed in varying the level of judicial review according to a perceived "preferred" status of a particular racial or ethnic minority are intractable. The concepts of "majority" and "minority" necessarily reflect temporary arrangements and political judgments. As observed above, the white "majority" itself is composed of various minority groups, most of which can lay claim to a history of prior discrimination at the hands of the state and private individuals. Not all of these groups can receive preferential treatment and corresponding judicial tolerance of distinctions drawn in terms of race and nationality, for then the only "majority" left would be a new minority of White Anglo-Saxon Protestants. There is no principled basis for deciding which groups would merit "heightened judicial solicitude" and which would not . . . The kind of variable sociological and political analysis necessary to produce such rankings simply does not lie within the judicial competence—even if they otherwise were politically feasible and socially desirable.

Analytic Considerations

Moreover, there are serious problems of justice connected with the idea of preference itself. First, it may not always be clear that a so called preference is in fact benign . . . Second, preferential programs may only reinforce common stereotypes holding that certain groups are unable to achieve success without special protection based on a factor having no relationship to individual worth . . . Third, there is a measure of inequity in forcing innocent persons in respondent's position to bear the burdens of redressing grievances not of their making.

By hitching the meaning of the Equal Protection Clause to these transitory considerations, we would be holding, as a constitutional principal, that judicial scrutiny of classifications touching on racial and ethnic background may vary with the ebb and flow of political forces. Disparate constitutional tolerance of such classifications well may serve to exacerbate racial and ethnic antagonisms rather than alleviate them . . . Also, the mutability of a constitutional principle, based upon shifting political and social judgments, undermines the chances for consistent application of the Constitution from one generation to the next, a critical feature of its coherent interpretation.

If it is the individual who is entitled to judicial protection against classifications based upon his racial or ethnic background because such distinctions impinge upon personal rights, . . . then constitutional standards may be applied consistently. Political judgments regarding the necessity for the particular classification may be weighed in the constitution balance, but the standard of justification will remain constant. This is as it should be since those political judgments are the product of rough compromise . . . When they touch upon an individual's race or ethnic background, he is entitled to a judicial determination that the burden he is asked to bear on that basis is precisely tailored to serve a compelling governmental interest. The Constitution guarantees that right to every person regardless of his background. . . .

Prior Cases

Petitioner contends that on several occasions this Court has approved preferential classifications without applying the most exacting scrutiny. Most of the cases upon which petitioner relies are drawn from three areas: school desegregation, employment discrimination, and sex discrimination. Each of the cases cited presented a situation materially different from the facts of this case.

The school desegregation cases are inapposite. Each involved remedies for clearly determined constitutional violations ... Moreover, the scope of the remedies was not permitted to exceed the extent of the violations ... Here, there was no judicial determination of constitutional violation as a predicate for the formulation of a remedial classification. The employment discrimination cases also do not advance petitioner's cause ... The courts of appeals have fashioned various types of racial preferences as remedies for constitutional or statutory violations resulting in identified, race-based injuries to individuals held entitled to the preference ... Such preferences also have been upheld where a legislative or administrative body charged with the responsibility made determinations of past discrimination by the industries affected, and fashioned remedies deemed appropriate to rectify the discrimination ... But we have never approved preferential classifications in the absence of proven constitutional or statutory violations.

Nor is petitioner's view as to the applicable standard supported by the fact that gender-based classifications are not subjected to this level of scrutiny ... Gender-based distinctions are less likely to create the analytical and practical problems present in preferential programs premised on racial or ethnic criteria. With respect to gender there are only two possible classifications ... There are no rival groups who can claim that they, too, are entitled to preferential treatment ... More importantly, the perception of racial classifications as inherently odious stems from a lengthy and tragic history that gender-based classifications do not share. In sum, the Court has never viewed such classification as inherently suspect or as comparable to racial or ethnic classifications for the purpose of equal protection analysis.

The State's Purpose

We have held that in "order to justify the use of a suspect classification, a State must show that its purpose or interest is both constitutionally permissible and substantial and that its use of the classification is 'necessary ... to the accomplishment' of its purpose or the safeguarding its interest ... The special admissions program purports to serve the purposes of: (i) "reducing the historic deficit of traditionally disfavored minorities in medical schools and the medical profession." Brief for Petitioner 32; (ii) countering the effects of societal discrimination; (iii) increasing the number of physicians who will practice in communities currently underserved; and (iv) obtaining the educational benefits that flow from an ethnically diverse student body. It is necessary to decide which, if any, of these purposes is substantial enough to support the use of a suspect classification.

If petitioner's purpose is to assure within its student body some specified percentage of a particular group merely because of its race or ethnic origin, such a preferential purpose must be rejected ... This the Constitution forbids. ...

The State certainly has a legitimate and substantial interest in ameliorating, or eliminating where feasible, the disabling effects of identified discrimination ... That goal was far more focused than the remedying of the effects of "societal discrimination," an amorphous concept of injury that may be ageless in its reach into the past.

We have never approved a classification that aids persons perceived as members of relatively victimized groups at the expense of other innocent individuals in the absence of judicial, legislative, or administrative findings of constitutional or statutory violations . . . After such findings have been made, the governmental interest in preferring members of the injured groups at the expense of others is substantial, since the legal rights of the victims must be vindicated. In such a case, the extent of the injury and the consequent remedy will have been judicially, legislatively, or administratively defined. Also, the remedial action usually remains subject to continuing oversight to assure that it will work the least harm possible to other innocent persons competing for the benefit. Without such findings of constitutional or statutory violation, it cannot be said that the government has any greater interest in helping one individual than in refraining from harming another. Thus, the government has no compelling justification for inflicting such harm.

Petitioner does not purport to have made, and is in no position to make, such findings. Its broad mission is education, not the formulation of any legislative policy or the adjudication of particular claims of illegality . . . Lacking this capability, petitioner has not carried its burden of justification on this issue.

Hence, the purpose of helping certain groups whom the faculty of the Davis Medical School perceived as victims of "societal discrimination" does not justify a classification that imposes disadvantages upon persons like respondent, who bear no responsibility for whatever harm the beneficiaries of the special admissions program are thought to have suffered. To hold otherwise would be to convert a remedy heretofore reserved for violations of legal rights into a privilege that all institutions throughout the Nation could grant at their pleasure to whatever groups are perceived as victims of societal discrimination. That is a step we have never approved. . . .

Petitioner identifies, as another purpose of its program, improving the delivery of health care service to communities currently underserved . . . But there is virtually no evidence in the record indicating that petitioner's special admissions program is either needed or geared to promote that goal. . . .

The fourth goal asserted by petitioner is the attainment of a diverse student body. This clearly is a constitutionally permissible goal for an institution of higher education. Academic freedom, though not a specifically enumerated constitutional right, long has been viewed as a special concern of the First Amendment. The freedom of a university to make its own judgments as to education includes the selection of its student body.

The atmosphere of "speculation, experiment and creation"—so essential to the quality of higher education—is widely believed to be promoted by a diverse student body. . . .

Thus, in arguing that its universities must be accorded the right to select those students who will contribute the most to the "robust exchange of ideas," petitioner invokes a countervailing constitutional interest, that of the First Amendment. . . .

Ethnic diversity, however, is only one element in a range of factors a university properly may consider in attaining the goal of a heterogeneous student body ... As the interest of diversity is compelling in the context of a university's admissions program, the question remains whether the program's racial classification is necessary to promote this interest. ...

It may be assumed that the reservation of a specified number of seats in each class for individuals from the preferred ethnic groups would contribute to the attainment of considerable ethnic diversity in the student body. But petitioner's argument that this is the only effective means of serving the interest of diversity is seriously flawed ... The diversity that furthers a compelling state interest encompasses a far broader array of qualifications and characteristics of which racial or ethnic origin is but a single though important element. Petitioner's special admissions program, focused *solely* on ethnic diversity, would hinder rather than further attainment of genuine diversity. ...

The Harvard Program

The experience of other university admissions programs, which take race into account in achieving the educational diversity valued by the First Amendment, demonstrates that the assignment of a fixed number of places to a minority group is not a necessary means toward that end. An illuminating example is found in the Harvard College Program. ...

In such an admissions program, race or ethnic background may be deemed a "plus" in a particular applicant's file, yet it does not insulate the person from comparison with all other candidates for the available seats. The file of a particular black applicant may be examined for his potential contribution to diversity without the factor of race being decisive when compared, for example, with that of an applicant identified as an Italian-American if the latter is thought to exhibit qualities more likely to promote beneficial educational pluralism. Such qualities could include exceptional personal talents, unique work or service experience, leadership potential, maturity, demonstrated compassion, a history of overcoming disadvantage, ability to communicate with the poor, or other qualifications deemed important. In short, an admissions program operated in this way is flexible enough to consider all pertinent elements of diversity in light of the particular qualifications of each applicant, and to place them on the same footing for consideration, although not necessarily according to them, the same weight. ...

This kind of program treats each applicant as an individual in the admissions process. The applicant who loses out on the last available seat to another candidate receiving a "plus" on the basis of ethnic background will not have been foreclosed from all consideration from that seat simply because he was not the right color or had the wrong surname. It would mean only that his combined qualifications, which may have included similar nonobjective factors, did not outweigh those of the other applicant. ...

It has been suggested that an admissions program which considers race only as one factor is simply a subtle and more sophisticated—but no less effective—means of according racial preference than the Davis program. A facial intent to discriminate, however, is evident in petitioner's preference program and not denied in this case. No such facial infirmity exists in an admissions program where race or ethnic background is simply one element—to be weighed fairly against other elements—in the selection process . . . And a Court would not assume that a university, professing to employ a racially nondiscriminatory admissions policy, would operate it as a cover for the functional equivalent of a quota system. In short, good faith would be presumed in the absence of a showing to the contrary. . . .

Summary

In summary, it is evident that the Davis special admission program involves the use of an explicit racial classification never before countenanced by this Court. . . .

. . . when a State's distribution of benefits or imposition of burdens hinges on the color of a person's skin or ancestry, that individual is entitled to a demonstration that the challenged classification is necessary to promote a substantial state interest. Petitioner failed to carry this burden. For this reason, that portion of the California court's judgment holding petitioner's special admissions program invalid under the Fourteenth Amendment must be affirmed.

In enjoining petitioner from ever considering the race of any applicant, however, the courts below failed to recognize that the State has a substantial interest that legitimately may be served by a properly devised admissions program involving the competitive consideration of race and ethnic origin. For this reason, so much of the California court's judgment as enjoins petitioner from any consideration of the race of any applicant must be reversed.

With respect to respondent's entitlement to an injunction directing his admission to the Medical School, petitioner has conceded that it could not carry its burden of proving that, but for the existence of its unlawful special admissions program, respondent still would not have been admitted. Hence, respondent is entitled to the injunction, and that portion of the judgment must be affirmed.

Opinion by Justice Brennan

[Mr. Justice Brennan assumed the role of chief defender of the Davis "quota." Brennan avoids the extreme position that "benign" or "remedial" racial classifications need not withstand "strict judicial scrutiny." However, Brennan accepts the remediation of the effects of past "societal" discrimination as a sufficient justification for affirmative action quotas. Here, Brennan along with Marshall, Blackmun and White) differs with Justice Powell. Like Powell, however, Justice Brennan rejects the contention that Title VI of the 1964 Civil Rights Act requires "color-blind" admissions programs.]

The Court today, . . . affirms the constitutional power of Federal and State Government to act affirmatively to achieve equal opportunity for all. The difficulty of the issue presented . . . and the mature consideration which each of our Brethren has brought to it have resulted in many opinions. . . . But this should not and must not mask the central meaning of today's opinions: Government may take race into account when it acts not to demean or insult any racial group, but to remedy disadvantages cast on minorities by past racial prejudice, at least when appropriate findings have been made by judicial, legislative, or administrative bodies with competence to act in this area. . . .

Applicability of Title VI

We agree with Mr. Justice Powell, that, . . . Title VI goes no further in prohibiting the use of race than the Equal Protection Clause of the Fourteenth Amendment itself. . . . Since we conclude that the affirmative admissions program at the Davis Medical School is constitutional, we would reverse the judgment below in all respects. Mr. Justice Powell agrees that some uses of race in university admissions are permissible and therefore, he joins with us to make five votes reversing the judgment below insofar as it prohibits the University from establishing race-conscious programs in the future. . . .

The Fourteenth Amendment, the embodiment in the Constitution of our abiding belief in human equality, has been the law of our land for only slightly more than half its 200 years. And for half of that half, the Equal Protection Clause of the Amendment was largely moribund . . . Worse than desuetude, the Clause was early turned against those whom it was intended to set free, condemning them to a "separate but equal" status before the law, a status always separate but seldom equal. And a glance at our docket and at those of lower courts will show that even today officially sanctioned discrimination is not a thing of the past.

Against this background, claims that law must be "color-blind" or that the datum of race is no longer relevant to public policy must be seen as aspiration rather than as description of reality. We cannot . . . let color blindness become myopia which masks the reality that many "created equal" have been treated within our lifetimes as inferior both by the law and by their fellow citizens. . . .

In our view, Title VI prohibits only those uses of racial criteria that would violate the Fourteenth Amendment if employed by a State or its agencies; it does not bar the preferential treatment of racial minorities as a means of remedying past societal discrimination to the extent that such action is consistent with the Fourteenth Amendment. . . .

. . .prior decisions are indicative of the Court's unwillingness to construe remedial statutes designed to eliminate discrimination against racial minorities in a manner which would impede efforts to obtain this objective. There is no justification for departing from this course in the case of Title VI and frustrating the clear judgment of Congress that race-conscious remedial action is permissible. We turn, therefore, to our analysis of the Equal Protection Clause of the Fourteenth Amendment.

Standards of Review

The assertion of human equality is closely associated with the proposition that differences in color or creed, birth or status, are neither significant nor relevant to the way in which persons would be treated. Nonetheless, the position ... summed by the shorthand phrase "(o)ur Constitution is color-blind,"... has never been adopted by this Court as the proper meaning of the Equal Protection Clause. ...

Our cases have always implied that an "overriding statutory purpose,"... could be found that would justify racial classifications. ...

We conclude, therefore, that racial classifications are not *per se* invalid under the Fourteenth Amendment. Accordingly, we turn to the problem of articulating what our role should be in reviewing state action that expressly classifies by race.

Respondent argues that racial classifications are always suspect and, consequently, that this Court should weigh the importance of the objectives served by Davis' special admissions program to see if they are compelling. In addition, he asserts that this Court must inquire whether, in its judgment, there are alternatives to racial classifications which would suit Davis' purposes. Petitioner, on the other hand, states that our proper role is simply to accept petitioner's determination that the racial classifications used by its program are reasonably related to what it tells us are its benign purposes. We reject petitioner's view, but, because our prior cases are in many respects inapposite to that before us now, we find it necessary to define with precision the meaning of that inexact term, "strict scrutiny."

Unquestionably we have held that a government practice of statute which restricts "fundamental rights" or which contains "suspect classifications" is to be subjected only if it furthers a compelling government purpose and, even then, only if no less restrictive alternative is available. ... But no fundamental right is involved here. Nor do whites as a class have any of the "traditional indicator of suspectness: The class is not saddled with such disabilities or subjected to such a history or purposeful unequal treatment, or relegated to such a position of political powerlessness as to command extraordinary protection from the majoritarian political process."...

Nor has anyone suggested that the University's purposes contravene the cardinal principle that racial classifications that stigmatize—because they are drawn on the presumption that one race is inferior to another or because they put the weight of government behind racial hatred and separatism—are invalid.

On the other hand, the fact that this case does not fit neatly into our prior analytic framework for race cases does not mean that it should be analyzed by applying the very loose rational-basis standard of review ... Instead, a number of considerations—developed in gender discrimination cases but which carry even more force when applied to racial classifications—lead us to conclude that racial classifications designed to further remedial purposes "must serve important governmental objectives and must be substantially related to achievement of those objectives."...

First, race, like "gender-based classifications" too often (has) been inexcusably utilized to stereotype and stigmatize politically powerless segments of society. ...

Second, race, like gender and illegitimacy,... is an immutable characteristic which its possessors are powerless to escape or set aside. While a classification is not *per se* invalid because it divides classes on the basis of an immutable characteristic, it is nevertheless true that such divisions are contrary to our deep belief that "legal burdens should bear some relationship to individual responsibility or wrongdoing.". . . and that advancement sanctioned, sponsored, or approved by the State should ideally be based on individual merit or achievement, or at the least on factors within the control of an individual. . . .

The "natural consequence of our governing processes (may well be) that the most 'discrete and insular' of whites . . . will be called upon to bear the immediate, direct costs of benign discrimination." Moreover, it is clear from our cases that there are limits beyond which majorities may not go when they classify on the basis of immutable characteristics. . . .

In sum, because of the significant risk that racial classifications established for ostensibly benign purposes can be misused, causing effects not unlike those created by invidious classifications, it is inappropriate to inquire only whether there is any conceivable basis that might sustain such a classification. Instead, to justify such a classification an important and articulated purpose for its use must be shown. In addition, any statute must be stricken that stigmatizes any group or that singles out those least well represented in the political process to bear the brunt of a benign program. Thus our review under the Fourteenth Amendment should be strict—not "strict" in theory and fatal in fact," because it is stigma that causes fatality—but strict and searching nonetheless.

The State's Purpose

Davis' articulated purpose of remedying the effects of past societal discrimination is, under our cases, sufficiently important to justify the use of race-conscious admissions programs where there is a sound basis for concluding that minority underrepresentation is substantial and chronic, and that the handicap of past discrimination is impeding access of minorities to the medical school. . . .

Congress can and has outlawed actions which have a disproportionately adverse and unjustified impact upon members of racial minorities and has required or authorized race-conscious action to put individuals disadvantaged by such impact in the position they otherwise might have enjoyed. Such relief does not require as a predicate proof that recipients of preferential advancement have been individually discriminated against; it is enough that each recipient is within a general class of persons likely to have been the victims of discrimination. Nor is it an objection to such relief that preference for minorities will upset the settled expectations of nonminorities. . . .

These cases cannot be distinguished simply by the presence of judicial findings of discrimination, for race-conscious remedies have been approved where such findings have not been made. Indeed, the requirement of a judicial determination of a constitutional or statutory violation as a predicate for race-conscious remedial actions would be self-defeating. Such a requirement would severely undermine efforts to achieve voluntary compliance with the requirements of law. And, our society and jurisprudence have always stressed the value of voluntary efforts to further the objectives of the law. Judicial intervention is a last resort to achieve cessation of illegal conduct or the remedying of its effects rather than a prerequisite to action.

Color Blindness Rejected

Nor can our cases be distinguished on the ground that the entity using explicit racial classifications had itself violated . . . the Fourteenth Amendment or an antidiscrimination regulation, for again race-conscious remedies have been approved where this is not the case. . . . Moreover, the presence or absence of past discrimination by universities or employers is largely irrelevant to resolving respondent's constitutional claims. The claims of those burdened by the race-conscious actions of a university or employer who has never been adjudged in violation of an antidiscrimination law are not any more or less entitled to deference than the claims of the burdened nonminority workers in *Franks* v. *Bowman,* 424 U.S. 747 (1976), in which the employer has violated Title VII, for in each case the employees are innocent of past discrimination. And, although it might be argued that, where an employer has violated an antidiscrimination law, the expectations of nonminority workers are themselves products of discrimination and hence "tainted," see *Franks, supra,* at 776, and therefore more easily upset, the same argument can be made with respect to respondent. If it was reasonable to conclude—as we hold that it was—that the failure of minorities to qualify for admission at Davis under regular procedures was due principally to the effects of past discrimination, then there is a reasonable likelihood that, but for pervasive racial discrimination, respondent would have failed to qualify for admission even in the absence of Davis' special admissions program.

Thus, our cases under Title VII of the Civil Rights Act have held that, in order to achieve minority participation in previously segregated areas of public life, Congress may require or authorize preferential treatment for those likely disadvantaged by societal racial discrimination. Such legislation has been sustained even without a requirement of findings of intentional racial discrimination by those required or authorized to accord preferential treatment, or a case-by-case determination that those to be benefited suffered from racial discrimination. These decisions compel the conclusion that States also may adopt race-conscious programs designed to overcome substantial, chronic minority underrepresentation where there is reason to believe that the evil addressed is a product of past racial discrimination. . . .

Encourage Voluntarism

A contrary position would conflict with the traditional understanding recognizing the competence of the States to initiate measures consistent with federal policy in the absence of congressional pre-emption of the subject matter. . . .

Indeed, voluntary initiatives by the States to achieve the national goal of equal opportunity have been recognized to be essential to its attainment. . . .

We therefore conclude that Davis' goal of admitting minority students disadvantaged by the effect of past discrimination is sufficiently important to justify use of race-conscious admissions criteria. . . .

Moreover, we need not rest solely on our own conclusion that Davis had sound reason to believe that the effects of past discrimination were handicapping minority applicants to the Medical School, because the Department of Health, Education, and Welfare, the expert agency charged by Congress with promulgating regulations enforcing Title VI of the Civil Rights Act of 1964, has also reached the conclusion that race may be taken into account in situations where a failure to do so would limit participation by minorities in federally funded programs . . . In these circumstances, the conclusion . . . that the lingering effects of past discrimination continue to make race-conscious remedial programs appropriate means for insuring equal educational opportunity in universities—deserves considerable judicial deference. . . .

No Stigmatizing Effect

The second prong of our test—whether the Davis program stigmatizes any discrete group or individual and whether race is reasonably used in light of the program's objectives—is clearly satisfied by the Davis program.

It is not even claimed that Davis' program in any way operates to stigmatize or single out any discrete and insular, or even any identifiable non-minority group. Nor will harm comparable to that imposed upon racial minorities by exclusion or separation on grounds of race be the likely result of the program. . . .

True, whites are excluded from participation in the special admissions program, but this fact only operates to reduce the number of whites to be admitted in the regular admissions program in order to permit admission of a reasonable percentage—less than their proportion of the California population—of otherwise underrepresented qualified minority applicants. Nor was Bakke in any sense stamped as inferior by the Medical School's rejection of him . . . Moreover, there is absolutely no basis for concluding that Bakke's rejection as a result of Davis' use of racial preference will affect him throughout his life in the same way as the segregation of the Negro school children in *Brown I* would have affected them. Unlike discrimination against racial minorities, the use of racial preferences for remedial purposes does not inflict a pervasive injury upon individual whites in the sense that wherever they go or whatever they do there is a significant likelihood that they will be treated as second-class citizens because of their color.

In addition there is simply no evidence that the Davis program discriminates intentionally or unintentionally against any minority group which it purports to benefit . . . The Davis program does not simply advance less qualified applicants; rather, it compensates applicants, whom it is uncontested are fully qualified to study medicine, for educational disadvantage which it was reasonable to conclude was a product of state-fostered discrimination. . . .

We disagree with the lower court's conclusion that the Davis program's use of race was unreasonable in light of its objectives. First, as petitioner argues, there are no practical means by which it could achieve its ends in the foreseeable future without the use of race-conscious measures. . . .

Character of Admissions Procedure

Second, the Davis admissions program does not simply equate minority status with disadvantage. Rather, Davis considers on an individual basis each applicant's personal history to determine whether he or she has likely been disadvantaged by racial discrimination. . . .True, the procedure by which disadvantage is detected is informal, but we have never insisted that educators conduct their affairs through adjudicatory proceedings, and such insistence here is misplaced . . . When individual measurement is impossible or extremely impractical there is nothing to prevent a State from using categorical means to achieve its ends at least where the category is closely related to the goal . . . And it is clear from our cases that specific proof that a person has been victimized by discrimination is not a necessary predicate to offering him relief where the probability of victimization is great.

Finally Davis' special admissions program cannot be said to violate the Constitution simply because it has set aside a predetermined number of places for qualified minority applicants rather than using minority status as a positive factor to be considered in evaluating the applications of disadvantaged minority applicants.

The "Harvard" program . . . as those employing it readily concede, openly and successfully employs a racial criterion for the purposes of insuring that some of the scarce places in institutions of higher education are allocated to disadvantaged minority students. That the Harvard approach does not also make public the extent of the preference and the precise workings of the system while the Davis program employs a specific openly state number, does not condemn the latter plan for purposes of Fourteenth Amendment adjudication . . . There is no basis for preferring a particular preference program simply because in achieving the same goals that the Davis Medical School is pursuing, it proceeds in a manner that is not immediately apparent to the public.

Accordingly, we would reverse the judgment of the Supreme Court of California holding the Medical School's special admissions program unconstitutional and directing respondent's admission, as well as that portion of the judgment enjoining the Medical School from according any consideration to race in the admissions process.

Opinion by Justice Stevens

[Mr. Justice Stevens spoke for the "bloc" of four Justices contending that the Davis admissions program violated Title VI. Stevens followed the maxim that courts should avoid a constitutional ruling where a case could be decided on statutory grounds. His opinion also attempted a narrow focus on the disposition of Bakke's case alone. Stevens was rebuffed by Powell and Brennan in both these attempts to narrow the focus of the Bakke decision, but

*the "bloc" for which he spoke provided four of the five votes needed to strike
down the Davis quota and order Bakke's admission.*]

This is not a class action. The controversy is between two specific litigants
. . . Whether the judgment of the state court is affirmed or reversed in whole or in
part, there is no outstanding injunction forbidding any consideration of racial
criteria in processing applications.

It is therefore perfectly clear that the question whether race can ever be
used as a factor in an admissions decision is not an issue in the case, and that
discussion of that issue is inappropriate. . . .

Our settled practice . . . is to avoid the decision of a constitutional issue if a
case can be fairly decided on a statutory ground. . . .

Petitioner contends . . . that exclusion of applicants on the basis of race does
not violate Title VI if the exclusion carries with it no racial stigma. No such
qualification or limitation of S. 601's categorical prohibition of "exclusion" is
justified by the statute or its history. The language of the entire section is
perfectly clear . . .

The legislative history reinforces this reading . . . the proponents of the
legislation gave repeated assurances that the Act would be "color blind" in its
application. . . .

It seems clear that the proponents of Title VI assumed that the Constitution
itself required a color blind standard on the part of government, but that does
not mean that the legislation only codifies an existing constitutional prohibition.
The statutory prohibition against discrimination in federally funded projects
contained in 601 is more than a simple paraphrasing of what the Fifth or
Fourteenth Amendment would require. . . .

However, we need not decide the congruence — or lack of congruence — of
the controlling statute and the Constitution since the meaning of the Title VI ban
on exclusion is crystal clear: Race cannot be the basis of excluding anyone from
participation in a federally funded program.

In short, nothing in the legislative history justifies the conclusion that the
broad language of 601 should not be given its natural meaning.

Accordingly, I concur in the Court's judgment insofar as it affirms the
judgment of the Supreme Court of California. To the extent that it purports to do
anything else, I respectfully dissent.

Opinion By Justice Blackmun

[*Mr. Justice Blackmun concurred in Justice Brennan's opinion, but added
a few "general observations" about the subtleties of the admissions process,
the meaning of the Fourteenth Amendment and the tension between affirmative action and abstract notions of equality.*]

It is somewhat ironic to have us so deeply disturbed over a program where
race is an element of consciousness, and yet to be aware of the fact, as we are,
that institutions of higher learning, . . . have given conceded preferences up to a
point to those possessed of athletic skills, to the children of alumni, to the
affluent who may bestow their largess on the institutions, and to those having
connections with celebrities, the famous and the powerful. . . .

I ... accept that ... the Fourteenth Amendment has expanded beyond its original 1868 conception ... This enlargement does not mean for me, however, that the Fourteenth Amendment has broken away from its moorings and its original intended purposes. Those original aims persist. And that, in a distinct sense, is what "affirmative action" ... is all about. If this conflicts with idealistic equality, that tension is original Fourteenth Amendment tension, constitutionally conceived and constitutionally imposed, and it is part of the Amendment's very nature until complete equality is achieved in the area. ...

I am not convinced, as Mr. Justice Powell seems to be, that the difference between the Davis program and the one employed by Harvard is very profound or constitutionally significant. ... for despite its two track aspect, the Davis program, for me, is within constitutional bounds, though perhaps barely so. ...

I suspect that it would be impossible to arrange an affirmative action program in a racially neutral way and have it successful. ... In order to get beyond racism, we must first take account of race. There is no other way. And in order to treat some persons equally we must treat them differently. We cannot—we dare not—let the Equal Protection Clause perpetrate racial supremacy.

Opinion by Justice Marshall

[*Mr. Justice Marshall, the only black ever to serve on the Supreme Court, concurred in Justice Brennan's opinion, but delivered an impassioned rebuke to the five-man majority overturning the Davis admissions program. Marshall's central thesis is that the legacy of systematic, state-sanctioned abuse of blacks provides an historic justification for racially-sensitive remedies under the Fourteenth Amendment.*]

... It is more than a little ironic that, after several hundred years of class-based discrimination against Negroes, the Court is unwilling to hold that a class-based remedy for that discrimination is permissible. In declining to so hold, today's judgment ignores the fact that for several hundred years Negroes have been discriminated against, not as individuals, but rather solely because of the color of their skins. It is unnecessary in 20th century America to have individual Negroes demonstrate that they have been victims of racial discrimination; the racism of our society has been so pervasive that none, regardless of wealth or position, has managed to escape its impact. The experience of Negroes in America has been different in kind, not just in degree, from that of other ethnic groups. It is not merely the history of slavery alone but also that a whole people were marked as inferior by law. And that mark has endured ... The dream of America as the great melting pot has not been realized for the Negro; because of his skin color he never even made it into the pot.

These differences in the experience of the Negro make it difficult for me to accept that Negroes cannot be afforded greater protection under the Fourteenth Amendment where it is necessary to remedy the effects of past discrimination. ...

It is because of a legacy of unequal treatment that we now must permit the institutions of this society to give consideration to race in making decisions about who will hold the positions of influence, affluence and prestige in America. . . . I do not believe that anyone can truly look into America's past and still find that a remedy for the effects of the past is impermissible. . . .

I fear that we have come full circle. After the Civil War our government started several "affirmative action" programs. This Court in the Civil Rights cases and *Plessy* v. *Ferguson* destroyed the movement toward complete equality. For almost a century no action was taken and this nonaction was with the tacit approval of the Courts. Then we had *Brown* v. *Board of Education* and the Civil Rights Acts of Congress followed by numerous affirmative action programs. Now, we have this Court again stepping in, this time to stop affirmative action programs of the type used by the University of California.

Opinion By Justice White

[*Mr. Justice White concurred in Justice Brennan's opinion, but expressed particular concern that the Court was losing sight of an important procedural issue: can an individual bring suit directly under Title VI of the 1964 Civil Rights Act?*]

I write separately concerning the question of whether Title VI . . . provides for a private cause of action . . . I am unwilling merely to assume an affirmative answer.

. . . there is no express provision for private actions to enforce Title VI, and it would be quite incredible if Congress, after so carefully attending to the matter of private actions in other titles of the Act, intended silently to create a private cause of action to enforce Title VI.

Chapter Six

Productivity, Efficiency, and Public Management

Introduction

In June 1978 California voters overwhelmingly approved Proposition 13, an initiative that placed a ceiling on the income derived from the property tax by governments. The measure cut most local government and school district budgets drastically. Consequently services were trimmed. If the state legislature had not provided new resources, massive layoffs and curtailments of many primary governmental functions would have occurred.

The proponents of the measure argued that no reduction of services was needed. The stated reason is familiar to any student of American politics. Governments spend their money inefficiently and when forced to economize, they can produce the same product for less money. This argument apparently fell upon receptive ears. A *Los Angeles Times* poll reported that a majority of those who supported the measure believed that no cut in services would be forthcoming.

The campaign for Proposition 13 was part of a larger problem with which public personnel administrators must deal. Confidence in the performance of the American political system is at a very low point. The Watergate abuses have caused much of the public to question the judgments of elected officials. Running against government has become a popular platform for prominent politicians like Jimmy Carter and Jerry Brown.

Many people thus assume that governments are run inefficiently. Investigative reporters and aspiring candidates look for examples of malfeasance and corruption. The public employee must continually prove that he or she is not wasting money.

Are Personnel Systems Inefficient?

Many people blame the inefficiency of government on characteristics of the personnel system. Why is this so? Savas and Ginsburg (Selection 19) argue that some of the blame must be placed on the structure of the civil service system. The desire to control the causes of the spoils system has left us with a personnel system that is unable to respond sufficiently to environmental changes and modify established policies adequately. Control of the abuses of the spoils system also restricts the ability of supervisors and department heads to influence employee actions.

Newland (Selection 20) finds other causes of government's failure to meet service demands. The growth of government, the expansion of unionization, and the use of legal action by public interest groups have added considerable complexity to the personnel process. The response of government has often been a centralization of decisions which has further limited the ability of agencies to respond to public problems.

Both these selections imply that public personnel organizations tend to discourage efficient and effective administration. To meet the challenge of restoring public confidence, new measures must be undertaken.

Toward an Efficient and Effective Public Service

The final selection in this chapter (Selection 22) addresses the challenge of creating an efficient and effective public service. It discusses two important developments that might dramatically change the future course of public management.

President Carter campaigned against waste, corruption, and inefficiency in the federal service. One of his first acts after taking office was the creation of the Federal Personnel Management project, the first thorough analysis of the United States civil service in forty years. The philosophy of the project team and some of its important recommendations are discussed in the selection (21) by Alan K. Campbell who chaired the United States Civil Service Commission. The proposals focused on providing more executive influence in personnel matters. Managers would be given more authority over their subordinates and the higher civil service would tend to have more allegiance to the President than to the agencies of employment.

In August 1978 Congress approved and President Carter signed the Civil Service Reorganization Plan. The plan's main provisions are:

1. Creation of a senior executive service—a corp of selected employees to be assigned wherever needed and eligible for annual bonuses for superior performance.
2. Authorization of incentive pay for many lower level federal managers and supervisors.
3. Division of the Civil Service Commission into two entities: the Merit System Protection Board to serve as a quasi-judicial body to hear employee complaints and appeals, and an Office of Personnel Management to be the management arm of the President.
4. Increased authority for managers in hiring and promoting employees.

The goal of these measures is the establishment of an efficient and responsive public service. This is to be accomplished by giving more authority to higher level management within the federal system by limiting the power of lower-level employees and certain interest groups such as veterans organizations and organized labor.

The reforms of the presidential management project must be assessed in light of the criticisms raised by Savas and Greenberg and Newland. What effect will these efforts have on inefficiencies resulting from increases in size and complexity?

Measuring Productivity

Many people tend to assume that productivity in the public sector cannot be measured. Lacking measures of profit, public organizations have no yardstick to measure efficiency and effectiveness. Walter Balk (Selection 22) questions this assertion and discusses several recent attempts to establish productivity measures in government. He sees these efforts as an important change in government's approach to productivity measurement.

Personnel Management and Productivity

The personnel manager must be concerned with productivity. Over 80 percent of most public budgets are spent on wages and salaries. If governments are to operate more efficiently, gains must be made in the amount of work accomplished by each employee. We tend to think of efficiency in terms of equipment such as computers and communication systems. While technological innovations are useful, they ultimately depend on the skills and motivations of those who operate them.

Are there means now at hand to bring forth improvements in productivity? Will the current interest in government efficiency result in the application of new techniques?

19
The Civil Service:
A Meritless System
E. S. Savas and Sigmund G. Ginsburg

The nation's basic civil service law was written in 1883, following the assassination of President Garfield by a disgruntled job seeker. The goal at the time was both noble and urgent: to assure that the merit principle, rather than

Reprinted with permission from *The Public Interest,* Vol. 32 (Summer, 1973), pp. 72-85. © 1973 by National Affairs, Inc.
E. S. Savas and Sigmund G. Ginsburg were members of the mayor's staff of the City of New York at the time of this writing.

the patronage principle, would be used for the selection and promotion of federal employees. Subsequently, in reaction to the excesses of the spoils system which had prevailed for the preceding half-century, a civil service reform movement swept the land, spreading through states, counties, cities, and school systems during the next few decades. Today, the so-called merit system—the name given to the elaborate web of civil service laws, rules, and regulations which embrace the merit principle—covers more than 95 per cent of all permanent federal (civilian) employees, all state and county employees paid by federal funds, most state employees, many county employees (particularly in the Northeastern states), most employees in more than three fourths of America's cities, and almost all full-time policemen and firemen.

However, vast changes in government and society have taken place in the last 50 years, and the rules and regulations appropriate for 1883 have now become rigid and regressive. After 90 years, the stage is set for a new era of civil service reform. Recent court decisions have ruled out several civil service examinations which had no demonstrable relation to the job to be performed; scholars and political leaders recognize the many shortcomings of today's civil service systems; and now the general public is stirring as well. The citizen sees that government—and tax collection—is a growth industry. (If we extrapolate the current rate of growth of the governmental work force, by the year 2049 every worker in America will be a government employee!) He sees that job security (tenure) exists for his "servants" but not for him. State and local governments spend as much as the federal government (excluding defense), and the citizen can see *their* work at close hand in his daily life. And what he sees is *not* a merit system—certainly not in the common usage of the word "merit." The low productivity of public employees and the malfunctioning of governmental bureaucracies are becoming apparent to an increasing number of frustrated and indignant taxpayers. The problem shows up all over the country in the form of uncivil servants going through pre-programmed motions while awaiting their pensions. Too often the result is mindless bureaucracies that appear to function for the convenience of their staffs rather than the public whom they are supposed to serve. It is the system itself, however, rather than the hapless politician who heads it for the minions toiling within it that is basically at fault.

Counterproductive Policies

Imagine a large, multi-divisional organization with an annual budget of 10 billion dollars. Imagine further that the organization has the following personnel policies and practices:

- Most entry positions are filled on the basis of written examinations scored to two or three decimal places.
- There is no scientifically supportable evidence that these examinations are related to subsequent on-the-job performance.
- Once a ranked list of examination scores is established, management must choose one of the top three names on the list regardless of special

qualifications, knowledge, experience, aptitude, or training of other applicants on the list.

• After an employee has spent six months on the job, he is virtually guaranteed the job for life, unless his superior files a special report urging that the employee be discharged or at least that the granting of tenure be deferred; it is very unusual for a supervisor to take such action.

• An employee, after acquiring such tenure, can be fired only on grounds of dishonesty or incompetence of a truly gross nature, and cannot be shifted to a less demanding assignment.

• An employee is "milked" of his ability and dedication, while given little significant opportunity for advanced training, personal development, career counseling, mid-career job change, or an enriched job that fully engages his evolving interests; no manager cares about this situation.

• Promotions are generally limited to employees who occupy the next lower position within the same division; qualified employees in other divisions of the organization are discriminated against, as are applicants from outside the organization.

• Promotions are made primarily through written examinations, with no credit given for good performance.

• Salary increases are virtually automatic and, with rare exception, are completely unrelated to the employee's work performance.

• Supervisors belong to unions, sometimes to the same unions as the employees they supervise.

• All personnel practices are regulated by a three-man commission, whose powerful chairman is the Director of Personnel Managers and supervisors must defer to his judgment on all personnel matters except those involving top-level executives.

• The employee unions have enough political power to influence the decision concerning whether or not the chief executive is permitted to stay on; furthermore, they also influence the appointment of top-level managers.

One does not have to be a management expert to be appalled at this array of counterproductive policies or to predict that the hypothetical organization employing such policies would be laughably ineffective.

Unfortunately, neither the policies nor the organization is hypothetical. The foregoing is an accurate description of the venerable civil service system under which New York City is forced to operate. In summary, the system prohibits good management, frustrates able employees, inhibits productivity, lacks the confidence of the city's taxpayers, and fails to respond to the needs of the citizens. While this bleak picture may not yet be fully representative of all civil service systems in the country, neither is it uncommon. Furthermore, considering that New York often serves as a leading indicator of societal problems, this pattern, if it has not already been reproduced elsewhere, may be soon—unless a groundswell of popular opinion leads to a new wave of reform.

More than half of New York's 9.4-billion-dollar budget is spent on the salaries and fringe benefits of its employees. In the last decade, personnel costs have risen by roughly 150 per cent, while the number of employees has increased by about 75 per cent—to 400,000. (Genghis Khan conquered Asia with an army less than half this size; however, he used certain managerial techniques of reward and punishment which are mercifully denied to today's more circumscribed and more humane chief executive.) Of this number, about a quarter of a million(!) constitute the "competitive class" of civil service—that is, employees who are hired and promoted on the basis of competitive examinations. This is the aspect of the civil service system dealt with here.

In order to understand fully the shortcomings of the current system in New York, it is useful to look in turn at each of its major elements: the jobs themselves, recruitment practices, examinations, selection procedures, promotions, and motivational rewards.

Jobs, recruitment, and examinations

Jobs

Very narrow, specialized jobs have gradually emerged, in part because this makes it much easier to produce an examination specific enough to given an appearance of relevance and fairness. Credentialism runs rampant, and prerequisites are sometimes introduced with no discernable value except bureaucratic convenience in the subsequent selection process. As a result, artificial and nonsensical divisions have proliferated, and New York City now has Methods Analysts, Management Analysts, and Quantitative Analysts, as well as Office Appliance Operators, Photostat Operators, Audio-Visual Aid Technicians, Doorstop Maintainers, and Foremen of Thermostat Repairers. When the human cogs in the General Motors assembly line at Lordstown stopped working, it was a clear and obvious revolt against the dehumanizing nature of their activity. Could it be that the human cogs in the municipal machinery stopped functioning long ago, for the same reason, and we are just now indirectly noticing their sullen revolt?

Recruitment

The recruiting process for civil service jobs is similarly arbitrary. The law requires only that advertisements of openings appear in certain specified, obscure places and in formidable terminology: the formal descriptions in "bureaucratese," of the narrow kinds of specialties mentioned above. The Personnel Department seldom goes far beyond this minimal legal requirement. This means that current employees (and their families) have an advantage over outsiders because they know where to look and how to decode the message. This fact, coupled with job qualifications of questionable value, serves to limit access into the service by other potential applicants.

In fact, this traditional process has been so ineffective that out of exasperation a competing recruiting organization was set up within the Mayor's office, not for dispensing patronage, but for recruiting the kind of professional and technical personnel without which modern government cannot really function. The most capable managers in the entire organization devote much of their effort and ingenuity to subverting and bypassing the regulations in order to hire such recruits from outside the system.

Examinations

About 400 civil service examinations are conducted each year in New York City, at great effort and expense, and about half of them consist primarily of written tests. *Yet not a single case could be found where the validity of a written test—with respect to predicting performance on the job—was ever proven.* That this problem transcends New York's borders is indicated by the following statement by the U.S. District Court in Massachusetts in regard to an examination for police officer:

> *The categories of questions sound as though they had been drawn from "Alice in Wonderland." On their face the questions seem no better suited to testing ability to perform a policeman's job than would be crossword puzzles.*

Heavy reliance on written examinations at least has the advantage of being "safe." No bureaucrat need be saddled with the difficult task of using his judgment somewhere in the selection process. Exclusive reliance on an "objective" test score creates a situation where no one can be accused of favoritism or overt bias, even though a test may demonstrate inherent discrimination against certain cultural minorities.

At present, candidates who pass an examination are ranked on any eligible list based on their adjusted final average, *carried to as many as three decimal places.* (Adjusted final average is derived from the candidate's scores on the individual tests which comprise an examination: written, practical, technical, oral, etc., plus veteran's preference credit, where applicable.) A manager must appoint one of the top three scorers. Now, no one seriously contends that a person who scores 92.463 on an examination of dubious validity is likely to perform better on the job than someone who scores 92.462, or even 91.462. This scientifically unsupportable custom is just another defense against accusations of bias and should be abandoned. Test scores should be rounded off, thereby creating more ties and giving managers more choice and flexibility in selecting their subordinates from among those candidates with the same score. The potential impact of this change, recently endorsed in New York City by Mayor Lindsay, can be indicated by noting that on the 1968 examination for Fire Lieutenant, 25 men scored between 86 and 87, and 203 scored between 81 and 82.

Another vexing problem with the existing system was described by one frustrated manager:

> *The City's unimaginative recruitment mechanism, combined with generally unappetizing work surroundings, makes it virtually impossible to recruit stenographers at the entry level. Accordingly, we keep filling*

entry-level stenographer positions with candidates who make it through a relatively undemanding stenography test which has been watered down to qualify those with minimal skills. No attempt is ever made to differentiate between candidates on the basis of intelligence, work attitudes, motivation, reading comprehension. Thus, we start with an entry group whose competence has not really been tested—and may well be minimal—and proceed to lock ourselves in by demanding that all candidates for higher level positions be selected from this pool, even though the pool may be drained of some of its best talent over time.

An example of the straitjacket created by this rigid procedure can be found in the agency that needed a mechanical engineer for maintenance of heating, ventilating, and air-conditioning equipment. The experience of the six highest-ranking candidates on the "Mechanical Engineer List" was inappropriate, consisting of machine design, drafting, and the like; the seventh-ranked engineer, however, was ideally suited for the job. Nevertheless, the agency was constrained by civil service rules to hire one of the top three. Only by finally persuading four of the top six to waive their legal claims to the job, thereby elevating Number Seven to Number Three, was the agency able to hire the man with the needed experience. If any one of the four who reluctantly withdrew had joined the other two of the top six in refusing to do so, the agency would have faced the choice of hiring either no one or someone with an inappropriate background, even though a suitable candidate was available only a few meaningless points further down the list.

Selection procedures: An Inverse Merit System

... Candidates with low passing grades are actually *more* likely to be hired than those with high passing grades! Furthermore, this perverse result seems to hold true for all skill levels.

This finding emerged from a careful study of three representative (written) examinations, which span a broad gamut of entry-level skills: Railroad Porter, a position which requires minimal education; Clerk, a position which requires some educational attainment; and Professional Trainee, a job which requires a college degree. Each examination showed the same general pattern—roughly speaking, the *lower* the percentile ranking, the *greater* the number of hires drawn from that percentile group! Conversely, the *higher* the percentile, the *fewer* the number of people hired from it.

Corroborating evidence was found by analyzing a 10 per cent sample of those 1970 and 1971 examinations which resulted in actual hiring: In almost half of the examinations analyzed (14 of 30), none of the four highest scorers was appointed; in a third of the examinations no one was appointed from the top 10 per cent; and in two of the 30 examinations, no one was appointed from the upper half of the eligible candidates.

These anomalous and unexpected results are presumably due to the long delay between the closing date for applications and the date of the first appointment. Delays are produced by a combination of administrative procedures and applicant-initiated protests, appeals, and law suits. The sample of examinations revealed that in 1970, the median delay was *seven months* and the maximum (of the sample) was *15 months*. If we assume that the "best" people score highest, then it seems reasonable to assume that many will find jobs elsewhere and that as time goes on a decreasing number of them will still be available when "their number is called." Analysis of the data showed that the greater the delay, the deeper into the lists one had to dig to find people still willing to accept appointment. When the delay was "only" three months, the openings were filled from the top 15 per cent of the list, but when the delay was six months, hires were drawn from the top 37 per cent, and when the delay was 15 months (for the Clerk examination), it was necessary to dip all the way down to 63 per cent in order to fill the vacancies.

One could argue that this finding is true but irrelevant, and that the 6,000th person on the Clerk list, for example, is really not significantly worse than the fifth, both of whom were hired. But if this assertion is accepted, then one is essentially admitting that the entire examination process is virtually useless.

In summary, as far as drawing new recruits into public employment via examination is concerned, the evidence strongly suggests that *New York City's civil service system functions as an inverse merit system* (something the public at large has cynically assumed for years). Although additional verification is needed before this finding can be generalized, at the moment the burden of proof must fall on those who would maintain that New York's civil service really is a merit system in this respect. Indeed, to anyone familiar with both public and private personnel systems, it is quite obvious that large corporations today are much closer to a true merit system than are our governments.

Promotion and Motivation

With regard to promotions, the civil service can be described more accurately as a seniority system than as a merit system. The rules discourage "lateral entry" into upper-level positions by outsiders. This means that one usually starts at the bottom and works his way up, which sounds fine: All organizations find it beneficial as a general practice to promote from within, and their current employees have a natural and desirable advantage over outsiders. In New York's civil service, however, this practice is carried to an extreme and becomes an exclusionary device that limits competition. One frustrated high-level city official offered a striking example of the problem:

> *In an occupational area like computer operations applying the usual rigid procedures denies us the option of hiring experienced computer program- mers, systems analysts, and data processing managers. It would force us to appoint only computer programming trainees and to wait for these to be trained and developed by years of experience. This is patently absurd.*

The current promotion procedure is as follows: Vacancies in positions above the lowest level in an agency are generally filled by promotion on the basis of competitive examination from among persons holding tenured positions in the next lower grade *in the same agency.* If the Civil Service Commission concludes that there are not enough people available at the lower grade to fill all the vacancies via promotion examination, it may decide to conduct an open-competitive examination as well. An open-competitive examination is open to individuals in other city agencies, to individuals in other grades within the same agency, and to complete "outsiders."

But this openness is illusory. Assuming that the "outsider" has somehow ferreted out the fact than an open-competitive examination is being conducted, he is still at a significant disadvantage compared to the "insiders" who take the promotion examination. Any "insider" who passes the promotion examination will be offered the vacant position before it is offered to anyone who passes the open-competitive examination. Even if one accepted the validity of the examinations, one can seriously question whether it is always better for the public to promote an "insider" who scores 70 than to hire an "outsider" who scores 99.

A study was made of 10 pairs of written open-competitive and promotion examinations given for such positions as engineer, accountant, stenographer, planner, and so on. For each position the promotion and the open-competitive examinations were almost identical. Though the results are not conclusive, they are suggestive, to say the least: The lowest-ranked "insider" was selected over the highest-ranked "outsider" despite the fact that the latter scored higher than the former in all cases but one; "insiders" who averaged 14 points below "outsiders" were nevertheless chosen before the latter. One can legitimately ask how the public interest is served by this policy.

Damning though such findings may be, the worst feature of the promotion system is that an employee's chance of promotion bears no relation to his performance on the job. It is the promotion examination that counts and not performance, motivation, or special qualifications. Distressing examples of the unfairness that this system produces are legion. For instance, a man responsible for the successful completion of an important health program failed to pass the promotion test for Senior Public Health Sanitarian. To all who were familiar with his excellent work, this result was positive proof that the examination was completely invalid. At the top of the list on that examination was someone who has never been able to supervise people and has been mediocre on the job. The demonstrated inability of such tests to predict supervisory competence remains one of the major weaknesses of the examination system.

Given the nature of the promotion procedures, there are relatively few ways in which an agency head, manager, or supervisor can motivate, reward, or penalize his workers. Yearly salary increases are authorized under union contracts, while cost-of-living and comparability adjustments occur automatically for non-union employees. In principle, an outstanding employee can receive a special salary increase, but in fact the vast majority of employees are never really evaluated for such increases, as few agencies and few positions come under this policy. How long will a highly motivated and competent individual be willing to put forth extra effort when he receives no real reward compared with others who do much less? A sensible individual would conclude that instead of spending extra energy and effort on doing his job well, his time would be better spent studying for promotion examinations, or simply relaxing. Also demoralizing for supervisors is the knowledge that it is almost impossible to penalize or discharge the barely competent or even incompetent permanent employee. The administrative procedures involved, the time lags, the large amount of managerial effort needed "to make a case," all force the manager to live with the problem rather than to solve it.

Collective Bargaining vs. Civil Service

The single most compelling reason for major reform of public personnel systems—even aside from the mounting evidence of their meritlessness—is the fact that a new system, collective bargaining, has grown up atop the old system, civil service. The enormous growth in membership, power, and militancy of unions of civil servants has resulted in increased protection, wages, and benefits for New York City employees—and in decreased productivity. The ultimate monopoly of power held by municipal unions raises fundamental and disquieting questions about public employee unionism that are not yet resolved.

It is an inescapable fact, however, that union power has produced a second personnel system overlapping and at times conflicting with and negating the civil service system. Job classifications and duties, recruitment, promotion paths, eligibility for advancement, and grievances all fall within the purview of the civil service system, yet all are in face negotiated, albeit informally, with the municipal unions. Initial selection of employees had remained the one area under the exclusive regulatory authority of the Civil Service Commission, but this, too, is now becoming subject to joint policy determination with the unions.

A strong argument can therefore be made for acknowledging reality and abolishing the civil service system, relying instead on the collective bargaining system. In effect, this has already been done in one area, the municipal hospitals, which have been taken over by the independent Health and Hospitals Corporation. Its employees are no longer civil servants but continue to be represented by a union, and there has been no discernible harm to them or to the body politic. At the very least, a "Blue Ribbon Commission" should be appointed to consider long-term, fundamental reform of New York's civil service system, with particular focus on the overlap between collective bargaining and civil service.

What Should be Done?

In trying to prevent itself from doing the wrong things—nepotism, patronage, prejudice, favoritism, corruption—the civil service system has been warped and distorted to the point where it can do hardly anything at all. In an attempt to protect against past abuses, the "merit system" has been perverted and transformed into a closed and meritless seniority system. A true merit system must be constructed anew, one that provides the opportunity for any qualified citizen to gain access non-politically, to be recognized and rewarded for satisfactory performance, and even to be replaced for unsatisfactory service. The improvements that are needed are obvious:

- The principal determinant of promotions should be a performance appraisal and potential assessment system, based upon performance standards and established with union cooperation. Such a system should include an employee's right to review and appeal the appraisal report.
- An individual's salary increase should be a function of his performance. Salary Review Boards with union representation should be established in each agency to set annual guidelines for allocating salary increases in the agency out of a lump-sum annual budget for raises; for example, "standard" performers might get a five per cent raise, "superior" performers a larger one.
- Examinations should be for broad categories of related positions, with "selective certification" used to appoint specialists from within the pool of qualified candidates.
- Written examinations should be employed only where their validity can be demonstrated. Oral examinations should be used more extensively for both selection and promotion. (We are not referring to the kind of "oral examination" now sometimes given—namely, a stilted interview in which competent interviewers are asked to camouflage their reasonable but subjective impressions of the interviewees by asking the exact same questions in the same sequence and giving numerical ratings to the responses. These "oral examinations" are then graded by employees who conscientiously average the interview scores.)
- In selecting new employees, the emphasis should be on evaluation of qualifications, experience, assessment by prior employers, and an oral or practical examination.
- The custom of scoring examinations to several decimal places should be abandoned. Round off the test scores; this will create more ties and give the appointing authority more freedom to use his judgment.
- Positions should be evaluated regularly to weed out rampant credentialism.
- More upper-level positions should be filled at the discretion of management. A good model can be found in the New York Police Department, where the highest rank attainable by examination is captain, and the Commissioner has the authority to assign captains to higher ranks as long as he is satisfied with their performance.
- The system should stop discriminating against "outsiders." Open-competitive and promotion examination lists for a given title should be merged into a single ranked list; alternatively, "outstanding" outsiders should be selected before "good" insiders, and so on. Experience in New York City government should be one of the criteria used in evaluating individuals.
- A flexible system of probationary periods should be instituted, with the duration of the period bearing some logical relationship to the job. The granting of tenure should require a positive act, as it does in universities.
- To improve the performance and motivation of employees, training

opportunities should be greatly increased. Job counseling and career planning should be introduced, and tuition-refund plans, evening courses, and released-time programs should all be utilized. Job responsibilities should be enlarged ("enriched") commensurate with employee acceptance. The constricted domain of the unfortunate doorstop maintainer might be expanded to include hinges and doorknobs, and in time even simple locks. So far Victor Gotbaum, the municipality's farsighted union leader, has done more for job training and enrichment than anyone on the management side.

The recommendations presented above would tend to make New York City's system more similar to the federal civil service. The federal system 1) makes far greater use of selective certification; 2) more readily accepts outside applicants for middle and upper positions, and evaluates them on the basis of their education and experience rather than by written examination; 3) bases promotions on performance rather than examination; 4) has a much shorter average time span for promotions; 5) identifies talented individuals early, at the time of the entrance examination; 6) encourages movement between government agencies; 7) is more concerned about training and identification of persons with higher potential; and 8) has a one-year probationary period for new appointees, with positive action by supervisors necessary for retention.

People who have served in both consider the federal system vastly superior to the one under which the city operates. However, some of the recommendations we have made would also apply to the federal government: 1) the need for evaluating duties and responsibilities of positions regularly to insure against demanding greater or different qualifications than the job requires; 2) strengthening the performance evaluation and potential assessment system; 3) doing away with automatic raises and tying them more closely to performance; and 4) making it easier to reward good performers and to demote or remove incompetent performers.

Racial and Ethnic Problems

The managerial virtues of such proposed changes are clear, but would they create an even worse problem of racial and ethnic patronage? In New York today, the civil service system is undergoing strain in part because of the widespread belief that to be successful in certain jobs one must possess traits that the system was designed to ignore: culture, class, neighborhood, and other such euphemisms for race and ethnicity. Hence the color-blind hiring practices which successfully staffed city agencies a half-century ago are not well suited for staffing the new municipal agencies that deal with problem families, drug addicts, and unemployed youths. Nor do they adequately provide the recruits needed by a police department whose job has changed significantly and now requires considerable community cooperation for effective crime control Cultural rapport is vital for success in both the new agencies and old ones facing new challenges.

Ingenious job descriptions (with the adjective "community" frequently in the titles), public employment programs aimed at reducing unemployment in particular neighborhoods, and carefully targeted recruitment campaigns are being used to get around the color-blind system, but such policies have hardly gone unnoticed. Those groups that are already well represented within the civil service decry the "decline in standards," and attack such hiring programs in the courts and at the bargaining table. They may recognize the irrationality of the system, but they fear that civil service reform and greater managerial flexibility will be used to advance newcomers at their expense.

Those major groups that are not yet proportionally represented, black and Spanish-speaking New Yorkers, recognize the irrationality of the system; they are successfully challenging discriminatory examinations which exclude them, and thereby introducing greater flexibility into the system. At the same time, though, they fear that a reformed civil service will allow supervisors the flexibility to discriminate against them.

We conclude that the civil service system is already enmeshed in all the strains of racial and ethnic politics in the grand New York tradition, and that a reformed system would be embroiled in similar, but hardly worse, fashion. This endemic condition, therefore, offers no grounds for abandoning the civil service changes advocated here, changes that are likely in time to provide improved delivery of public services to all citizens and neighborhoods.

The Prospects for Reform

How can civil service reform be brought about? At first glance, the picture is not very promising. Elected chief executives are understandably wary of the issue, on two counts. First, an attempt at reform might easily lead to demoralization of the work force, with employee resentment leading to a further drastic decline in government performance, to the chagrin of its head. Second, elected officials fear the voting power of the growing army of civil servants. In New York City, the conventional wisdom runs as follows: There are some 400,000 employees. Each one votes himself and influences several relatives and friends. Hence municipal employees represent a voting bloc of more than a million votes, more than enough to ensure victory or defeat. Therefore, the logic goes, don't do anything that might antagonize the work force—and be sure to treat it especially well in election years.

It is not at all clear, however, that this simplistic arithmetic really applies: At least one seventh of the work force lives out of town and is therefore ineligible to vote in New York's municipal elections; voter registration, turnout, and bloc voting may be no greater for civil servants than for other groups; many of those influenced by government employees are themselves in public service and should not be counted twice; and other friends who are not on the public payroll might resent the "good deal" that they attribute to the tenured civil servant, and hence would approve of reform.

Furthermore, candid discussions with many public employees reveal support for civil service reform; able and devoted civil servants—and there are many thousands of them— resent it when they see incompetent co-workers receive equal pay and pass promotion examinations, and they are tired of being vilified by the public for the lethargy of such colleagues. They would respond favorably to sensible improvements, for the overwhelming majority want to be effective in their work and to have pride in their organization. Therefore, the irreconcilable opposition to civil service reform probably numbers far, far less than one million, and political leaders should be able to deal with such opposition by mobilizing the many latent forces for reform.

But for too long there has been a mutually convenient conspiracy of silence among civil service employees, their unions, and public officials about the quantity and quality of work performed, the productivity of government agencies, and the level of service delivered to the public. Employees received security, generous fringe benefits and pensions, and constantly improving salaries. (The top civil service salary is now close to $40,000.) The unions acquired members and political power. The public officials' reward was the possibility of reelection or reappointment. However, that era is drawing to a close as taxpayers demand better performance and as alert political leaders sense the popular mood.

The time now seems right for a long-overdue reform of the civil service. The intent of reform should be to adapt the civil service system to changing times and changing needs in order to bring about more efficient and more effective government. Several of the steps recommended by us were accepted in New York and are being implemented. Although the procedures will generally vary from state to state, many of the changes needed in the nation's civil service system can be effected by the direct and indirect authority of the chief executives. Other changes may require enlightened rule-making by appointed civil service commissions. Still others will require action by state legislatures.

Inevitably, there will be opposition to any changes, and the dread spectre of the 19th-century spoils system is already being exhumed and summoned to the battlements. Certainly, safeguards will be needed. But the surest safeguard of all is the fact that current political realities have greatly reduced the threat of the spoils system. Today an elected official can best secure his own reelection by creating and maintaining an efficient and effective organization to deliver governmental services to the public. He cannot do this without a competent work force. Trite though it may sound, the best protection against abuses is an enlightened citizenry, demanding performance and accountability of its government, and aided by a vigilant free press. These conditions exist today in New York, and in other places as well.

The argument for reform is overwhelming. The potential future imperfections of a revitalized personnel system are small and distant compared to the actual weaknesses, large and immediate, of today's illusory merit system. Undoubtedly, the perscription should be applied selectively. Some states and cities are still suffering under a corrupt spoils system and can benefit from the kinds of changes introduced long ago by the *first* wave of civil service reform. By far the most common affliction, however, is the rigor mortis of overdeveloped and regressive civil service systems. If these are reformed, no doubt the time will come again, in another 50 or 100 years, when the disadvantages of the system advocated here will outweigh its advantages. At such time, new reforms—reforms that meet the needs of those new conditions—will again be in order, for no system devised by man works well forever.

20
Public Personnel Administration: Legalistic Reforms vs. Effectiveness, Efficiency, and Economy

Chester A. Newland

Public personnel administration in the United States has been the subject of political conflicts and doctrinaire reform movements throughout the nation's history, but while it has often been at the center of controversy, it has generally remained at the peripheries of power, at best. The resulting impact on practice in the field since the 1930s has been development of a complex variety of activities held together by increasingly legalistic and bureaucratic organizational structures and processes, with key functions like personnel ceilings often dominated by "non-personnel" agencies. These complex arrangements have been complicated further by three developments of recent decades: (1) the enormous growth of governments since the 1940s; (2) the rapid growth of unions and of collective bargaining since the 1950s; and (3) the widespread growth of litigious, public service-rights populism since the 1960s.

Objectives of public personnel administration—the employment of people under reasonably just compensation and working conditions for effective, efficient, and economical conduct of government—may be obscured or nearly lost sight of altogether in the complicated mazes of legislation, executive orders, judicial decisions, civil service and labor relations regulations and decisions, auditors' opinions, and agency rules which presently dominate the personnel field. Although personnel and labor relations specialists have multiplied more than proportionately to the growth of public employment since the 1930s, their professional effectiveness in the face of political "reforms" and controls has been increasingly limited to procedural accomplishments. They have been required to devote major energies to compliance with legalistic procedures at the expense of expeditious and economical employment services to the public, employees, and operating agency managers.

Reprinted with permission from *Public Administration Review*. Vol. 36, No. 5, (Sept.-Oct. 1976), pp. 529-537.
Chester Newland is Professor of Public Administration, University of Southern California.

Responsible public executives, employee unions, and many employees alike share in complaints that the most pervasive and persistent problems of public personnel administration are the impersonal, slow, unresponsive, rigid, and expensive personnel processes which scarcely accomplish public employment objectives. Meanwhile, policy-level professionals and politicians remain largely preoccupied by personal or bureaucratic battles over turf or by conflicts between extremes of political values and power, generally around traditional themes of spoils vs. merit and of collective bargaining. In the more professional of these conflicts, the debates today center upon the proper bureaucratic organization for performance of personnel functions: neutral independence vs. executive control; centralization and prescription vs. dispersion and differentiation; and labor-management integration vs. collective bargaining.

Political Reforms and Bureaucratization

Although the well-known history of spoils vs. merit does not bear repetition here, merit concepts are so fundamental to the little framework of basic ideas in public personnel administration that they do warrant repeating, if only to emphasize their widespread acceptance. They were identified, as follows, in the Intergovernmental Personnel Act of 1971:

(1) recruiting, selecting, and advancing employees on the basis of their relative ability, knowledge, and skills, including open consideration of qualified applicants for initial appointment;

(2) providing equitable and adequate compensation;

(3) training employees, as needed, to assure high-quality performance;

(4) retaining employees on the basis of the adequacy of their performance, correcting inadequate performance, and separating employees whose inadequate performance cannot be corrected;

(5) assuring fair treatment of applicants and employees in all aspects of personnel administration without regard to political affiliation, race, color, national origin, sex, or religious creed and with proper regard for their privacy and constitutional rights as citizens; and

(6) assuring that employees are protected against coercion for partisan political purposes and are prohibited from using their official authority for the purpose of interfering with or affecting the result of an election or a nomination for office.

Today's problems rarely derive from public disagreement with those merit concepts. Except for relatively infrequent incursions of partisan politics and spoils, such as the limited but serious violations during the Nixon Administration, characteristics of bureaucracy and multiplicity of conflicting laws account for most current complaints against the "merit system"—that it is impersonal, unresponsive, legalistic, like swimming in glue. This suggests that it is past time for public personnel administration to reexamine its functions, processes and organizations to determine the extent to which they merely reflect worn-out concepts of bureaucracy instead of merit. It also points up a need to simplify the hodge-podge of conflicting and overlapping legal provisions in personnel administration to produce human, responsive, reasonable government which gets the right things done with acceptable efficiency.

Generally, reformist approaches to improvements in public personnel administration have resulted instead in increased legalistic complexity and bureaucratization, with both the benefits which bureaucracy denotes and the many faults which it connotes. The reformers' efforts have taken two dominant directions: changes in structures and changes in processes. These concerns have often dominated the field at the expense of goals and objectives to be served.

Principal structural reforms have pulled in these competing directions: toward neutral independence and toward central executive control. Procedural reforms have often gone in conflicting and ambiguous directions, given unity only through increasing centralization.

Neutral Independence vs. Executive Control

Merit processes were generally limited to examining and appointment of some lower-level employees during the 50 years from the 1880s to the 1930s, and independent civil service commissions were the favorite structures for performing those functions during that era of quite limited government. But with the emergence of more comprehensive public personnel administration by the 1930s and broadening of merit coverage coincident with the growth of big government, the key issue of merit vs. spoils took a dramatic new form: how to reconcile merit protectionism with responsible executive leadership in personnel management. Only highlights of that well-known history merit repetition here.

The principal concepts of the field of public administration from the publication of Woodrow Wilson's essay in 1887 through its first 60 years were centralization, economy and efficiency, and separation of politics from administration. Centralization became the bureaucratizing thrust of the discipline, most evident by the close of the Progressive Era in the city management movement and in state government reorganization efforts. The traditional bureaucratic model of public administration was complete by the 1930s, with these "principles" to guide the One Best Way:

1. External policy direction and control.
2. Hierarchical conformation and executive leadership.
3. Coordinated staff services under a chief executive.
4. Departmentalization according to functions.
5. Merit selection and protection of personnel—and objective detachment.
6. Organizational compliance based on internalization of society's basic values.

Such "principles" became the absolute of Reform. Luther Gulick guided Virginia's Governor Harry Byrd, Sr., through these paths in search of economy and efficiency in the 1920s, for example, and he then went on to join Louis Brownlow and Charles Merriam in recommending similar administrative reorganization of the federal government. With respect to personnel administration, the 1937 Brownlow Committee Report provides the strongest statement in favor of executive management as an alternative to neutral protectionism:

> *Personnel management is an essential element of executive management. To set it apart or to organize it in a manner unsuited to serve the needs of the Chief Executive and the executive establishments is to render it impotent and ineffective.*
>
> *Finally, a satisfactory personnel agency would occupy a position close to the Chief Executive. Such an agency cannot develop its highest usefulness without the active interest of the Chief Executive, and he, in turn, cannot perform his important personnel functions in a satisfactory manner without the constant assistance of a central personnel agency worthy of his respect.*[1]

In 1938 President Roosevelt followed this concept in an order to establish personnel directors and offices in all of the departments and larger agencies. But the Brownlow Committee recommendations with respect to the U.S. Civil Service Commission were specifically rejected by Congress in the Reorganization Act of 1939.[2]

From that time through the nation's Bicentennial the issue of neutrality vs. executive direction has been joined many times. Following Watergate and several serious political assaults on the merit system in the 1970s, the pendulum swung from an extreme which favored "responsiveness to the elected Chief Executive" to another extreme of neutral protectionism. Legislation proposed in 1976 would have moved so far as creation of a seven-member Board of Federal Employee Appeals independent of the Civil Service Commission and its enforcement functions.[3] Influential proposals behind that legislation would have moved the Commission itself into a much more neutral role, *vis-a-vis* the Executive Office of the President.[4]

The major consequence of the domination of public personnel administration by such heated controversies over spoils vs. merit and neutrality vs. responsiveness has been ever-growing bureaucratization and legalistic complexity in the field. This has resulted in part from pressures on personnel commissions to develop complicated machinery to guarantee political neutrality while seeking efficiency and economy through bureaucratic structures and processes designed for executive-responsiveness models of administration. Agency personnel offices, on the other hand, have labored under similarly ambiguous pressures to respect requirements of political neutrality while functioning within a traditional bureaucratic model, dominated by the concepts of hierarchy and executive leadership.

Centralization and Prescription vs. Dispersion and Differentiation

Centralization of functions and legal prescription of conflicting but relatively uniform processes for all of government have been the dominant formulae of bureaucratization of public personnel administration. The prototype of this tendency is the federal government, in which, for example, at least 27 different "special emphasis" programs for employment of various interest groups (veterans, handicapped, women, minorities, etc.) require enforcement, covering a vast majority of people in one special category or another. To make this jumble of legal requirements, sometimes called merit, at all workable, the U.S. Civil Service Commission has been required to become not only a central management policy and legal control organization, but also a center of litigation as well as a major operating agency in recruiting and examining and in special program areas. Within this framework, agency personnel offices may exert some creative initiatives, but legal limitations set by Congress, OMB, and the Commission on differentiated approaches to individual agency needs are so extensive that agency personnel administrators may easily fall into more of a compliance-officer role than one of creative professional leadership.

The development of the present dominant, centralizing, prescriptive operation of the U.S. Civil Service Commission is highlighted by the history of the Federal Personnel Council and its successor, the Interagency Advisory Group. The Council came into being in 1931. It served as a vehicle for leadership by agency personnel directors in the field of public personnel administration, and it resulted in some dynamic and creative tension between them and the U.S. Civil Service Commission. The Council was abolished pursuant to the Independent Offices Appropriation Act of 1953, and its functions were transferred to the office of the Commission's Executive Director. The Interagency Advisory Group was established in January 1954 to fill the void, but, compared to the Council, the IAG has been largely dominated by the Commission's professional staff.

Recruiting and examining is another and more visible illustration of long-felt needs to centralize operations as well as policy guidance in the U.S. Civil Service Commission, a parallel to situations common in state and local governments. While several agencies (State, ERDA, CIA, etc.) exercise extensive authority for their own recruiting and examining, dominant reform proposals of 1976 called for further limitations on such agency authorities and enlarged concentration of operations in the U.S. Civil Service Commission. In short, further bureaucratization according to models out of the 1930s continued as proposed personnel reforms, whereas, in the larger field of public administration, such deficiencies as do exist have come to be attributed in recent years to excesses of bureaucratization and overly detailed legislation about as much as to other causes.

In the larger field of public administration, excesses of bureaucracy like those which characterize personnel administration have been ameliorated a bit with the development of changed management concepts and technologies during the past 25 years. Effectiveness has come to rank with economy and efficiency as a concern of administrators; dispersed, open-systems models of organization have become workable; goal and objectives-oriented management approaches, such as PPB, MBO, and program evaluation, have become dominant as agency approaches to getting the right things done. These changes have been easier to implement in program management than in staff or administrative management. That is likely to continue to be the situation, since staff functions, like personnel, are at the heart of bureaucracy—and a large measure of traditional bureaucracy may be essential in staff functions to permit larger movements to open-systems management of programs. But imaginative management efforts to implement MBO in the U.S. Civil Service Commission since 1973 demonstrate that clarification of objectives can go a long way toward making bureaucracy workable. The limited gains made by stressing objectives could encourage personnel professionals and political leaders to attempt other efforts to reverse the increasing bureaucratization of the field. To accomplish this will require less doctrinaire approaches than those associated with traditional reforms of organization and processes. It will also require creative conceptualization to cut through the present hodgepodge of functions which have grown up as disconnected "add-ons" in the context of growing bureaucratization.

Labor-Management Integration vs. Collective Bargaining

The greatest personnel "add-on" of all times is labor-management relations, a development since the 1950s that threatens or promises (depending on one's viewpoint) to reverse which function is the add-on and then to become the central thrust of public personnel administration. Organizationally, central public personnel functions have generally been classifiable as control (enforcing rules), staff (employment services, counseling), or services (performing relatively unrelated functions, i.e., Voter Rights Act enforcement). The control and staff functions include several specialities, often relatively unassociated with one another in practice: recruiting, examining, and placement; position classification and job evaluation; training, development, and career advancement; wage, salary, and benefits administration; performance evaluation, motivation, and productivity improvement; safety and occupational health; workforce and position management; and personnel management evaluation or inspections. Labor-management relations has been gradually added to such lists since the 1950s.

These functions have often developed in relative independence of one another. For example, training and development programs are sometimes not directly associated with career advancement, and often traditional merit concepts would be violated by linking formal education or training to promotion. Even pay and fringe benefits have scarcely been related, with little attention to total compensation packages before the advent of collective bargaining. Position management has generally meant enforcement of arbitrary personnel ceilings, usually derived from political decisions relatively unrelated to functions to be performed, and that has often passed for workforce planning.

Pressures of collective bargaining and of workforce planning and management are now such that they require intensive conceptual reexamination of the public personnel field. That necessity should be taken as an occasion to reexamine past tendencies to growing bureaucratization as the vehicle to administer the hodgepodge of functions which have defined public personnel administration in the past.

Statistics of the growth of exclusive recognitions in the federal government
... show the trends adequately. Generally, the concerns during this development have been more pragmatic than conceptual:

1. Legalization of collective bargaining in governments.
2. Relationships between collective bargaining and merit.
3. Administration of labor-management relations systems.
4. Definition of government management and clarification of supervisors'
   roles.

But while pragmatic in approach, several practical management responsibilities
have often been ignored in collective bargaining precisely because of failures to
link problems and practices through adequate conceptualization. The following
areas have been particularly neglected:

1. Workforce planning, forecasting, and utilization.
2. Financial impact of collective bargaining decisions both on government
   and on the general economy.
3. Productivity management, including measurement systems which relate
   costs and accomplishments.
4. Relationships to social change, including identification of social indicators
   and evaluation of accomplishments in terms of general governmental goals
   and objectives.

More serious than the failure to relate labor-management relations decisions to
these immediate management responsibilities may be pressures under collective bargaining to even greater bureaucratization of public personnel administration. These pressures derive from three major sources: (1) the historical
development of collective bargaining out of the bureaucratic organizations of
the industrialization era and the consequent acceptance of bureaucracy by
many labor-management relations specialists as natural and inevitable; (2) the
legal character of collective bargaining and the consequent tendency to
approach it legalistically in a bureaucratic sense, instead of reasonably, in the
sense of the value of rule of law; and (3) the tendency in public personnel
administration to treat collective bargaining as just another "add-on" function to
be incorporated into traditional bureaucracy.

To ameliorate these pressures to increased bureaucratization, the basic
concepts of collective bargaining need to be understood in the context of its
conceptual definition: Ideally, it is a legally defined system for resolving
conflicts, solving problems, and promoting common goals of management and
organized employees. In private enterprise, by law, it is a labor-management
relationship which is characterized by periodic negotiations resulting in a
written agreement on a basic rule system to govern the work relationship and
organized arrangements for resolving disagreements and problems as they arise
day-to-day. Under that broad definition, the following concepts may be identified:

1. Exclusive representation within legally established bargaining units.
2. Enforcement of good faith bargaining through legal maintenance of the
   bargaining processes but without prescription of bargaining ends.
3. Legal enforceability of agreements for a fixed time period.

4. Legal differentiation between types of disputes and remedies.
5. Bargaining processes and legal remedies, such as arbitration, based on concepts of fairness and flexibility—a search for organizational justice or reasonableness.

Public personnel administration could be well served by taking a cue from the last—the most fundamental—of those concepts as an approach to escape from its ever-mounting bureaucratization. The field needs to move away from narrow legalisms and toward a goal and process-orientation of law as a search for reasonableness. Instead of probing these basic concepts, collective bargaining is still treated by many simply as an intrusion of class warfare on an imagined universe without distinctions between labor and management—a universe of one integrated public service. Unfortunately, collective bargaining is often presented by its more doctrinaire proponents in equally unreal terms of inevitable labor/management conflict, with little room for intervention of critical thought processes. In such circumstances, further bureaucratization has been a tempting refuge in the face of doctrinaire "reform."

Complicating Developments

As noted at the outset, the bureaucracies of public personnel administration have been pushed to the brink of ineffectiveness by three complications of recent decades: (1) big government; (2) unionization; and (3) litigious populism. The complications of unionization and collective bargaining have been of a character to force both attention and some action, however hesitant and shallow, as noted above. But relatively little creative thought has been devoted to the complications of bigness now imposed on personnel structures which were originally conceived for small, limited governments. And populist legislation of the late 1960s and 1970s, adopted for the central government by Congresses without party responsibility for execution of the laws, has not been subjected to systems analysis for workability, or often even to rudimentary comparison and contrast with other legal requirements for elemental clarity for administrative implementation.

Big Government and Workforce Management

Probably the clearest problem imposed on public personnel administration by the rise of big government is uninformed hostility toward federal government employees. With over one-third of GNP spent by or flowing through government in the United States, there is a tendency to assume that proliferation of federal bureaucrats is the chief cause, when in fact government costs have risen most due to expansion of welfare programs, services, military hardware, and public works, while expansion of the federal workforce has been severely limited by often arbitrary ceilings which are sometimes inconsistent with program performance requirements established by law. These sharply conflicting realities—legally mandated program responsibilities and rigid low personnel ceilings—often make effectiveness, efficiency, and economy in government impossible.

The second side of this coin of relatively low labor-intensity and high money expenditure of federal government is high labor-intensity of state and local governments, with their responsibilities for delivery of services such as education, public safety, health, and welfare. The financial resources of these service governments are particularly sensitive to economic fluctuations— inflation and unemployment pressures—and, as high labor-intensive organizations, their problems tend quickly to multiply adverse impacts of economic instability and to send their reverberations throughout their regions and the nation's whole economy.

The largest personnel *organization* problem of big government is that dominant personnel institutions were created to serve small, limited governments, they must now serve large, powerful governments; and they have been adapted to their enlarged functions essentially by increased bureaucratization, with relatively little creative, adjustive organizational change.

For example, when the Pendleton Act was adopted in 1883, it covered only 13,780 of the government's 131,208 employees—10.5 per cent. Fifty per cent coverage was not reached until Theodore Roosevelt's Administration, and government's size remained small, even though federal employees had more than doubled in number in less than 20 years. The independent Civil Service Commission's functions remained quite limited—examining and appointment of lower-grade employees. By the Hoover Administration, 80 per cent of federal employees were under the classified service, but that fell to 60.5 per cent by 1936, with the growth of the New Deal. When President Eisenhower entered office, over 86 per cent of the 2 1/2 million employees were covered, and the per cent has remained near that ever since. The size of the overall federal workforce has scarcely grown proportionate to population growth since the 1950s, however, while government programs and costs have multiplied well beyond that rate and while state and local government employment has more than tripled.

With the growing size and complexity of government and with the extension of the classified service to higher grades, the original examining and certification function of the U.S. Civil Service Commission has reached demanding levels of diverse expertise scarcely imagined 50 or even 30 years ago when still-dominant concepts of centralized bureaucratic organization were adopted to serve this function. Meanwhile, with the assignment of new functions to the Commission, bureaus and offices have been added on in traditional bureaucratic fashion, with relatively little effort until quite recently to relate different functions and to develop institutional approaches based on systems perspectives oriented to shared objectives. Instead, bureaus and offices have been responsible for particular turf, and incentives have been to protect and nourish these separate organizational domains. These incentives have generated pressures to centralize operations as well as policy guidance and control functions in the Commission.

One most neglected aspect of public personnel administration in this era of big government is *workforce information and planning.* Where practiced at all, workforce planning and management in government have been oriented in four directions: (1) position management, usually consisting of enforcement of arbitrary personnel ceilings which have been based more on cosmetic consider-ations than on functional requirements; (2) aggregate workforce (or man-power) planning, generally performed outside of public personnel organiza-tions, as by the U.S. Department of Labor's Employment and Training Adminis-tration; (3) specialized workforce information services, as in the U.S. Civil Service Commission's Bureau of Executive Manpower publications and ser-vices; and (4) organizational workforce planning, generally limited to relatively large governments or large agencies of the federal government. . . .

Litigious Populism

The highly legalistic, bureaucratic character of public personnel adminis-tration makes it especially vulnerable to the 1970s phenomenon of litigious, public service-rights populism. But thus far organizational guerilla-warfare has probably reinforced bureaucratic qualities in personnel about as much as it has led to more functionally oriented approaches.

Criticism of the U.S. Civil Service Commission by Ralph Nader associate Robert Vaughn, for example, favored a return to quite negative policing of agency personnel management by the Commission—a rigid, bureaucratic approach hostile to consultative-interdependent modes of organizational change.[5] Yet these simplistic, traditionally bureaucratic views ultimately suc-ceeded through litigation,[6] seriously limiting the Commission's innovative efforts and progress since 1971 away from a negative inspections stance by the Commission toward more collaborative, organizational development ap-proaches.

On the other hand, Freedom of Information Act amendments of 1974 and the Privacy Act of the same year have tended to require some revisions which may move personnel administration toward more open processes in perfor-mance of some public functions, such as timely provision of information of a policy or administrative nature. Yet, both Acts are amenable to use for harassment of government agencies through requests and litigation which may consume large resources of time, personnel, and money. The personal liability provisions of the Privacy Act seem particularly conducive to bureaucratic caution and legalistic behavior.

The feature of populist-oriented 1970s legislation which may be most disruptive of highly legalistic, bureaucratic organizations—whether personnel or program agencies—is its tendency to drive public administrators to even greater legalistic extremes. Instead of selective enforcement of laws and provision of public services, agencies are increasingly forced into 100 per cent performance of a multitude of legal provisions. With respect to public person-nel, for example, there has been a tendency to require different agency action programs to implement each of the multitude of special interest employment provisions adopted in recent years. In a litigious environment this may be hostile to selective and coordinated enforcement which has been the classic approach to reasonable execution of law under the consent system of American constitutional government. Such administrative discretion has saved rule of law from transformation into the legalistic rigidity which is one negative impulse of bureaucracy. But, freed of party responsibility for Executive Branch enforcement after 1969, Congresses tended in the 1970s toward legislation of an uncoordinated hodgepodge of absolutes as a method of disciplining an Administration found guilty of Watergate.

These legal absolutes which limit discretion in the execution of laws may provide incentives to replace with more functional approaches the bureaucratic organizations and processes which have generated support for such rigid legislation. Public personnel administration is a prime target for such change since it is often the epitome of bureaucracy.

Conclusions

The old debates of public personnel administration—spoils vs. merit and neutral independence vs. executive management—have continued relevance today, as revealed by Watergate events and reactions to them. But it is past time to move beyond the simple conceptual level of those conflicts, which are likely to be around and require attention forever, and move toward creative efforts to deal also with other issues which are overtaking the field while professionals and politicians remain preoccupied with the old and the obvious.

Other great issues in urgent need of creative attention are collective bargaining, workforce planning and management, and, most of all, overwhelming bureaucracy and legal complexity.

Progress may be made in dealing with these personnel issues by directing the field toward more functional, process-oriented organizations; goals and objectives-oriented management; decentralization of operations to line agencies; and clear articulation of personnel functions with basic values of American constitutional democracy: human dignity and rule of law. Put more simply, great improvements may be possible by moving deliberately away from highly centralized bureaucratic approaches of administrative management and toward more differentiated, objectives-oriented approaches of contemporary program management. Much progress in that direction, however, depends on simplification of the proliferating maze of legalistic reforms which presently frustrate effectiveness, efficiency, and economy in public personnel administration.

Notes

1. President's Committee on Administrative Management, *Report with Special Studies* (Washington, D.C., U.S. Government Printing Office, 1937), pp. 7-14 and 59-133.

2. The details are most thoroughly reviewed in Richard Polenberg, *Reorganizing Roosevelt's Government: 1936-1939* (Cambridge: Harvard University Press, 1966). It is instructive to compare the history reported in that book with the efforts of the Nixon Administration as reported in Richard P. Nathan, *The Plot That Failed, Nixon and the Administrative Presidency* (New York: John Wiley, 1975). Together, these case studies forcefully summarize the political pulling and hauling which have dominated public personnel administration in the United States in the name of Reform.

3. H.R. 12080, February 25, 1976, 94th Cong., 2d Sess. Bill introduced by Chairman David N. Henderson, House Committee on Post Office and Civil Service.

4. Bernard Rosen, *The Merit System in the United States Civil Service* (Washington, D.C.: U.S. Government Printing Office, 1975), 94th Cong., 1st Sess., Committee Print No. 90-10, esp. pp. 89-90. This monograph, prepared in 1975 for the U.S. House Committee on Post Office and Civil Service, contains an exceptionally clear summary of historical developments in the federal government.

5. Robert Vaughn, *The Spoiled System: A Call for the Reform of the Civil Service System* (New York: Charterhouse Books, Inc., 1975).

6. *Vaughn* v. *Rosen,* 383 F. Supp. 1049 (D.C., 1974), Affirmed 523 F.2d 1136 (October 9, 1975).

21
Revitalizing the Civil Service
Alan K. Campbell

Since taking over as Chairman of the Civil Service Commission, I have found the work to be vital and exciting. The responsibilities of public service have been especially challenging and inspiring in these first few months of this administration. Yet the best feature I have found about the civil service has been the quality of the *people* in it, while the worst appears to be the personnel *system.*

As one who has spent the greater part of my professional life training young men and women for the public service, I already knew the quality and commitment of my former students. To discover that their attributes were typical of most government workers was not a surprise but was reassuring. Federal employees today are more highly educated, more experienced, and more capable than ever before.

Right now, the competition to get a Federal job is higher than ever. Last year there were 76 inquiries and 12 applications for every job filled, yet all forecasts predict that these ratios will continue to climb.

However, we are not going to rely solely on the competition for jobs to ensure the highest quality work force we can get. We are actively going out and seeking top candidates and encouraging them to enter the Federal service.

Remarks delivered at the National Conference in Government, National Municipal League, Denver, Colorado, November 15, 1977. Reprinted from *Civil Service News.*

Alan K. Campbell, formerly chairman United States Civil Service Commission, is director of the Federal Office of Personnel Management.

One of my first steps upon taking office was to recommend the Presidential Management Intern Program. This program is designed to bring into the Federal service each year 250 outstanding graduate students in public management—men and women of exceptional management potential who have received special training in planning and managing public programs and policies. If they can demonstrate their management ability during the intern period, and if the agency is satisfied with their performance, they will be eligible for conversion to the career service without further competition at the end of the internship.

Another program just authorized is the Graduate Level Work-Study Program. This will allow us to hire students in relevant education programs for positions in general management. The objective is to combine graduate study with work experience for the students, while providing Federal agencies with a source of quality employees both before and after graduation day.

Not only will these programs attract "the best" people to Federal service, they will simultaneously aid us in meeting the affirmative action mandate that the President specified when he signed the Executive orders creating the programs. We believe these programs will be an important and new avenue for well-qualified minorities and women to demonstrate their potential as future managers in government.

With all the efforts to maintain and improve the quality of the Federal work force, however, those of us who work for the Federal Government must still live with a paradox.

Charges of Inefficiency

It seems that every time we open a newspaper or read a magazine we find another article bemoaning the low quality and general ineffectiveness of Federal employees. One need only examine recent issues of The Wall Street Journal, the Reader's Digest, U.S. News and World Report, or any of a number of other popular publications to find charges of Federal employees not working very hard and Federal managers unwilling or unable to take the disciplinary action such situations call for.

Although charges of inefficiency have been made for as long as there has been a government, the accusations today are coming with a greater frequency and intensity than ever before. Nor are they coming from just a bunch of disgruntled, crackpot radicals, but rather from many respected, middle-of-the-road analysts. Not long ago David Brinkley, in his commentary on the NBC nightly newscast, chose to attack the Federal Government and Federal employees. He said,

> . . . the Federal government, through good times and bad, sucks in the money from all over the country and spends a good deal of it on itself and its employees. People get paid whether they produce anything or not, whether they work hard or not at all. And it's almost unheard of for anyone to be fired. Government pay is higher than civilian pay for the same work. So are the benefits. And people get raises by just staying on, regardless of merit.

David B. Wilson, from the Boston Globe, wrote,

*The bureaucratic life rewards conspiracy, sycophancy, ideological confor-
mity, caution and class solidarity. It punishes innovation, originality, and
the work ethic.*

The issue is not merely what appears in the media, however, for these
reports reflect a view that is fairly widely held among the public, the taxpayers
who supply the money to run the government. A recent Gallup Poll indicated
two-thirds of the people in the country believe that Federal employees are paid
more than their private sector counterparts; two-thirds believe that government
benefits are excessive; and three-quarters believe that government workers do
not work as hard as their private sector counterparts.

The reasons for the public's disenchantment with the government are
varied. Partly it's a result of those who openly brag about what they get away
with as Federal employees. There is the high ranking economist at HUD who
brags that for two years he has done nothing but write free-lance articles, yet he
defies the Assistant Secretary to fire him. (I know the assistant Secretary in that
case, by the way, and I believe the economist *will* be fired.)

Then there was the typist interviewed on a news broadcast who claimed
that she spends her days doing nothing but filling out crossword puzzles.

I believe another reason is a carryover from a growth in distrust caused by
the merit abuses during the Watergate era. Previously the career civil service
system was thought to be nonpolitical and inviolate; those abuses led to a belief
that, in fact, the system could be politically manipulated.

But I believe the most important reason for the disenchantment was
revealed in a poll taken by *Psychology Today* magazine. They started by asking
people to rate government workers as a group, and got results similar to those in
the Gallup survey. However, they went on to ask the same people to rate the
individual Federal workers with whom they've had contact—over 70 percent
said they were satisfied or very satisfied with the service they had received.

The problem here is not unlike the one faced by Congress, where over 80
percent of the people across the country indicate they lack a trust and faith in
Congress *generally,* while an equal proportion also believe their *individual*
Congressman is doing fine. It is this contrast between the institutions themselves and the people in them that causes the paradox.

I said earlier that there has been a skepticism about government for as long
as there has been a government, and I believe that within a framework of
underlying trust, such skepticism is healthy. As the custodians of public power,
we should indeed be carefully watched and checked. There *are* problems with
the system that need correcting, and to that degree the public perceptions are
accurate.

We need to be responsive to that portion of those perceptions that are
accurate, and attempt to change the system to deal with the problems. This, I
would argue, is exactly what the President has in mind with his general

reorganization plans. It is not a mere shuffling of organization charts, but an effort to improve, to make more efficient and effective, the management of government programs. It is this motivation which, in my judgment, makes the revitalization of *management* the heart of the President's overall reorganization.

The President's Goals

In my first conversation with the President about the Chairmanship of the Civil Service Commission, he made it abundantly clear that he felt some fundamental changes in Federal personnel management practices were necessary to his own goals.

First, to aid the reorganization itself, he wanted changes so that the inflexibility of personnel rules would not stand in the way of the kind of revitalization of the system he had in mind.

Second, he believed that in the long run, streamlining Federal personnel practices could make a major contribution to increased effectiveness, efficiency, and responsiveness of government.

It was with that mandate that we established the Federal Personnel Management Project in June of this year. Task force members came from the public service itself, with only a few outside business and academic people as advisors. So, this will not be another report to gather dust; those who wrote it will also help make it happen. . . .

Our general philosophy is based on the belief that managers need to have the authority and power necessary to manage, that managers need greater flexibility, but must also be held accountable for the job done. This means greater flexibility in examining applicants for jobs, in rewarding, in assigning and reassigning employees, in disciplining, in discharging, and in all the rest of the actions associated with managing people.

The system is currently so encrusted with rules and regulations that too many managers feel it is almost impossible to take personnel actions. We did a series of case studies of the time it took to perform personnel actions and found that, in one sample, it took seven months to hire, and between eight months and three years for various kinds of discipline. Added to this is an appeals system that drags on and on, due in part to a lack of attention by managers.

We saw one case where a supervisor attempted to remove an employee whose work was so bad that everyone in the office agreed she should be fired, and at the end of that time the supervisor received an unfavorable performance rating, because he had spent so much time on this case that he ignored his other duties.

These rules and regulations originated as a defense against the spoils system and the poor government that it provided, but they now result in as much inefficiency as they were designed to prevent.

In baseball, no one argues against the need for a batter to wear a protective helmet, or the need for some players, like the catcher, to have special protective gear. However, if you dressed the entire team in a complete set of catcher's pads, they could not hit, field, or throw too well no matter how talented they might be.

In our reorganization we are trying to remove the *unnecessary* protections that hinder performance.

We also are trying to open up the system to accomplish affirmative action and equal employment opportunity goals. Taking credit where credit is due, the Federal Government's record, looking at the total work force, is quite good compared to that of the private sector. However, if you look at the top jobs, it is *not* that good. Only three percent of the supergrades are minorities and only three percent are women. By the way, until a year ago that figure was approximately two percent in each case, and the improvement has been produced entirely by non-career Presidential and secretarial appointments, not by any improvement in career appointments.

The civil rights issue, in my judgment, is now entering a new phase, one that will be much tougher, if that is believable, than the first. In the first phase we were opening up public institutions, schools, and public facilities on an integrated and equal basis to all. But, in that opening up we were not denying spaces or access to anybody. There were not fewer seats on the buses or in the public schools or wherever; it was simply that they were to be made to be generally available. We now enter the stage where we are dealing with limited spaces, whether in academic graduate programs or in Federal employment.

I think it is safe to predict that the size of the Federal work force will remain fairly stable. Since the pool of talent to fill top jobs comes from grades 13, 14, and 15, and these grades have only 5.7 percent women and 5.9 percent minorities, it is obvious that fantastically strenuous efforts, including reaching outside the service, must be made if we are to meet the President's mandate of bringing a full range of talent to the Federal service, especially at the top.

Our third broad objective is to try to eliminate the schizophrenic organization of the Civil Service Commission, caught between trying to be judge and jury for individual employees in personnel appeals while simultaneously trying to serve as the President's personnel officer and to carry out the personnel programs to achieve management's goals.

Employees see our appeals processes as management-oriented, and feel they can't get a fair shake. Managers feel that our torturous appeals routes are a tremendous hindrance on their ability to take disciplinary action. As a result, we are damned by both sides, and I don't believe any amount of empirical evidence could change those views.

Therefore, we are suggesting splitting off the quasi-judicial appeals functions of the Commission and establishing something that might be called the Merit System Protection Board. It would have bipartisan members, appointed for fixed terms, and not subject to reappointment. This is a way to create a genuine independent agency to deal with those functions.

Simultaneously, for the positive side of the Civil Service Commission's functions in recruiting and examining, in personnel evaluation, in areas such as equal employment opportunity, we would create a new, more effective agency, perhaps the Office of Personnel Management. It is my dream that such an agency would sit alongside OMB and make the management of people just as important as the management of money.

Specific Recommendations

Let me now give you a few of the specific recommendations we are making.

We propose to establish at the top of the personnel system a senior executive service, where grade and rank would be assigned to *persons* rather than *positions*. The pay system would be one with freedom for management discretion within a limited range of salaries. There would be no automatic pay increases, but there would be a possibility for earning substantial bonuses.

The executive management service would include not just the super-grades, but executive levels IV and V as well. It would have a strict limitation on the proportion of appointments that could be non-career, a proportion certainly no greater than it is now, that would be written into law, which it is not now, thereby providing a real protection against further politicalization of the career service.

We believe the executive management service would give top management substantial freedom in assigning talented people to critical new program needs, and in forming new units to help achieve the goals of that organization. It would be a new kind of flexibility for top managers in the Federal Government, and I can assure you that, in individual conversations as well as cabinet meetings, these top managers express great frustration about their inability to take the kinds of action designed to improve management.

One of the problems with public management is that most people in the top positions, whether President, Secretary of a Department, Chairman of the Civil Service Commission, or what have you, have a relatively short-range view due to their limited terms of office. Therefore, to make their mark quickly, they are likely to turn away from trying to make basic improvements in management of the government's business unless they have some ability to move on the management side.

The country today has the great good fortune of having a President who is management-oriented, who is willing to use enough of his time and energy to improve the government's managerial system. Such Presidential interest is rare, occurring perhaps once in a generation, and I hope those of us who have an interest in, and commitment to, public management have the necessary talent and knowledge to help the President accomplish his management goals.

We must improve the public service, both in reality and in perception. I am convinced that the quality of our society is determined not only by the quality of its public institutions but also by the people's views of those institutions.

All institutions in this country today—whether government, business, religious, or educational—suffer from a lack of public confidence. I think the way to turn that around is for the Federal Government to do as the President directed, which is to bring new light to the public sector.

I'm sure that as we open up our Federal agencies, and simplify their procedures—in this case personnel procedures—the good things we do will spill over into other institutions.

When we issue the final personnel reorganization report, that will merely mark the beginning of the job. The government must then do its part to implement the improvements; the public must ensure that government remains on the right track.

We need a combined effort from all citizens to achieve these goals, and we *must* have it, because a society that allows the quality of its government to falter will itself fail.

22
Technological Trends
in Productivity Measurement
Walter L. Balk

To say that we want to measure something is quite a mouthful. Generally we use the term "measure" to refer to the process of observing objects and events and making them correspond to the rules of mathematical logic. Our purpose, in productivity measurement, is to distinguish trends and evaluate occurrences so that we can predict and control outcomes. But some of us have a very rigid meaning for measurement. We want a "hard" measure; a thermometer type of arrangement which will give us a precise idea of where we are. In this paper, an attempt is made to consider problems of "hardness" of data. My conclusion is that we'll also have to learn how to handle "softer" productivity measurement information and that this will affect the way we manage things.

Only a few years ago, the case I will make would not have had much meaning. The feeling was that most tasks in large organizations were highly routinized, and we were committed to reasonably rigid bureaucratic organizational ideas. But the nature of work is changing throughout our culture with a considerable impact upon the valuable ideas of yesterday. This transition has been recently and very ably documented by Daniel Bell.[1] A rapid shift is occurring from a goods-oriented economy to a service orientation. This will not signal the end of scarcity, as was once believed, so productivity and its measurement will continue to be a vital necessity. As this change goes on, my feeling is that the ground rules for measurement of productivity will be affected.

Progress to Date

There is no real technological difficulty in measuring a large percentage of the work we do in government. The reason is that many tasks are relatively

Reprinted with permission from *Public Personnel Management,* Vol. 9, No. 2, (March-April, 1975), pp. 128-133.
Walter Balk is a professor in the Graduate School of Public Affairs, State University of New York, Albany.

routine and we can apply well-established techniques to understand the nature of the work being performed. In some cases it is possible to develop "engineered work standards." The approach is to (a) divide each job into basic work increments, (b) assign a time to each increment, (c) add these times up to get a "standard time" per unit of output, and (d) match the actual to the ideal time in order to measure efficiency. Engineered work standards (or EWS) have been the happy hunting ground of industrial engineers since the turn of the century. They have the advantage of providing a reasonably scientific basis to measure individual performance in many manufacturing, clerical, and maintenance jobs. A number of excellent texts and manuals exist to tell one how to go about measuring these tasks.[2][3] But there's a fly in the EWS ointment.

Over the years it has become apparent that engineered work standards can be applied to only a small amount of government work ... my guess is from fifteen to thirty percent, depending upon such factors as size of operation, the nature of the work, and the level of government. So many of us have started to look at more complex, less routine work with reasonably tangible outputs. One approach has been to consider the work done by an entire group of people and to develop efficiency ratios, the most common being number units produced per average person in a group. For example, let us consider a hypothetical automobile registration operation. In this group effort, people switch jobs from day to day, the types of registrations differ in complexity as well as format and load can vary according to the weather or time of day. It is valuable to divide the numbers of each category of registrations completed by the manhours used each month. This gives so many registrations of such and such a type per average work hour. Now, if we do this each month, then a pattern emerges showing trends of performance over time. The technology for this has been quite well developed, especially, by such organizations as the U.S. Government Accounting Office[4] and the Ontario Committee on Government Productivity.[5] In my opinion, such trend measurements apply to about another fifteen to thirty percent of our government effort; again this will vary with the work situation.

From a measurement technology point of view, engineered work standards are much more elegant than work load trends. However, we have recognized that there is something about the nature of the work which makes EWS impractical or impossible to attain. Therefore the tendency has been to collect data about output load and observe trends. This means, of course, sacrificing a certain amount of measurement delicacy and its attendant scientific flavor. With this in mind, it seems reasonable to say that proven measurement technology exists for about half of government work. What gives us all headaches is the remainder of our operations which are surely not adaptable to EWS and only partially to work load trends. You can record the case loads of social service workers, for example, but how do you know they are doing a "good job?" The same problem applies to education and student-faculty ratios. Truly, we are at a measurement impasse, and solutions are not easy to come by. One point of this paper is that we are perhaps "frozen" in the measurement modes described above because the concepts of productivity and work are not understood well enough and commonly enough for more progress to take place. My purpose is to develop an argument about both of these concepts and suggest some implications about measurement technology.

What Is Productivity?

A logical way to think of productivity is to consider its relationship to the production process. Using systems language, inputs are transformed into outputs which are supposed to meet desired standards. Each of these elements has factors which help us to analyze the process. In the following figure, some of these factors are listed beneath the appropriate element:

Figure 1
The Production Process and Its Elements

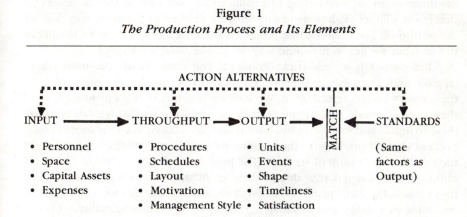

The general process statement above is that inputs are converted to outputs and matched with standards (or expectations of results) to see if the process should continue and what improvements might be made. If outputs do not meet standards we can revise factors under the elements of input, throughput, or change standards. In order to control this process we measure and use ratios. For example it is common to set up ratios of dollars spent per employee, or dollars spent per square foot. Interesting as these numbers are, they are only gauges of input, hence very limited in what they tell us. To increase our understanding of the process, we develop more extensive ratios. Comparison of output to input is known as efficiency. The familiar manning tables of units produced per employee are a good example of efficiency ratios. As already stated, productivity has historically been seen as the simple ratio of output to input. But this is deceptive, because it assumes that all output units meet a quality standard. (This is the matching of output to standards shown in Figure 1 above). A more complete statement would have to incorporate a quality (technically, this is called effectiveness) concept. Industry and classical economics have used the simple output to input ratio because quality is a step in the manufacturing process. In service industries, customers are assumed to buy only "satisfactory"

outputs. These market mechanisms do not operate in much of the public sector. Thus a productive process is one which optimizes efficiency and effectiveness ratios. To put it in simple terms:

Productivity = efficiency + effectiveness
or = O/I + O/S

Several interesting notions come to mind as we think of productivity in such process and these dual ratio terms.

In the first place efficiency and effectiveness must arrive at some kind of balance. Thus the common sense notion that "quality fights quantity" is confirmed by the formula shown above. Also, our ability to define output is the keystone to an understanding of productivity. Not only is this necessary to determine efficiency, but standards must be defined in the same way that we define output. The reason is that standards are what we expect; so we had better define what we get in the same way we define what we expect.

But output is a very tricky concept. The term means the results have tangible and intangible properties. Physical properties are the ones we have traditionally concentrated upon. We look for quantity of units produced, see if they meet schedule, and define their shape and form so that we can compare these to inputs and standards. But output also has intangible characteristics such as client satisfaction, value to the community and other "feelings" we have about the results of government services. The problem is that while these emotional outputs can be gauged, they do not seem to "fit" the notion of productivity and they present the usual problems of psychological measurement . . . that is to say problems of validity and reliability. Finally, we are uncomfortable with less tangible characteristics of output since we don't know when to apply them. My argument will now be that we may improve our ability to resolve some of these problems if we can better understand the nature of work, especially what is known as task ambiguity.

Work and Task Ambiguity

It is a common sense notion that more routine work is easier to measure than is less routine work. If this is true, then the amount of routine in certain categories of work should determine the types of measures we can get and the way we use the numbers. While this is recognized by most, surprisingly little has been done to measure the degree of routine in work. This would involve defining "routine" so that it can be observed and developing a scale to determine the amount of routine in work.

We have started to approach this problem of defining routine at the Graduate School of Public Affairs and our progress was summarized in a recent publication.[6] In this research we looked at characteristics of tasks such as variety of work, control over input, dependence on others and skill requirements in order to develop a scale of what is called "task ambiguity." This has been tried out in several locations, most recently in mental health sites. We find that it is possible to discriminate between degrees of task ambiguity and that degrees of task ambiguity can be related to styles of measurement. For example, tasks with low ambiguity (or high routine) are best measured by EWS. As tasks become moderately ambiguous, they are often more appropriately measured by work-load criteria (*e.g.,* units per man days over time). Highly ambiguous tasks appear to be best measured by program elements and schedules. . . .

Here are a series of propositions:

As task ambiguity increases, then:

1. Measurement reliability and validity *decrease.*
2. The utility of efficiency ratios *decreases.*
3. The importance of effectiveness ratios *increases.*
4. The possibility of a single measure to define a productivity situation *decreases.*

   Therefore, as task ambiguity increases, managers must increasingly:

5. Have employees help them to interpret results of productivity measurement.
6. Rate productivity upon a group basis rather than upon an individual performance basis.
7. Take higher risks in predicting outcomes.

We are checking out some of these hypotheses, and they seem to hold at this time. In any event, we are certain that different management styles are predictably tied in with measurement modes. This has revolutionary, if disturbing implications for the way we run organizations. Disturbing because we have to understand the details of work and the way productivity is measured before we can evolve appropriate productivity policy. Some implications for personnel management people are taken up at the end of this paper.

Other Aspects of Measurement Technology

Most of us who are in the productivity measurement field find tremendous amounts of data available; yet there is little systematic guidance to select the most appropriate measures. Our work on task ambiguity should be of help in this respect. But, beyond this, there is a need to build measurement styles into information systems which will serve to improve controls. One of our most persistent problems today is that we have too much unorganized, almost random data polluting our decision channels.

A long term answer to the problems of "data pollution" could be found by better understanding how the mind processes information in order to make decisions. The absorbing and interpretation of data is called perception. This is an organizing process which appears to occur in steps of increasing complexity. The most basic event is that information must have an intensity or disturbance level in order to get absorbed. This, in effect, gets our attention. Next we locate the source of the information and assign patterns and rates of change. Once this is done, it enables the mind to go on to an evaluation cycle which considers relationships to previous perceptions, and then control strategies evolve. Repeated experience enables us to devise principles and guides for action which become the basis for making decisions. The success of decisions has to do with learning so that we can consider data and respond by ignoring them, using routines (or rote activities), programming innovative responses, or reorganizing previous perceptual styles. The value of routines cannot be overestimated because they result in low processing effort responses. These patterns hold us in place and give us identity. They provide the freedom to engage in creative programming of information and the reorganization of previous perceptions. By now it is evident that there are striking similarities between how organizations attempt to deal with information and the workings of the mind. Small wonder, because organizations *are* collections of minds. The danger in this line of thought is to make too close a parallel between mind and agency organization. This would overlook important differences. For example, agency organizations include interacting and exchanging groups ... properties which individual minds do not possess. The purpose of all this is to suggest that some very fruitful research might result in the area of productivity measurement, evaluation and systems analysis if we could better relate the way organizations work to the way the mind works. While this appears promising our knowledge of mind and social organization is quite formative. As important as such research is, progress would be slow and difficult, and I see no practical results for administrators within a period of several years.

Another area worth exploring in more detail is that of the intangible or effective nature of output. A few months ago a food service organization in a large government organization contacted me because, while they had a good handle on EWS and workload data, there was no measure of "quality" of food service. My suggestion was that they develop a rating committee of clients and administrators, determine dimensions of food service quality and have the committee rate trends and compare results of various locations. Surely there is a reservoir of talent to develop this approach among psychological attitude measurement experts. As another example, in the urban field the quality of street cleanliness is judged by panels who simply look at photographs; these are taken using sound sampling techniques. Many of our technicians recoil from these types of measurements because they involve the complexity and uncertainty of attitude testing. However, I think it's considerably better than nothing and we are missing the boat by not being more active in this vein of research.

Policy Consequences of the New Measurement Technology

From the above, we may conclude that the need for new measurement technologies will push us further into the area of grappling with ambiguous tasks. This has inevitable associations with management style. In addition, we will have to take more risks by measuring attitudes and using a number of measures, both "hard" and "soft" to guide us in making better and more productive decisions. This means an emphasis upon informality, less of an attachment to machine models of organization and making more impressionistic decisions at the expense of unattainable precise, instrument-like measurements. These trends should affect the functions of personnel managers drastically:

1. Employees and managers will "share" more and more productivity data in

the future. This means that *employees* will have to understand the technology of measurement in order to help management interpret the results.

2. Productivity evaluations will have to be done for groups instead of centering upon individual performance. This should have a sizable effect upon performance evaluation systems and collective bargaining.

3. Items 1 and 2 above have pervasive training implications for both managers and employees. Surprisingly enough it means a good deal of emphasis upon the technical content of measurement, and perhaps less on broad notions of "human relations."

Elaboration of the above implications would require another paper. My only purpose is to demonstrate that the technology of measurement cannot be left, nor will it stay solely in the hands of industrial engineers and work measurement experts. Productivity measurement has become the concern of all management. The reason, of course, is that the world around us and the nature of work is changing.

Notes

1. Daniel Bell, *The Coming of Post-Industrial Society* (Basic Books, 1973).
Efforts to improve productivity occur within a broad social context. Bell sees some trends for the future. Heavy going at times, but his treatment of scarcity, planning and the shift from goods to services are most central to the problem of state governments.

2. Gerald Nadler, *Work Design* (Irwin, 1963). A very detailed handbook, mostly devoted to the more routine tasks and operations. Concentrates on the industrial sphere, but useful to government administrator.

3. Dennis A. Whitmore, *Measurement and Control of Indirect Work* (American Elsevier, 1971). A very complete manual for the more routine clerical operations. Typical industrial engineering approach. Necessary knowledge, but limited to certain types of work.

4. U.S. General Accounting Office, *The Permanent Measurement Systme,* Volumes 1 and 2, October and December 1973.
Replete with examples of measurement methods, trends, and output indicators for specific types of work.

5. Committee on Government Productivity, *Report Number 10, A Summary* (Government of Ontario, March 1973).
Taking productivity in its broadest meaning, the commission outlines some policy proposals. A useful source for general ideas and approaches.

6. Walter Balk, "Productivity Controls and the Measurement of Task Ambiguity," *Technical Papers* (American Institute of Industrial Engineers, 1973).
Task Ambiguity is seen as a major variable in understanding the measurement of work and management control styles. The question is: Can we develop a scale showing the relative amount of ambiguity in jobs?

Chapter Seven

The Future and Public Personnel Policy

Introduction

We can infer much about the future of public personnel policy from the material presented up to this point in this book.

1. Public employee organizations and unions will continue to grow in size and their importance in the policymaking process will increase. State and federal laws and court cases will shape the growth and influence of employee groups but it is unlikely that the thrust of the immediate past will be greatly affected. Public managers will need to become accustomed to dealing with employee organizations. If we can learn from the experience of the private sector, future labor-management relations may be much smoother than they are at present.

2. Efforts to improve equal employment compliance will be a part of the policymaking process in the years to come. Court rulings and new laws may have a more direct effect in this area, because it is a less clearly established one. However, as long as the deprived groups are important voting blocs and potential sources of agitation, it may be assumed that their influence on personnel policy will be felt.

3. Concern for government productivity likewise will continue. Many say we are moving into an era of limits where production must be altered to preserve the environment and conserve energy. Competition from other nations will mean that American goods will no longer be as much in demand. Future generations thus may have to accept a standard of living lower than that which we now experience. A lower standard of living would require important personal and psychological adjustments by the public. If the necessities of life become more expensive, people will become much more concerned with the public services they must pay for. Hence concern for efficiency, effectiveness, and economy in the public sector is likely to become more important.

A Society of Constant Change?

According to Fredrick Mosher (Selection 23) future generations will live in an environment of frequent change. Government will be deeply involved in the direction of change and new leadership skills will be required. Personnel administrators will need to develop methods of recruiting, training, and motivating a new breed of public administrator.

Mosher sees the future public personnel administrator as one who is more intimately involved in policy matters. As demands and needs change, the administrator must adapt his or her policies and actions accordingly. As problems become more interdisciplinary in nature and less clearly based on the past, innovative thinking will be required.

The Mosher piece was written in early 1970 in reaction to the tumult of the previous decade. It remains relevant today, however, because, as indicated in each chapter of this book, the world of the public personnel administrator has become more turbulent and the standard techniques of successful performance much less useful. Only by venturing into new fields of knowledge and developing innovative approaches can the modern personnel policymaker deal with current problems.

The Employer of Last Resort?

Changes in the American economy suggest a larger and more important role for the personnel administrator. Most economic policymakers have assumed that unemployment can be prevented through government actions to stimulate the private sector. Increases in the demand for the products of private industries will result in the employment of the unemployed. Consequently, as business demand expands, unemployment will decrease.

In recent times, however, increased production has not caused large reductions in unemployment. In fact, large numbers of people remain unemployed in times of vigorous business activity.

The "Dual Market" Theory

Some economists have provided an explanation for this occurrence. They suggest that changes in the business cycle affect only certain kinds of workers — those with background traits and educations compatible with the needs of modern industry. Businesses today, they argue, have less need for unskilled labor and more demands for skilled paraprofessionals, sales personnel, and white collar support staff. The requirements of these jobs emphasize language skills, social poise, and proper dress. People who lack at least a high school education and have not acquired certain class-based traits are likely to be excluded from these positions. They become members of the "secondary market."

Members of the secondary market cannot obtain permanent employment even when economic conditions are favorable. An upturn of the business cycle provides more jobs for those in the primary market only. For those without primary market skills, jobs are rarely permanent and low in wage.

Changing the number of unemployed requires basic changes in the skills of those in the secondary market. Government programs to train those lacking primary market traits are frequently suggested. Government efforts could provide training for the unemployed and gradually advance these people into the primary market as they acquire marketable skills. Such programs could also become a means for finding work for those unable to locate employment elsewhere. The selection by Thurow (Selection 24) discusses the implications of the dual market theory for government employment.

A much larger role for public personnel administration follows if this line of reasoning is accepted. Public personnel officials would become responsible for creating basic changes in the economy. The number of public sector employees must expand if government becomes the employer of last resort, and finding meaningful work for individuals in the secondary market is added to the responsibilities of the public administrator.

All these ideas are speculations of a future we cannot predict. Others deserve mention. A decline in the birthrate, for instance, diminishes the need for certain services. Public personnel administrators will have to be concerned with retraining those who become displaced by such changes. As health standards continue to improve, more emphasis will be placed on utilizing the skills of senior citizens and developing creative leisure time. Again, public personnel administrators will need to be involved. Whatever the future holds, a more complicated and innovative career for the public personnel policymaker is the consequence.

23
The Public Service
in the Temporary Society
Fredrick C. Mosher

This essay is addressed to two related questions: With respect to the public administrative services in the United States, where are we and where are we going? and how can and should we prepare our public services to meet probable future demands in our systems of higher education and of public-service management?

Reprinted with permission from Dwight Waldo (ed.) *Public Administration in a Time of Turbulence* (Chandler, 1971), pp. 234-252. Copyright 1971 by Harper & Row, Publishers, Publishers, Inc. By permission of Harper & Row, Publishers, Inc. Footnotes omitted.
Fredrick C. Mosher is Doherty Professor of Government, University of Virginia. He is author of *Democracy and the Public Service* and *Governmental Reorganizations: Cases and Commentary*.

But there is another question, basic to these, which requires attention first. It concerns the changing nature and probable future directions of the society from which the public services are drawn, within which they operate, and which they are presumed to serve. This paper therefore begins with some observations about the society and its demands upon government, including some of the underlying dilemmas which seem to me most salient to the public service of the near future. The second part is a discussion of the probable implications of these social directions and dilemmas for public-administrative organizations, the public service, public-personnel systems, and the universities.

I pretend no expertise in that increasingly popular field of study and speculation known as futuristics. No predictions are offered here about the public services and the society of the United States in the year 2000. My ambition is more modest. It is to cull from our experience of the last few years ... some probabilities about the next few ... and to deduce from these what we in public administration should be doing. The didactic tenor of many of the sentences which follow, the frequent use of the unqualified verb "will," falsely conveys a sense of confidence. All my statements should be qualified by the adverb "probably"; and I would hesitate to give a numerical value to the margins of error. The prognostications are tentative and hopefully provocative, not definitive.

"The Temporary Society" is an expression cribbed from the book of that title by Warren G. Bennis and Philip E. Slater and is used here in two senses, only the second of which is theirs. In the first sense, the society is temporary in that it is changing rapidly and will, in effect, be transformed into another society within a relatively short span of years, say ten or fifteen; furthermore, the transformation is widely acknowledged and appreciated. Societies of the past have of course changed, particularly in the West, but none with such speed and few with such self-awareness. Basic social changes of long ago could be described by historians in terms of eras; later, in terms of centuries; more recently in terms of generations. But the "social generation" of today is considerably shorter than the "human generation." The parent of the seventies is preparing his infant to live in a society that is not the same as his own and not even once removed from his own—it is more nearly twice removed.

The second sense in which our society may be described as temporary concerns the institutions and organizations within it and the attachments, the moorings, of the individuals who compose it. Bennis, in his chapters of *The Temporary Society,* uses the term to connote the allegedly changing nature of productive organizations and the evolving patterns of individual roles and associations within those organizations:

> *The social structure of organizations of the future will have some unique characteristics. The key word will be "temporary." There will be adaptive, rapidly changing temporary systems ... of diverse specialists, linked together by coordinating and task-evaluating executive specialists in an organic flux—this is the organization form that will gradually replace bureaucracy as we know it.*

Although he acknowledges that "the future I describe is not necessarily a 'happy one.'" Bennis is basically optimistic about the prospect for releasing the individual; encouraging his revitalization; and legitimizing fantasy, imagination, and creativity. Slater, in his discussion of the social consequences of temporary systems and particularly of their effects upon the family, is less reassuring.

Both of these senses of the term "temporary society" may exaggerate and overdramatize. As any student of anthropology or reader of Arnold Toynbee knows, no society is permanent, although some manage to survive with little change for some centuries. And, clearly, there are still many stable organizations in the United States and a good many people who do have firm organizational and institutional moorings—probably a solid majority, in fact. But in both senses the trend toward temporariness seems likely, and both have significance for the American public service of the future.

Other Observations and Assumptions

First among the other assumptions that seem to me most significant for purposes of this discussion is one that is negative, though, from my point of view at least, optimistic: that in the next several years there will be no nuclear holocaust, no civil war between races or other groups, no revolution which suddenly overthrows governments or other established institutions or which reverses existing systems of values and beliefs. In other words, while social transformation and changes in institutions and behavior will continue with a rapidity at least equal to that of the present, steps in the future will be made from footprints marked today and in the recent past.

A second assumption has to do with the extent, the depth, and the application of human knowledge. The developments since World War II have been variously labeled: the postindustrial revolution, the scientific revolution, the professional revolution, the information revolution, the cybernetic revolution, the knowledge explosion, the technological era. The emphases among these various labels differ, but the central themes are compatible: Knowledge, particularly in the hard sciences and in technology, is growing at a rapid rate and, as it is applied to the affairs of people, it is bringing about rapid and tremendous changes in the nature of society and the capabilities, the values, and the behavior of human beings. Furthermore, in the words of Paul T. David, "... the oncoming world of the future, however described, will evidently be a world of increasing potential for human intervention and control both good and bad." As a correlate, knowledge itself and its procreation and its application have assumed greater and greater importance in the eyes of men, as have the institutions which develop, apply, and transmit it. Wealth, or income-producing ability, is increasingly perceived in terms of knowledge and its application and decreasingly in terms of property. I am assuming here that this emphasis will continue.

A third assumption concerns the role of government in determining the strategies, the courses and means of action, for the future. Government has ceased to be merely the keeper of the peace, the arbiter of disputes, and the provider of common and mundane services. For better or worse, government has directly and indirectly become a principal innovator, a major determiner of social and economic priorities, the guide as well as the guardian of social values, the capitalist and entrepreneur or subsidizer and guarantor of most new large-scale enterprises. This development has added to both the scope and the range of American politics and public administration. Both enterprises now have a centrality and importance for which the only precedents are their conduct during the World Wars and the Great Depression of the thirties. Virtually every major problem and every major challenge and opportunity leads us to turn to government. The range of those problems and challenges is vast: for example, the cultivation of the ocean bottom, control of the weather, exploration of outer space, training the disadvantaged for jobs, providing day-care centers for working mothers, controlling population growth, eliminating discrimination on the basis of race or sex, juggling the interest rate, reducing the impact of schizophrenia, rescuing a bankrupt railroad, safeguarding children from dangerous toys, or cleaning the air. True, government can turn its back on problems, but if they continue to fester and grow, it eventually has to confront them. It is true also that government relies heavily upon private organizations and individuals to carry out many of its programs, but it cannot escape the responsibility for guidance, regulation, often financial support, and results.

Finally, the variety and range of governmental responsibilities, coupled with the continuing development of new knowledge and new techniques for dealing with them, have increased enormously the reliance of the whole society upon the people who man governmental posts, who collectively make the decisions. This is true of officials in all three branches of government, but it is most conspicuous and probably most significant with regard to the elective and appointive officers in the executive agencies. As the range of public problems and programs broadens, and as knowledge relevant to each grows and deepens, it becomes less and less possible for politically elected representatives to get a handle on more than a few of the significant issues. Even with respect to issues they do deal with directly, they must rely heavily upon the information, analysis and judgment of appointive public servants. This reliance upon administrative personnel will, I assume, continue to grow. . . .

The emerging public administration, the truly "new" public administration, will bear responsibilities of a range and an importance that are hardly suggested in any current textbook. It will have to anticipate and deal with changes in a society that is changing more rapidly than any in human history. It too will have to have the capacity for rapid change and flexibility. It will have to press for greater rationality and develop and utilize ever more sophisticated tools for rational decisions, at the same time accommodating to forces that seem unrational. It must concern itself more than in the past with human goals—"life, liberty, and the pursuit of happiness"—but without doing damage to the processes which make democracy viable, and these goals must be more sophisticated than simple quantitative growth. It must recognize the functional and geographic interdependence of all sectors of the society without too much sacrifice to the values of professional specialism and local interest. It must develop collaborative workways whereby centralization and decentralization proceed simultaneously, and assure high competence at every level of government.

These are tall orders for public administration. Their implications are described more specifically in the balance of this paper.

Implications for Public Organizations

The statements about public organizations which follow are not purely predictive. All have some basis in observations of current developments. And all are responsive to the societal trends and problems described earlier.

First in our consideration of the implications of the "new" public administration are the increasing emphasis in and among organizations upon *problems* and *problem solving,* and the growing distrust of established and traditional routines which have failed to provide solutions.

There will be increasing dependence upon, and increasing acceptance of, *analytical techniques* in planning and evaluating public programs, centering upon specialized units near the top of agencies but spreading downward to the lower and operating echelons seeking rationalized defenses of their programs. One might also anticipate a broadened and more sophisticated approach to analytic techniques which take into account elements beyond purely economic and quantitative considerations. There will be increasing concern about long-term objectives, alternative measures for reaching such objectives, social—as distinguished from purely economic—indicators, and improved information systems concerning both costs and effects of programs. There will also be more efforts toward experimentation in undertakings whose prospects are untried and unproven.

As the interconnection and interdependence of social problems are increasingly perceived, there will be growing reliance upon *ad hoc problem-solving machinery*—task forces, commissions, special staffs to executives, interagency committees, and institutionalized though *ad hoc* mechanisms within agencies.

Both the second and third developments cited above will force increased attention on the inherently obstinate problems of translating new or changed program decisions into effective action through—or in spite of—existing and traditional agencies and operations. In fact, one of the weakest links in public administration today is that of giving operational meaning to planning decisions, however sophisticated may be the analysis behind the plans and however effective the collaboration in reaching agreement on the plans.

Political executives, under unrelenting pressure from elements in the society and dissatisfied with the answers available from the established bureaucracy, tend to develop and utilize machinery directly responsible to them for *developing new programs* and *changing old ones.* At the national level, this tendency is manifest in the emergence of the National Security Council, the new Domestic Council, and a number of presidential program initiatives. Governors like Rockefeller and mayors like Lindsay have responded in substantially comparable ways. So have strong department heads, dissatisfied with recommendations, or lack thereof, from established line bureaus.

There will continue to be vigorous *attacks against "entrenched" bureaucracies* within departments and agencies. Such attacks may be expressed by reorganizing a bureau out of business, or scattering its functions, or taking over key activities such as planning, personnel, and budget, or politicizing its top positions.

Partly in self-defense, bureaus and comparable agencies will undertake to *broaden their bases and broaden their capabilities* through the engagement of people in relevant specializations who are not typical of the elite profession of the bureau. They will also increasingly seek and welcome collaborative relationships with other bureaus and agencies and with other levels of government. And they too will become more problem-oriented.

As these characteristics of problem orientation and collaboration develop at one level of government, particularly the federal, *comparable approaches at other levels* with which it deals will be encouraged and sometimes enforced.

As local constituencies become more vociferous and more vigorous, and as the capabilities of personnel in federal regional offices, the states, and local governments are upgraded, there will be growing demand for *the decentralization of decision-making power.* My guess is that this kind of decentralization will proceed only a little more slowly than the centralization process implied above.

Finally, there will be a growing premium on *responsiveness* to social problems and *speed* in planning and taking action on them. These demands will be enforced, in part, by the politics of confrontation.

In short, administrative organizations will be more *political,* especially at the leadership levels, in the broad, Aristotelian sense of politics. But the change will not result in any loss of brain power or specialized knowledge; the movements toward and the need for them will continue to grow. Agencies, though continuing to reflect a heavy functional emphasis in their structure, will necessarily look beyond their specific functions to related functions and agencies. And they will be more flexible.

These developments will not occur equally in all public agencies any more than they have to date. Indeed, there are a good many public activities for which they will not occur at all. The changes will be most evident in those problem areas resulting in articulate public concern and in connection with new or radically changed programs; that is, in controversial fields. There will be an abundance of President Truman's "kitchens" around Washington and in other capitals in the United States. One can foresee no diminution of intra- and interorganizational conflict.

Partly as a result of the developments suggested above, there will probably be profound changes within administrative organizations in their patterns and behavioral styles. The old Weberian description of bureaucracy, with its emphasis upon formal structure, hierarchy, routinization, and efficiency in the narrow sense, is rapidly becoming obsolete in many organizations. This model is particularly inadequate for "thought" organizations, agencies which operate within a particularly turbulent political environment, agencies facing increasing complexity in their programs, and agencies staffed heavily with highly professional or scientific personnel. If such organizations are to survive, they must be responsive, adaptive, flexible, creative, and innovative. This means, among other things, that they will be increasingly structured around projects or problems to be solved rather than existing as permanent, impervious hierarchies of offices, divisions, and sections. Permanent hierarchical structures will remain for a variety of administrative purposes and for the affixing of final responsibility, but work itself will be organized more collegially on a team basis. Generalist decisions will be reached through the pooling of the perspectives and techniques of a variety of specialists. Leadership will be increasingly stimulative and collaborative and less and less directive.

This projection of the "new" style of bureaucracy is not wholly wishful, nor is it simply the paraphrasing of the writings of social psychologists about what an organization ought to be. The movement toward it is evident in many public and private enterprises and dominant in a few, particularly those involved in research and development such as units of NASA, NIH, and the scientific laboratories. It is more and more prevalent in the social fields, as illustrated by their growing reliance upon intra- and interagency task forces, work groups, and committees. It is reflected also in the nature and assignments of a large portion of the so-called "political" appointees who are not politicians and whose party regularity is incidental if not, in some instances, totally irrelevant. Many of these appointments appear to be predicated upon the individual's professional competence in an appropriate field, ability to apply skills to a variety of problems, and competence in working with and through (rather than over) others.

Implications for the Public Service

More than half of the products of the nation's universities and colleges, graduate and undergraduate, are educated in specializations that are intended to prepare them for professional or scientific occupations. Not including housewives, the majority of the other college graduates will later return for professional graduate training or will enter upon some line of work, like the foreign service, wherein they will acquire the accoutrements of professionalism on the job. Ours is increasingly a professional society or, more accurately, a professionally led society. And American governments are principal employers of professionals. Very probably, within a few years as many as two-fifths of all professionals in this country will be employed directly or indirectly by governments. I perceive no signals that this trend toward professionalism in government will decline. The programs now developing to help the underprivileged find satisfying careers in government and elsewhere may involve lowering educational requisites for some kinds of jobs. But the extent that such programs are successful will be measured by the numbers of their participants who rise to professional or at least paraprofessional levels. What is challenged in this case is not professionalism but the orthodoxy of the traditional routes to attain it.

Books can and should be written about the impact of professionalism upon the public service. I would like to mention very briefly only a few implications that seem salient to this discussion:

• Professionals generally, though not universally, have an orientation to problems or cases; they are prepared to move from one problem to another, somewhat different problem, or to keep several balls in the air at the same time. The problem orientation described above in connection with public organizations is entirely in keeping with the professional way of life.

• All professions (with the possible exception of the ministry) view themselves as rational, but their ways of viewing and defining rationality vary widely. Rationality is no monopoly of administrators, economists, or lawyers. Probably the nearest approach to "pure" rationality, with respect to any given problem, is the product of a mix of differing professional perspectives on that problem.

• Professional study and practice has tended to foster increasing specialism, and increasing depth but decreasing breadth of scope by both student and practitioner in the professions. This circumstance has been further encouraged by the explosion of knowledge in most fields. Until quite recently it has tended to crowd out the consideration of general social consequences of professional behavior and the philosophical consideration of social values in both education and practice. In most fields, it has also minimized education or practice in politics, administration, or organization.

• Insofar as professionalism requires many years of training and experience (varying in different fields) in specialized subjects, it has an inhibiting effect upon movement from one occupation to another. But it encourages mobility from place to place and from organization to organization (or to self-employment), especially when the move promises new and greater challenges. This is probably truest among the best qualified, most innovative, and most problem-oriented individuals.

• Professional behavior tends to be conditioned more by the norms, standards, and workways of the profession than by those that may be imposed by an employing organization. Within those standards professionals seek a considerable degree of autonomy and discretion in the application of their particular skills. They resist working *under* close supervision of others, especially when the others are not members of the same profession.

• When professionals work on problems requiring a number of different occupational skills—and these include almost all problems in the social arena—they prefer to work with others on an equal or team basis, founded in mutual respect.

• Most of the professions are increasingly grounded in some branches of science. Science is in turn grounded in the search for truth and, for any given problem, the finding of the *correct* answer. Scientists—and many professionals—are intolerant of ambiguity, of politics, and all too often of other ways of looking at problems.

These alleged attributes of professionalism do not apply equally to all professions or all members of any given profession. Where and to the extent that they do apply, it may be noted that some of them are entirely congruent with and encouraging to the kind of organizational behavior suggested in the preceding section. Such attributes include orientation to problems, projects, and cases; mobility or willingness to move from place to place and from job to job; and collegial relationships in working with others on common problems.

But in certain other respects, the education for and practice of typical professions is a good deal less than optimal for the public service of tomorrow. First, there is insufficient stress upon and concern about human and social values. All professions allege their dedication to the service of society, and most take for granted that activities their members perform within professional standards are useful and beneficial to the public. The reexamination of these assumptions has been rather sparse in the face of a rapidly changing society and the rapid expansion of governmental responsibilities. And individual practitioners are given little motivation or intellectual grounding to stimulate concern about general social values in relation to their day-to-day problems. This is only incidentally a matter of professional codes of ethics; most codes are essentially negative and very few even mention any special ethical problems arising from public service, even when substantial portions of the profession are employed by governments. The kind of need I perceive is more of the order of the following examples:

•that engineers who plan highways or airports or sewage plants take into consideration the secondary and tertiary effects of these undertakings on the quality of life in America and in the places for which they are planning;

•that lawyers look beyond due process, *stare decisis,* the adversary system, and the like to the roots of our social difficulties;

•that economists look beyond primary and quantitative costs and benefits, the market analogy, and the GNP growth rate to where we as a society and as individuals are going—both as a whole and in relation to individual economic decisions.

Second and closely related to the values question is the need for a great many more professionals who have a sophisticated understanding of the social, economic, and political elements and problems of our times, including an understanding of the relation of their own work to that setting.

Third is the need for humility and for tolerance of others, and of their ideas and perspectives, whether or not they are professionals. This includes an ability to communicate with others on shared problems.

Fourth is an ability to work in situations which are uncertain and on problems for which there is no *correct* solution—in short, a tolerance for ambiguity.

Fifth is an understanding of organizations and how they work, particularly in the context of American politics and government, plus management skill in the sense of getting things done with and through other people.

Sixth, there should be greater incentive for—and much less discouragement of—creativity, experimentation, innovation, and initiative.

Seventh is the need for a much higher degree of mobility—within agencies, between agencies, between governments, and in and out of government.

Despite the observation made earlier that professionalism encourages such mobility, public employment by and large has inhibited it, even for its professionals. One result is that the majority of those who rise to the near top have had effective experience in only one agency, often in only one division of that agency. The absence of challenge and of different and broadening kinds of experiences resulting from the lack of mobility is a disservice to the individual. It is a loss for the government as well because it tends to solidify bureaucratic parochialism and, to some degree, discourage the problem approach which was stressed earlier. Ten years of experience in one job may be merely one year of experience repeated ten times. The idea of temporariness should extend much farther than it has in the civil services of governments.

Finally, the able young, the underprivileged, and women are in need of greater opportunities for challenge and rapid advancement. In government, this means providing opportunities for professionalizing the nonprofessionals and making rapid advancement through a variety of challenging assignments possible for those who prove effective.

Implications for Personnel Systems

Obviously, the strengths and weaknesses of the public service can be attributed only partially to personnel systems—the systems whereby people are employed and deployed, advanced, and retired. And changes in these systems have only a partial and usually rather gradual influence in changing the nature and caliber of the public service. Yet I doubt that there is any other manipulable element with as much potential impact. The system and its popular image condition the kinds and the capabilities and expectations of people who seek entrance. It also influences the expectations of those already on the job, their motivation, the rewards and penalties of differing kinds of behavior, their movement from job to job, and the way they work together.

Since World War II but particularly in the decade of the sixties, personnel administration has been undergoing a radical transition in the national government and, in varying degrees, in the states and cities. This transition has been marked by the following characteristics:

• decentralization and delegation from central civil-service agencies in the direction of line managers;

• growing emphasis upon personnel as a management service rather than as a control or police activity;

• growth of employee- and executive-development programs, particularly through institutionalized training;

• growth and recognition of employee organizations and collective bargaining;

• concern about and programs for equal opportunity for the handicapped, underprivileged, minority groups, and women;

• relaxation of rules and requirements for standardized personnel actions, particularly as they apply to professionals;

• "positive" recruitment in the educational institutions and elsewhere.

The extent and significance of these and other changes are not, I think, sufficiently appreciated. If one were to compare an annual report of the United States Civil Service Commission of a prewar year such as 1939, or even 1955 with *Blueprint for the Seventies,* the Commission's report for 1969, he would have difficulty in believing that they were produced by the same agency though a glance at the appendices might make the identity of the three more recognizable. Most of these changes have been consonant with the changing nature and needs of the society.

Yet there linger some tenets of civil-service administration—and the image of those tenets as perceived by both bureaucrats and the general public—which seem inconsistent with the directions of the society and dysfunctional in terms of the demands upon the public service. I should like to focus upon two of such tenets, both born of reform movements and both having a distinguished history of half a century or longer. The first, here referred to as *careerism,* is that feature built upon the expectation that individuals will be recruited soon after completion of their education; that they will spend the bulk of their working lives in the same organization; that they will be advanced periodically as they gain experience and seniority, such advancement being made on the basis of competition with their peers; and that they will be protected in such advancement against competition with outsiders. The second is *position classification*—the thesis that the content of a given position or class of positions be the hub around which other personnel actions and indeed management generally should revolve.

Careerism has historically been associated with such commissioned corps systems as the Army, Navy, and Foreign Service, but it is now clear that it is equally or more virile in many of the well-established agencies under civil service in all levels of government. Typically, in the United States, and in most other industrialized nations of the world, careers are associated with individual agencies—departments, bureaus, services, divisions—rather than with the government as a whole. And careers are usually identified with a particular type of professional specialization, dominant or subordinate, within the given agency. Careerism may contribute to managerial flexibility in the provision of a corps of qualified people within the organization who are available for different kinds of assignments. At the same time, it inhibits over-all elasticity in terms of quick changes in total manpower resources or the provision of persons with different kinds of skills and perspectives. It discourages lateral entry or the ingestion of new blood above the bottom, or entering, level—some agencies have absolutely banned such entry. More often than not, careerism provides built-in, though usually unwritten, incentives for individuals to pursue orthodox careers within the agency and to avoid unusual assignments which might sidetrack or delay advancement. Over-all, careerism probably significantly acts to discourage creativity, innovation, and risk-taking because of the perceived or imagined dangers of stepping out of line. And insofar as it assures that the older officers within the system will hold the top positions of the agency, it assures continuity, stability, and conservatism in agency policy. It is probably the principal ingredient of the cement which binds an agency into a strong, autonomous, and perhaps impervious entity against outsiders—whether from above, in the executive branch, or from outside, in the legislature or the public.

It is apparent that many aspects of careerism run counter to effective governmental responsiveness to the needs of the temporary society. Among the activities it discourages are collaborative relationships with other agencies and specializations toward the solution of common problems; interchange of personnel among agencies, among jurisdictions of government, and between government and the private sector; *ad hoc* but temporary assignments that are unorthodox in terms of career advancement; responsiveness and rapid change to meet rapidly changing conditions. Insofar as the gates of entry to a government career are based upon orthodox educational credentials—and most of them are—careerism inhibits employment programs for aspiring potential professionals of minority groups. The bar against lateral entry effectively shuts out mature and qualified women after they have raised their families. And the whole image of government as life-long career systems in single agencies discourages some of the most alert, idealistic, and action-oriented of American youth.

Like careerism, position classification is not necessarily a dysfunctional process. Indeed, it is hard to imagine any sizable organization operating without at least a skeleton of a classification plan, even if it is unwritten. The problem arises from the centrality and dominance which positions and their classification have come to assume in personnel administration, in management generally, and in the psychology of officers and employees. Thirty years ago, classification had become the jumping-off point for most activities in the field of personnel; it determined pay, recruitment and selection, placement, promotions, transfers, efficiency ratings, even training. It provided the blocks for what some have called the building-block theory of organization—an essentially static and mechanistic concept. It was the restraining leash around the necks of aggressive public managers, and the more successful of them were often the ones who could successfully slip or unfasten it. Classification has subtler though perhaps more important negative effects upon such matters as status, motivation, willingness to work with others on common problems, communications, flexibility and adaptability—in short, it generates pervasive impairment to what Argyris has labeled "organizational health."

The whole concept of position classification runs somewhat counter to the concept of organization as a fluid, adaptive, rapidly changing entity, oriented to problems and motivated by organizational objectives. To the extent that it is coercive and binding, detailed and specific, and difficult to change, classification has the effects of retarding organizational change and adaptation; discouraging initiative and imagination beyond the definition of the position class; inhibiting special, *ad hoc* assignments or otherwise working "out of class"; and discouraging recognition of unusual contributions and competence through rapid advancement.

Bennis confidently predicted that "[p]eople will be differentiated not vertically according to rank and role but flexibly according to skill and professional training." His forecast is not totally reassuring, since "skill and professional training" sound suspiciously like credentialism, and differentiation by credentials can certainly be vertical. But it is clear that the dominance of classification in government has declined a great deal and nearly vanished in some sectors except as a convenience to management. In the federal government, the flexibility of the management-intern and FSEE programs at the lower rungs of the ladder and, to a slight degree, of the executive Manpower System at the upper rungs are examples. But clearly in many federal agencies and state and local governments we need to go much further and faster.

I have not intended in this section to suggest that governments cease assuring careers to prospective and incumbent employees nor that position classification be abandoned. Both seem to me essential. But some of the unintended consequences of both could and should be alleviated in terms consonant with the trends of the society and its demands on government. What is really needed is a PPBS-type analysis of public-personnel practices in terms of their long-range costs and benefits for governmental objectives. My prediction is that such analyses would indicate the need for

• a deemphasis of careerism and tenurism;
• more lateral entry, exit, and reentry;
• more mobility and flexibility in assignment and reassignments;
• rewards rather than implicit penalties for broadening experience in other agencies, other governments, and the private sector;
• more emphasis in rank, status, and rewards upon the man and his performance, less upon his position description;
• declining reliance upon examinations and rank-order lists in entrance and advancement and more reliance upon performance and references;
• more opportunities for reeducation and retraining, and for broadening education and training, especially for professional personnel;
• more emphasis upon rewards and recognition for initiative and work well done, with less concern about discipline and penalties for nonconformity;
• broadening of the subjects of negotiation in collective bargaining and, with some exceptions, recognition of the right to strike. ...

24
The Economic Status of Minorities and Women: Some Facts and Conclusions

Lester C. Thurow

While many statistics could be used to explore the economic position of any minority group, the essential nature of a group's position can be captured in four basic statistics. First, what is the group's probability of being employed relative to the majority group? Second, given those members of the group that are employed, what is their earnings relative to that of the majority group? Third, are members of the group making a breakthrough into the high income jobs of the economy? And fourth, what is the group's level of economic welfare as measured by its average family income relative to that of the majority?

In each case it is necessary to look not just at current data but at the group's economic history. Where has it been in terms of employment and earnings opportunities? Where is it going and how fast is it progressing? Since the current recession or depression is so severe as to have a radically different impact than previous post World War II recessions, data will be presented on the progress or retrogression of groups through 1973, and then a separate analysis will look at what has been happening in the current recession.

The data on family income and ethnicity reveals only three major groups with incomes below average—blacks, Spanish heritage, and American Indians. Of the almost 100 million Americans who think of themselves as having an ethnic origin, all have incomes above those of people who do not identify with an ethnic group. Interestingly the groups with the highest average family incomes in 1972 were Russians ($13,929), Poles ($12,182), and Italians ($11,646). Ethnic Americans may believe they are economically deprived, but they have on average reached to the top of the economic ladder.

Blacks Versus Whites

Since World War II no significant change has occurred in the employment probabilities of blacks and whites. At all points in time—good or bad—black unemployment rates are approximately twice as high as those of whites. This was true prior to the civil rights and anti-poverty decade of the sixties, and it is true now. While the monthly data for early 1975 are not shown, exactly the same relationship has held as unemployment escalates. Month by month, black unemployment is twice that of whites.

Reprinted with permission from *The Civil Rights Digest,* Vol. 8, No. 2-3 (Winter-Spring, 1976), pp. 3-9.

Lester Thurow is Professor of Economics and Management, Massachusetts Insitiue of Technology.

While the current relative employment probabilities of blacks are no worse than they have been since World War II, the problem should not be minimized. Absolute rates are the highest they have been since the Great Depression for both whites and blacks. Relative to the sizes of their respective populations, two black men or women are thrown out of work for every white man or woman during a period of rising unemployment.

Analysis indicates that we are dealing with a longrun, deeply embedded, structural relationship in the economy. The rapidly escalating black unemployment rates of this recession or depression are not a temporary phenomenon. They are exactly what would have been expected given the structure of the economy. Little has changed in the past 30 years.

While there are a variety of earnings statistics on blacks and whites, the earnings of full-time, full-year workers are the best summary measure of earnings for those who have escaped the problems of unemployment. These earnings statistics completely eliminate the effect of unemployment (total or partial) and those individuals who do not seek full-time, full-year work.

The relative employment probabilities of blacks have not improved in the post World War II period, but relative earnings have (see Table 1). Between 1955 and 1973, the earnings of black males have risen from 56 to 66 percent of white males, and earnings of black females have risen from 56 to 86 percent of white females. (Over the period under consideration, however, white females have fallen relative to white males.) While the earnings of both black males and females have improved, the relative gains of black females have been three times as large as those for males.

It is interesting to note, however, that the rate of gains for blacks was just as fast in the 1950s as it was in the 1960s. The civil rights and poverty programs of the 1960s might have been necessary to sustain the rate of increase started earlier, but they did not serve to accelerate it.

More to the current point, however, are the data since 1970 or 1971. Since 1970, little evidence exists of any advance in the relative earnings of black males,

Table 1

Relative Earnings of Full-Time Full-Year Workers
(Black Males to White Males and Black Females to White Females)

Year	Males	Females
1955	56%	56%
1960	59	68
1968	61	77
1969	62	81
1970	65	83
1971	65	87
1972	65	88
1973	66	86

and since 1971 little evidence exists of any advance in the relative earnings of black females. These data are interesting because they antedate the current recession which started in the first quarter of 1974. While the data contain enough sampling error to warn against calling a 3-year hiatus in gains a trend, it is nonetheless disturbing. The movement of the 1960s toward greater equality in earnings seems to be broken.

One could also predict a fall into the ratio of black to white full-time, full-year earnings over the course of the current depression. Most of the progress that has been made in the past has not been made by altering the relative earnings of older workers, but by altering the earnings of individuals just entering the labor force. Thus the greatest relative gains have been made among young blacks.

As far as an employer is concerned, this type of change causes the least disruption. Young whites lose relative to young blacks, but they lose something they did not yet have. To alter the relative position of older workers, it is necessary to reshuffle existing jobs or expected promotions. In either case, white employees are aware of the fact that they lost something and are in a position to exert countervailing power.

But in a recession, the whole process is reversed because of seniority provisions (formal and informal) in hiring and firing. The youngest workers are most apt to lose their jobs, and they are the workers where the ratio of black to white earnings is most likely to be near parity. Therefore, a recession shifts the weight of those remaining fully employed toward older groups who have larger relative earnings differences.

Regardless of whether the current hiatus is or is not significant, relative earnings—especially for black males—also result from a long-run structural problem. If current rates of progress were to continue, black females would achieve parity with white females in about 10 years, but black males would not reach parity for another 75 years. Since there is no trend toward parity between white males and females, achieving parity with white females is hardly the end of the economic problem.

Looking at the jobs in the top 5 percent of the earnings distribution, some improvement has occurred in the relative position of black males. In 1960, black males were only about 9 percent as likely as white males to hold a job in the top 5 percent of the earnings distribution. By 1973, they were 19 percent as likely to hold such a job. Black females held none of the top jobs in 1960 and essentially none in 1973. The position of white females actually deteriorated over this period, from being 6 percent as likely to hold a job at the top in 1960 to only 4 percent as likely in 1973 (see Table 2).

Black family incomes have risen and fallen relative to white family incomes depending upon the phase of the business cycle. From 1947 to 1952, black family incomes rose from 51 percent to 57 percent of white family incomes at the peak of the Korean War; declined to 51 percent with the recession of 1957-58; rose to 64 percent under the pressures of the Vietnam War and the civil rights movement; and then once again started to fall, reaching 60 percent in 1973.

Table 2

Probability of Holding a Job in Top 5 Percent
Of Earnings Distribution Compared to White Males

	1960	1973
Black males	9%	19%
Black females	0.0	0.06
White females	6	4

The most recent decline was not, however, caused by the business cycle. Instead the decline has been produced by a reduction in the proportion of black families with two or more workers and an increase in the proportion of white families with two or more workers. The proportion of white families with two or more workers now exceeds that of blacks. This is a process that is apt to continue and will lead to an increasing gap in average family incomes.

Spanish Heritage Families

Extensive data over time are not available for Spanish heritage Americans, but it is possible to report on their economic position in 1969 and a few changes from 1969 to 1973. During this period, Spanish heritage families have risen from a position of economic inferiority relative to both black and white families to a position of superiority relative to black families.

In 1969 the average black family income was 63 percent of the average white family income, but the average Spanish heritage family had only 58 percent as much as the average white family. By 1973 the average black family had dropped to 60 percent of the average white family, but the average Spanish heritage family had risen to 69 percent of the average white family.

Among Spanish heritage families the most spectacular gains were made by the Cuban, Central and South American, and Spanish segment of the Spanish heritage families (see Table 3). Mexican Americans have, however, also made sharp gains in a rather limited period of time.

Rising relative family incomes can be caused by falling relative unemployment rates, rising relative earnings, or rising family labor force participation rates.

Table 3

Family Incomes of Spanish Origin Families
Relative to White Family Incomes

	1969	1973
Total	58%	69%
Mexican American	56	67
Puerto Rican	51	64
Other	65	89

White it is not possible to trace the sources of Spanish heritage family income gains definitely, it is possible to determine some of the causes.

In 1970, unemployment rates were similar for black and Spanish heritage workers with males showing a slightly lower rate and females a somewhat higher one. By 1974 female rates were still slightly higher, but male rates were 25 percent lower. As a result, a substantial fraction of the improvement in Spanish heritage family incomes can be attributed to falling relative unemployment rates for male Spanish heritage workers.

In addition, while female unemployment rates have not fallen relative to whites or blacks, Spanish heritage female participation rates have been rising in pace with those of whites and faster than those of blacks. In 1970 female participation rates were 9 percentage points lower for Spanish heritage females than for black females and approximately equal to those of white females. By 1974 Spanish heritage female participation rates had risen in pace with those of white females and into approximate parity with those of black females. Spanish heritage males maintained their position of parity with white males and had participation rates approximately 8 percentage points higher than that of black males.

Higher male participation rates have a greater payoff for Spanish heritage families than they do for black families, since fully employed male workers are much closer to parity with fully employed white workers. In 1969 the average full-time, full-year Spanish heritage male worker earned 80 percent as much as the corresponding white, while the average fully employed Spanish heritage female worker earned 89 percent as much as white females. Like blacks, Spanish heritage females were closer to parity with white females than Spanish heritage males were with white males, but the male gap was much smaller.

Similarly, Spanish heritage males are much more likely to hold high earnings jobs. In 1969 a black male was only 12 percent as likely as a white male to hold a job earning $25,000 or more per year, but a Spanish heritage male was 38 percent as likely to do so. This situation deteriorated slightly between 1969 and 1973, however, since by 1973 Spanish heritage males were only 21 percent as likely to hold a top job. Females witnessed little change, with black and Spanish heritage females half as likely as white females to hold such jobs, but with white females only 8 percent as likely to hold such jobs as white males.

As a result, the economic progress of blacks and Spanish heritage workers has been substantially different during the 1970s. The 1970s have been a period of relative economic stagnation for black Americans, but a period of rapid economic gains for Spanish heritage Americans. These gains have in turn been caused by falling relative unemployment rates for Spanish heritage males and rising relative participation rates for Spanish heritage females.

American Indians

American Indians are the smallest and poorest of all of America's ethnic groups. They are also the least well described and tracked by U.S. statistical agencies. Despite the existence of the Bureau of Indian Affairs, only the roughest estimates exist of the economic situation of American Indians. Based on reports from approximately half of all of the U.S. reservations to the Economic Development Administration, the median family income of American Indians was $3,300 in 1969 with a range from $1,000 on several reservations to $15,000 on one reservation. This means that the median income of an Indian family is something on the order of one-third of that of a white family.

Given the lack of data and the range of error, no one is in a position to say whether the population of American Indians is or is not making any economic progress. Regardless of whether they are or are not making economic progress, American Indians stand in a class by themselves when it comes to suffering economic deprivation relative to the rest of the population.

Female Workers

From 1960 to 1974, unemployment rates deteriorated for both white and black females. White females went from unemployment rates 10 percent higher than those for white males to rates 40 percent higher, and black females went from unemployment rates 12 percent lower than those for black males to unemployment rates 18 percent higher. Interestingly, the earnings of fully employed females did not move in a symmetrical manner. Full-time, full-year white female earnings fell from 61 to 56 percent of white male earnings from 1939 to 1973, while black female earnings were rising from 51 to 69 percent of fully employed black males.

As Table 2 shows, the probability of black females holding a job in the top 5 percent of the earnings distribution has improved minutely, while the probability of a white female holding a job in the top 5 percent of the earnings distribution has deteriorated. While white females are still much better off than black females, all of the relevant variables, except participation rates, are moving in the direction of lowering the relative earnings of white females.

Total white female earnings are up relative to white males and black females, but only because their participation rates rose from 31 to 45 percent from 1948 to 1974, while black female participation rates were only rising from 46 to 49 percent. Shortly, white females will probably have higher participation rates than black females.

Male participation rates have been declining for both white and black men, but white men have fallen from 87 percent to 79 percent while black men were falling from 87 percent to 73 percent from 1948 to 1974. As a result, both male and female participation rates are changing such that white income is rising relative to black income.

Minorities and the Recession

While preliminary data are available for 1974, the real impact of the current recession will not be seen until 1975 data become available. The Gross National Product peaked in the fourth quarter of 1973, but the rapid escalation in unemployment rates did not occur until the fourth quarter of 1974 and the first quarter of 1975. As a result, the effects of radically higher unemployment rates are not really visible in 1974 data.

In 1974 real family incomes declined for all groups, but somewhat surprisingly, the declines were larger for whites than for blacks or Spanish heritage families. While the median white family income was falling 4.4 percent, the median black family income was falling 3.2 percent and the median Spanish heritage family income was falling only 1.2 percent. Spanish heritage families continued to make economic progress relative to both black and white families, and black families made a small gain relative to white families.

In terms of absolute purchasing power, the average white family lost $600 while the average black family was losing $250 and the average Spanish heritage family was losing $100. While the rising relative income of Spanish heritage families was spread across the country, the small gain in relative family incomes for blacks was completely concentrated in the northeast. While white incomes were declining by 4 percent in the northeast, black incomes were rising by 2 percent. These gains were caused by rising real incomes for fully employed black females and males at the same time that fully employed white males and females were experiencing cuts in their incomes in the northeast.

The gains in the relative income position of Spanish heritage families can be traced to gains in the earnings of Spanish heritage female workers. While the incomes of white and Spanish heritage males both declined 6 percent, the income of Spanish heritage females rose 4 percent, while the white females incomes fell 1 percent.

Unemployment rates indicate that minorities and women continue to suffer from a higher probability of being unemployed, but the 1974 recession, somewhat surprisingly, hit the earnings of year-round, full-time white male workers the hardest. The real incomes of fully employed white males declined 5 percent, while the incomes of fully employed black and Spanish heritage males declined 1.5 percent.

Among females, fully employed white females experienced a cut in income of 4 percent, while fully employed black females were experiencing a 3 percent increase in income, and fully employed Spanish heritage females were experiencing a 0.5 percent increase. As a result, the increase in incomes for Spanish heritage females was almost completely concentrated among those who work part-time or part-year.

Since overtime was slashed sharply during 1974, the decline in earnings for fully employed whites must be traced to the disappearance of overtime. Evidently, other groups receive little overtime and therefore have less to lose when overtime disappears.

EEOC and the Economy

During the previous discussion of the income advances and retreats of different groups, no mention has been made of the effects of the Equal Employment Opportunity Commission. The absence of any mention of EEOC is not meant to imply that it has had no impact on the distribution of earnings. EEOC was not mentioned because of a fundamental fact that is often overlooked. The United States has a very large economy: an economy so large that no agency the size of EEOC could be expected to have noticeable effect on aggregate data.

The Gross National Product is approaching $1,500 billion per year. The labor force totals almost 95 million individuals, with 103 million individuals working at some point during the year. There are 55 million families and 18 million unrelated individuals. In an economy this large, it is not possible for an agency with an annual budget of $55 million (fiscal year 1975) to have a noticeable effect on the distribution of earnings.

The success or failure of EEOC as an institution must rest on the results that it has obtained in the cases which it entered. Economywide data point up where we have been and where we are going. They define the size of the remaining task, but they do not provide a basis for evaluation of the costs and benefits of EEOC.

The size of the remaining task does, however, raise questions about the litigation premises upon which EEOC is built. Is it possible to make the kinds of changes that EEOC was designed to accomplish, given the legal structure upon which it is based? One could argue that a legal case approach where the burden of proof is on those charging discrimination will not solve the problem. This is not to advocate that the current approach be scrapped. It clearly has an integral role to play in redressing individual economic grievances, but the current approach is too cumbersome and time consuming to cause major changes in the distribution of earnings.

If the current rate of change in the distribution of earnings is inadequate, some other mechanism must be built that can augment that now in place. The question to be addressed is not the narrow success or failure of EEOC, but the nature of a mechanism that might narrow or eliminate the earnings gaps that now exist.

The AT&T case, which involved a companywide consent decree, is an obvious improvement over the individual grievance procedure, but it does require at least the threat of going to court to make the negotiations take place. It is also easy to exaggerate the ease with which such a procedure can work. All it would take to bring this procedure to a halt is the strong opposition of one large company.

Based on our experience with antitrust cases, it is clear that one large, strongly-opposed company could tie up all of EEOC for 15 to 20 years, even if it were obvious that the company would lose in the end. Just to put the problem in perspective, many observers think that the entire Justice Department does not have enough resources to take on both IBM and AT&T at the same time in the antitrust area. Antitrust cases easily take 15 to 20 years to reach a final conclusion, and they can tie up hundreds of lawyers.

To make either the individual case approach or the companywide consent decree approach work, it is necessary to create economic pressures that make it less likely the Government will run up against opponents that are willing to fight to the end. Something approaching full employment is probably essential to the success of EEOC, but it isn't enough. Even at full employment, the economy generates unemployment probabilities that are twice as high for blacks as for whites. If this recession is eventually cured, future recessions will occur.

Now is the time for those who are interested in EEOC's goals to push vigorously for a comprehensive guaranteed job program or a real "right to work." Employment is also the area where antidiscrimination laws have been least successful. While some progress has generally been made in terms of relative wages for those who do work, no progress has been made in closing the gap in relative employment probabilities.

While there is a lot of talk now about public service employment and even rising appropriations, it is important to understand that a comprehensive right to work program is not a large temporary public employment program. It is a permanent, open-ended public employment program where everyone who wants work gets work. Congress does not get to determine its size, but simply agrees to appropriate whatever is necessary—just as it does for farm price supports.

The program must be open-ended for a very simple reason. To the extent that the program is closed, discriminatory decisions can be made as to who gets into the program and who does not. To offset differences in employment probabilities in the private economy, public employment must stand ready to hire anyone that the private economy refuses to hire. At the moment, many public service employment programs are simply being used to hire back previously laid-off public employees. Chances are that the discriminatory quotient embedded in the current public service employment program is not significantly different from that in the rest of the economy.

On one level it is surprising that a society that stresses the value of work as much as ours is so resistant to the guaranteed job. The right to work is not only compatible with the work ethic, it is a logical concomitant of it. No logical society can define something as ethical (work) and then make it impossible to be ethical (there is no work to be had).

As in most cases of inconsistent behavior, the answer is to be found in conflicting moral principles. We also preach the virtues of private enterprise. But private enterprise cannot guarantee the right to work. The right to work can only be guaranteed by public enterprise. If the government is to guarantee that right to work, then it must be involved in the employment of large numbers of people and as a consequence, it is going to be producing some large quantum of goods and services. To be for open-ended permanent public employment is to be for public ownership of some fraction of the means of production.

While one can argue that the Federal Government is already heavily involved in economic production, the guaranteed job would so significantly escalate the degree of involvement that it should be considered a shift in kind rather than degree. This conclusion must be faced. As John Kenneth Galbraith has noted, if one wants well-run, efficient state industries, one must believe that state industries are the first-best way to run many industries, and not the second-best way.

Similarly, if one wants a well-run guaranteed job program, one must believe that guaranteed public jobs and equal access to employment opportunities is the first priority. It is not a program designed to mop up some of the unfortunate side effects of private enterprise. Precisely the converse is true. Private enterprise has an important but subsidiary role to play in guaranteeing employment opportunities for everyone.

Given that the current recession or depression has produced a high unemployment rate that is likely to last for several years, now would seem to be the time to press for the guaranteed job for everyone. Groups are being hurt by unemployment that have not been hurt since the Great Depression. For the first time in a long time, they are being forced to realize that unemployment can be caused by factors other than laziness. Given what many believe is a high degree of economic bungling in Washington, these groups may not be hurt for another 35 years.

As a result, minority groups and those interested in their problems should push for an open-ended, permanent guaranteed job for everyone regardless of race, creed, color, sex, or age. But one must remember that from the point of view of minorities, it is absolutely vital that the program be universal and open-ended. Anything less would be unlikely to have an impact on relative earnings and employment; large scale public employment is not an adequate substitute.

INDEX

Accountability, 11-12
Affirmative action, 201-202
American Federation of State, County and
    Municipal Employees (AFSCME), 97
Arbitration, 130-135
Angel, Frank, 164

Bargaining. *See* Collective Bargaining
Blacks, 162-171, 172-191, 276
Blackman, Justice Harry, 218-219
Boulding, Kenneth, 155-156
Bramwell, Jonathon, 166-167
Brennan, Justice William, 196-197, 211-
    217
Brinkley, David, 248-249, 298
Brookings Institution, 90-91
Budgeting, 29-38
Burger, Justice Warren, 179-183
Burnham, David T., 137-146
Buzan, Bert C., 191-202

Campbell, Alan K., 247-253
Career mobility, 49
Case, Fredrick, 162-163, 169
CETA. *See* Comprehensive Employment
    and Training Act
Chapman, Brian, 24
Chicano. *See* Mexican-American; Employ-
    ment discrimination
City Government. *See* Local government
City management, 27-43
Civil service, 2-4, 120, 223, 247
Civil Service Commission. *See* United
    States Civil Service Commission
Civil Rights Act. *See* United States Congress
    Civil Rights Act
Civil Service Reform Act, 1978. *See* United
    States Congress
Collective bargaining, 102-130, 137-146,
    231, 241-43
Compensation, 122
Comprehensive Employment and Training
    Act, 70-71, 86-95

Dahl, Robert A., 111
David, Paul T., 265
Department of Justice, 68
Department of Labor, 67-69
Donnelly, Harrison H., 86-95
Douglas v. *Hamilton*, 165
"Dual market theory," 262

Earnings, 277-278
EEOC. *See* Equal Employment Opportunity
    Commission
Efficiency, 11-12, 16, 243, 255-259
Elected officials, 3-4
Employment discrimination, 72-77, 147-
    202
Employment discrimination, American In-
    dian. *See* American Indian
Employment discrimination, blacks. *See*
    Blacks
Employment discrimination, Mexican
    Americans. *See* Mexican Americans
Employment discrimination, Spanish
    heritage. *See* Mexican Americans
Employment discrimination, women. *See*
    Women
Employment tests, 4, 175-191, 165
Employment quotas, 191-220
Engineered work standards (EWS), 254-
    259
Equal Employment Opportunity Coor-
    dinating Council, 165
Equal Employment Opportunity Commis-
    sion, 67, 69, 165, 168, 170, 282-284
Equal employment opportunity, 152,
    171-178
Equity, 11-12
Examinations, 222, 232

Federal government, 9, 45-62, 150-160,
    167, 247, 284
Federal government, black employment,
    169-171

Female. *See* Women; Employment discrimination, women
Fourteenth Amendment, 65

Galbraith, John Kenneth, 284
Greer, Charles R., 130-135
Ginsburg, Sigmund G., 223-236
Griggs v. *Duke Power Company*, 165, 179-183

Heclo, Hugh, 45-62
Helburn, I.B., 137-146
Higher civil servants, 45-62
Horton, Raymond, 117-130

Inefficiency, 223-236, 248
Interest groups, 1
Intergovernmental Personnel Act, 237

Judicial system, 64-66

Kaufman, Herbert, 114
Kennedy, Robert F., 163
Krislov, Sam, 20-21
Kuhn, James W., 117-130

Labor relations of government employees, 24
Lewin, David, 117-130
Local government, 26-43, 86-95, 117, 171-178, 184-191, 223-236

Manpower Development and Training Act, 87
Marshall, Justice Thurgood, 256-257, 219-220
Merit system, 2-3, 16, 228-9
Mexican-Americans, 171-178, 279-280
Minority groups, 1
Mosher, Fredrick C., 21, 263-276
Municipality. *See* Local government

Negroes. *See* Blacks
Neutrality, 22
Newland, Chester A., 236-247
"New" public administration, 266

Office of Federal Contract Compliance (OFCC), 68, 69

Office of Personnel Management (OPM), 251

Performance evaluation, 54
Political rights of civil servants, 22-24
Political science, 15
Polsby, Nelson W., 114
Position classification, 34-35
Powell, Justice Lewis, 197-199, 203-211, 217-218
Private enterprise. *See* Private sector
Private sector, 8, 156-157
Productivity, 25-36, 253-259
Professions, 269-271
Promotion, 229
Proposition 13, 221
Position classification, 273-274
Public employee unions, 24-25, 97-101
Puryear, Mahlon, 163

Recruitment, 226-227
Rees, Albert, 103
Referenda, 137-146
Reform, 12-13, 17, 234-235, 237
Rehnquist, Justice William, 78-85
Report of the Council of Economic Advisors, 103-104
Representative bureaucracy, 20, 46
Responsiveness, 11-12
Rosenbloom, David H., 15-25

Saltzstein, Grace Hall, 171-178
Sayas, E.S., 223-236
Schurz, Carl, 17
Seidman, Harold, 21-22, 26
Senior executive service, 252
Seniority, 229
Sevareid, Eric, 163
Slater, Phillip E., 264
Spanish heritage families, 279-280
Spoils system, 235
Stahl, O. Glenn, 2, 3, 16
Stevens, Justice John Paul, 195-196
Stewart, Debra, 150-160
Strikes of public employees, 130-135

Test validity, 18, 185-191
Tiger, Lionel, 153
Thompson, Frank J., 26-43
Thurow, Lester C., 276

United States Civil Service Commission, 45, 47, 48, 53, 55, 240, 244, 245, 247, 281

United States Constitution, 64-65, 81, 85

United States Congress, 79-80
   Civil Rights Act, 1964, 67, 70, 71, 72-77, 108, 147-148, 179, 192, 203-220
   Civil Service Reform Act, 1978, 247-253
   Fair Labor Standards Act, 78-85
   Comprehensive Employment and Training Act. *See* Comprehensive Employment and Training Act (CETA)

United States government. *See* Federal government

United States Supreme Court, 78-85, 179-220

Wage and Hour Division, Department of Labor, 68, 69

Warren Court, 65

Weber, Max, 19

Wellington, Harry, 102-117

White, Justice Byron, 182-191, 220

Wilson, David B., 249

Wilson, James Q., 9-15

Winter, Ralph K., 102-117

Women, 150-160, 171-178, 276, 281